W9-BSR-019

STATE POWER AND WORLD MARKETS

STATE POWER AND WORLD MARKETS

The International Political Economy

Joseph M. Grieco and G. John Ikenberry

Duke University and Georgetown University

W. W. NORTON & COMPANY

NEW YORK AND LONDON

Copyright © 2003 by W. W. Norton & Company, Inc.

All rights reserved
Printed in the United States of America
First Edition

The text of this book is composed in Fairfield Light
with the display set in Meta
Composition by PennSet
Manufacturing by the Maple-Vail Book Manufacturing Group
Book design by Chris Welch

Library of Congress Cataloging-in-Publication Data

Grieco, Joseph M.
   State power and world markets : the international political economy / Joseph M. Grieco
and G. John Ikenberry.
      p.   cm.
   Includes bibliographical references (p.) and index.
   ISBN 0-393-97419-7 (pbk.)
      1. International economic relations.   2. International economic integration.
   3. Commercial policy.   I. Ikenberry, G. John.   II. Title.

HF1359 .G73 2002
337—dc21

                                                                2002025505

W. W. Norton & Company, Inc., 500 Fifth Avenue, New York, N.Y. 10110
                        www.wwnorton.com
W. W. Norton & Company Ltd., Castle House, 75/76 Wells Street, London W1T 3QT
  2 3 4 5 6 7 8 9 0

To Joseph Grieco's brother, Peter, and sister, Rita,
and to John Ikenberry's parents, Gilford J. and
Nelda B. Ikenberry

CONTENTS

ACKNOWLEDGMENTS

We would first and foremost like to thank Roby Harrington for his encouragement and especially his patience during the writing of this book. In addition, we thank Avery Johnson, who during the summer and fall of 2001 played a vitally important coordinating role in bringing this project to completion, and who offered innumerable helpful suggestions regarding the content and structure of the book. We also thank Stephen Erfle (Dickinson College), Raymond Hopkins (Swarthmore College), Timothy McKeown (University of North Carolina, Chapel Hill), and Mohan Penubarti (University of California, Los Angeles) for their excellent commentaries on and suggestions for improvement of earlier drafts of the manuscript. We also thank Traci Nagle for her superb copyediting work on the manuscript, which included insightful substantive suggestions as well as helpful stylistic recommendations.

Joe Grieco would like to thank Giacomo Chiozza for his research assistance and the students at Duke who have taken his courses: the International Political Economy of Trade, the International Political Economy of Money and Finance, International Business–Government Relations, and Understanding and Managing Global Capital Markets Crises (the last co-taught with Enrique Mendoza). I would also like to thank my students at the Postgraduate School of Economics and International Relations at the Catholic University of Sacred Heart, in Milan, Italy. I have always been inspired by my students' dedication to and enthusiasm for the study and exploration of the world political economy. I also thank Enrique Mendoza, who guided me through the economics of financial crisis contagion; the Ford Foundation, for assistance under a grant to Duke University for curricular innovation in the social sciences; and Gary Gereffi, director of Duke's Markets and Management Studies Program.

John Ikenberry would like to thank the students at Princeton, the University of Pennsylvania, and Georgetown who have taken his various courses on international political economy. As co-director of the Lauder Institute at Penn, an innovative program that combines a master's degree in business administration from the Wharton School of Business and a master's of international studies from the School of Arts and Sciences, I enjoyed developing a core course on globalization and world political economy for these students. I also thank the students of the Graduate Institute of Peace Studies at Khung Hee University in Korea and the Postgraduate School of Economics and International Relations at Catholic University in Milan, Italy, who have also taken my course of international political economy.

STATE POWER AND WORLD MARKETS

Chapter 1

Introduction

Everywhere around us is evidence that economic and technological changes are transforming the international landscape. Economies and people around the world are more closely linked than ever before. Information circles the globe in an instant. Business is conducted largely without regard to international borders. Capital markets are integrated worldwide. Decisions made in London or New York are felt in Tokyo and Jakarta. Only a few decades ago, most businesses operated within national economies and overseas markets mattered little, but today the world's major corporations are truly global. Countries that only a few decades ago were economically inconsequential—such as those in Southeast Asia or Latin America—are today closely tied to the advanced industrialized economies through trade and investment. Financial instability in one seemingly remote country can threaten economies around the world, as Filipinos, Russians, Brazilians, and Americans saw in the case of the collapse of the Thai currency, the baht, in 1997.

Growing economic interdependence is changing the political landscape of the world, as well. Countries rise and fall depending on their ability to operate within a rapidly evolving world economy. Fueled by trade and investment, China is rising to global prominence, following in the footsteps of Japan and the smaller East Asian trading countries. The Cold War ended in part because the Soviet Union could not compete with the dynamic growth and modernization of the Western capitalist countries. Now postcommunist leaders are seeking to integrate their countries into the international capitalist order. By pursuing market-friendly trade and investment strategies in the last few decades, many countries in the developing world have experienced rapid economic growth and rising living standards, but they have also felt the insecurity and dislocations of currency crises and market fluctuations. The European Union is engaged in a bold experiment to link its societies and economies in ways that transcend the nation-state. In the meantime, political struggles have erupted in Europe, the United States, and elsewhere in recent years over globalization and the threat it poses to sovereignty, cultural traditions, environmental protection, and worker rights. Great rewards and sobering risks greet countries that open themselves up to the expanding global economic system.

The interconnectedness of societies is creating new sorts of challenges. Environmental pollution is increasingly spreading beyond national borders. The destruction of the Brazilian rain forest harms the entire planet's atmosphere. The unwillingness of the administration of U.S. president George W. Bush to sign the Kyoto Protocol—an international agreement that obligates countries to reduce pollutants that cause global warming—has angered governments and environmental groups around the world. Acquired immunodeficiency syndrome (AIDS) and other deadly diseases cannot be easily contained within national borders. Terrorism is increasingly easy to spread around the world. The Internet facilitates communication and cooperation between peoples, but it also empowers transnationally organized criminal and hate groups. Rising populations and income inequality in the developing world are intensifying refugee flows into the rich, industrialized countries and igniting ethnic and social conflict. With global interdependence comes both promise and peril.

But the growing interconnectedness of the world economy is not automatic or irreversible. Globalization is not simply the unfolding of an iron law of economics. Politics and governmental decisions are at the heart of the process. In some respects, nation-states and their governments are limited and constrained by an integrating world economy. But across the centuries, it has been nation-states—and especially the leading great powers—that have made the critical choices to construct a world economy.

This basic insight about the pivotal role of the advanced economies informs this book. States and markets are deeply intertwined: states need markets and markets need states. The world economy depends on national governments and the institutions, legal rules, and protections they provide. The age-old competition between nation-states has also stimulated the construction and regulation of international markets. At critical historical turning points in the nineteenth and twentieth centuries, leading states have used military and diplomatic power to promote world economic openness. In turn, the dynamic economic forces that have been unleashed by states have enriched societies, boosted the power of some states, and undermined others.

This book provides a critical survey of the field of international political economy, a field whose central concern involves the reciprocal relationships between state interests and power on the one hand, and world market structures and economic dynamics on the other. The book will look at how these dual logics of state and market operate and how their interactions are shaping the world political economy today. The questions we want to explore are several:

- What are the sources of openness and stability in the world economy? In other words, what accounts for a world economy that is characterized by relatively free trade, convertible currencies, and unfettered movement of capital?
- How do major states seek to shape the organization of economics in a way that promotes their national interests, and how do less powerful states adjust their national policies to these major-state interests and policies?
- What challenges do the world economy and exposure to international markets present to states, even powerful states?
- How have states sought to manage economic stability and openness and to tackle the challenges resulting from their integration into the world economy?

We will seek answers to these questions by examining a wide range of theory and economic history. In this introduction, we will look more closely at the historical dynamics of states and markets, particularly during the two great eras of globalization in the nineteenth and twentieth centuries. Then we will look at each side of the relationship: the impact of states on the organization of markets and the impact of markets on states. Finally, we will preview the main themes and objectives of the rest of this book.

Two Great Eras of Globalization

In the mid-nineteenth century, the world entered the first age of globalization. Trade and investment spread rapidly around the world, spurred by revolutions in communication and production technologies and a stable gold standard. Behind the scenes stood the United Kingdom, pre-eminent in manufacturing, finance, and naval power. The United Kingdom championed free trade throughout the Victorian era, beginning with the celebrated repeal of its protectionist Corn Laws in 1846. The free trade movement spread to other countries with the Cobden-Chevalier Treaty of 1860, which lowered French tariffs but also introduced to the world the ***most-favored-nation clause***, whereby each party to a treaty agrees to extend to the other party any tariff reductions it grants to a third country. Within the next two decades of this "Golden Era" virtually all the countries of Europe reduced their tariffs in a series of bilateral agreements. In the meantime, a succession of British governments championed the cause of open markets in a wide range of commercial agreements, London banks put capital to productive use abroad, and the Royal Navy ensured open access to world markets and resources. The result was an unprecedented flow of goods, capital, and people, and the rise of the first truly open world economy.

In 1900 there was every reason to expect and welcome a future world of continued economic openness. Nineteenth-century globalization advocates such as Richard Cobden and John Bright argued that free trade fostered growth and created vested interests in favor of stable and peaceful relations between countries. After all, the United Kingdom's trade missions to continental Europe during this period were not just business initiatives but peace missions as well. This optimism was soon to end, however. The open world economy came crashing down in 1914, a victim of rapidly shifting power relations, escalating strategic rivalries within Europe, and war.

Today the world is well into the second great age of globalization, propelled by technological revolutions and the advanced industrialized states' commitment to the liberalization of trade and capital. This time, the United States has put its geopolitical weight behind developing the open world economy—creating multilateral institutions, sponsoring trade negotiations, opening its own markets to imports, and singing the praises of commercial liberalism. After World War II, in support of open markets, the United States worked with other countries to create the General Agreement on Tariffs and Trade (GATT), the International Monetary Fund, the World Bank, and other international trade-related organizations. Based on principles of multilateralism and nondiscrimination, GATT sponsored a series of postwar negotiating rounds that rolled back tariffs from their prewar peaks. In the first multilateral agreement negotiated under GATT—the Geneva round, in 1947—tariffs were reduced, on average, by 35 percent. Successive negotiating rounds in the decades that followed—most recently the Uruguay round, concluded in 1994—have virtually eliminated tariffs on manufactured goods. In 1995, the World Trade Organization (WTO) was established to replace GATT and to guide the expansion of a global, rule-based trading system, armed with elaborate new procedures for settling trade disputes.

The two eras of globalization have both been characterized by rising trade and capital flows. From the mid-nineteenth century to the outbreak of World War I, exports expanded at about 3.5 percent a year, outpacing the rise of domestic production, which rose at 2.7 percent a year. The share of exports in world output reached its peak in 1913, a high point that was not surpassed until 1970.[1] The expansion of the world economy in the nineteenth century was also fueled by the massive flow of capital from the United Kingdom and continental Europe to North America, Australia, and elsewhere. At its highest level, the outflow of capital represented 9 percent of British gross national product (GNP) and almost this amount from Germany, France, and the Netherlands. Before 1914, capital moved around the world with few restrictions, much of it flowing into bonds that financed the building of railroads in North America and into long-term government debt. This openness was facilitated by the gold standard, which allowed currencies to be converted easily at stable prices.

The major trading countries made great strides in reducing trade barriers during the post–World War II era. Most important, they cut tariffs from an average of about 40 percent of the value of imported goods in 1946 to about 5 percent in the 1990s. This liberalization of trade, together with reductions in the costs of transport and communications, caused international commerce to explode over the past 50 years and prompted a major overall increase in international economic integration. As Essential Economics 1.1 shows, the volume of world merchandise exports increased by a factor of more than 19 between 1950 and 1999. By way of comparison, total world production of goods and services, or the world's gross domestic product (GDP), increased during the same period by a factor of somewhat more than 6. The picture that emerges is of the steady increase in cross-border exchanges of goods and services and a resulting increase in the integration of the world's advanced economies.

ESSENTIAL ECONOMICS 1.1

Growth in World Merchandise Exports and World Real Gross Domestic Product, 1950–99

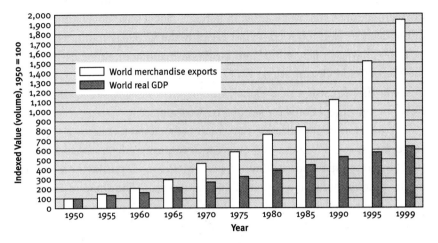

Note: The WTO data employ 1990 as the base year; data in this figure have been recalculated to employ 1950 as the base year.

Source: World Trade Organization, *International Trade Statistics 2000* (Geneva: WTO, 2000), Table II.1, p. 27, available at www.wto.org/english/res_e/statis_e/longtermtrends_e.htm.

> *Core Principle*
>
> **S**ince 1950, trade liberalization has caused exports to skyrocket. The steady increase in cross-border exchanges of goods and services has led to an increasingly integrated world economy.

This increasing integration of the world's major economies can be observed in Essential Economics 1.2, which presents, both for the world as a whole and for each of the seven leading industrialized democracies, the ratio of real merchandise exports to real GDP. Reflecting the trends captured by Essential Economics 1.1, we observe that, although merchandise exports equaled a bit more than 5 percent of world GDP in 1950, they grew to somewhat more than 10 percent in 1973 and to more than 17 percent in 1998. Similarly, the figure indicates that the economy of each of the industrialized democracies has become increasingly integrated with the world economy: note that for countries such as Germany and Canada, by the end of the

✳ ESSENTIAL ECONOMICS 1.2

Real Merchandise Exports as a Percentage of Real Gross Domestic Product, 1950–98

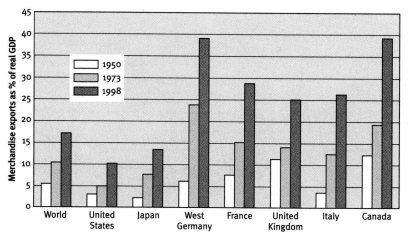

Note: Both exports and GDP are based on 1990 constant international dollars.

Source: Angus Maddison, *The World Economy: A Millennial Perspective* (Paris: Organization for Economic Cooperation and Development, 2001), Table F-5, p. 363, Table A1-b, p. 184 (for Italy and Canada), and Table F-2, p. 361.

> ### Core Principle
> **S**ince 1950, the economies of the world's major countries have become increasingly interconnected.

1990s, merchandise exports accounted for more than one-third of their respective total economies.

The growth of American exposure to the world economy in the post–World War II era can also be observed in Essential Economics 1.2. To show in more detail this most important instance of international economic integration, Essential Economics 1.3 reports on changes across time in U.S. imports and exports as a share of the U.S. GNP. As can be observed in the figure, in the early 1950s imports and exports amounted to about 10 percent of U.S. GNP, but by the 1990s, imports and exports had grown to equal almost a quarter of U.S. GNP. More and more American workers and businesses depend on participation in the world economy.

Just as a century ago, the march of global capitalism appears irresistible

✳ ESSENTIAL ECONOMICS 1.3

U.S. Trade as a Percentage of U.S. Gross National Product, 1900–98

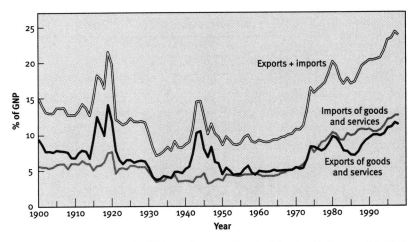

Source: Council of Economic Advisers, *Economic Report of the President: 2000* (Washington: U.S. Government Printing Office, 2000), p. 203, available at w3.access.gpo.gov/usbudget/fy2001/pdf/2000erp.pdf.

> *Core Principle*
>
> The United States has become increasingly integrated into the world economy since 1900, as evidenced by the growing contribution of trade to the country's GNP. More and more American workers and businesses depend on participation in the world economy.

today. The rise of a global economy in the last half-century also appears to have brought with it the promise of more peaceful and cooperative relations among the major countries. After all, with today's economies so tightly linked, it is difficult to imagine that governments would place at risk the jobs and wealth that come with economic interdependence. But it is worth recalling that this was also the optimistic view of many observers a century ago. "International finance has become so interdependent and so interwoven with trade and industry that . . . political and military power can in reality do nothing. . . . These little recognized facts, mainly the outcome of purely modern conditions (rapidity of communications creating a greater complexity and delicacy of the credit system), have rendered the problems of modern international politics profoundly and essentially different from the ancient." These words were written by Nobel Peace Prize–winning author Norman Angell in *The Great Illusion,* a book that has sold over a million copies in seventeen languages—but that was published in 1910. The outbreak of war in 1914 made it clear that economic interdependence and the flow of markets are not the last word or the bottom line in world politics.

To be sure, the character of globalization is much different today than it was on the eve of World War I. The linkages of trade, finance, and investment are more deeply embedded in the industrial societies and international institutions that facilitate the management and stabilization of economic and political relationships. But market orders do rise and fall, and the geopolitical struggles of states do not necessarily obey the rational dictates of markets. To make sense of our era of globalization—and to grasp its logic and its future— it is necessary to look more closely at the complex and dynamic relations between the world of states and the world of market capitalism.

State Power and Interests and Their Impact on Markets

Nation-states have keen interests in the workings of markets. These interests have led governments to get intimately involved in the way in which national and international market relations are organized.

Nation-states emerged in the modern world within a competitive state system that rewarded governments that had access to a thriving economy. The power of the state has always been ultimately dependent on the wealth and productivity of the society of which it is a part. As a result, state leaders have tended to actively foster economic advancement and growth and seek ways to harness the resulting wealth for geopolitical goals. The fiscal and political structures of France, the United Kingdom, and the other European governments have been shaped in critical respects by centuries of military struggle on the continent. The countries that had the most efficient tax systems and most stable banking systems tended to be more capable of raising revenue and armies for war. In the late-nineteenth century, for example, Japan's imperial government undertook a modernization of the social and industrial structure of the country, building Japan up as a powerful state alongside the European great powers. The Japanese state mobilized society and promoted industrial modernization in order to bring Japan into the top ranks of the industrialized world. The United States built a modern administrative state, capable of regulating and mobilizing the national economy, in the 1930s and 1940s in response to the national crisis brought on by Depression and World War II. With an eye on the country's national security, the U.S. government led the way during the Cold War in the creation of entire industrial sectors such as atomic energy and aeronautics. Today governments around the world, seeking to keep their countries on the cutting edge of industrial competitiveness, spend billions of dollars on scientific and technological research and development.

Major states have also conducted foreign economic relations to advance their geopolitical goals. After World War II, the United States used its economy as a tool in building Cold War security partnerships with countries in Asia and Europe. The U.S. government actively sought to integrate Japan into the Western world economy by encouraging Japanese imports into the American domestic market. Officials hoped that expanded trade would boost the Japanese economy and stabilize the Japanese political order—goals that U.S. officials embraced for their most important security partner in Asia. The United States also encouraged the integration and unification of the post-1945 European economies through the massive Marshall Plan and the Atlantic security pact that facilitated the reintegration of West Germany into the European economy. The encouragement of European economic integration served several American purposes: it was hoped that integration would lead to greater economic growth, which would help dampen political instability and opportunities for communist inroads in Western Europe, and it would make Europe a better trade and security partner for the United States. The U.S. government's more recent promotion of trade relations with China, and its support for Chinese membership in the WTO, has been driven partly by the anticipated political impact that greater Chinese integration in the world economy will have on Chinese foreign policy. U.S. officials hope that by creating stronger economic ties with the outside world, the government in Beijing will have additional incentives to pursue cooperative relations with the United States and China's neighbors.

States have also used the promotion of regional economic integration as a tool of political control and security policy. The United States pursued the North American Free Trade Agreement in part to reinforce Mexico's liberalizing reform movement. By connecting Mexico's economy more closely with that of the United States and facilitating foreign investment south of the border, U.S. officials hoped that the resulting integration would make it more difficult for future Mexican governments to backtrack toward inward-looking, nationalist policies. After World War II, the French pursued strategic economic integration with West Germany to bind the two countries together and make it more difficult for Germany to rebuild as a military power and threaten Europe and, in particular, France. Toward this end, the European Coal and Steel Community was created to ensure multi-country ownership of the industries most needed for military mobilization, embedding Germany's strategic industries within a Europe-wide framework. France could have pursued a more traditional strategy of power balancing against Germany, but by tying itself to Germany and Germany to a Europe-wide economic grouping, France was able to ensure its own security while also gaining the economic benefits of a more integrated European continent.

Governments are also constantly concerned about the impact of trade and investment agreements on the economic position of domestic workers and businesses. When governments engage in trade liberalization negotiations, they tend to give a great deal of attention to the impact of trade pacts on their country's businesses. Elaborate private-sector advisory groups often play a part in government planning and negotiations. Governments around the world are responsive to domestic interest groups. Korea has high tariffs on the importation of foreign rice because of pressure from the domestic agricultural lobby. Japan's ruling Liberal Democratic Party, which has led the country for most of the postwar era, is heavily dependent on the support of rural agricultural interests, and this dependence has resulted in a highly protected agricultural sector in Japan. U.S. trade policy has used trade laws to protect a wide array of domestic commercial industries, including steel, autos, and textiles. The French government made its membership in the European Economic Community in the 1950s contingent on the protection of French farmers against the more competitive German producers. The result was the Common Agricultural Policy, which continues to be an integral part of the political bargain between France and Germany. Recently, the European Union's commitment to expand its membership to include more eastern European countries has stalled because of fear by France and other member states that their agricultural sectors will be injured by agricultural producers in Poland and other former Soviet-bloc countries. In the United States, a recent poll indicated that 69 percent of Americans believe that trade restrictions are justified to protect jobs. The same poll revealed that only 52 percent of the public believes that trade helps the economy.

Governments also attempt to use trade and investment to manipulate the policies of other states. The use of economic sanctions lies at the heart of efforts by states to punish or pressure other states without the direct use of military force. But sanctions are a difficult instrument of policy. For example, the United States and the United Kingdom, working through the United Nations (UN), sought to use sanctions as a signal to Iraqi dictator Saddam Hussein that Iraq's August 1990 invasion of Kuwait was unacceptable and might bring on a war with the United States; Iraq failed to reverse its course of belligerence, and a full-scale Anglo-American military attack was required in early 1991 to push Iraq out of Kuwait. Later, the United States and the United Kingdom sought to use economic sanctions under the auspices of the United Nations to constrain Saddam from renewing his country's programs to acquire weapons of mass destruction (that is, nuclear, chemical, and biological weapons); international support for these sanctions progressively weakened over the course of the 1990s, and by 2001 the UN sanctions regime against Saddam had effectively collapsed. However, although sanctions by themselves neither reversed the Iraqi invasion of Kuwait nor stopped Saddam from moving ahead with his weapons programs, we should not conclude that they were without value. As we will see in Chapter 6, even when sanctions do not achieve their immediate ends, they may have important value.

In all these various ways, national governments have attempted to establish, extend, and manipulate markets for political goals. It is sometimes thought that governments primarily attempt to disrupt or regulate markets, whereas businesses seek open markets. But actually the opposite is often the case. Promoting market relations—through regional integration, deregulation, trade liberalization, and so forth—can serve the state's geopolitical goals. The impulses that lead governments into the economy are more varied and complex.

World Markets and Their Impact on States

Just as states shape and manipulate markets, so too do markets shape and constrain states. The organization and evolution of world markets—trade, monetary, and financial systems—have varied and pervasive impacts on the power and choices of states. Consider the following examples.

In a flexible exchange-rate system (the details of which will be discussed in Chapter 3), a country's currency and, as a result, its economy can be punished by "incorrect" economic policies. When François Mitterrand was elected president of France in 1980, he pursued an ambitious socialist agenda aimed at the nationalization of banks and industry and the expansion of welfare spending. At the time, the other major industrialized countries—the United States, the United Kingdom, and Germany—were led by conservative parties committed to deregulation and *restrictive monetary policies*. Currency markets responded negatively to Mitterrand's economic agenda and the value of the French franc on the international exchange market began to fall, eventually forcing the new president to return to more centrist economic policies. In the spring of 1998, in the wake of the Asian financial crisis and a few months before national elections, Indonesian president Suharto violated the terms of an agreement it had negotiated with the International Monetary Fund (IMF) by proposing new spending measures. This action triggered an abrupt plunge in Indonesia's currency, requiring the negotiation of a new currency-support package with the IMF. Suharto was re-elected, but he was nonetheless caught between a collapsing economy and IMF-mandated austerity measures. Social unrest continued to build and, a few months later, Suharto resigned from office. During the same period, South Korea, Brazil, Russia, and other countries struggled in the wake of the collapse of the Thai baht to stabilize their currencies and also entered into financial-support agreements with the IMF. They, too, found themselves with little freedom of action, dependent on external assistance and forced to enact particular policies.

When states become more integrated into the world trading system—that is, when a growing share of domestic economic production is tied to imports and exports—the domestic political constituencies in favor of stable and continuous relations with the outside world grow. The costs of disruptions go up. When China and the United States confronted each other in the spring of 2001 over the downing of an American intelligence-gathering plane off the coast of China, Beijing had to weigh the economic consequences of a prolonged crisis. One Western observer commented, "The more China's economy is integrated with the world economy, the more dependent she is on the outside world and the less she can afford to embark upon some adventurous course."[2] Aggressive moves toward Taiwan and other neighbors risk disrupting trade and investment, which amounts to approximately 30 percent of China's GDP. The opening to the world economy also provides China with technology, management techniques, and financial expertise critical to the government's ambitious modernization goals. The more belligerent China is in its foreign policy, the more ammunition other countries have to act against China's interests. Moreover, Taiwan's economic investment in mainland China also creates incentives for Beijing to seek a peaceful resolution of its dispute with Taiwan. Taiwan has invested more than $50 billion in the mainland, and trade across the Taiwan Strait reached $30 billion in 2000, making Taiwan China's sixth-largest trading partner. "Over the long run I believe that economic integration will lead to some kind of social and political integration," argues Lin Chong-ping, vice-chairman of Taiwan's Mainland Affairs Council.[3]

As economic linkages grow between countries, vested interests—that is, interest groups with a direct economic stake in trade relationships—emerge and can help shape foreign policy. The dense economic connections between the United States, Europe, and Japan have been matched by the rise of business councils and other groupings of commercial interests that seek to promote openness and stable economic relationships across the Atlantic and the Pacific. In Japan, the leading business organization, Keidanren, is a strong voice within the political establishment, favoring Japan's commitment to open multilateral trade and investment relations. In the United States, leading business groups weigh in with Congress and the executive branch, seeking the expansion of trade and investment opportunities in China and elsewhere around the world. Within the Republican Party and the Bush administration, there are policy groups deeply suspicious of China that favor a hard-line policy of limited economic ties. But other voices in the party reflect the views of American business with strong trade connections with China. The foreign policy that actually emerges is shaped by a mix of views, including those of people who speak, at least indirectly, for these commercial interests.

The expansion of foreign direct investment across the industrialized world has created new and more complex national economic interests that have important implications for countries' foreign and economic policies. During the 1980s, Japanese auto companies, including Toyota and Honda, established assembly plants in the United States. In part they were responding to worries about American trade protectionism and exchange-rate instabilities. But they were also seeking to create vested interests inside the United States—among American workers—who henceforth would have a stake in stable trade and investment relations with Japan. Former secretary of labor Robert Reich captured this new reality in an op-ed piece he wrote: "American companies are making things everywhere and selling them everywhere. And Americans are working for global companies headquartered all over the place. General Motors makes cars in Germany for export to Japan. Companies such as Compaq get their hard-disk drives from Taiwan. Dell and

Hewlett-Packard get their computer modems there. IBM and Motorola make all sorts of gadgets in South Korea, Taiwan, and the Philippines. Boeing's aircraft parts come from 17 different countries."[4]

The new software and Internet business world tends to take this borderless logic to the extreme. One software start-up company, for example, has a mailing address in California, its software is designed by a team in Croatia, its chief-executive is a Canadian who has been working in Hong Kong, its vice president for technology is Russian, and its vice president for sales is German but is living in Tokyo. If national economies are increasingly woven together by cross-cutting foreign investment and complex transnational production and service networks, how do national governments define and pursue the "national interest"? At the very least, it is more difficult for national leaders to separate one country's economic interests from another's. Protection may be increasingly self-defeating. Governments may still want to act on behalf of the national economy—its businesses and workers—but they may no longer know how to do so.

The expansion and deepening of the world economy leaves states in a delicate position. Countries that open themselves up to trade and investment do tend to benefit through greater economic growth and advancement. Governments are often the initiators of economic openness and integration. But economic interdependence also alters the array of domestic interests and changes the calculations that states must make in their foreign and security policies.

Looking Ahead

These complex dynamics between state and market will be explored in the chapters that follow. In Chapter 2, we look at the basic economic logic of international trade relations. Modern economic theory provides a strong basis for the view that nations have an interest in constructing mechanisms that enable international trade flows because they achieve gains from international economic specialization and factor mobility. But these same theoretical insights suggest that particular factor owners may lose from integration with the international trading system and thus have a rational basis to prefer protection over trade competition.

Chapter 3 will explore monetary and financial relations. Like trade, monetary flows provide a basis for national benefits but also pose potential costs, particularly the erosion of national policy autonomy. These theoretical constructs help identify where the gains and losses are to be found in world economic relations. They do not tell us, however, how states will perceive and act on these interests and incentives.

Chapter 4 explores the logic of state power and competition in the organization of the world economy. We show the varied motivations that lead states to push for greater openness or closure. States tend to want it both ways: to experience the gains that come from exposure to the world economy but to also avoid the losses. The anarchy of the international system, a situation that creates incentives for states to enhance their own power and be suspicious of others, prompts states to promote market openness when it leads to domestic economic growth and wealth creation. But the same competitive pressures can lead states to restrict trade or manipulate commercial relations to achieve greater gains than do their rivals. Powerful states—such as the United Kingdom in the nineteenth century and the United States after World War II—have incentives to overcome the problems of anarchy and to use their commanding position to create an open and stable world economic system. Likewise, international institutions can be used by states to overcome competitive pressures and to reinforce stable commitments to economic openness.

Chapter 5 looks more directly at the circumstances that lead states to enhance their power and pursue geopolitical goals through market integration. The United States, emerging from World War II as the world's leading state, sought to create an institutionalized system of free trade and convertible currencies. As we shall see, the Cold War played an important role in creating the incentives for the United States to seek the reintegration of Germany and Japan into this open system. The same logic led the United States to promote European integration. Open, multilateral relations within Europe were championed by the United States and reinforced by the Atlantic security pact as a way to extinguish rival nationalism, prevent the re-emergence of German militarism, and create binding political ties that would stabilize relations between old adversaries. Political bargains helped cement this postwar liberal multilateral order—an order that still serves as the foundation of today's globalizing world economy.

Chapter 6 turns the tables to consider the ways in which states have used economic sanctions and economic incentives to achieve political goals. Both types of instruments have had a decidedly mixed record of success, and this chapter identifies the various conditions under which they tend to work.

Chapter 7 shifts the angle of analysis yet again. Rather than looking at how states shape the international economy, Chapter 7 looks at how international economic integration can induce political change and conflict within and between nations. In particular, it looks at how processes of economic globalization can create economic inequities. Greater economic integration can activate conflicts within countries over worker rights and health standards and can make it more difficult for governments to react to financial shocks. Cultural conflicts can also be brought to life by globalization. Greater economic integration can create new incentives for countries to resolve their differences and contain political conflict, but it also creates new conflicts between states and within countries.

Chapter 8 looks at the policy dilemmas that face developing countries within the world economy, looking at the variations in the economic experiences of developing countries in the postwar era. International economic integration has been a necessary element of economic development but it is not, in itself, sufficient to ensure development. In our examination of these issues we identify critical institutional factors within countries and international linkages that are important for successful economic development.

Chapter 9 looks at the challenges of global economic governance. Governance in the postwar era has tended to come in several varieties. The most ambitious has been rule-based governance—realized most fully in the WTO—that embeds cooperation between countries in binding institutional mechanisms. But governance has also been provided by informal, smaller-group mechanisms, in which processes of consultation and ad hoc policy coordination are pursued. Regional groupings are another way in which states are seeking to govern international economic relations. The challenge ahead is to find ways to integrate nongovernmental organizations into global and regional multilateral institutional mechanisms.

In Chapter 10 we will probe the key challenges facing the international political economy in the future. These include the fate of the U.S. engagement policy toward China, the uncertain course of European monetary and political union, reform of the international financial system, and the dynamics unleashed by growing world economic inequality. A stable and open world economy hinges on the ability of states to find mechanisms that allow them to overcome competitive protectionist pressures, renew commitments to joint economic management, and discover ways to tackle new threats of conflict and instability.

Notes

[1]"Globalization in Historical Perspective," in International Monetary Fund, *World Economic Outlook, May 1997* (Washington, D.C.: IMF, 1997), p. 112.

[2]James Kynge, "China's Binding Ties," *Financial Times,* May 10, 2001.

[3]Craig S. Smith, "Signs in China and Taiwan of Making Money, Not War," *New York Times,* May 15, 2001.

[4]Robert B. Reich, ". . . And Does Anyone Know How to Define an 'American' Interest?" *Washington Post,* November 21, 1999.

Chapter 2

The Economics of International Trade

Introduction

OBJECTIVES

- Understand the three elements of microeconomic theory that serve as the building blocks for trade theory: consumption indifference curves, production possibilities frontiers, and optimized market equilibrium.
- Explore the Ricardian (classical), constant-costs model of comparative advantage and mutually advantageous trade.
- Explore the neoclassical, increasing-costs model of trade and the contribution made by the Heckscher-Ohlin theorem to our understanding of the bases of comparative advantage.
- Examine the Stolper-Samuelson theorem that trade, although beneficial to a country as a whole, may create losses for particular groups within that country, thus giving them a rational basis to prefer protection over trade.
- Understand the new areas of economic research regarding the possible contributions of trade to national economic growth (trade and endogenous growth) and changes in the composition of trade (intra-industry vs. inter-industry trade).

Y ou are living in Des Moines, Iowa. You wake up in a house built with lumber from Canada. You wear clothes fabricated in India or Honduras and shoes from Italy or Brazil. You prepare a breakfast that includes orange juice from Brazil and cereal from Switzerland; you use silverware made in China, South Korea, or Finland; and you sit at a breakfast table manufactured in Thailand or Denmark. You drive to work in an automobile built in Japan or Germany or Sweden and use gasoline that was refined from oil imported from Venezuela, Nigeria, or Saudi Arabia. At lunch you have a salad consisting of tomatoes from Belgium, bell peppers from the Netherlands, lettuce from Mexico, grapes from Chile, olives from Greece, and cheese from France. You have to make a phone call during lunch, and to do so you use a cell phone made in Finland or Sweden. After work you return home and watch the news on a television set made in Mexico; you catch up on your e-mail using a laptop computer assembled in Taiwan of components made in Singapore and China; and you listen to some music by placing a German-made CD into a Japanese-made CD player. Before you retire for the evening, you turn off the lights in your house, which were made in Mexico. You reflect, as you drift off to sleep, on your upcoming visits to Prague and Budapest, with a brief layover in London.[1]

International trade affects what we eat, what we wear, what we watch and listen to, how we move about, where we go, and how we earn a living. But how exactly is it possible for consumers in Iowa to obtain tomatoes from Belgium? How do people in Finland know that people in Des Moines wish to buy cell phones? How, in other words, does trade come about? What determines who sells what, and who buys what? And is all this trade a good idea?

We will see in Chapters 4 and 5 that politics determines the answers to these questions to a remarkably large degree. However, the discipline of economics during the past two centuries also has developed a powerful understanding of the sources, mechanics, and effects of international trade. By understanding international trade theory we can identify some of the most important and interesting political issues relating to the world political economy.

Hence, in this chapter we present the main elements of international trade theory. We begin our review with a brief consideration of the building blocks for trade theory that are taken from microeconomics. Using these analytical building blocks, we introduce the two basic models of trade, the Ricardian or classical model, and the more contemporary neoclassical model, emphasizing both what they have in common and where they diverge. Both models, we shall see, reach the same fundamentally important result: trade improves the overall welfare of nations by allowing them to make the best use of their scarce productive resources, and to improve their overall consumption by producing certain things themselves and obtaining other goods and services from other nations. In light of the tremendous gains that trade holds for nations, economists are skeptical of most arguments that are made against international commerce. However, although trade may benefit a nation as a whole, groups within a nation may in some circumstances lose from freer trade and therefore may have a rational reason to resist more open trade. Finally, we shall explore two frontiers of research in international trade theory, one relating trade to national economic growth, and another focusing on the tendency of many countries to trade similar rather than dissimilar goods. Both of these new lines of inquiry, we shall see, have led economists to rethink some elements of their theory of trade, and both point to important new developments in the world trading system.

Analytical Building Blocks

Economists rely on three analytical tools in their exploration of the bases for and benefits of trade: consumption indifference curves, production possibilities frontiers, and an analysis of optimized production-consumption equilibrium in the absence of trade.

Consumption Indifference Curves

Economists assume that individuals derive happiness, or utility, from their consumption of goods. Different combinations of goods, or what economists term "market baskets," may each provide an individual with the same level of utility. For example, an individual may be exactly as happy consuming a market basket containing five pairs of shoes and two computers as he or she would be consuming a market basket containing six pairs of shoes and one computer. As a result, if presented with a choice between two such baskets, the individual would be *indifferent* as to which of these two market baskets is preferable, for each would provide the same level of utility. A graphical representation of the different combinations of shoes and computers that would provide the individual with a constant level of satisfaction would be that person's **consumption indifference curve** with respect to shoes and computers.

Economists have employed the concept of an individual's consumption indifference curves in their analyses of trade between countries. They assume that it is possible to aggregate the satisfaction levels that all residents of one country attain from the consumption of different baskets of goods, and therefore that it is possible to create *national* consumption indifference curves. In this book, when we refer to consumption indifference curves, we are referring to the consumption indifference curves for countries taken as a whole.

Examples of hypothetical consumption indifference curves for the United States are presented in Essential Economics 2.1(a). Let us begin with indifference curve U_0. The different combinations of computers and shoes along that curve—for example, those represented by points *A, B, C,* and *D*—provide the country with exactly the same level of aggregate satisfaction.

U_0 is convex with respect to the origin, not straight or concave. The premise underlying this characteristic of the indifference curve is that of **declining marginal utility from consumption** of additional increments of any given good. That is, as an individual consumes more and more increments of one good, each increment delivers less and less satisfaction than the preceding increment, and therefore the individual becomes less and less willing to forgo other goods to obtain that next increment. By consequence, if the United States is at point *A* on U_0 and is asked how many pairs of shoes it is willing to forgo to obtain 2 million more computers, all the while retaining the level of satisfaction it enjoys at point *A*, its response would be 40 million pairs (this new market basket is represented by point *B* on U_0). However, if the United States is at point *C* on U_0, in response to the same question the answer would be not 40 million pairs, but only 10 million pairs (shown by point *D* on U_0).

Economists therefore suggest that a curve like U_0 reveals a declining **marginal rate of substitution** of computers for shoes on the part of the United States. The marginal rate of substitution at any point along an indifference curve is the absolute value of the slope of the indifference curve at that point. Because the slope of U_0 declines as we move along the curve from left to right, so does the marginal rate of substitution decline.

One other key observation can be derived from Essential Economics 2.1(a). What happens if the United States is no longer presented with the combinations of shoes and computers depicted by U_0, but instead can

✳ ESSENTIAL ECONOMICS 2.1

Three Building Blocks for Economic Analysis

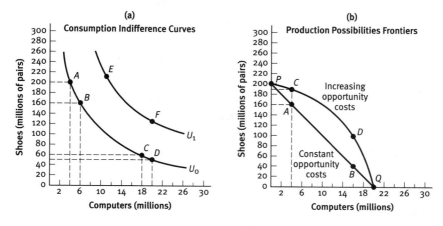

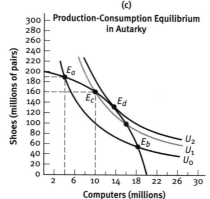

Consumption indifference curves (panel a) graphically represent the different combinations of two goods that would provide a nation with a constant level of satisfaction. Production possibilities frontiers (panel b) show the trade-offs that countries make in the production of two different goods. The optimization of both consumption and production in autarky is shown by the point of tangency between the production possibilities frontier and the highest possible consumption indifference curve (panel c).

Core Principle

Consumption indifference curves, production possibilities frontiers, and production-consumption equilibrium in autarky all show a country's production and consumption options in the absence of international trade.

choose among a new set of market baskets, each of which contains more computers, more pairs of shoes, or more of both? Such market baskets are represented by the curve labeled U_1. Since points on U_1, such as E and F, represent combinations of goods that mark an increase, as compared with points on U_0, in American consumption of shoes or computers or both, the United States must be enjoying a higher level of satisfaction along each point of U_1 than it is at any point along U_0.

Hence, and this concept will be crucially important in our later discussion of the effects of trade, anything that permits the United States to increase its consumption of at least one good must be improving overall American satisfaction and must therefore be producing a movement by the United States to a *higher indifference curve*. Trade, as we will see later in this chapter, is precisely such a mechanism; it provides a way for countries to improve their overall levels of consumption and thereby to move to higher indifference curves, signifying higher levels of overall societal satisfaction.

Production Possibilities Frontiers

The second analytical device we need to acquire for our discussion of trade theory is the concept of a **production possibilities frontier.** A production possibilities frontier represents the different combinations of goods that a country can produce during some period of time (in our illustrative discussion below, one year), given the full exploitation of the productive resources available in the country during that period of time. Two basic types of production possibilities frontier are presented in Essential Economics 2.1(b): the first is built on the premise of *constant opportunity costs,* and the second is built on the premise of *increasing opportunity costs.*

Production Possibilities Frontiers with Constant Opportunity Costs

Let us begin with the production possibilities frontier in Essential Economics 2.1(b) closest to the origin. Notice that this frontier has a negative slope, and that it is a straight line. The first characteristic of the frontier—that its slope is negative—indicates that **opportunity costs** are present in production. As can be observed of the inner frontier in Essential Economics 2.1(b), if the United States puts all its productive resources into shoe manufacturing, it can reach point P on that frontier and produce 200 million pairs of shoes in one year. If it decides to produce not just shoes but also computers, it would need to take some of its resources out of shoe manufacturing and reallocate them to the production of computers. For example, if the United States elects to build 4 million computers, that is, to go from point P to point A on the inner frontier, it needs to reduce its production of shoes by 40 million pairs. In this example, then, the cost of building one computer in the United States is the opportunity to produce ten pairs of shoes. In the language of economics, the opportunity cost of producing one computer is the production forgone of ten pairs of shoes. This notion of opportunity costs is absolutely central to our upcoming discussion of the bases for and dynamics of trade.

As we have noted, the inner production possibilities frontier in Essential Economics 2.1(b) is drawn as a straight line. This second characteristic of the frontier indicates that the opportunity cost of producing computers in terms of shoes forgone remains *constant* (as we have drawn the frontier, constant at ten pairs of shoes forgone for each computer built) no matter how many additional increments of computers the United States chooses to build. By virtue of the assumption of constant opportunity costs, if the United States wants to go from point B to point Q on the frontier, that is, from 16 million to 20 million computers produced, then it needs to forgo the production of 40 million pairs of shoes, the same amount it must forgo when moving from point A to point B on the frontier.

Production Possibilities Frontiers with Increasing Opportunity Costs

We will be using a production possibilities frontier that is based on constant opportunity costs later in this chapter when we discuss the first major economic theory of trade. However, in more recent years economists have built their models of trade, which we will also discuss later, on the basis of the assumption that production possibilities frontiers should represent *increasing* opportunity costs. In other words, they assume that successive, equal increases in the production of one good will require forgoing the production of larger and larger increments of the other good. The rationale for this switch to an assumption of increasing opportunity costs is that it is usually more reasonable to assume that, although the first redeployment of an increment of productive resources from one use to another might produce very large results, eventually, as more and more increments of resources are so redeployed, decreasing ***returns to scale*** for the resource increments are likely to come into effect.

To see how decreasing returns might arise, and how decreasing returns create increasing opportunity costs, let us assume the following about a country:

- It has land on which it can grow either grapes or wheat;
- Some of the land is better suited for grapes than for wheat, whereas some of the land is better suited for wheat than for grapes; and
- At first, the country is using all available land to produce grapes.

If this country were to decide to grow some wheat, it would need to select plots of land to take out of grape production, and then use those plots to plant wheat. In order to maximize the production of wheat and to minimize the reduction in the production of grapes, the country would select the plots of land that are the least suited for grapes and the most suited for wheat. In doing so, it would find at first that forgoing a relatively small amount of grapes results in the production of large amounts of wheat. But what if the country wanted to produce more and more wheat? Eventually, it would have to use plots of land that were progressively less suited for wheat and more suited for grapes. As a result, the amount of additional wheat harvested per plot of additional land so allocated would decline. In the face of such decreasing returns in wheat production with respect to land, an effort by the country to produce successive equal increments of wheat would require forgoing the production of ever larger volumes of grapes—that is, there would be *increasing* opportunity costs for wheat in terms of grapes forgone.

The outer frontier in Essential Economics 2.1 (b) is an example of a production possibilities frontier for computers and shoes that is characterized by such increasing opportunity costs. Note that movement from point *P* to point *C* on the outer frontier, that is, increasing U.S. computer production from 0 to 4 million computers, requires a reduction in U.S. shoe production by 10 million pairs. However, because we are assuming decreasing returns as America shifts resources from shoes to computers, if we instead start at point *D* and increase computer production by the same amount, 4 million computers, to reach point *Q*, we must accept a vastly greater drop in shoe production, about 100 million pairs.

More generally, and in contrast to the inner production possibilities frontier in Essential Economics 2.1(b), the outer frontier reflects increasing opportunity costs for computers in terms of shoes forgone, and what economists term an increasing **marginal rate of product transformation** between computers and shoes. The marginal rate of product transformation at any point along a production possibilities frontier is the absolute value of the slope of the curve at that point. Insofar as the outer frontier in Essential Economics 2.1(b) depicts a requirement that more and more shoes must be forgone in order to build each additional fixed increment of computers, the slope of the outer curve is increasing, indicating an increasing marginal rate of product transformation between shoes and computers.

Optimized Production and Consumption in Autarky

Essential Economics 2.1(c), in which consumption indifference curves and production possibilities frontiers are superimposed on one another, provides a final key analytical building block for our understanding of the sources and benefits of trade. This panel presents economists' conception of the manner in which a country achieves its highest level of satisfaction in the context of *autarky*, that is, in the absence of trade. This analysis of optimization in autarky, we will see in the following discussion, allows us to appreciate how a country can enjoy greater satisfaction if it moves from autarky to participation in the international trading system, and therefore why countries choose to participate in world trade.

We begin with another hypothetical production possibilities frontier, which we assume is characterized by increasing opportunity costs (i.e., its slope is increasing as we move from left to right). As with the curves in Essentialized Economics 2.1(b), this frontier depicts the different combinations of computers and shoes that the United States can produce in one year with its current resources. Because we are assuming that absolutely no trade is taking place, the production possibilities frontier also sets the limits on what the United States can consume: Americans are able to consume only the combinations of the two goods that are on or inside the frontier. Assuming that all goods that are produced are consumed, the effective range of choice for the United States in terms of optimum consumption is the locus of points that constitutes the production possibilities frontier.

In these circumstances, the United States produces the combination of shoes and computers that provides the maximum level of satisfaction possible.

Consider the country's reasoning if it finds itself at point E_a. How much would it have to give up in terms of shoe production forgone in order to consume 10 million rather than 4 million computers—that is, what is the drop in shoe production that is associated with a move from E_a to E_c? The answer, if we move along the production possibilities frontier, is about 30 million pairs of shoes. Yet how many pairs of shoes would the United States be *willing* to forgo to obtain those extra 6 million computers while being no worse off in terms of its level of satisfaction? The answer, as we move down along the consumption indifference curve U_0, is about 90 million pairs. By shifting resources from shoes to computers and moving from E_a to E_c, the United States could have all the satisfaction it enjoys at E_a, plus the satisfaction of the 60 million pairs of shoes that it would be *willing* to forgo, but would not have to forgo, in order to obtain the 6 million extra computers. Recalling our discussion about consumption indifference curves in Essential Economics 2.1(a), it is clear that, by moving from E_a to E_c, the United States is enjoying a higher level of satisfaction and therefore must have shifted to a higher indifference curve—specifically, curve U_1.

Clearly, then, the combination represented by point E_a, at which the United States is producing and consuming 4 million computers and 190 million pairs of shoes, is not an optimum outcome. At point E_a, the United States would be willing to forgo consuming many more shoes in exchange for computers than it would actually have to forgo producing in order to make those computers. More theoretically, at E_a, the country's marginal rate of substitution exceeds its marginal rate of product transformation; equivalently, at E_a, the slope of the country's consumption indifference curve is greater than the slope of its production possibilities frontier. Likewise, if the United States found itself at point E_b, it would find it in its interest to shift resources out of computers and into shoes. At point E_b, the slope of the production possibilities frontier is greater than the slope of the consumption indifference curve, which means its marginal rate of product transformation exceeds its marginal rate of substitution.

Where, then, does the country maximize its happiness in light of its production possibilities frontier? Maximum satisfaction is found at point E_d, which is associated with the indifference curve U_2. At that point, the marginal rate of substitution of computers for shoes is exactly equal to the marginal rate of product transformation between the two goods. That is, at point E_d, given its preferences for the two goods and its ability to make them, the United States cannot improve its satisfaction further by changing its production or consumption choices. This situation can change, however, if we introduce the opportunity for the United States to engage in international trade.

Why Do Nations Engage in Trade?

The Ricardian Model: Two Countries, Two Goods, and Constant Opportunity Costs

Using these basic building blocks, economists have demonstrated that countries can gain from trade and thereby have an incentive to engage in such transactions across their borders.

To make this issue concrete, consider the following questions:

- From 1996 to 2000, the United States bought about $400 million per year in coffee and coffee products from Brazil. Coffee, however, was not the largest product category of Brazilian exports to the United States during this period; the highest it ranked was second, in 1997. On average, the biggest category of Brazilian export products going to the United States during 1996–2000 was footwear, which averaged $1.1 billion per year during that period.[2] Now, it might be obvious why the United States buys coffee from Brazil: it cannot be grown readily in the U.S. climate and it can be in Brazil. But how, in light of the fact that the United States is an industrial powerhouse, could the United States possibly benefit from importing from Brazil something as simple to make as shoes?

- The biggest single category of U.S. exports to Brazil between 1996 and 2000 was telecommunications equipment: it averaged about $1.2 billion per year during this period. Yet the biggest overall area of U.S. exports to Brazil during the late 1990s, at an average level of $1.8 billion per year, was information technology—that is, computers, computer parts, and parts for other office equipment. What is remarkable about these U.S. information-technology hardware exports to Brazil during the late 1990s is that it followed a 20-year period during which Brazil had been seeking and had made some progress in nurturing a domestic Brazilian computer industry.[3] Given this apparent Brazilian national interest in promoting an indigenous computer industry, why didn't Brazil simply prohibit computer imports and thereby create a market for local computer producers? How, in other words, does Brazil gain from buying U.S. computers rather than building them at home?

➤ TIMELINE 2.1

The Development of International Trade Theory

1776	Adam Smith argues his free-market critique of mercantilism
1817	David Ricardo develops Ricardian (classical) model
1879	Alfred Marshall proposes offer curves and trade
1919	Eli Heckscher ⎱ develop what comes to be known as the
1930	Bertil Ohlin ⎰ Heckscher-Ohlin theorem
1930	Gottfried Haberler explores increasing opportunity costs and trade
1932	A. P. Lerner explores increasing opportunity costs and trade
1933	Wassily Leontief explores increasing opportunity costs and trade
1939	Paul Samuelson advocates the gains from trade
1941	Wolfgang Stolper and Paul Samuelson propound the Stolper-Samuelson theorem
1975	H. G. Grubel and P. L. Lloyd examine intra-industry trade
1981	Paul Krugman and Elhanan Helpman theorize on increasing economies of scale and trade
1986	Paul Romer develops endogenous growth theory

The foundations of the neoclassical model (1930 Haberler – 1939 Samuelson)

To understand why the United States and Brazil exchange shoes for computers today, we can usefully employ the logic of ***comparative advantage.*** The benefits of freer trade were highlighted by Adam Smith in his foundational 1776 work, *The Wealth of Nations,* and the logic of comparative advantage as the underpinning for this view was presented by David Ricardo in 1817.[4]

Let us, for the following discussion, stipulate these assumptions:

- There are only two countries, Brazil and the United States;
- Brazil and the United States produce only two goods, computers and shoes;
- There are no transportation costs for goods shipped between Brazil and the United States;

ESSENTIAL ECONOMICS 2.2

Hypothetical Output Levels, United States and Brazil

	OUTPUT PER WORKER PER YEAR		OPPORTUNITY COST	
	Computers	*Pairs of shoes*	*1 computer*	*1 pair of shoes*
United States	50	200	4 pairs shoes	.25 computer
Brazil	5	175	35 pairs shoes	.03 computer

> *Core Principle*
>
> **A**n absolute advantage in manufacturing does not necessarily imply a comparative advantage.

- Only one input, labor, is required for the production of either computers or shoes;
- There are constant opportunity costs between the two goods in each country, or, in graphical terms, the production possibilities frontiers for both countries for computers and shoes, while possessing different slopes, are straight lines;
- The United States and Brazil each have one million labor-years of total labor supply; and
- Any one worker in the United States and Brazil is able to produce in one year the number of computers or pairs of shoes depicted in the first two columns of Essential Economics 2.2.

Any one worker in the United States, in this scenario, can produce more computers than can any one worker in Brazil (50 in America as opposed to 5 in Brazil), and any American worker can also produce more pairs of shoes than can a Brazilian worker (200 as opposed to 175 pairs). The United States, in other words, has an *absolute advantage* over Brazil in both computers and shoes. In these circumstances, it might appear to be highly unlikely that the United States could gain anything from trade with Brazil.

The key to appreciating the potential basis for mutually profitable trade between these two countries lies in the differences in opportunity costs each faces with respect to shoes and computers. As we discussed earlier, if the United States wants to produce more shoes, it can do so only by moving workers out of computer manufacturing. Over the course of one year, for each worker it shifts from computers to shoes, 50 fewer computers are built and 200 pairs of shoes are produced. For each additional pair of shoes produced, then, the United States must forgo the production of 1/4 of a computer (50 computers whose production is forgone ÷ 200 pairs of shoes thereby produced = 1/4 computer forgone per additional pair of shoes produced). Hence, the opportunity cost of each additional pair of shoes produced in the United States is the production forgone of 1/4 of a computer. If the United States prefers to have more computers and thus shifts workers from shoe making to computer manufacturing, then, for each worker so shifted, computer production goes up by 50 units over the year while shoe production goes down by 200 pairs. Therefore, the opportunity cost of 1 additional computer is the production forgone of 4 pairs of shoes (200 pairs of shoes whose production is forgone ÷ 50 additional computers thereby produced = 4 pairs of shoes forgone per additional computer produced).

By the same token, in Brazil, each worker shifted from computers to shoes causes production of the former to go down by 5 computers while allowing production of the latter to go up by 175 pairs; the opportunity cost of 1 additional pair of shoes made in Brazil is the production forgone of about .03 computer. Each Brazilian worker shifted from shoe production to computer manufacturing causes the former to go down by 175 pairs while allowing the latter to go up by 5 computers; the opportunity cost of 1 additional computer produced in Brazil is the production forgone of 35 pairs of shoes. These opportunity costs for the United States and Brazil are shown in the third and fourth columns of Essential Economics 2.2.

Now comes the critical point. If we ask where it is relatively cheaper to build additional computers in terms of pairs of shoes forgone, we see in the third column of Essential Economics 2.2 that the answer is in the United States, where only 4 pairs of shoes must be forgone to build each additional computer, as opposed to the 35 pairs that must be forgone in Brazil. The United States, then, has a comparative advantage over Brazil in the making of computers. By the same token, if we ask where it is relatively cheaper to manufacture additional pairs of shoes in terms of computers forgone, we see in the fourth column of Essential Economics 2.2 that the answer is in Brazil, for there only .03 computers must be forgone to produce each additional pair of shoes, whereas in the United States, .25 computers must be forgone. Brazil, therefore, has a comparative advantage over the United States in the production of shoes.

We can now employ the analytical tools developed in the preceding section to appreciate how the logic of comparative advantage produces opportu-

✳ ESSENTIAL ECONOMICS 2.3

The Ricardian Model of Trade

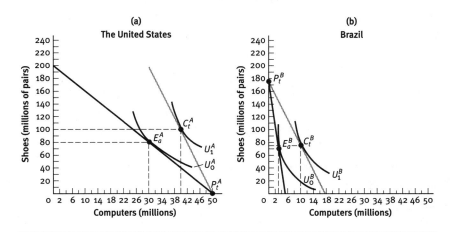

C o r e   P r i n c i p l e

Trade between two countries allows each of them to specialize and increases each country's level of overall satisfaction.

nities for mutually beneficial trade between countries. Consider the two graphs in Essential Economics 2.3: the solid straight lines in panels (a) and (b) represent the production possibilities frontiers for the United States and Brazil, respectively. At the moment we are assuming constant opportunity costs between computers and shoes in each country, so the production possibilities frontier for each country is drawn as a straight line. Furthermore, the slopes of the two countries' production possibilities frontiers differ from one another, reflecting the different opportunity costs each country experiences in production of the two goods.

We begin with the situations in the United States and Brazil under the assumption of autarky. In autarky, as we discussed earlier, the only consumption opportunities available to each country are those defined by their respective production possibilities frontiers. Let us assume that, in autarky, demand conditions in Brazil and the United States are such that each allocates 600,000 labor years to computers and 400,000 labor years to shoes. In these circumstances, market equilibrium in the United States is at point E_a^A in Essential Economics 2.3(a), at which the United States is producing and

consuming 30 million computers and 80 million pairs of shoes and is enjoying a level of satisfaction that is represented by consumption indifference
curve U_0^A. Brazil's market equilibrium in autarky is at point E_a^B in Essential
Economics 2.3(b), at which it is producing and consuming 3 million computers and 70 million pairs of shoes and is enjoying a level of satisfaction
that is represented by consumption indifference curve U_0^B.

What happens now if trade becomes possible between the United States
and Brazil? If trade becomes possible, then the United States specializes on
the basis of its comparative advantage: it stops making shoes and increases
its production of computers from 30 million to 50 million units. This is
noted in Essential Economics 2.3(a) by the movement downward along the
U.S. production possibilities frontier from E_a^A to P_t^A. Brazil also specializes
on the basis of its comparative advantage, ceasing the production of computers and, using the labor so released, increasing its shoe production from
70 million pairs to 175 million pairs. This is captured in Essential Economics 2.3(b) by the movement of Brazil upward along its production possibilities frontier from E_a^B to P_t^B.

Now that the United States is producing many more computers and
Brazil is producing many more pairs of shoes, each might seek to obtain the
good it no longer produces locally by offering to enter into an exchange. The
key requirement is that both countries agree on the terms of trade—that is,
the rate at which U.S. computers will be exchanged for Brazilian shoes.
Given the domestic opportunity costs between computers and shoes in the
two countries, we know that certain offers will not be accepted:

- If Brazil offers fewer than 4 pairs of Brazilian shoes for each U.S.
  computer received, then the United States will decline to trade: it
  would be cheaper for the United States to make its own shoes again
  by reallocating labor from computers back to shoes, and thereby obtain 4 pairs of American-made shoes for each computer forgone.
- If the United States indicates that it will provide a computer to
  Brazil only if it received more than 35 pairs of shoes in return,
  then Brazil will decline the chance to trade: it would be cheaper for
  Brazil to acquire computers by shifting labor out of shoes and back
  into computers, since it can obtain each locally produced computer
  by forgoing only 35 pairs of shoes.

Thus, for each partner voluntarily to accept the opportunity to specialize and
to trade, the terms of trade between the two countries need to fall some-

PRIMARY DOCUMENT 2.1

David Ricardo and International Trade

Under a system of perfectly free commerce, each country naturally devotes its capital and labour to such employments as are most beneficial to each. This pursuit of individual advantage is admirably connected with the universal good of the whole. By stimulating industry, by rewarding ingenuity, and by using most efficaciously the peculiar powers bestowed by nature, it distributes labour most effectively and most economically: while, by increasing the general mass of productions, it diffuses general benefit, and binds together by one common tie of interest and intercourse, the universal society of nations throughout the civilized world. It is this principle which determines that wine shall be made in France and Portugal, that corn shall be grown in America and Poland, and that hardware and other goods shall be manufactured in England.

Source: David Ricardo, *On the Principles of Political Economy and Taxation*, Chapter 7, Intelex Past Masters series, available at pastmasters2000.nlx.com/display.cfm?&clientID=1332338&depth=2& infobase=pmbritphil.nfo&softpage=GetClient42&view=browse.

Core Principle

David Ricardo believed that trade, when combined with specialization on the basis of comparative advantage, can provide benefits to all participants, and that it does so through the allocation of labor to its most productive uses and thus through the production and consumption of a greater amount of goods globally than would be possible in the absence of trade. Ricardo also suggests in this passage that freer trade yields other benefits, including the fostering of technological innovations and the forging of common interests among nations.

where between 1 U.S. computer for 4 pairs of Brazilian shoes and 1 U.S. computer for 35 pairs of Brazilian shoes. For the purposes of analysis, let us assume that the demand for computers and shoes in both the United States and Brazil is such that they negotiate terms of trade setting 1 computer equivalent to 10 pairs of shoes (this is noted by the dashed lines in Essential Economics 2.3(a) and 2.3(b)), and they agree to exchange 10 million U.S.-made computers for 100 million Brazilian-made pairs of shoes.

Americans' consumption therefore grows from 30 million computers in autarky to 40 million computers with trade, and from 80 million pairs of shoes without trade to 100 million pairs of shoes with it. Graphically, we see in Essential Economics 2.3(a) that U.S. consumption moves off the U.S. production possibilities frontier: specifically, it moves from E_a^A to C_t^A. Given that the United States is consuming more of both computers and shoes after it has specialized and engaged in trade than it had in autarky, it must be enjoying greater satisfaction than it had during autarky, and this is represented by its attainment of a higher consumption indifference curve, U_1^A rather than U_0^A. Similarly, Brazil's consumption of computers grows from 3 million to 10 million, and its consumption of shoes rises from 70 million to 75 million pairs. Graphically, we see in Essential Economics 2.3(b) that Brazil's consumption point also moves off its production possibilities frontier, going from E_a^B to C_t^B. Given that Brazil with trade is now consuming more of both computers and shoes, it must be enjoying greater satisfaction than it had in autarky, and this is represented in Essential Economics 2.3(b) by Brazil's movement from consumption indifference curve U_0^B to U_1^B. Thus, the combination of specialization and trade allows both countries to improve their welfare.

David Ricardo's model of comparative advantage and trade is of profound historical and contemporary importance, and the power and persuasiveness of his thinking can be appreciated even in the very brief extract from his presentation of that model that is presented in Primary Document 2.1. The model's brilliance and endurance over time have resulted from its capacity to demonstrate that countries that choose specialization and trade can escape the seemingly tyrannical limits imposed on their consumption levels by their individual production possibilities frontiers. In other words, countries can use specialization and trade to achieve greater consumption and thus greater satisfaction than was possible in autarky.

Yet Ricardo's model, as powerful as it is, leaves two key problems unresolved:

- If specialization on the basis of comparative advantage is the path to enhanced national welfare, why do we not observe countries fully specializing in the good(s) in which they have a comparative advantage?
- What causes one country to have a comparative advantage in one good, and another country to have a comparative advantage in another good? Why, for example, does the United States have a comparative advantage in computers and Brazil have a comparative advantage in shoes?

The Neoclassical Model of Trade: Two Countries, Two Goods, and Increasing Opportunity Costs

In addressing the first of these unanswered questions, we may recall that, in our discussion so far of the Ricardian model, we have assumed that the United States, as it shifts labor from shoes to computers, can produce each additional computer at the opportunity cost of 4 pairs of shoes, and that this opportunity cost remains the same no matter how many more computers the United States produces. Neoclassical economic theory (in contrast to the "classical" approach articulated by such economists as Ricardo) argues persuasively that constant opportunity costs between goods are not likely to hold as a country progressively specializes in one or another good. Instead, as we noted earlier in this chapter, such specialization is likely to encounter increasing opportunity costs. To make this case, the neoclassical approach begins with two key adjustments to the Ricardian model's assumptions about the production of either computers or shoes:

- Rather than being produced with only one factor of production, shoes and computers are produced with at least *two* factors of production: in the discussion that follows, we will assume that these two factors are labor and capital (machinery and buildings).[5]
- Technical knowledge allows both computers and shoes to be made with different amounts of labor and capital. However, compared to shoes, the most efficient ways of making computers all use relatively more capital than labor, whereas, compared to computers, the most efficient ways of making shoes all use relatively more labor than capital.

With these modified assumptions, the neoclassical model would expect that, although at first the United States may be able to build one more computer by shifting the labor and capital previously used to make four pairs of shoes, eventually it would need to forgo progressively larger numbers of shoes to make each additional computer. This is because, in comparison to the optimal mixture of capital and labor to make a computer, the reduction in shoe production releases too much labor and too little capital. The computer industry would respond by turning to relatively more labor-intensive manufacturing processes, but, given that computers are optimally made using capital-intensive techniques, the productivity of the computer industry as a whole would at some point begin to decline. As a result, to keep building additional increments of a given number of computers, shoe production would have to drop by progressively larger and larger amounts. Returning to our example, rather than being able to produce one more computer by shifting the labor and capital that had been used to make four pairs of shoes, it would become necessary at some point to shift the labor that otherwise would yield five pairs of shoes, and then seven pairs, and so on.

The result, according to neoclassical economic theory, is that the opportunity cost of computers in terms of forgone pairs of shoes increases as the United States makes more and more computers and fewer and fewer shoes. By the same logic, the opportunity cost of pairs of shoes in terms of forgone computers increases as Brazil makes more and more shoes and fewer and fewer computers. Eventually, as the United States and Brazil undertake specialization and trade, additional U.S. computer production becomes so expensive in terms of forgone shoes, and extra Brazilian shoe production becomes so costly in terms of forgone computers, that the opportunity costs between computers and shoes become equal across the two nations. At that point, which in all likelihood would occur prior to full specialization, neither of the two countries would have an incentive to specialize further. Hence, in the neoclassical model of increasing opportunity costs, the dual process of specialization on the basis of comparative advantage plus trade is mutually beneficial to the nations involved, but it is not likely to lead to full specialization by either partner in the good in which it has a comparative advantage.

We can observe the implications of increasing opportunity costs for trade in Essential Economics 2.4. As can be observed in the two graphs in the figure, increasing opportunity costs characterize the production possibilities frontiers for both the United States and Brazil: both are concave with respect to the origin. In autarky, as shown in Essential Economics 2.4(a), the United States is at the production-consumption equilibrium point E_a^A, at which it produces and consumes 14 million computers and 150 million pairs of shoes and enjoys a satisfaction level represented by the consumption indifference curve U_0^A. Brazil, as we can see in Essential Economics 2.4(b), finds itself in autarky at E_a^B, at which it produces and consumes 12 million computers and 70 million pairs of shoes and enjoys a level of satisfaction that is associated with the consumption indifference curve U_0^B.

With the possibility of trade, the United States begins to shift productive resources out of shoes and into computers, the good for which it has a comparative advantage, while Brazil begins to shift productive resources out of computers and into shoes, the good for which it is has a comparative advantage. However, as we observed in connection to the outer frontier in Essen-

The Neoclassical Model of Trade

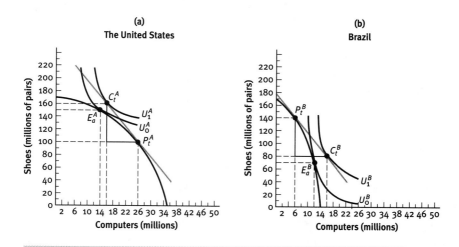

(a)
The United States

(b)
Brazil

Core Principle

Increasing opportunity costs for trade cause specialization to end where opportunity costs and market clearance converge. Even partial specialization, when combined with trade, produces a consumption outcome for both countries that is superior to what is optimally possible in autarky.

tial Economics 2.1(b), we see in the panels of Essential Economics 2.4 that, as the United States produces more and more computers, its opportunity cost for one more computer in terms of pairs of shoes forgone increases, and as Brazil produces more and more shoes, its opportunity cost for one more pair of shoes in terms of computers forgone also rises. As a result, opportunity costs between shoes and computers come to be similar in each country.

The point at which specialization ends in both countries reflects both this tendency toward a convergence in opportunity costs and the clearing of the markets in both countries for computers and shoes (both domestically produced and demanded from the trading partner). Let us assume that markets clear at the hypothetical exchange ratio, both domestically and internationally, of 1 computer for 6 pairs of shoes. This exchange ratio is depicted by the faintly-drawn lines in the two panels in Essential Economics 2.4. With these mutually agreed-upon terms of trade, the United States moves its production from E_a^A to P_t^A in Essential Economics 2.4(a), reducing its domestic production of shoes from 150 million to 100 million pairs and, with the productive resources thus released, increasing its computer output from 14 million to 26 million units. It then exports 10 million computers to Brazil in exchange for 60 million pairs of shoes; rather than consuming at E_a^A, the United States is now consuming at C_t^A.

If we compare C_t^A to E_a^A in Essential Economics 2.4(a), we find that even partial specialization, when combined with trade, produces a consumption outcome for the United States that is superior to what is optimally possible in autarky. Prior to trade, the United States is able to consume 14 million computers and 150 million pairs of shoes; with partial specialization and trade, it is able to consume 16 million computers and 160 million pairs of shoes. With partial specialization and trade, the United States, with no increase in resources, increases its consumption of both computers and shoes, and this is reflected in its movement from consumption indifference curve U_0^A to the higher curve U_1^A.

Brazil also faces in these circumstances the opportunity for an improvement in its consumption and overall satisfaction. If trade becomes possible, Brazil moves along its production possibilities frontier from E_a^B to P_t^B in Essential Economics 2.4(b): it produces 6 million computers rather than 12 million, and with the freed-up resources it increases shoe production from 70 million to 140 million pairs. As noted in the preceding paragraph, it then sends 60 million of those pairs to the United States in exchange for 10 million computers. This brings Brazil to the consumption point C_t^B, at 16 million computers and 80 million pairs of shoes. Brazil, then, also increases its consumption of both computers and shoes as a result of partial specialization and trade. This increased satisfaction is reflected in Brazil's movement from U_0^B to the higher indifference curve U_1^B in Essential Economics 2.4(b). Hence, even in the face of increasing costs, Brazil, like the United States, reaches a higher indifference curve by abandoning autarky and embracing specialization and trade.

Accounting for Differences in Comparative Advantage: Relative Factor Abundance and the Heckscher-Ohlin Theorem

In response, then, to the first of the questions that emerged from our exploration of the Ricardian model of trade—why we do not witness full special-

ESSENTIAL ECONOMICS 2.5

Similarities and Differences between the Ricardian and Neoclassical Models of Trade

	RICARDIAN MODEL	NEOCLASSICAL MODEL
Similarities in assumptions		
Number of countries	2	2
Number of goods	2	2
Technology	Similar across countries	Similar across countries
Transportation costs	0	0
Differences in assumptions		
Factors of production	1 (labor)	2 or more (land, labor, capital)
Opportunity costs	Constant	Increasing
Differences in results of trade		
Specialization in production	Complete	Partial
Improved consumption	Yes	Yes

Core Principle

The Ricardian and neoclassical models of trade differ in their views of opportunity costs and specialization. The neoclassical model answers the Ricardian model's question about full specialization by highlighting the importance of increasing opportunity costs.

ization in the presence of international trade—neoclassical theory argues the following: countries can mutually benefit if they undertake specialization and trade because in the absence of trade they differ with regard to opportunity costs between goods, but specialization and trade eventually eliminate these differences and thus eliminate the incentive to trade or to specialize further. The key similarities and differences between the Ricardian and neoclassical models of trade are summarized in Essential Economics 2.5.

But what about the second question? Why is it that the United States has a comparative advantage in computers rather than shoes, whereas Brazil has a comparative advantage in shoes rather than computers? The Swedish economists Eli Heckscher in 1919 and Bertil Ohlin in 1930 provided a helpful response to this question by investigating the implications of adding to the neoclassical model the following assumptions:

- Compared to the availability of capital and labor in one country, another country will have relatively more or less capital than labor (for example, the United States is a capital-abundant country, whereas Brazil is a labor-abundant country).
- Preferences or tastes for one commodity over another are similar across countries. Differences in the relative amounts of two goods that are produced and consumed in two countries prior to specialization and trade are therefore a reflection not of relative demand for those two goods but of differences in the relative costs of producing them in the two countries.

Working with these assumptions and those listed earlier under the neoclassical theory, Heckscher and Ohlin developed a crucially important line of analysis about trade. What has come to be known as the ***Heckscher-Ohlin theorem*** of the bases of trade suggests that a country will have a comparative advantage in, and thus will tend to export, those goods whose production requires the intensive use of the factor of production that it has in relative abundance.

In the Heckscher-Ohlin framework, because the United States, compared to Brazil, is abundant in capital rather than labor, the cost of capital, relative to wages, is likely to be lower in the United States than in Brazil. Given the earlier assumption that economically efficient production techniques are capital-intensive for computers and labor-intensive for shoes, the United States can produce computers at a lower cost and therefore at a lower price relative to shoes than can Brazil, and Brazil can produce shoes at a lower cost and price in comparison to computers than can the United States. This is equivalent to saying that the opportunity cost for producing an additional computer in terms of shoes forgone is lower in the United States than in Brazil.

The Heckscher-Ohlin line of inquiry thus suggests that differences across countries in their endowments of the factors of production, plus differences in the mixtures of factors of production with which different goods are optimally made, can explain why Brazil has a comparative advantage in shoes and the United States has a comparative advantage in computers. Given that the United States and Brazil face different relative prices of computers and shoes (and therefore different opportunity costs of one in terms of the other) as a result of the differences in their factor endowments and the factor intensities associated with the two products, the United States best improves its prospects for increasing its overall consumption of both computers and shoes by specializing in computers and exchanging some for Brazilian shoes, whereas Brazil best improves its consumption opportunities by specializing in shoes and exporting some to the United States in exchange for computers.[6]

Why Protectionism? The Problem of the Domestic Distribution of the Gains from Trade

In our discussion so far, we have found that both the Ricardian and the neo-classical theories of trade yield the same basic argument about why nations engage in trade: nations are better off trading than remaining in autarky. Trade and specialization on the basis of comparative advantage are clear examples of the power of human ingenuity and rationality, for the increases in welfare in the two trading states result not from increases in capital or labor in the two countries, but rather from the more efficient use by each of its existing capital and labor resources and the construction of a new human institution: voluntary exchange across national boundaries.

Given these core findings, economists have generally supported freer trade among nations and have been highly skeptical of arguments favoring restrictions on trade, generally referred to as protection. Indeed, given the big gains that nations may attain from trade, it is hard to understand how anyone could rationally question the wisdom of efforts by nations to facilitate international commerce, or how someone could rationally support national policies that impair such exchange.

However, as we will see in this section, modern trade theory has identified and explored at least one dynamic associated with specialization and trade that could lead some groups within a country to have a perfectly rational basis for opposing freer trade, even though the country as a whole would benefit from more open trade.

To appreciate how economists have come to the view that there might in fact be a rational basis for some groups within a country to prefer protection over liberalization of trade, we proceed in three steps: first, we specify the main types and effects of protection; second, we review arguments for protectionism that economists find highly unpersuasive; and third, we present the argument for protection that, from the viewpoint of economic theory, may be persuasive or even compelling.

Types of Protection and Their Impact on National Welfare

Instruments of Trade Protection

Governments have three basic classes of protectionist measures at their disposal: tariffs, quotas, and non-tariff barriers.

TARIFFS

A ***tariff*** is a tax imposed by government on imported goods or services. Tariffs can be of two types. *Specific tariffs* impose a tax of a fixed amount on each unit of an item being imported. For example, the United States might charge $5 for each and every pair of shoes imported into its territory, regardless of the import prices of different types of shoes. *Ad valorem* tariffs, by contrast, are based on the value of the items being imported. So, for example, the United States could impose a 25 percent tariff on each and every imported pair of shoes.

QUOTAS

As an alternative to a tariff, a government might impose a ***quota*** or a quantitative limit on the amount of a good or service that may be imported during a period of time. For example, at a given price for shoes in the United States, imports might total ten million pairs in a given year, but the United States might impose a quota of five million pairs on the importation of shoes per year, thus creating a shortage of five million pairs of shoes compared to what would have been supplied had the quota not been imposed.

NONTARIFF BARRIERS

A third option available to a government is to put into place policies that have the effect of increasing the cost of importing goods into the country; such policies are called ***nontariff barriers.*** For example, the United States might put into place a law that requires the U.S. military to purchase boots and other footwear only from U.S. sources, or the U.S. government could require health and safety certifications for imported shoes that are more onerous than such requirements for domestically produced shoes, or it could require burdensome and expensive paperwork for importers who seek to bring shoes through customs.

The Effects of Protection on National Welfare

Tariffs, quotas, and nontariff barriers raise the domestic prices of imported goods and thus reduce the price advantages in the domestic market that might otherwise be enjoyed by suppliers from countries with a comparative advantage in the good against which protection is being imposed. As a result, protection makes it less profitable for foreign producers to shift resources into the production of the protected good even though they have a comparative advantage in that good. At the same time, protection reduces the incentive for local producers to shift resources out of the production of goods for which their country does not have a comparative advantage and into goods for which the country does have a comparative advantage.

So, for example, if by virtue of imposing some form of extreme protection the U.S. government were to cause the relative prices of shoes and computers to be equal in both the United States and Brazil, U.S. consumers would no longer demand Brazilian shoes. As a result, the price of shoes in Brazil relative to computers would not go up, and Brazilian manufacturers would have no incentive to shift resources out of computers and into shoes. At the same time, with no additional supply of shoes from Brazil, or no Brazilian demand for U.S. computers, American producers would have no interest in shifting resources from shoes to computers. The imposition by the United States of extreme protection against shoe imports would, therefore, unwind the entire sequence of steps we have explored whereby the United States and Brazil specialize in the goods for which each has a comparative advantage and then engage in mutually attractive exchange. Both countries, as a result of protection, would lose the substantial increases in satisfaction that can be attained by specialization and exchange, even in the face of increasing opportunity costs.

Arguments for Protection Strongly Resisted by Economists

Economists, looking at the sort of welfare gains that are forgone when protection is imposed against imports, are unreceptive to most arguments in favor of protection. Two arguments are particularly unappealing to economists.

The "Unfair" Cheap Foreign Labor Argument

One argument in favor of protection that is often put forward in the United States and in Europe is that protection is legitimate and necessary because foreign countries compete on the basis of very cheap labor. Economists respond to this argument by emphasizing that absolute differences in labor costs by themselves do not create differences in comparative advantage across countries. Workers in a poor country may be paid 15 cents an hour while workers in the United States are paid $15 an hour. However, if, as a result of having little in the way of shoe machinery, each worker in the poor country can produce only 1 pair of shoes per hour while an American worker using efficient machinery can produce 100 pairs an hour, then, from the viewpoint of labor cost per pair of shoes, shoe production would be as costly in the poor country (15 cents per pair) as in the United States (again, 15 cents per pair). It is not differences in the cost of any single factor of production, economists emphasize, but differences in the cross-national relative abundance and thus the cross-national *relative costs* of factors of production that drive comparative advantage.

The Infant-Industry Argument

Producers and workers in an industry that might be opened to trade or that is already under pressure from less-expensive imports sometimes bring forward the argument that, if their industry were given temporary protection, it would in fact become (or would again become) as competitive as foreign suppliers. Just as a cruel and unfair world imperils children, who therefore need the protection of their parents when they are young or they might not survive, so too, these producers and workers suggest, can trade prevent their "infant" industry from reaching its true potential as a world competitor. Similarly, just as children need less assistance from their parents as they grow up, so too, these claimants for protection suggest, would their industry eventually outgrow that temporary protection from foreign competition.

Economists emphasize that one key flaw with this ***infant-industry argument*** is that a government is likely to be unable to decide which among the many industries putting forward requests for protection on the basis of infant-industry claims are in fact worthy of protection. In addition, once an industry is afforded protection on infant-industry grounds, that industry has few incentives to become more competitive (after all, it has a protected market). As a result, the government may soon find itself confronting an uncompetitive industry and a hard choice between allowing that industry to remain in place, at the opportunity cost of the welfare gains that trade would afford, and permitting trade but forcing a larger and perhaps more painful reallocation of national resources across sectors than would have been necessary had it not afforded protection to the infant industry in the first place.

The Stolper-Samuelson Theorem and a Rational Preference for Protection

From the viewpoint of modern trade theory, cheap-labor and infant-industry arguments for protection are usually ill founded. However, from the viewpoint of that theory, at least one possible set of circumstances could provide some groups within a country with a rational basis for opposing freer trade. The line of analysis that identified and explained that set of consequences was put forward by economists Wolfgang Stolper and Paul Samuelson (the latter a Nobel laureate) in 1941, and the important result of their analysis is known in economics as the ***Stolper-Samuelson theorem.***

This theorem explores the effects of the opening of a country to trade on the returns and hence the incomes of factor owners (for example, workers, capital owners, or landowners) as their countries specialize on the basis of comparative advantage as envisioned in the Heckscher-Ohlin framework—that is, as the country specializes in those goods whose most efficient production employs intensively the factor of production that is in abundance in that country. The Stolper-Samuelson theorem suggests that such specialization can cause the owners of the relatively abundant factor to experience a gain in their returns and real incomes, but can cause the owners of the relatively scarce factor to sustain a drop in their returns and real incomes. This dichotomy will result from changes in the demand for factors of production as specialization proceeds on the basis of comparative advantage.

For example, in our case involving the United States and Brazil, when trade commences, U.S. computer manufacturers will encounter an increase in demand for their product, and to meet that increased demand they will want to expand production. To do so they will need some additional labor and a lot of additional capital equipment, for computers are a capital-intensive product. In our earlier discussion, we identified the source from which both sets of additional inputs would come: the shoe industry. But we did not reflect on why capital will move from the shoe industry to the computer industry. The answer is that computer manufacturers, in dire need of capital, will be willing to pay higher prices for it, and it is the prospect of receiving such higher returns that induces some of the owners of capital equipment in the shoe industry to provide it to the computer makers. Only the payment of that higher price by shoe manufacturers will prevent other capital owners from also abandoning the shoe industry.

Hence, higher demand for computers will lead to higher demand for capital equipment, and, in the face of that higher demand for capital, capital owners in both the computer and the shoe industries will enjoy a higher return and thus an increase in their incomes. Prices of computers in the United States would also go up as computer demand escalated in the face of the new export market in Brazil, but the Stolper-Samuelson model suggests that the percentage increase in the return to capital would be greater than the percentage increase in the price of computers. Therefore, capital owners would enjoy not just an increase in the returns to their factor of production, but also an increase in their **real income** (that is, an increase in their income after taking into account price changes) even if they purchased only computers. Thus, owners of the relatively abundant factor of production gain from an opening of trade.

Owners of the relatively scarce factor—in the present discussion, labor—face a different situation when specialization and trade go forward. As we have just seen, the computer industry will expand its production by drawing both capital and labor from the shoe industry. Let us also recall that, by assumption, compared to each pair of shoes, each computer is made using a great deal of capital and not much labor. Therefore, compared to the optimal combination of capital and labor needed to make computers, too much labor is being released relative to the amount of capital that is becoming available as shoe production contracts. As a result, more workers are available than are required for employment in the computer industry and the now-reduced shoe industry, *given the current production methods using capital and labor in the two industries.* Workers laid off from shoe factories who were unable to get jobs in the expanding (but capital-intensive) computer industry would respond to their situation by offering to accept lower wages if offered a position in either industry, and, in the face of decreasing costs for labor, both industries would hire these less costly workers and maintain overall output by moving to more labor-intensive manufacturing processes. Hence, in the face of specialization and trade, owners of the relatively scarce resource in the United States (labor) would experience a decline in their returns (that is, their wages), and, according to the Stolper-Samuelson theorem, this decline in wages would not be offset by the percentage decline in the prices of shoes as the latter became more plentiful through imports from Brazil. Workers would, in sum, experience a decline in their real incomes.

In sum, although specialization and exchange with Brazil would make the

United States as a whole better off, the Stolper-Samuelson theorem provides a basis for finding that a particular group within the United States—U.S. workers—would be worse off as a result of such a move to specialization and commerce. Hence, although the United States as a national community might have a rational incentive to pursue trade liberalization, U.S. workers would have a rational basis for resisting such a liberalization of exchange. Similarly, although the Stolper-Samuelson theorem would help us understand why workers in Brazil, as the owners of the relatively abundant factor of production in that country, would unambiguously gain from trade and thus rationally would have an incentive to press for trade with the United States, the theorem would also lead us to expect that Brazilian capital owners would rationally oppose such trade.

The main response by modern trade theory to the implication of the Stolper-Samuelson theorem (that some groups within a country may have a rational preference for protection) is that the gains from exchange are so great that those who win from trade liberalization could offer compensatory payments to those who lose, and both groups would still be better off with trade than with autarky. Will that occur, and if so, what will be the form of compensation? Will the country instead respond to demands for protection by imposing restraints on trade to some degree, even if this reduces the nation's overall gains from trade? Or will the country pursue liberalization without compensating domestic losers? These questions concern the politics and political institutions of the country considering liberalization, the subjects of Chapters 4 and 5.

Recent Developments in International Trade Theory

Ricardo's insight into comparative advantage and mutually advantageous trade, the neoclassical identification of increasing costs as a constraint on specialization, the Heckscher-Ohlin understanding of the sources of comparative advantage, and the Stolper-Samuelson theorem regarding possible problems with the distribution of the gains from trade remain at the heart of the analysis by modern economists of the sources and consequences of trade. In recent years, economists have sought to engage and, to some degree, amend the neoclassical model in order to press ahead on two important research frontiers regarding trade: trade's relationship to economic growth, and the importance of intra-industry rather than inter-industry exchanges across nations.[7]

The Benefits from Trade:
From Greater Consumption to Higher Economic Growth

Our exploration of economic theory has shown how trade can yield new opportunities for countries to achieve higher levels of consumption. In recent
years, economists have also turned their attention to the way in which trade
might also help nations enjoy faster long-term rates of economic growth.

The capacity for international trade to improve the aggregate growth rate
of a country during the period in which integration is occurring has long
been recognized by employment of the model of trade outlined in this chapter.[8] The fundamental insight of this model is that, as a country opens itself
to world markets, it specializes in the production of a narrower range of
goods, the precise choice of which depends on the country's endowment of
productive factors, local and world tastes for and prices of goods, and the
state of world technology (which is assumed to be available to all nations for
any given good). This narrowing of a country's product range may in turn create opportunities for the enjoyment of increasing returns to scale over some
range of the production runs of these goods. For example, by making more
shoes, Brazil may enjoy economies of scale resulting from larger runs of particular types of shoe. This enjoyment of economies of scale permits an increase in the country's aggregate growth rate. However, according to the
increasing-costs model of trade described earlier, declining economies of
scale would eventually curtail the capacity of this specialization to boost the
rate of economic growth for the country as a whole.[9]

Yet recent economic analysis highlights opportunities for trade to increase
the long-term economic growth rates of countries well beyond that anticipated by the standard model of trade described in this chapter. What is often
termed "endogenous growth theory" identifies the ways in which economic
growth and especially intense inter-firm competition in the context of a
growing economy may motivate entrepreneurs to seek out technological innovations. Technological innovations, in turn, produce increases in the productivity of labor and capital, which, in turn, boost the rate of national
growth.[10] Openness to trade, the new theory suggests and a number of empirical tests appear to confirm, can enhance the long-term growth trajectory
of nations, because trade expands market opportunities for home producers
as well as instigates greater competition for them, and thereby it both encourages and compels these firms to seek out and to invest in new technology. Moreover, trade creates new opportunities for local firms to gain access
to new, superior technologies from abroad. Through these and other mecha-

nisms, economists find, trade has a good chance of increasing the productivity of the factors of production and thereby enhances national growth rates.[11]

Economists caution, however, that although trade between advanced industrialized countries—that is, between countries that are similarly well endowed with capital and technological capabilities—is likely to act as described above, it is at least possible that developing countries that are lacking in such resources may not find that trade with industrialized countries will impart to their developing economies the same pressures and opportunities to innovate. Thus, it is not certain that trade with industrialized countries, by prompting the search for and facilitating the acquisition of new technology, will necessarily place developing countries on higher long-term growth trajectories than would be possible in the absence of trade.[12] For example, while emphasizing that they do not suggest that developing countries would necessarily be better off by closing their economies to the world, economists central to endogenous growth theory have noted that if the products in which developing countries are prompted to specialize as a result of trade are not associated with substantial opportunities for technical improvements, then trade might not contribute very much to the rate of technological advance in those countries and thus it might not deliver the positive dynamics identified in endogenous growth theory.[13]

The Content of International Commerce: From Inter-Industry to Intra-industry Trade

The neoclassical increasing-costs model of trade that we presented in this chapter is concerned with explaining why two countries would gain from the trade of two commodities that are constituents of very different industries (in our examples, shoes and computers). For some time, however, economists have recognized and have sought to understand why much of the international commerce we actually see in the world consists not of such *inter-industry trade*, but of *intra-industry trade.*

Intra-industry trade consists of the exchange between countries of goods in the same industry.[14] For example, the biggest single category of U.S. exports to *and* imports from Mexico in 1998 consisted of electrical machinery, equipment, and related parts. This category of goods constituted about 24 percent of the total dollar value of U.S. exports to Mexico that year, and it also constituted 27 percent of the total dollar value of U.S. imports from Mexico. More generally, in the late 1990s, intra-industry trade accounted for about 57 percent of all U.S. trade, 60 percent of all trade by European countries, and 20 percent of all trade by Japan.[15]

This large volume of intra-industry trade has prompted economists to reflect upon a number of features of the neoclassical model of trade. For example, in our discussion of that model, it was assumed that goods are *homogeneous* across producers both within and among countries: for example, the shoes made in the United States are all exactly the same as those made in Brazil. Economists have noted that, from the viewpoint of consumers, goods are in fact often *differentiated*: for example, automobiles are differentiated in the eyes of consumers in terms of being speedy or being fuel-efficient. Hence, one reason we might observe intra-industry trade, economists have suggested, is that while some consumers in a country may prefer one variety of a given good, others may prefer another variety of the same good, and whereas one country might have a comparative advantage in the one variety, another country might have a comparative advantage in the other.

But how might this difference in comparative advantage come into being? Here again, economists have reconsidered elements of the neoclassical model of trade. As we have seen, that model assumes increasing opportunity costs as a country shifts from the production of one good to the production of another. One reason for such increasing costs was emphasized in our discussion regarding U.S. specialization in computers: as the United States increases computer production by drawing resources from the shoe industry, it must make use of progressively larger amounts of the "wrong" factor for computer manufacturing—that is, labor. A second reason might also explain increasing opportunity costs between shoes and computers: *decreasing returns to scale*. As firms in the computer industry grow bigger and bigger, each proportional increment of labor and capital used in production may result in fewer and fewer additional computers being built. A variety of circumstances may cause decreasing returns to scale. Managers, for example, may experience "bureaucratic diseconomies of scale"—that is, they may become progressively less able to coordinate production at their firms as those firms become larger and larger.

Yet recent economic analyses have suggested that often we see not decreasing but *increasing returns to scale* within a firm, at least up to a point. In other words, the larger the number of computers already being built by a firm, the cheaper it is to build the next increment of computers, at least up to some very large number of computers produced. The consequence of increasing returns to scale might be an inversion of the production possibilities frontier facing a country: over some significant range of production possibilities, the curve might be convex rather than concave! If this is correct, then as the firms in a country specialize in a particular variety of a good, they will enjoy an ever-greater comparative advantage in that particular variety. Although it might be chance that determines which countries specialize in which varieties of goods, once they begin to specialize, increasing returns to scale may prompt them to devote ever-greater resources to those varieties in which they started to specialize in the first place.

Finally, we noted earlier that the Stolper-Samuelson theorem provides a basis for expecting some elements of society to lose from trade and thus to have a rational basis for seeking to prevent or to undo efforts by countries to pursue trade liberalization. This line of reasoning may be correct with respect to the effects of inter-industry trade on domestic income distribution. However, economists have suggested that *intra*-industry specialization does not require the sort of large redeployments of resources across industries that may be associated with inter-industry trade.

In the neoclassical model of inter-industry trade, workers in a capital-abundant country experience a decline in their real wages as the country moves from the production of labor-intensive to capital-intensive goods. However, if intra-industry trade prompts the movement of labor within that country from one segment of a given industry into another segment of the very same industry, then wages are likely to be adversely affected to a much smaller degree, and, given that intra-industry trade augments the variety of goods available within the country, workers might actually experience a net improvement in their overall welfare through such trade.[16] Intra-industry trade then, is less costly in terms of domestic adjustment, less disruptive in terms of inducing shifts in national income distributions, and less likely to prompt demands for or movements toward protection as a country opens itself to the world trading system. These characteristics of intra-industry trade may in turn have prompted governments to liberalize trade since World War II in a manner that has fostered and perhaps even accelerated the development of intra-industry trade.[17]

Conclusion

In this chapter we have offered a thumbnail sketch of how economic theory helps us understand why states engage in international trade. Trade occurs between countries because it can be mutually advantageous. Two states can both benefit if each specializes on the basis of comparative advantage and engages in mutually voluntary trade. A country's comparative advantage is likely to reflect its endowment of such resources as labor, capital, and land.

Although a nation as a whole stands to gain from international trade, some segments of society within a nation may lose. In particular, owners of the relatively scarce factor of production may experience a reduction in their incomes. Society as a whole may choose to compensate those who lose from an opening of the country to trade. However, economic theory cannot tell us whether that will happen, how it will happen, the degree to which it will happen, whether the nation will instead choose economic closure, or whether society will choose openness without compensation of those left behind. Those questions require analysis of political institutions and dynamics both within and across nations, which we will turn to in Chapters 4 and 5.

Notes

[1]This paragraph is inspired by the famous economist John Maynard Keynes's reflections on life in 1914 for "an inhabitant in London" at the height and, as it turned out, the end of the first "Golden Era" of global economic integration. See Primary Document 7.1 on page 206 for those reflections.

[2]U.S. Department of Commerce, International Trade Administration, "U.S. Trade by Commodity with Brazil," available at www.ita.doc.gov/td/industry/otea/usfth/top80cty/brazil.cp. Brazilian aircraft exports to the United States grew in importance at the end of the 1990s: these totaled about $1.2 billion in 1999 and $1.5 billion in 2000, surpassing footwear exports in each of those years.

[3]On efforts by Brazil to foster the emergence of an indigenous computer-hardware industry, with only limited success, see Peter B. Evans, *Embedded Autonomy: States and Industrial Transformation* (Princeton: Princeton University Press, 1995).

[4]For a superb analysis of Ricardo's model of trade and the overall historical development of international trade theory, see Douglas Irwin, *Against the Tide: An Intellectual History of Free Trade* (Princeton: Princeton University Press, 1996); and John S. Chipman, "International Trade," in John Eatwell, Murray Milgate, and Peter Newman, eds., *The New Palgrave: A Dictionary of Economics* (London: Macmillan, 1991), esp. pp. 937–52.

[5]There might be additional factors of production that are economically meaningful for some goods, such as land with respect to agricultural goods.

[6]However, if tastes in the United States were such that its consumers had a much stronger preference for computers over shoes than did Brazilians, then it might be the case that, in light of increasing costs, local demand-driven high production of computers in the United States could cause the opportunity costs between (and therefore the relative prices of) computers and shoes to be equal to those in Brazil, thus undermining the basis for specialization by either or trade between them. It is for this reason that the Heckscher-Ohlin theorem assumes that tastes

between countries are not so dissimilar as to bring about a demand-led equalization of opportunity costs.

[7]A third characteristic of international trade is garnering increasing attention—namely, the large incidence of intra-firm exchanges as a component of total world trade. According to an analysis by the United Nations Conference on Trade and Development (UNCTAD), for example, exports by firms to their own affiliates in other countries totaled about $2.3 trillion in 1998, which is about 34 percent of the total of $6.7 trillion in world exports recorded that year. See UNCTAD, *World Investment Report 1999* (Geneva: UNCTAD, 1999), Table 5, p. 10.

[8]Very useful overviews of the theoretical and empirical studies relating economic openness to national economic growth are provided by Sebastian Edwards, "Openness, Trade Liberalization, and Growth in Developing Countries," *Journal of Economic Literature* 31 (September 1993), pp. 1358–93; and Sebastian Edwards, "Openness, Productivity, and Growth: What Do We Really Know?" *Economic Journal* 108 (March 1998), pp. 383–98.

[9]For a helpful graphical treatment of how, according to the basic increasing-costs model of trade, an outward movement of the production possibilities frontier results from the achievement of economies of scale after specialization and trade, see Richard E. Caves, Jeffrey A. Frankel, and Ronald W. Jones, *World Trade and Payments: An Introduction* (Reading, MA: Addison-Wesley, 1999), pp. 36–39.

[10]In this model, the sources of technological change and thus future economic growth are internal, or *endogenous*, to current economic processes, thus yielding the term "endogenous growth theory."

[11]A key early statement of endogenous growth theory was put forward by Paul M. Romer, "Increasing Returns and Long-Run Growth," *Journal of Political Economy* 94 (October 1986), pp. 1002–37. Romer presents an important intellectual history of the development of the endogenous growth research program in "The Origins of Endogenous Growth," *Journal of Economic Perspectives* 8 (winter 1994), pp. 3–22. A useful juxtaposition of the main elements of endogenous growth theory with that of the traditional model of growth, formulated by Robert Solow, is presented by David M. Gould and Roy J. Ruffin, "What Determines Economic Growth," *Economic Review of the Federal Reserve Bank of Dallas* (2nd quarter 1993), pp. 25–40. For empirical studies that link international economic openness to investments in innovations and thus medium-term greater economic growth, see Edwards, "Openness, Productivity, and Growth," and Robert Z. Lawrence and David E. Weinstein, "Trade and Growth: Import-Led or Export-Led? Evidence from Japan and Korea," National Bureau of Economic Research Working Paper 7264 (July 1999), available at www.nber.org/papers/w7264.

[12]As a result, Luis Rivera-Batiz and Paul Romer, for example, emphasize that their work on the manner in which trade prompts technical advances and thus growth is restricted to the circumstance in which both countries have advanced research-and-development capabilities. See Luis A. Rivera-Batiz and Paul M. Romer, "Economic Integration and Endogenous Growth," *Quarterly Journal of Economics* 106 (May 1991), esp. pp. 532 and 550.

[13]Gene M. Grossman and Elhanan Helpman, "Endogenous Innovation in the Theory of Growth," *Journal of Economic Perspectives* 8 (winter 1994), pp. 440–41.

[14]For a key early work on this subject, see H. G. Grubel and P. L. Lloyd, *Intra-industry Trade: The Theory and Measurement of International Trade in Differentiated Products* (New York: Wiley, 1975).

[15]Roy Ruffin, "The Nature and Significance of Intra-Industry Trade," *Economic and Financial Review of the Federal Reserve Bank of Dallas* (4th quarter, 1999), pp. 7–8.

[16]See Paul R. Krugman, "Intraindustry Specialization and the Gains from Trade," *Journal of Political Economy* 89 (October 1981), pp. 959–73.

[17]For interesting discussions of the political implications of intra-industry trade, see Howard P. Marvel and Edward John Ray, "Intraindustry Trade: Sources and Effects on Protection," *Journal of Political Economy* 95 (December 1987), pp. 1278–91; Charles Lipson, "The Transformation of Trade: The Sources and Effects of Regime Change," in Stephen D. Krasner, ed., *International Regimes* (Ithaca: Cornell University Press, 1983), pp. 258–62; and Beth V. Yarbrough and Robert M. Yarbrough, *The World Economy: Trade and Finance* (Fort Worth: The Dryden Press, 1994).

Chapter 3

The Economics of International Money and Finance

Introduction

OBJECTIVES

- Understand the functions and operations of the foreign-exchange market and understand the basic choice governments face between flexible exchange rates and exchange rates that fix the value of their currencies against another currency or a "basket" of currencies.
- Understand a nation's balance of payments.
- Explore the meaning that the balance of payments has for a country from the viewpoint of operating a fixed as opposed to a flexible exchange-rate regime.
- Understand how the combination of high levels of trade and low barriers to the entry or exit of capital significantly constrains the capacity of most countries to affect such key economic variables as national growth and employment.

In Chapter 2 we discussed the bases for and gains from trade without regard to money. We were assuming that trade takes place on the basis of barter—that is, on the basis of a direct exchange of goods for goods. But of course, U.S.-made computers are not traded directly for Brazilian shoes in the real world. An American manufacturer, whose expenses (such as wages, materials, and equipment) will be mostly in dollars, will typically require payment from customers in dollars. Therefore, if a foreign resident (either a person or a firm) wants to buy that American manufacturer's product, that foreign resident will need to acquire dollars.

In Chapter 2 we also pointed out that countries where capital is relatively scarce will tend to have relatively higher costs for borrowing capital—that is, interest rates—than those of capital-abundant nations. If investors from the capital-abundant countries had some way to purchase financial instruments issued in the capital-scarce countries, such as stocks, bonds, money-market accounts, or interest-bearing checking accounts, or real assets such as property, they could earn a higher return than would be available in their respective home countries. But again, the investors would need to acquire the currency of the capital-scarce countries in order to purchase such assets.

Hence, both trade and financial transactions require for their completion the acquisition and use of foreign currencies and the entry by traders and financiers into the foreign-exchange market. Smooth and steady participation by a country in the worldwide foreign-exchange market is an essential ingredient for taking full advantage of the opportunities afforded by international trade and financial integration. And yet, participation in the foreign-exchange market and in international markets for financial assets can pose serious challenges to a country. As we shall see in this chapter, if a country develops serious imbalances in its international currency or financial transactions, it can find itself in need of painful adjustment, including losses in the international purchasing power of its currency and possibly reduced short-term prospects for national economic growth.

How different countries structure their participation in the foreign-exchange market, why some countries have problems with foreign-exchange markets while others do not, and how foreign-exchange markets and international markets for financial assets may impinge upon a country's national economic policies are among the key subjects to be discussed in this chapter.

We will begin with a description of the two basic approaches a country can take to participate in foreign-exchange markets: it can use either a fixed exchange-rate regime or a flexible exchange-rate system. We will then describe the basic features of a country's balance of payments. We do this in order to identify and to explore the different problems that disruptions in a country's balance of payments may pose, depending on which type of exchange-rate regime it has elected to follow. We will also discuss the consequences of enhanced capital mobility among countries in recent years for the capacity of national governments to manage macroeconomic conditions, such as increasing overall national employment. We will find that increased international capital mobility has, for the most part, constrained the capacity of governments to affect national economic conditions. Thus, while international financial integration affords countries many opportunities, it also creates new risks and challenges for them as custodians of national economic stability and well-being.

The Foreign-Exchange Market

The foreign currency market is governed by supply and demand, just as is the market for any other good or service. Residents of a country *supply* their country's currency on the foreign-exchange market by purchasing imported goods and services and foreign financial assets. The *demand* for a country's currency on the foreign-exchange market reflects demand by residents of foreign countries for the goods and services that country exports and for its financial assets.

Foreign currencies are typically traded on the foreign-exchange market: the major foreign-exchange markets include those in London, New York, Frankfurt, and Tokyo. The price that a person must pay in his or her own country's currency to purchase one unit of a foreign currency is the ***exchange rate.*** The various exchange rates among the world's major currencies are published each day by newspapers and on the Internet. Essential Economics 3.1 provides a snapshot of the exchange rates among several key currencies on November 27, 2001.

Two Types of Exchange-Rate Regimes

A key policy issue that nations must decide is whether to allow forces of demand and supply to determine the exchange rate between their currency and those of others. If a government allows market forces to determine the exchange rate, then the government is pursuing a ***flexible (or floating) exchange-rate*** regime. If the government instead announces that the currency will trade at a government-specified rate against a key currency or group of currencies, and the government undertakes financial interventions in the foreign-exchange market to keep those rates in place, then it is pursuing a ***fixed (or pegged) exchange-rate*** regime.

Essential Economics 3.2 provides a glimpse of the exchange-rate experiences from the early 1990s through mid-2001 of two countries, Switzerland

⁑ ESSENTIAL ECONOMICS 3.1

Exchange Rates among Major Currencies, November 2001

MARKETS I CURRENCIES

currencies home

Powered by **FT** Market**W**atch**.com**

currency converter

USD vs EURO	USD vs GBP	USD vs YEN
+5% +0% -5% Sep	+5% +0% -5% Sep	+5% +0% -5% Sep
©BigCharts.com 12/9/2001	©BigCharts.com 12/9/2001	©BigCharts.com 12/9/2001

World Currencies | Spot Prices | International Currency Rates | Money Rates

World Currencies Summary				12Sep2001
Currency	**USD**	**GBP**	**EUR**	**JPY**	**DEM**
USD	–	0.68339	1.10415	119.45097	2.15953
GBP	1.46330	–	1.61570	174.79257	3.16003
EUR	0.90568	0.61893	–	108.18384	1.95583
JPY	0.00837	0.00572	0.00924	–	0.01808
DEM	0.46306	0.31645	0.51129	55.31351	–

Source: "Currencies Home" section of the *Financial Times* Web site, available at mwprices.ft.com/custom/ft-com/html-currency-summary.asp.

Core Principle

Exchange rates among the world's currencies can fluctuate daily. This excerpt from the Web site maintained by the *Financial Times* reports foreign-exchange rates among several of the world's major currencies as of November 27, 2001, as well as short-term trends in those exchange rates. Reading down any column of the table tells us the foreign-exchange rate between the currency listed at the head of the column and the currency listed along the left side of the table. For example, as we move down the first column, we find that, on November 27, the price of one British pound sterling (listed as GBP) is about $1.46; the price of one euro (EUR) is about 91 cents. Moving along each row tells us how much foreign exchange one unit of the currency listed along the left side can acquire: one

German deutsche mark (DEM) could acquire about 46 cents or about 55 Japanese yen (JPY). The Web site also provides a link to a page that reports the exchange rates of other countries, and a "currency converter" that permits rapid calculation of the exchange rate between any two of the world's traded currencies.

and Mexico, in terms of the value of their respective currencies, the Swiss franc and the Mexican peso, against the U.S. dollar. Mexico from the late 1980s through 1994 sought to maintain a fixed exchange-rate regime; that regime, for reasons we will discuss in a moment, came apart at the end of 1994. Switzerland throughout the 1990s maintained a flexible exchange-rate regime.

A Flexible Exchange-Rate Regime

Before we discuss the sustainability of the two types of foreign exchange-rate regimes, let us concentrate on how each operates. To assist in this exploration, Essential Economics 3.3 depicts hypothetical changes in supply and demand curves relating the U.S. dollar to the Swiss franc over the course of a particular year. Panel (a) of the figure presents a scenario in which demand for Swiss francs increases. Let us begin by noting that the initial demand function for Swiss francs, D_0^f, is downward sloping. The downward slope of D_0^f means that, holding other determinants of demand constant, if Americans are faced with the option of paying 50 cents per franc rather than 60 cents per franc, then they will purchase more francs. Why? One reason concerns the relative attractiveness of Swiss goods at different exchange rates. Consider the attractiveness to an American consumer of a Swiss watch that sells for 200 francs in Switzerland. If we ignore transportation and transaction fees, at an exchange rate of 60 cents per franc, the watch costs $120 in New York; at an exchange rate of 50 cents per franc, the watch costs $100 in New York. As the dollar–Swiss franc exchange rate goes down, or as the U.S. dollar *appreciates* against the Swiss franc (or, from the opposite perspective, as the Swiss franc *depreciates* against the dollar), Americans are likely to want to purchase more and more Swiss watches and other Swiss products, and therefore U.S. demand for Swiss francs increases as the price of the franc, or the dollar-franc exchange rate, decreases.

Notice, too, that the supply function in Essential Economics 3.3(a) for Swiss francs, S_0^f, is upward sloping. Consider the attractiveness to a Swiss

✳ ESSENTIAL ECONOMICS 3.2

The Value of Swiss Francs and Mexican Pesos against the U.S. Dollar, 1990–2001

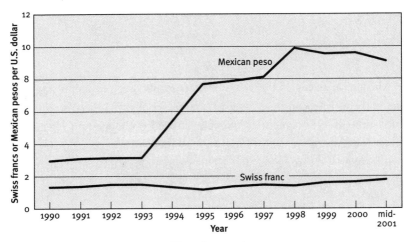

Note: Exchange-rate values are as of December 31 each year.

Core Principle

Fixed exchange-rate regimes can easily lead to more economic disruption that do flexible exchange-rate regimes. As this figure shows, although Switzerland has a flexible exchange-rate system, its exchange rate against the dollar has remained very stable; although Mexico sought during the early 1990s to maintain a fixed exchange rate between the peso and the dollar, it experienced currency turbulence, and the peso fell sharply against the dollar during the mid-1990s.

---

consumer of a $20 U.S.-made compact disc. At 50 cents per Swiss franc, the compact disc costs 40 Swiss francs; at 60 cents per Swiss franc, the compact disc costs about 33 Swiss francs. Hence, as the Swiss franc becomes more valuable against the dollar, or in other words, as the Swiss franc *appreciates* while the dollar *depreciates,* Swiss consumers will supply more and more Swiss francs to the foreign-exchange market so that they can purchase what from their viewpoint are progressively less expensive American goods.

Let us imagine that the equilibrium market-based exchange rate between the U.S. dollar and the Swiss franc is about 55 cents to 1 Swiss franc (this is the approximate exchange rate that obtained in mid-2001). This suggests

Determination of Exchange Rates: Flexible Exchange-Rate System

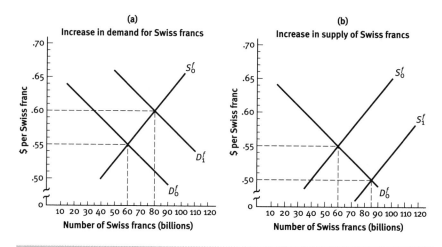

Core Principle

Demand and supply of a currency on the world market determine that currency's exchange rate under a flexible exchange-rate system.

that demand for Swiss francs and supply of Swiss francs equalize at 55 cents per franc. Hence, in Essential Economics 3.3(a), D_0^f and S_0^f intersect at 55 cents per franc, and over the course of a year U.S. residents offer $33 billion in exchange for 60 billion Swiss francs.

Now let us imagine that one or more of the following circumstances develop:

- Tastes in the United States change in favor of a range of Swiss-made products (pharmaceuticals, precision-made capital equipment, and consumer goods such as watches and, of course, chocolate!), resulting in an increase in U.S. demand for Swiss-made products.
- U.S. incomes increase dramatically, and hence U.S. demand for all foreign goods, including Swiss products, increases greatly.
- Swiss investments suddenly offer better returns than do U.S.

investments, and thus U.S. investors decide to increase their purchases of Swiss-denominated investment instruments such as bonds and equities.

As one or more of these circumstances come into effect, U.S. residents would want to obtain more francs in order to satisfy their enhanced demand for Swiss products and financial instruments. For example, with the change in their preferences, if they were presented with a need to pay 63 cents per Swiss franc, Americans over the course of a year may wish to purchase not 20 billion Swiss francs, as had been true when the character of U.S. demand was associated with D_0^f, but 65 billion Swiss francs; and, at the exchange rate of 55 cents per Swiss franc, Americans, after the change in conditions cited above, may wish to purchase not 60 billion Swiss francs but 105 billion Swiss francs. Thus, the increase in U.S. demand for Swiss francs at each exchange rate brings about an outward shift in the U.S. demand curve for Swiss francs, from D_0^f to D_1^f.

Let us assume that Swiss preferences for U.S. goods and financial instruments do not increase in this new situation: Americans, then, continue to face a supply indicated by S_0^f. However, S_0^f, as we discussed above, is upward sloping: the Swiss are willing to supply more francs as the price of Swiss francs goes up. At the new intersection of supply and demand, where S_0^f and D_1^f intersect, the new equilibrium price is 60 cents per Swiss franc, and the new quantity of Swiss francs that is demanded and supplied is 80 billion. Hence, in the face of an enhanced U.S. preference for Swiss products and financial instruments, and a resulting increased U.S. demand for Swiss francs, the franc experiences an appreciation in its value against the dollar in the foreign-exchange market, or, put a different way, the dollar experiences a depreciation in its value against the Swiss franc.

Let us next turn to Essential Economics 3.3(b). Using the same logic pursued above, an increase in Swiss preferences and demand for U.S. goods or financial instruments, holding other conditions constant, induces a shifting outward of the Swiss franc supply function, which in turn brings about an appreciation of the dollar and a depreciation of the Swiss franc. First, let us assume that Swiss residents increase their demand for U.S. goods, services, and financial instruments. Second, and as a consequence of their increased demand for American goods, services, and financial instruments, at each exchange rate, Swiss residents are willing to offer more Swiss francs than in the past: this shift in Swiss preferences is represented in Essential Economics 3.3(b) by an outward shift from S_0^f to S_1^f. Third, given that U.S. demand for Swiss francs continues to be depicted by D_0^f, the increased supply of Swiss francs in the foreign-exchange market brings about a decrease in the dollar–Swiss franc exchange rate, from 55 cents per Swiss franc to 50 cents per franc, with the demand and supply equaling one another at 85 billion Swiss francs.

Thus, with a flexible (floating) exchange rate, the value of a currency in terms of another currency fluctuates with the demand for and supply of the currency in question.

A Fixed Exchange-Rate Regime

In a fixed exchange-rate regime, on the other hand, the government of a country intervenes to ensure that the value of its currency remains stable, at a rate (peg) chosen by the government. Essential Economics 3.4 presents hypothetical demand and supply curves relating dollars to pesos, with the assumption that the Mexican government is seeking to maintain a fixed peg at 35 cents per peso, a peg similar to that which it sought to maintain in the early 1990s.[1] In this case, supply and demand conditions are still operating in the foreign-exchange market, but the Mexican government does not let those interactions determine the dollar-peso exchange rate. Instead, the Mexican government commits to maintain the exchange rate at 35 cents per peso through currency-market interventions (that is, purchases or sales of currency by the government) or through changes in the country's fiscal and especially its monetary policy.

In Essential Economics 3.4(a), we begin with the assumption that the Mexican government has fixed the peg at the point where, in the foreign-exchange market, supply and demand for pesos are in equilibrium; in Essential Economics 3.4(a), S_0^P and D_0^P intersect at that point, corresponding to a exchange rate of 35 cents per peso and a quantity of pesos demanded and supplied over the course of a year of 320 billion. If these conditions remain constant, then the peg remains in effect without any need for intervention by the Mexican government.

But what happens if U.S. demand for pesos increases, shifting the demand curve from D_0^P to D_1^P? In that case, if there were no peg, the price of a peso would go up to about 42.5 cents, and this would bring about a new supply-demand equilibrium, whereby 350 billion pesos would be traded for dollars. However, the Mexican government has stated that it wants the rate to be 35 cents per peso. At that price, and given the outward shift in demand to D_1^P, demand for pesos would be 380 billion pesos, but supply would re-

🔆 ESSENTIAL ECONOMICS 3.4

Determination of Exchange Rates: Fixed Exchange-Rate System

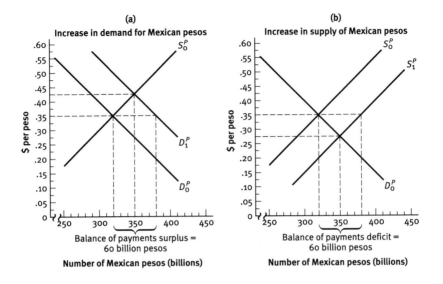

(a)
Increase in demand for Mexican pesos

(b)
Increase in supply of Mexican pesos

Balance of payments surplus =
60 billion pesos

Number of Mexican pesos (billions)

Balance of payments deficit =
60 billion pesos

Number of Mexican pesos (billions)

Core Principle

Supply and demand do not determine the exchange rate in a fixed exchange-rate system because the government maintains an official rate through currency-market interventions and fiscal and monetary policy.

---

main at 320 billion; demand over the course of the year would therefore exceed supply by 60 billion pesos. The Mexican government would be obliged, in order to maintain its fixed exchange rate, to satisfy that new demand for pesos. If it did not satisfy that demand, a black market would likely develop wherein individuals who wanted pesos but could not find them (in light of their scarcity at 35 cents per peso) would offer whatever amount would in fact bring them pesos. The black-market rate would be higher than the official rate, and some peso sellers might even divert pesos from the legal to the illegal market, further exacerbating the shortage of pesos in the open market.

If the Mexican government did not want this to occur, its most likely response would be to supply pesos in exchange for dollars in an amount sufficient to meet the shortage of 60 billion pesos. It would exchange its own reserves of pesos for the currencies held by those wishing to buy pesos. The effect, then, of an increase in demand for a currency whose peg is undervalued compared to the open-market equilibrium is a currency shortage and, in order to maintain the peg, a buildup in the foreign-currency holdings of the government.

What would happen in the event of an increase in the demand for dollars on the part of Mexicans, or, in other words, an increase in the supply of Mexican pesos that are being offered in the currency market in exchange for dollars? This brings us to the situation in Essential Economics 3.4(b): the supply curve for pesos shifts from S_0^P outward to S_1^P. If there were no peg, a new market-based equilibrium would be established whereby the peso's exchange rate would decline to 27.5 cents per peso, and supply and demand would again equal one another as 350 billion pesos changed hands. Given the pegged exchange rate of 35 cents to the peso, however, the new supply of pesos that has come onto the market exceeds the demand for pesos: in Essential Economics 3.4(b), demand for pesos remains at 320 billion, but supply moves out to 380 billion. If the government does nothing, then a black market in dollars may develop. To prevent that, and to maintain the integrity of the peg, the Mexican government would be obliged to come to the foreign-exchange market and, using its own supply of dollars, buy the 60 billion excess pesos, so that supply and demand would continue to clear at 35 cents to the peso.

Hence, a government that has elected to pursue a fixed exchange-rate regime but finds that the official value of its currency is higher than the interplay of supply and demand on the foreign-exchange market would otherwise dictate will be required to use its own reserves of foreign exchange to buy the local currency and so maintain the official peg. As will be discussed in the next section of this chapter, this creates a risk that the government will exhaust its holdings of foreign currencies and, in the end, be unable to maintain the official peg; in that event the government would be forced to permit the exchange rate to decline to some new level.

Specific terminology is used to refer to changes in exchange rates associated with flexible as opposed to fixed exchange-rate systems. As a matter of convention, increases and decreases in the official value of a currency in a fixed-rate regime are called ***revaluations*** and ***devaluations*** of the currency, respectively. Market-induced increases and decreases in the value of a currency in a flexible-rate regime are called ***appreciations*** and ***depreciations*** of the currency, respectively.

The Choice of an Exchange-Rate Regime

So why would a government choose to adhere to a fixed exchange rate and thereby risk exhausting its foreign-exchange reserves in an attempt to prevent a currency devaluation? One central reason usually concerns the government's prior problems as the custodian of the country's economic stability.[2] Consider a situation in which a country has a flexible exchange rate and the government of that country has a poor track record of preventing domestic price inflation, and in fact has in the past fueled inflation through deficit spending and overly expansive monetary policy (for example, by printing currency). With that government track record, holders of the country's currency would constantly worry that their real purchasing power both at home and abroad is at risk, and any slightly adverse development in the domestic economy would therefore induce them to sell the currency for whatever the market will offer them, in order to get their savings and investments into more stable funds. In the absence of a peg, such sales would push the value of the currency downward in foreign-exchange markets. That depreciation, in turn, would cause import prices to rise, thereby causing domestic inflation; inflation would force the government to raise interest rates or reduce government spending, measures that would bring about slower economic growth and perhaps even a recession (negative growth) in the economy.

The government, wishing to promote growth and fearful of the domestic political repercussions of not doing so, would want to find a policy mechanism that would signal domestic and foreign residents alike that it is now committed to achieving domestic price stability as a precondition to sustainable economic growth. One such mechanism is to "peg" the exchange rate of the country's currency to the currency of a country with a low rate of inflation, thereby announcing that the government will do whatever it takes to maintain the fixed rate, including using fiscal and monetary policies that will slow the nation's economy if it overheats, rather than permit inflation to erode the external value of the currency. If holders of the currency believe the government is serious about maintaining the official peg, they will be more likely to keep their holdings in the face of short-term economic shocks, thereby short-circuiting the downward spiral sketched above, and giving the country a better chance to achieve economic growth.

For the most part, governments hope that they will be able to maintain the peg largely by interventions in the foreign-exchange market—by buying and selling their own currency and those of other countries. The big tests of a fixed-rate regime, as we shall see later in this chapter, are likely to come when the government must make good on its commitment to adjust interest rates or even fiscal policy in order to maintain the peg. However, to appreciate fully why a country's reserves of foreign currencies are crucial to maintaining a peg, in order to prevent the government from resorting to the more demanding measures associated with monetary and fiscal policy, we need first to appreciate some basic elements of the accounting system used to record a nation's international transactions.

The Balance of Payments

Definitions and Conventions

A nation's **balance of payments** summarizes the economic transactions of its residents with residents of countries in the rest of the world during a fixed period of time, such as a quarter (three months) or a year. A country's balance-of-payments reporting is based on the following three conventions:

- "Residents" may be individuals, firms, or governments.
- Balance-of-payments reporting employs "double-entry" bookkeeping: for example, if a good is exported, the transaction appears once as the recording of the value of the good being shipped out of the country and once as the recording of the payment for that good coming into the country.
- Transactions are listed in the balance of payments as credits (+) or debits (-). Credits are those transactions that involve the receipt by a domestic resident of a payment from a foreign resident. Debits are those transactions that involve a payment by a domestic resident to a foreign resident.

Balance-of-Payments Accounting

Essential Economics 3.5 provides an example of a country's statement of its balance of payments in a given year—specifically, the United States in 1997. For a country such as the United States, the balance of payments has two major components: the **current account** and the **capital account.**

✳ ESSENTIAL ECONOMICS 3.5

The U.S. Balance of Payments, 1997

	LINE ITEM	AMOUNT (MILLIONS OF $)
1	*Exports of goods, services, and income*	*1,179,380*
2	Goods, adjusted, excluding military	679,325
3	Services	258,268
4	Transfers under U.S. military agency sales contracts	18,269
5	Travel	73,268
6	Passenger fares	20,895
7	Other transportation	26,911
8	Royalties and license fees	33,676
9	Other private services	84,465
10	U.S. government miscellaneous services	784
11	Income receipts on U.S. assets abroad	241,787
12	Direct investment receipts	109,407
13	Other private receipts	128,845
14	U.S. government receipts	3,535
15	*Imports of goods, services, and income*	*−1,294,904*
16	Goods, adjusted, excluding military	−877,279
17	Services	−170,520
18	Direct defense expenditures	−11,488
19	Travel	−51,220
20	Passenger fares	−18,235
21	Other transportation	−28,949
22	Royalties and license fees	−9,411
23	Other private services	−48,421
24	U.S. government miscellaneous services	−2,796
25	Income payments on foreign assets in the United States	−247,105
26	Direct investment payments	−45,674
27	Other private payments	−113,959
28	U.S. government payments	−87,472
29	*Unilateral transfers, net*	*−39,691*
30	U.S. government grants	−12,090
31	U.S. government pensions and other transfers	−4,193
32	Private remittances and other transfers	−23,408

Line Item	Amount (millions of $)
33 **U.S. assets abroad, net**	**-478,502**
34 U.S. official reserve assets, net	-1,010
35 Gold	—
36 Special drawing rights	-350
37 Reserve position in the International Monetary Fund	-3,575
38 Foreign currencies	2,915
39 U.S. government ssets, other than official reserve assets, net	174
40 U.S. credits and other long–term assets	-5,302
41 Repayments on U.S. credits and other long-term assets	5,504
42 U.S. foreign currency holdings and U.S. short-term assets, net	-28
43 U.S. private assets, net	-477,666
44 Direct investment	-121,843
45 Foreign securities	-87,981
46 U.S. claims on unaffiliated foreigners reported by U.S. non-banking concerns	-120,403
47 U.S. claims reported by U.S. banks, not included elsewhere	-147,439
48 **Foreign assets in the United States, net**	**733,441**
49 Foreign official assets in the United States, net	15,817
50 U.S. government securities	-2,936
51 U.S. Treasury securities	-7,270
52 Other	4,334
53 Other U.S. government liabilities	-2,521
54 U.S. liabilities reported by U.S. banks, not included elsewhere	21,928
55 Other foreign official assets	-654
56 Other foreign assets in the United States, net	717,624
57 Direct investment	93,449
58 U.S. Treasury securities	146,710
59 U.S. currency	24,782
60 U.S. securities other than U.S. Treasury securities	196,845
61 U.S. liabilities to unaffiliated foreigners reported by U.S. non-banking concerns	107,779
62 U.S. liabilities by U.S. banks, not included elsewhere	148,059
63 **Allocations of special drawing rights**	**—**
64 **Statistical discrepancy (sum of above items with sign reversed)**	**-99,724**

Source: Christopher L. Bach, "U.S. International Transactions, Fourth Quarter and 1998," *Survey of Current Business*, April 1999, p. 47, available at www.bea.doc.gov/bea/Articles/Internat/BPA/1999/0499bop.pdf.

C o r e   P r i n c i p l e

A country's balance of payments summarizes its international transactions over a fixed period of time.

The Current Account

In Essential Economics 3.5, items that constitute the current account run from lines 1 to 32. The current account records three basic types of international transactions undertaken by U.S. residents and residents in other countries:

- Trade in goods and services: U.S. exports of goods and services (lines 2 and 3) to the rest of the world give rise to payments received from abroad and are therefore listed as credits (+)[3]; U.S. imports of goods and services (lines 16 and 17) give rise to payments to foreigners and are therefore debits (-).
- Income receipts: U.S. receipts of payments on assets that U.S. residents hold abroad (line 11), such as earnings or dividends arising from foreign investments, are credits; U.S. payments to residents abroad (line 25) by virtue of their ownership of U.S. domestic assets are debits.
- Unilateral transfers: The receipt by the United States of any sort of foreign assistance or worker remittances from abroad are credits, whereas foreign aid provided by the United States, or worker remittances sent abroad are debits. In Essential Economics 3.5, these credit and debit transfers are combined (line 29) in one "net transfers" figure.

Putting these three classes of current transactions together, we find that

$$\textbf{Current Account Balance =}$$
$$\textbf{Current Receipts − Current Expenditures.}$$

For example, from Essential Economics 3.5 we can calculate that U.S. current expenditures (lines 15 and 29) in 1997 exceeded U.S. current receipts (line 1) by about $155.2 billion, and for that reason we would say that the United States ran a *current account deficit* of $155.2 billion that year.

The Capital Account

The second main component of the U.S. balance of payments is its capital account, which consists of those financial transactions that are undertaken by residents of a country for the normal business purposes; these transactions are called **autonomous transactions.** (By contrast, transactions undertaken for the sole purpose of bringing the country's payments position into balance are called **official transactions.**) Before we identify the main elements of the capital account, it will be helpful to consider what is entailed when an individual makes or disposes of an investment, or undertakes lending or borrowing, or adds cash to or draws cash from a checking account.

An individual who buys a financial asset exchanges some form of payment (let us assume it is cash) for the documentation indicating ownership of that asset. When an individual sells an asset, that person exchanges the relevant ownership document for cash. Thus, for example,

- An individual who purchases shares of a company provides cash in exchange for those shares, and receives a certificate indicating that he or she owns a certain stake in the company.
- An individual who extends a loan provides cash in exchange for a promissory note that indicates how much interest will be paid as well as the date by which the loan will be repaid. The borrower "sells" that promissory note in exchange for cash.
- An individual who deposits funds in a checking account is giving cash to the bank in exchange for receipts documenting that the bank is holding the individual's money. When that person writes a check, he or she is receiving cash in exchange for documentation acknowledging that the bank is now holding less cash on behalf of that person.

Keeping these basic concepts in mind, let us turn back to Essential Economics 3.5 to study some of the key elements of the capital account:

- Direct investments: U.S. residents (firms or individuals) move money abroad when they purchase shares or some equivalent title of ownership sufficient for the U.S. resident to exercise managerial control over an enterprise, and thus such investments (totaled in line 44) are debits.[4] At the same time, direct investments in the

United States by foreign residents (line 57) consist of the movement inward of capital and thus are recorded as credits.

- Purchases of securities: Purchases by U.S. residents of foreign securities (line 45), such as bonds and equities in amounts that do not confer managerial control, involve outward movements of capital, and therefore are debits; purchases by foreign residents of comparable U.S. securities (lines 58 and 60) are credits.

- Borrowing and establishment of checking accounts: Borrowing by non-U.S. residents from U.S. financial entities or establishment by them of U.S. checking accounts (lines 46 and 47) entails a movement of capital out of the United States and is recorded as a debit; borrowing by U.S. residents from foreign financial entities (lines 61 and 62) involves an inflow of capital and is recorded as a credit; increases in holdings by foreigners of U.S. currency (line 59) are also credits.

These three broad classes of capital transactions together yield the following:

Capital Account Balance = Capital Inflows – Capital Outflows.

For example, in Essential Economics 3.5, capital inflows into the United States not relating to changes in foreign official (government) reserve assets, which we will discuss in a moment, totaled $717.6 billion in 1997 (line 56); capital outflows from the United States other than those relating to U.S. official reserve assets totaled $477.8 billion (line 43 minus line 39). Thus, the U.S. capital account balance was $239.8 billion in 1997.

The U.S. Balance of Payments on Autonomous Transactions

Putting together both the current account balance and capital account balance, we can assess the impact of autonomous transactions—that is, those that were undertaken without regard for their impact on the balance of payments. This assessment will help us evaluate the country's payments situation. The balance of payments arising from autonomous transactions is

Balance of Payments = Current Account + Capital Account.

Thus, in the case of the United States during 1997, its balance of payments (from autonomous transactions) was $84.6 billion. Hence, although the

United States ran quite a large deficit in its current account in 1997, it ran a large surplus in its capital balance. Put most simply, increasing private inflows of capital into the United States more than compensated for the fact that the country imported more goods and services than it exported.

In this accounting framework, if the total amount of credits exceeds the total amount of debits, the country has a ***balance of payments surplus,*** and if total autonomous credits are less than total autonomous debits, the country has a ***balance of payments deficit.*** As Essential Economics 3.5 shows, the United States enjoyed a balance of payments surplus in 1997 in autonomous transactions.

Bringing the Accounts into Balance

Before we turn to how such a payments imbalance is rectified in a flexible as opposed to a fixed exchange-rate regime, and the political implications for resolving such an imbalance, let's examine exactly how the United States brought its payments position into equilibrium—that is, made its total receipts equal its total payments—in 1997. Recall that the United States wound up with an autonomous surplus of about $84.6 billion. It is the official transactions on the balance-of-payments report that bring the accounts into balance. Observe that foreign official assets held in the United States (that is, holdings of U.S. currency or U.S. Treasury bills and bonds by foreign central banks and other monetary authorities) increased by $15.8 billion (line 49 in Essential Economics 3.5) in 1997, while during the same period, U.S. holdings of official reserve assets (that is, holdings of foreign currencies or foreign government debt by the U.S. Federal Reserve System) decreased by $1.0 billion (line 34), producing a net change of $14.8 billion and pushing the U.S. surplus in payments to about $99.4 billion ($84.6 billion plus $14.8 billion). To account for this large surplus, the U.S. government assumes that there must have been errors in the reporting of transactions, or else some payments were made to foreigners but were not reported; hence, we see the offsetting figure of –$99.7 billion on line 64, the "statistical discrepancy." As we shall see in the next section, not all governments can accommodate their payment imbalances so easily!

Bringing About Balance-of-Payments Equilibrium: Flexible and Fixed Exchange-Rate Systems

How a country resolves its external payments imbalances is determined largely by whether it has chosen a flexible exchange-rate regime or a fixed exchange-rate regime.

Adjustment under a Flexible Exchange-Rate Regime

If a country with a flexible exchange-rate system were to begin to run a surplus in its overall balance of payments (for example, by beginning to experience a surplus in both its current account and its capital account), demand for its currency would begin to exceed supply, and the price of the country's currency would begin to appreciate. The country's exports, as a result, would become more expensive for foreigners, who would therefore reduce their purchases of its goods and services. Meanwhile, imported products would become cheaper for domestic residents and thus demand for them would increase. As a result of both trends, the country's current account surplus would begin to decline. At the same time, foreign financial assets would become less expensive to purchase, and local financial assets would become more expensive: this adjustment would encourage an increase in capital outflows and a resulting reduction in the capital account surplus. The combined effect of these developments in the current account and the capital account would cause what had been a payments surplus to contract and to move back toward balance.

If, in contrast, a balance of payments deficit were to start to develop, the oversupply of the nation's currency in the foreign-exchange market (caused by excess purchases of foreign goods and excess investments in foreign assets) would cause the country's currency to begin to depreciate. As a consequence, imports and foreign assets would become more expensive for local residents, exports and local assets would become cheaper for foreigners, and the resulting shifts in current and capital account transactions would push the balance of payments back from a deficit toward overall balance. Hence, by establishing a flexible exchange-rate regime, the government in principle needs to do nothing to bring about equilibrium in the country's balance of payments; supply and demand in the markets for foreign exchange and for exports, imports, and financial assets accomplish the task.

Adjustment under a Fixed Exchange-Rate Regime

In our discussion of Essential Economics 3.4(b), we found that changes in preferences for currencies could cause a government-set peg to be either too high or too low in relation to the market-clearing exchange rate. It is also possible that, from the outset, a government had pegged the exchange rate either above or below the market-clearing rate. In either event, if a pegged rate is overvalued, the supply of the country's currency will exceed demand for it as a result of a deficit either in the current account (that is, obligations to make payment exceed receipts), the capital account (that is, investment outflows exceed inflows), or both. To prevent a devaluation, or a drop in the value of the national currency, the government must come to the foreign-exchange market, as we discussed earlier, and buy up the "excess" supply of national currency with its foreign-exchange reserves. Conversely, if the peg had been set too low, a shortage of the local currency would develop in the foreign-exchange market as a result of a payments surplus in the current account, the capital account, or both. To prevent a revaluation of the currency, the government would be required to make up for the shortage of local currency by selling that currency in exchange for foreign currency, which it then would add to its foreign-exchange reserves.

Currency-market interventions by the government seek to offset imbalances in the current account or the capital account; these efforts are called *official transactions,* or "compensatory transactions," insofar as they are meant to compensate for payments imbalances in the autonomous transactions that are recorded in the current and capital accounts. Compensatory transactions are recorded in the *official settlements account* of the nation's balance of payments. Let's consider how such compensatory interventions appear in a country's official settlements account under conditions of a payments surplus or a payments deficit.

Situation 1: Mexican Payments Surplus Arising from Autonomous Transactions

If a country has a payments surplus as a result of autonomous transactions in the current and capital accounts, its foreign-currency receipts are greater than its foreign-currency payments. What then happens? Let us imagine that Mexico has a fixed exchange-rate regime and is running a balance of payments surplus with the United States as a result of autonomous transactions. Some economic agents in that country (Mexican exporters, let's say) would have more dollars on hand than they could sell at the pegged rate. So, rather than agree to accept fewer pesos in order to dispose of their dollars, they submit those dollars to the Mexican central bank in exchange for pesos at the official rate. The Mexican central bank might then transfer those dollars to New York City and purchase a U.S. Treasury bond that had been kept on hand for such purposes by the Federal Reserve Bank of New York. Hence, an increase in Mexico's official foreign-reserve holdings (associated with a payments surplus in Mexico's autonomous transactions) brings about a capital outflow from Mexico and would be listed as a debit in the official settlements portion of Mexico's balance of payments.[5]

Situation 2: Mexican Payments Deficit Arising from Autonomous Transactions

If, on the other hand, Mexico had a payments deficit with the United States as a result of autonomous transactions, then the supply of pesos in the foreign-exchange market would exceed demand for them at the official rate of exchange. In the absence of intervention, the value of the peso would go down. To prevent that, the Mexican central bank would have to buy the excess supply of pesos with dollars. Where does it get those dollars? One option would be to sell back its U.S. Treasury bond in exchange for dollars and, by using those dollars to buy up the excess supply of pesos, close the gap between peso supply and demand. So, from the viewpoint of Mexico, a reduction in its holdings of foreign-exchange reserves (which in this case had been in the form of Mexican central bank holdings of U.S. Treasury bonds) brings about a capital inflow for Mexico, documented as a credit in the official settlements account component of Mexico's balance of payments.[6]

Thus, the balance of payments for a country with a flexible exchange-rate regime consists, from a policy viewpoint, of the current and capital accounts. In contrast, the balance of payments for a country with a fixed exchange-rate regime consists of these two components plus the official settlements account, which records the transactions undertaken by the government to compensate for the imbalances in autonomous transactions reflected in the current and capital accounts (imbalances that, in the absence of such compensatory transactions, would undermine the official peg).

Asymmetry between Surplus and Deficit under a Fixed Exchange-Rate Regime

Countries that choose to pursue a fixed exchange-rate regime face significantly different constraints when experiencing a surplus than they face when experiencing a deficit. As we have seen, compensatory intervention by a country facing an autonomous payments surplus consists of purchases of foreign currency by the central bank with local currency. The constraint on the "surplus country's" central bank in creating local currency for use in purchases of foreign currency from local residents is the risk that, as more local currency is injected into the national economy, price inflation will increase. The central bank can, of course, counteract such inflationary pressures by "sterilization" operations: selling government bonds denominated in the local currency, and thereby "soaking up" the local currency it had previously sold for foreign currency.

Intervention by a country facing a payments deficit, as we also saw earlier, consists of sales of foreign currency by the central bank in exchange for local currency. The constraints on the "deficit country's" central bank in undertaking such sales are its holdings of foreign currency and its ability to borrow foreign currency, both of which are likely to be limited. Hence, whereas surplus countries have substantial leeway to maintain a peg so long as they are willing to sterilize, deficit countries are constrained by their finite foreign-exchange reserves and foreign borrowing capabilities.

At the extreme, a deficit country might find that investors do not believe that the central bank will be able to maintain the peg at the official rate; these investors must weigh the possible benefits of making money by selling the currency at a profit against the risk of losing money if they cannot sell the currency or must sell it at a loss. How might this come about? Why and how might foreigners so reduce their investments in a country that doing so would threaten that country's pegged exchange rate?

To address this question, it is useful to consider one particular type of foreign investment available in a country: very short-term lending by a commercial bank. Suppose an American bank extended a 90-day loan denominated in U.S. dollars to a Mexican commercial bank, with both principal and interest to be repaid in dollars after 90 days. At the end of those 90 days, the U.S. bank might renew the loan, or it might elect not to do so and choose instead to repatriate the principal and interest back to the United States or to use those dollars to extend a dollar loan to a bank or other residents in a third country.

If the U.S. bank continually renewed (or "rolls over") its loan, the Mexican bank would have a solid source of short-term funds on the basis of which it could buttress its own (probably longer-term) lending operations, such as for mortgages, or land, or industrial development. Problems could develop very quickly, however. As Mexican bank lending to local residents increased as a consequence of the new cash it had on hand from the foreign loan, domestic price inflation could set in, thereby spurring imports and dampening exports. This trend might cause Mexico to experience progressively larger current-account deficits. At some point, foreign investors might come to believe or to fear the pegged peso-dollar rate of exchange to be unsustainable, and that likely to drop.

As a consequence, to go back to the example of the Mexican and U.S. banks, the U.S. bank, increasingly fearful that the Mexican bank might not be able to generate sufficient peso revenues to pay its (increasingly expensive, in peso terms) dollar-denominated debts, might decide, if there were any negative developments in Mexico, to stop making new dollar loans to that Mexican bank, or to call in existing loans, if possible. If many foreigners and Mexicans reached this conclusion and thus began to call in loans, stop making new ones, or sell off other Mexican assets, such as Mexican dollar-denominated certificates of deposit, two problems might ensue:

- A domestic credit shortage: Mexican banks might find themselves unable to meet all the demands by foreign lenders for repayment of loans without calling in their own loans to Mexican residents and firms, or by declining to make new ones; these actions would create a credit crunch in Mexico.
- A rapid liquidation of peso holdings: If both foreigners and Mexicans began to fear that a devaluation of the peso were coming, they would try to liquidate their peso assets (such as certificates of deposit or equity shares) and buy dollars; this would create more downward pressure on the peso-dollar rate of exchange.

In these circumstances, Mexican bond and equities markets could collapse, and, as a result of the credit crunch, many firms and households could be thrown into bankruptcy. Simultaneously, the Mexican central bank, seeking to protect the peso, would be compelled to raise interest rates sharply. The combined effect of these developments would be a severe contraction in aggregate economic growth in Mexico. In the absence of other government efforts to maintain price stability and other elements of social stability, a

➤ **TIMELINE 3.1**

Mexican Peso Crisis, January 1994–February 1995

1994

January	Chiapas uprising begins
Early March	Mexican foreign reserves at $28 billion
March 23	Presidential candidate Luis Donaldo Colosio is assassinated
End April	Mexican foreign reserves at $17 billion
April–November	Mexican foreign reserves stabilize around $17 billion
December 1	Ernesto Zedillo becomes president of Mexico
December	Violence re-erupts in Chiapas
December 10	Mexican foreign reserves at $10.5 billion
December 22	Mexican foreign reserves at $6.5 billion; Mexico abandons peg
End December	Peso depreciated 40% since peg abandoned

1995

January	First effort by Clinton administration to organize bailout fails
February 21	$52 billion U.S. bailout plan announced for Mexico

pegged exchange rate may have within its operation the sources of its own destruction.

The Breakdown of a Peg: Mexico, 1994–95

Indeed, this is just what happened to the Mexican peg of the early 1990s.[7] The crisis and eventual demise of the Mexican exchange-rate peg was, as is summarized in Timeline 3.1, both sudden and dramatic. After spending approximately 75 percent of its foreign-exchange reserves over a period of eight months in an attempt to maintain the peg, on December 22, 1994, the Mexican government ceased its efforts to keep the peso fixed against the dollar, and by late January 1995, when the United States intervened with a massive bailout package for Mexico, the peso had lost 40 percent of its value.

What had happened to Mexico and its peg? First, in the context of important but still partial economic liberalization under President Carlos Salinas de Gortari in the late 1980s and early 1990s, Mexico began to experience fast economic growth and, with it, rising current-account deficits, which grew from 2.5 percent of Mexican gross domestic product (GDP) in 1988–89 to nearly 7 percent in 1992 and 1993. Second, although foreign capital inflows had been helping to offset Mexico's growing current-account deficits in the early 1990s, these inflows contracted in 1994 in response to increases in U.S. interest rates and to serious political instability—most dramatically, the outbreak of a rebellion in January in Chiapas, a rural province in southern Mexico, and the assassination on March 23 of Luis Donaldo Colosio, the presidential candidate of the ruling Institutional Revolutionary Party (PRI). Mexicans and foreigners began to withdraw capital from the country: from a starting point of a bit more than $28 billion dollars on March 23, international reserves held by the Mexican central bank fell to about $17 billion by the end of April.

At first, it appeared that Mexico might be able to defend its peg by a combination of raising domestic interest rates (which doubled, from 9 percent to 18 percent) and taking on loans of dollars from the United States and Canada (in the amount of $6.75 billion). The government's international reserves appeared to stabilize from April to November in the range of $16 billion to $17 billion; the exchange rate steadied, and Mexican interest rates actually began to decline. Yet political uncertainties remained high in Mexico after President Ernesto Zedillo (also from the PRI) came into office on December 1. A renewal of the rebellion in Chiapas that month and a growing perception in Mexico and abroad that the Mexican government could not meet its public-debt repayment obligations led Mexicans and foreigners to sell pesos: international reserves dropped to $10.5 billion by December 20, and to about $6.5 billion on December 22, when the government abandoned the peg.

Abandoning the peg, however, did not lead to a stabilization of the peso; it lost 40 percent of its value in the span of a few days. Renewed interventions by the government, not to maintain a fixed rate but simply to slow the decline of the currency, were unsuccessful, producing a sense of crisis in the country and raising the possibility of a complete exhaustion of the country's foreign reserves.

At this point the U.S. government again intervened. In early January 1995, the Clinton administration tried to put together a $40 billion official government loan to Mexico, but Congress balked at President Clinton's request to go forward with such an arrangement. The administration then put together an international rescue package for Mexico, announced on February 21, that totaled close to $52 billion and did not require congressional authorization. The administration committed $20 billion in loans drawn from the U.S. Exchange Stabilization Fund, managed by the U.S. Treasury Department; it pushed through a $17.8 billion loan for Mexico from the International Monetary Fund; it generated a further $10 billion loan from the Bank for International Settlements; it negotiated a loan package of about $4 billion for Mexico from Canada and from several Latin American states; and finally, it arranged for $3 billion in loans for Mexico from a number of commercial banks.[8]

In the wake of the peso crisis, Mexico's economy experienced a sharp contraction: Mexican GDP dropped by 6 percent during 1995, after having grown by an average of almost 4 percent each year between 1989 and 1994. However, the Mexican government, with international support, put into place a new stabilization and growth strategy and rapidly repaid its loans to the United States, other bilateral creditors, and international financial institutions. The Mexican economy recovered and achieved an average rate of growth of 5 percent between 1996 and 2000.[9] The government's new economic strategy had many components, but absent among them was a fixed exchange-rate system; instead, after December 1994, the Mexican government, although it intervened modestly in the foreign-exchange market to foster what is called "orderly foreign-exchange market conditions," elected to pursue a moderately flexible exchange-rate policy for the peso. The events of 1994–95 in Mexico showed that fixed exchange-rate systems, if not supported by a wide range of public policies aimed at sustaining the peg and helping it contribute to economic stability, carry with them serious risks of periodic financial crises and even of financial collapse.

Macroeconomic Policy in an Open Economy

To understand more fully the domestic effects of government efforts to maintain a peg, as well as the limits on the capacity of governments with flexible exchange-rate systems to manage their economies, we next move to the subject of the macroeconomics of countries that are highly integrated into the world economy. First, however, we should review the basic language with which economists analyze trends in the overall level of economic activity in a country during some period of time—that is, the country's macroeconomic conditions.[10]

Central Concepts in Macroeconomic Analysis

Economists interested in understanding the dynamics of a country's economy look at its **gross national product (GNP),** which is the money value of the final goods and services produced by residents of a country during some period of time, usually a quarter or a year.[11] They are particularly interested in knowing whether GNP is growing, whether it is being generated at a level that makes full use of the productive resources of the country (especially its labor force), and whether national supply and demand conditions surrounding the generation of GNP are in balance and thus producing neither unemployment nor price inflation.

Economists study GNP for a particular period by examining a country's **national income** (Y), which is the total income earned during that period by the owners of the country's different factors of production (the most important of which are labor, capital, and land). Analysis of national income is undertaken not in terms of the *actual* income received by the different factor owners, but instead in terms of the *types of expenditures* that brought about the production of the goods and services as a result of which the different factor owners received income. Four types of expenditures are of keen interest to economists as they study the production of GNP and the associated generation of national income:

- *Consumer expenditures* (C): expenditures by domestic households;
- *Investment expenditures* (I): expenditures by domestic firms to bring about future production;
- *Government expenditures* (G): net expenditures by the government (that is, government spending minus taxes collected);
- *Net exports* $(X\text{-}M)$: the difference between expenditures by foreigners on domestically produced goods and services (exports, or X) and expenditures by residents on foreign-produced goods and services (imports, or M).

Putting these concepts together, economists characterize the national economy in the following terms:

$$Y = C+I+G+(X–M).$$

The right side of this equation relates the sources of demand for goods and services—that is, the country's level of aggregate demand—to the level of goods and services thereby produced and, therefore, to Y, the national income received by different factor owners (the left side of the equation).

Many governments have sought since the 1930s to employ **macroeconomic stabilization policies** as a way of managing the level of aggregate demand and thus the generation of national income within their borders. They have used such policies for the purposes of promoting growth, preventing unemployment, and, since the 1970s, mitigating pressures toward price inflation. These policies come in two main forms:

- **Fiscal policy:** Governments have sought to increase G and thus Y when the latter has been less than the level that is associated with politically acceptable employment conditions. Governments can adjust G by raising government expenditures, by reducing taxes, or by pursuing some combination of the two.
- **Monetary policy:** When economic conditions have been such that national income falls short of the level that would fully employ the nation's productive resources, governments have pursued an **accommodative monetary policy,** in which, working largely through their central banks, they seek to reduce interest rates and thereby buttress aggregate demand by encouraging consumer and business spending. When aggregate demand has exceeded the productive capacity of a country, inducing factor shortages and price inflation, governments have turned to a **restrictive monetary policy,** in which they seek to increase interest rates, thereby reducing C and I, and thus reducing aggregate demand.

Macroeconomic Policy in a World of Economic Openness

Many industrialized and developing countries have experienced significant increases in recent years in the degree to which their economies have become integrated in both international trade and financial flows. This enhanced international economic openness has had major repercussions for the efficacy of fiscal and monetary policy. In a nutshell, whether a country is pursuing a fixed or a flexible exchange-rate system, the efficacy of fiscal policy has declined as a result of enhanced international economic integration, while the efficacy of monetary policy has declined for fixed-rate systems and has increased for flexible-rate systems.

To provide a sense of how economic openness affects the efficacy of macroeconomic policy, in the discussion that follows we assume that a country begins in a state of external balance (that is, the country's balance of payments due to autonomous transactions is neither in surplus nor in deficit) but at a level of national income, Y, that is associated with unemployment beyond what is considered politically tolerable by the government. We then investigate how economic integration complicates the use of either monetary or fiscal policy to spur national income and thereby employment, depending on whether the country is pursuing a fixed or a flexible exchange-rate regime.

Fixed Exchange Rates, Capital Mobility, and the (Hypothetical) Increasing Efficacy of Fiscal Policy

If the government's goal is to stimulate Y, the traditional fiscal policy response would be to increase aggregate demand by increasing government spending or by reducing taxes, or some combination of the two. In response to such measures, national income, employment, and prices would all go up, *as would interest rates*. This increase in domestic interest rates would induce a capital inflow from abroad in search of the higher returns now available in the country's financial markets. The magnitude of the capital inflow would probably exceed the increase in expenditures on imports that would result from people's increased incomes. The result would be a payments surplus in the capital account that exceeded the deficit in the current account, and thus an excess supply of foreign currency at the pegged rate for the national currency, and finally, in the absence of central-bank intervention, a revaluation of the national currency in the foreign-exchange market. To prevent that revaluation, the central bank would be required to buy up the excess supply of foreign currency with national currency, thereby increasing the supply of money in the country, decreasing interest rates, sparking additional private investment and consumer expenditures, and thus further raising national income.

Fiscal policy would seem then to be highly effective for a country with a fixed exchange-rate regime in a world of high capital mobility. One might have expected, then, that such western European countries as France and Spain, which had pegged their currencies against the German deutsche mark in the framework of the European Monetary System, would have been able to use fiscal policy to reduce the high rates of unemployment that plagued their economies in the early to mid-1990s. Yet France and Spain specifically avoided such fiscal expansionism. Why did these countries not use fiscal policy when it seemed to be the obvious solution?

The answer takes us to a key assumption made earlier about the reaction of investors to the increase in interest rates induced by fiscal expansionism. We assumed that investors would react by buying financial assets in the country in order to take advantage of the higher returns, and that this additional inflow of capital would exceed any current account deficit that might develop as Y increased. However, this chain of developments requires investors to estimate that the country's exchange rate would remain stable over time, or even that it would appreciate in the face of enhanced capital inflows. Investors might make that estimation, but they might also worry that the increase in national aggregate demand induced by fiscal expansionism would spark not only greater economic activity and higher interest rates, but also *much higher prices in the future*. This trend toward higher domestic prices, investors might conclude, could ultimately erode the international competitiveness of the country (exports would become less competitive and imports more competitive) and thereby bring about a progressively larger current account deficit.

At some point, as we envisioned earlier in this chapter, investors might come to believe that the risk of an official devaluation brought on by a growing current account deficit might outweigh the gains brought about by holding financial assets of the country. As a consequence, investors would begin to sell those assets and the country's currency. To prevent such an outflow of capital, which would undermine the peg, the central bank of the country would be compelled to raise interest rates as a way of compensating investors for the perceived relatively greater risk associated with holding that country's currency and assets. This move to raise interest rates would choke off both I and C, thus reducing aggregate demand and counteracting the growth-inducing effects of expansionary fiscal policy.

Thus, although in principle fiscal policy is effective when combined with a fixed exchange-rate regime and global financial integration, in fact this is true only while investor confidence is strong that fiscal expansionism will not engender price inflation and unsustainably large current account deficits in the future.

Fixed Exchange Rates, Capital Mobility, and the Declining Efficacy of Monetary Policy

Monetary policy is not effective for a country with fixed exchange rates and a high level of exposure to the world economy. Let us again assume that the policy goal is to stimulate national economic activity, and that the central bank seeks to do so by increasing the monetary supply, thereby reducing interest rates, and ultimately stimulating I, C, Y, and hence employment. But the reduction in interest rates would trigger a capital outflow in search of higher returns abroad. The supply of national currency would therefore exceed demand for it on the foreign-exchange market, and the central bank, obliged to maintain the exchange rate, would need to intervene and purchase the excess supply of national currency with its foreign-exchange reserves. The government would thereby reduce the stock of national currency circulating in the national economy, and this in turn would induce an increase in interest rates, a decrease in I and C, and ultimately a contraction of Y. Hence, monetary expansionism, too, would have little or no efficacy if the country is committed to a fixed exchange-rate regime and is open to international capital flows.[12]

Flexible Exchange Rates, Capital Mobility, and the Declining Efficacy of Fiscal Policy

Fiscal policy is also likely to be ineffective for a country maintaining a flexible exchange-rate regime if there is high international capital mobility. If a government in those circumstances were to increase spending or to decrease taxes as a way of spurring economic activity, interest rates in the country, as noted above, would probably increase. This would in turn spark inflows of capital into the country (in search of high rates of return), and these inflows would likely be much greater than increases in imports arising from enhanced national economic activity. Thus, there would be a net increase in demand for the national currency. Because supply and demand would be determining the exchange rate, the national currency would appreciate in value, causing imports to become less expensive for domestic consumers and exports to become more expensive for foreign buyers. Thus exports would drop and imports would increase. National production of goods and services would not go up, and it might actually decrease if exports dropped and imports increased substantially. Thus, the reduction in net exports $(X-M)$ by the country would put downward pressure on Y and employment that would match, and even perhaps be greater, than the expansionary effect that had been brought about by the government's fiscal policy.

Flexible Exchange Rates, Capital Mobility, and the Increasing Efficacy of Monetary Policy

Monetary policy by a government with a flexible exchange-rate regime is the only macroeconomic tool that has been strengthened as the world has become more integrated. Why? If a country sought to expand national income and employment through expansion of the money supply and an associated reduction of interest rates, the response by investors would be to take their capital out of the country in search of financial assets abroad that were providing relatively higher earnings. This would bring about a depreciation of the country's currency, which in turn would make the country's exports cheaper for foreigners and imports more expensive for local consumers. Net exports would increase and further boost aggregate demand and national income. Hence, capital flows and associated shifts in the exchange rate would magnify the effects of monetary policy. Thus monetary policy can be highly useful if a country is pursuing a flexible exchange-rate regime and is highly open to international capital and trade.

Conclusion

This chapter's thumbnail sketch of economic theory and international money and finance has taught us two main points. First, and as with trading ties, international financial transactions occur because such transactions can be mutually advantageous to the participants in the transaction. International financial transactions support trade, provide the opportunity for private economic actors to achieve higher returns on their investments, and help bring about more efficient use of the world's resources of savings.

Second, a country that chooses to take advantage of openness to international finance exposes itself to a number of risks, including the possibility of externally induced financial panics and the lessening of its own autonomy in the field of macroeconomic policy. Whether a country that experiences such a loss in policy autonomy is likely to remain committed to financial openness, or how it might act individually and with others to try to cope with the loss of autonomy while remaining part of the world economy, or whether it might choose to reverse course and restrict economic transactions with the outside world, cannot be answered by economic analysis alone. As with trade issues, a full understanding of international monetary affairs requires that we supplement economic theory with a political analysis of international economic relations. It is to that important task that we now turn.

Notes

[1]This section draws in particular from the analysis of a hypothetical Mexican fixed exchange-rate system that is presented in William J. Baumol and Alan S. Blinder, *Macroeconomics: Principles and Policy*, 7th ed. (Fort Worth: The Dryden Press, 1997), pp. 408–10.

[2]This discussion of the credibility rationale for adoption of a fixed exchange-rate regime draws largely from International Monetary Fund, "Exchange Rate Arrangements and Economic Performance in Developing Countries," Chapter 4 of IMF, *World Economic Outlook: October 1997* (Washington, DC: IMF, 1997), pp. 78–97.

[3]Credits are typically listed without the positive (plus) sign, whereas debits are always indicated either by a negative (minus) sign or by being enclosed in parentheses.

[4]In Chapter 8, we will discuss the nature of foreign direct investments more fully and contrast them with such instruments as portfolio and very short-term investments.

[5]We may also look at things from the U.S. perspective. It has a balance-of-payments deficit with Mexico in this example on current-account and capital-account transactions. As a result, the Mexican central bank is depositing dollars in a U.S. institution—the Federal Reserve Bank of New York, let's say—by purchasing a U.S. Treasury bond. An increase in official holdings by foreign central banks (or other government agencies) in the form of U.S. Treasury bonds in the United States would appear as a credit in the U.S. balance of payments (line 49 in Essential Economics 3.5; also recorded in the subcategory lines numbered 50 and 51).

[6]From the U.S. viewpoint, a decrease in official holdings by foreign central banks (or other foreign official agencies) in the form of U.S. Treasury bonds in the United States would appear as a debit in the U.S. balance of payments (line 49 in Essential Economics 3.5; also recorded in the subcategory lines numbered 50 and 51).

[7]This discussion of the Mexican crisis of 1994–95 is based on International Monetary Fund, "Factors Behind the Financial Crisis in Mexico," Annex I of IMF, *World Economic Outlook: May 1995* (Washington: IMF, May 1995), pp. 90–97; Moises Naim, "Mexico's Larger Story," *Foreign Policy*, no. 99 (Summer 1995), pp. 112–30; Moises Naim, "Latin America the Morning After," *Foreign Affairs* 74, no. 4 (July/August 1995), pp. 45–61; Guillermo A. Calvo and Enrique G. Mendoza, "Mexico's Balance-of-Payments Crisis: Chronicle of a Death Foretold," *Journal of International Economics* 41 (December 1996), pp. 235–64; Jeffrey Sachs, Aaron Tornell, and Andres Velasco, "The Mexican Peso Crisis: Sudden Death or Death Foretold?" *Journal of International Economics* 41 (December 1996), pp. 265–83; and Arne Kildegaard, "Foreign Finance and the Collapse of the Mexican Peso," *Journal of Economic Perspectives* 31 (December 1997), pp. 951–67.

[8]On this package see Arne Kildegaard, "Foreign Finance," note 10; and *Keesing's Record of World Events*, January 1995, p. 40353.

[9]For a helpful overview of Mexico's post-1994 economic strategy and economic performance, see Organization for Economic Cooperation and Development, *OECD Economic Surveys: Mexico* (Paris: OECD, May 2000), pp. 23–43.

[10]This discussion of macroeconomics and the national income accounts follows Paul R. Krugman and Maurice Obstfeld, *International Economics: Theory and Policy*, 2d ed. (New York: HarperCollins, 1991), pp. 287–96.

[11]A related concept of national income that is used by most foreign governments, and is increasingly employed by the U.S. government, is that of **gross domestic product (GDP).** As noted in the text, a country's GNP is the money value of final goods produced by residents of that country during some period of time; these residents may in fact be in the country, or they may be located abroad. A country's GDP, on the other hand, is the money value of final goods produced just *within* that country's borders during the period under review. For most countries, GNP is approximately the same as GDP.

[12]This finding is summarized in modern economic theory in the "Mundell-Fleming conditions," which posit that countries may *at most* have two of the following attributes: monetary policy autonomy, capital mobility, and fixed exchange rates.

Chapter 4

The Political Foundations of the World Economy

OBJECTIVES

- Explore the nature and meaning of states and the distinctions between states and societies as they relate to the international political economy.
- Understand how the inherent insecurity of the competitive international system affects the ways that states operate in the international economy.
- Consider the fluid relationships between states and markets, identify the contradictory choices facing states regarding the international economy's benefits and pitfalls, and understand how states
  navigate these decisions.
- Examine the roles of hegemonic states and international organizations as actors in the world economy.

Introduction

If we simply looked at the world economy as a system of markets, it would
be a busy place of producers, buyers, and sellers. Markets would operate
according to the laws of supply and demand and comparative advantage.
Competition would be fierce, based on the price and quality of the goods
and services being offered in the marketplace. The world economy would ex-

pand and eventually become a single, integrated whole. Governments would provide only the basic necessities—the rule of law, property rights, protections against crime—and would otherwise let the dynamic workings of capitalism improve the economic fortunes of all peoples in all places. There is only one problem with this picture: it does not capture the actual workings of the world economy, past or present. Thus we are going to need more than just economic theory to understand the rise and changing character of the world economy.

The modern world economy presents a puzzle. For one thing, if the world economy responded only to the logic of efficiency and comparative advantage, it would be substantially more integrated than it is today. Yet if governments wanted only to protect their societies from the potential losses and instabilities that inevitably accompany open markets, the world economy would be a lot less open than it is today. The world economy is and always has been a mixture of openness and closure, and during the last two centuries it has moved back and forth dramatically between those two extremes. In the decades before World War I, the world economy flourished, with trade and capital flowing across the industrialized world and into the periphery. In the interwar period, trade and investment collapsed, and the world moved in the direction of antagonistic regional blocs. In the post-1945 period, the world again experienced a great increase in trade, investment, and capital movement. An open world economy re-emerged.

The great historical shifts over time in the world economy and the ongoing struggles between openness and closure suggest that more is going on within the world economy than can be captured by simple economic models. To explain this puzzle, it is necessary to explore the full range of forces at work, including the fundamental role of the state and the competitive state system in opening, directing, and restricting the world economy.

States are political organizations that command a national territory. Throughout history, states have varied widely in their principles of organization and styles of rule: the world has seen absolutist, authoritarian, socialist, monarchical, and liberal democratic states, and many other types as well. But regardless of their specific political character, all states have tended to look after and promote their own country's security and welfare. When state leaders look outward at the world economy, they ask questions about how an open world economy will advance their own political and social goals, which can range from the simple (win re-election and stay in power) to the complex (modernize society or rapidly industrialize so as to catch up with other countries), and from responding to special interests (do favors for the capitalist class, organized labor, or specific interest groups) to seeking protection and advancement of the entire society (promote social welfare or mobilize for war). To understand the workings of the world economy, it is necessary to understand how states and their various goals interact with the logic of world markets.

As we discussed in Chapter 2, the world economy is shaped by great tensions between openness and closure. But this struggle is not simply between businesspeople and traders, who want openness, and politicians and bureaucrats, who may at times want closure. In fact, sometimes these roles are reversed. States, for example, often seek to open their countries to world markets because of the promise of faster economic growth and rising living standards, but they may nevertheless be worried about social instability and the political costs that result when domestic workers and businesses lose out to foreign competitors. State leaders—presidents, prime ministers, dictators, parliamentarians—must make difficult trade-offs between these various goals and conflicting domestic pressures.

Throughout history, states operating in the world economy have exhibited as much variety as there are characters in Shakespeare's plays. We find the great free-trade idealists, such as the United Kingdom in the nineteenth century and the United States after World War II; both were champions of unfettered trade and investment. Then we have come across dark enemies of openness, such as Japan and Germany in the 1930s, each of which erected high walls of protection against the outside world. Clever opportunists, such as Japan in the postwar era, have sought out export markets but carefully limited imports. And ideologues and sophisticates, such as France and Germany, have proven themselves highly skilled in presenting elaborate ideas about the workings and ultimate goals of a market society. If the world economy were a play, it would be at various moments a drama, a satire, a comedy, and, on occasion, a tragedy.

The motivations that inform the actions of states and their societies within the world economy are many and complex. This chapter presents the basic logics of politics that together push the world economy in one direction or the other—toward greater openness or toward closure. We begin by looking at the central logic of states within the world economy and by emphasizing the distinction between the state and society. Then we discuss the ways that the competitive and insecure world system in which states operate systematically affects states' goals and actions within the world economy. States want it both ways: they want to benefit from open markets, and indeed to participate in helping to create them, but they also want to avoid the losses—to specific sectors of political importance or to the absolute or relative standing of the country as a whole—that can accompany economic openness.

States and Societies

States operate in the world economy, but they also operate at home within their own societies. As a starting point, it is useful to think of the state as an organizational entity that is at least partially separate from the larger society of which it is a part. Whereas the society encompasses the wider territorial entity, the state is the political organization that asserts rulership of the society. It is the collection of administrative, legal, and political institutions that together monopolize legitimate force and territorial sovereignty within the country's borders. This is the view associated with the writings of the German sociologist Max Weber, who defines states as compulsory associations claiming control over territories and the people within them. "Administrative, legal, extractive, and coercive organizations are the core of any state," argues political sociologist Theda Skocpol. "These organizations are variably structured in different countries, and they may be embedded in some sort of constitutional-representative system of parliamentary decision making and electoral contests for key executive and legislative posts."[1] Indeed, the forms of the state have varied widely over the centuries and across the regions of the world: princes and monarchs were early state rulers; dictatorships and single-party monopolies have also assumed command of states; elected leaders and representative assemblies have given many states a modern democratic form.

Yet regardless of the specific character of the state, its organization and the leaders who make up the state are in a distinctive position, lodged between the domestic society and the larger international economy and state system. Thus the state is a sort of "gatekeeper" between the inside society and the outside world. The state and its leaders are uniquely positioned to speak for the society as a whole and are charged with looking after the security of the country. We should expect, therefore, that state leaders will be particularly sensitive to outside threats, dangers, and opportunities.[2]

It is useful to think of the state as Janus-faced, or double-sided. It has one face looking outward at the world system and another looking inward at its own society and economy. In historical perspective, the state's relationships with the outside world and with its domestic society are related: the rise of the modern state in Europe involved the simultaneous process of fighting off foreign rivals while also carving out and formalizing the state's relationship with the society and its economy. The more intense the interstate competition, the more the state needed to mobilize and extract resources from society, and this need in turn provided incentives to encourage a productive economy and a legitimate role for the state within the society. The more the state needed to make demands on the society and the economy, the more incentives it had to make its rule legitimate and effective.

As states interact with their own societies, the institutions and traditions of government and society impose constraints on what state leaders can do. States differ in terms of their relations with society, and these differences shape how states can operate both at home and within the world system. These differences can be understood as variations in the *capacities* of states. Some states are more centralized and insulated from society than are other states, and as a result they are better able to act in an independent and strategic manner. Other states are more decentralized and less autonomous, and as a result their policies will tend to more directly reflect the class or group interests within society. Some states are very capable, able to formulate policies and strategies that are independent of society and to implement them effectively. Other states are less capable, are unable to act coherently, and lack the policy tools with which to pursue independent goals.[3]

A variety of factors can shape the capacities of states. Perhaps most fundamental are the integrity of the state and the state's military and administrative control of the territory, or its **sovereignty**. The ability of the state to implement policies will be enhanced by loyal and able bureaucrats and by its access to financial resources. The authority and coherence of state offices will be influenced by the ability of the state to attract well-educated and motivated bureaucrats, which in turn will hinge on the social prestige attached to bureaucratic careers in government and the regular flow of graduates from elite universities. France and Japan, for example, have long, established traditions of government service, so that government agencies can successfully compete with the private sector in attracting the top university graduates to public service. The financial resources of the state depend on the prevailing mechanisms of taxation and ultimately on underlying conditions of economic growth. States also differ in terms of the ability of their central ministries to influence corporate investment and the long-term structure of the economy. Japan and France are also distinguished among the postwar industrialized democracies in having the most sophisticated capacities to channel credit to specific industries and firms, and by so doing to pursue state-led strategies of economic development.[4] In contrast, Russia in the 1990s experienced a dramatic decline in its state capacity as the government in Moscow lost control over society: the rule of law broke down, businesses and households evaded taxes, and organized crime plundered major parts of the economy.[5]

The capacities of a state to operate within the world economy are at least partly determined by the institutions and traditions that define the state's relations with its own society and economy. These institutions and traditions usually stay more or less fixed, the result of distinctive historical, political, and economic experiences. State leaders must make choices and pursue policies within this context of state-society relations. These long-standing relations that connect the state to society shape what state leaders can do as they operate within the world economy.

States in a World of Anarchy

States exist within a competitive international state system, and this fact powerfully affects how states operate within the world economic system. World markets must co-exist with sovereign, territorial states that are driven to compete and cooperate with one another by the political dynamics of interstate relations. The two systems—the capitalist world economy and the international state system—emerged together on the world stage in the seventeenth century. They have had an uneasy relationship ever since. Each system has a logic of its own. Capitalism is inherently transnational; states are inherently territorial. Each system has at various moments been threatened or destabilized by the other: market booms and busts and rapid economic change have undermined the political standing of ruling regimes and have fueled political conflict within and between states; likewise, interstate competition—and, at the extreme, war—has disrupted international flows of trade and investment and set limits on the integration of world markets. But the two systems have also been profoundly symbiotic in important ways: states have devised rules and property rights to safeguard trade and investment, and capitalism and its dynamic system of wealth creation have provided states with the power and wherewithal to compete with other states.

The *realist* tradition of international relations theory has provided the most systematic understanding of how the system of states operates and affects politics and economics. According to realists, the most basic and consequential feature of the international system is its organizational principle: *anarchy*. It is a decentralized system of sovereign states, with no centralized and authoritative governing power, such as a single global empire or world government.[6] States are left to their own devices. There is no "higher authority" than the states themselves. This is the fundamental definition of state sovereignty: no authority above states exists that can act authoritatively to dictate the policies of states. Sovereignty ends at the water's edge. States can raise armies and levy taxes—this ability is fundamental to what it means to be a sovereign state—but institutions and groups above or between states are not empowered to do so.[7] States have the final word and the ultimate veto.

Implications of Anarchy for States

If anarchy is the most fundamental feature of the international system, *insecurity* is its most fundamental implication. States can never be fully certain that they are safe in an anarchic world of competing sovereign states. A state can never be completely sure that other states will not act against it—militarily, economically, or politically. States seek security, but because other states can always become threats, that security is never absolute. Moreover, a state can never be absolutely certain of the intentions of other states. Promises are never absolute or guaranteed. A state, for example, can never be completely certain that its current allies will remain allies in the future or turn into adversaries. War is never completely out of the question—even among countries that are currently quite friendly and cooperative. As a result, the material capabilities of states matter a great deal. These capabilities are best understood in relative terms: in an insecure world of anarchy, states have an incentive to be powerful and to enhance their capabilities *relative* to the capabilities of other states.

How do these circumstances shape the goals of states within the world economy? There are no absolute or simple deductions that can be made from anarchy, but the general structure of interstate relations does create incentives for states to promote national economic gains, protect national autonomy, and be responsive to the relative power consequences of international economic relationships.[8] In short, states will bring considerations of power and social purpose to their decisions about involvement in the world economy. But international anarchy is not an absolute and unchangeable circumstance; its structural properties will intrude on the politics of international economic relations in different ways and to different degrees, depending on the situation, and states can actively seek ways to mute or overcome the intensity and consequences of anarchy.

Promote National Economic Growth and Capacity

One immediate implication of the insecurity of anarchy is that state elites will seek to enhance or promote the state's power and the power resources available to it within society. Thus, *economic growth and capacity are vital components of state power.* In a competitive international system, states are likely to care a great deal about the wealth and prosperity of their respective societies. In the short run, it might be possible for states that are searching for security within the international system to forcefully extract resources from their societies and build up their military capabilities, taking capital and other assets away from more productive uses. But in the long run, the power of the state will depend on the wealth of the society that it commands. As a result, we should expect states to encourage economic growth and the accumulation of wealth. There may be other reasons why the leaders of a state may want to promote economic growth and wealth creation at home, such as

 PRIMARY DOCUMENT 4.1

Mercantilism

In a letter to his cousin, France's foreign minister under King Louis XIV, Jean-Baptiste Colbert, wrote, "Trade is the source of finance and finance is the vital nerve of war."

★ ★ ★

In a letter to Louis XIV, Colbert urged the monarch to "limit all the industrial activity of your subjects as far as possible to such professions as may be of use in furthering these great aims, that is to agriculture, trade, war at sea and on land."

Source: Eli Hecksher, *Mercantilism II* (London: G. Allen and Unwin, 1935), pp. 16, 17.

Core Principle

The mercantilist understanding of the international political economy holds that a country's commerce is a foundation of its military power, and therefore government should control the country's relationship with the world economy.

responding to interest-group politics or creating a prosperous electorate that will re-elect those leaders. But the structure of the state system itself—and the demands of security and of the mustering of state power that arise within it—provide a simple and powerful incentive for states to care about the health and welfare of the national economy.

This basic state goal does not necessarily lead directly to a simple and absolute view about participation within the world economy. As we saw in Chapter 2, the neoclassical theory of trade would suggest that it does—that trade openness promotes specialization and maximizes economic gains. Contemporary theories of economic growth also stress the importance of productivity gains and the importance of technological advancement to such gains, which in turn are maximized by exposure to the world economy and its productivity-enhancing competitive pressures. But states interested in promoting long-term economic growth may also find reasons to protect domestic industries at their initial stage of development and shelter critical industries and technologies from foreign competition.

Protect Autonomy

Another implication for states operating within an anarchic system is that states will have incentives to *protect the country's autonomy*. States will not want their economy to be too dependent on others: being dependent puts the country's security at risk.[9] An open system of world markets may stimulate the growth of the national economy, something a power-sensitive state wants, but too much exposure to the world market can create dangerous dependencies. There are two sides to this coin. States will try to prevent themselves from becoming dependent on other states, particularly if the other states could eventually become adversaries. But a state might also try to make other states dependent on it by providing favorable terms of trade—drawing other states into a dependent relationship that gives the first state more advantages and power. The U.S. government's active encouragement of Japanese imports to the United States after World War II, for example, was aimed both at stimulating economic revival in East Asia (and thereby warding off communist-led political instability) and at drawing Japan into the emerging U.S. Cold War alliance system as a reliable junior partner. In these circumstances, states must make difficult choices between interdependence and autonomy.

We can look more closely at the problem of autonomy and dependence. Imagine that state *A* has allowed itself to become dependent on the vital natural resources located in state *B*. State *A*'s steel production, for example, is tied directly to its ability to import from state *B* coal and other materials that are necessary for industrial production. But in becoming dependent on another state for the continued flow of resources, state *A* is putting its economy and overall security at risk, at least to some extent. There is no guarantee that state *B* will continue to sell its resources to state *A*. The importing state is not relying on the goodwill or moral character of the exporting state; it is, after all, paying for the resources, so there is reason to believe that at the right price, the resources will continue to flow. But what if the broader relationship between states *A* and *B* were to deteriorate? If state *A* is dependent on state *B* for vital resources, state *B* has the upper hand: it can threaten to discontinue the export of the critical resources if state *A* does not bend to its desires, or it could actually discontinue the flow of these resources and cripple state *A*'s industry.

A state that opens itself up to dependence on another state must make a series of calculations.[10] The threat of a cutoff of critical resources is not as straightforward as it seems. It is useful to make a distinction between "sensitivity" and "vulnerability" to resource cutoffs. If state *A* is able to shift the source of its resource imports from state *B* (which has threatened to cut off the flow of resources or has actually done so) to state *C* (which is eager to sell the same resources to state *A*), the security implications of dependence on state *B* are not that serious. State *A* is merely sensitive to disruptions. Alternatively, state *A* might be able to undertake domestic efforts to substitute for the discontinued flow of resources with other materials that serve the same purpose. In this situation, again, the implications of disruption are not severe; dependence is therefore a matter of sensitivity and not ultimate vulnerability.

The United States, for example, is highly dependent on imported oil from Saudi Arabia and other Middle Eastern oil producers. Saudi Arabia could attempt to wield power by threatening to cut off oil imports to the United States, and indeed such a disruption in the flow of oil would dramatically boost oil prices and harm the U.S. economy. But whether the United States is merely sensitive to these potential supply disruptions or actually quite vulnerable hinges on whether other oil producers—domestic or foreign—could make up for the shortfall in Saudi Arabian imports by supplying more oil to the United States, and on whether the United States could reduce in a timely fashion and without severe damage its economy's dependence on oil.

To return to the general argument, let us assume that other states are not available to make up for the disruption of resources from state *B*, and that state A cannot find a domestic substitute, either. In this situation, the dependence on state B is more severe: it is a vulnerability with serious implications for the security of state A. If one state is dependent on another for the import of vital resources, a potential power relationship exists. State A is putting its security at risk—at least in part—by allowing itself to become dependent. In a world of anarchy, states must worry constantly about their security, and where possible they will try to minimize such dependence. If a state develops resource or trade dependence on another state, we should expect the dependent state to broaden and diversify its imports and trade relationships to limit the power of the supplier state; the dependent state may well try to find domestic substitutes for the resources as well.

Small states in the world economy, such as the small European countries, are in this dependent situation, and they must find ways to cope with their external dependence on trade and resource imports. They have done so by developing flexible domestic institutions that allow them to respond quickly to changing external economic conditions, and by seeking the protection of larger states that can bring some stability to the region in which they operate.[11] Japan, too, relies heavily on the import of raw materials for manufacturing and on the export of goods to specific countries. In particular, the United States is a crucial market for Japanese products, while Japan is a much smaller market for American goods. In this situation, Japan is asymmetrically dependent on the United States. If trade between the two countries were disrupted, Japan would be much more severely harmed than the United States would be. As we might expect, Japan has responded to this situation of dependence: it has cultivated and maintained strong security ties to the United States, thereby lowering the risks that the bilateral relationship will break down and threaten economic disruption; it has tried to diversify its exports to other parts of the world, such as Southeast Asia; and it has strategically promoted Japanese investment inside the United States, such as in the automobile industry, to promote closer economic relations and to create vested interests within the United States that favor maintaining stable and harmonious relations. These strategies are Japan's response to the underlying risks to its autonomy.

To look at the flip side of the coin, a state that is seeking to expand its power and enhance its own autonomy might want to promote the dependence of other states on it.[12] In the classic study of this strategy, economist Albert Hirschman looked at Germany's interwar trade relations with the small countries in southeastern Europe. As part of its pre–World War II grand strategy, Germany drew these states into trade relationships that made them dependent on Germany over the longer term; Germany's goal was to enhance its own autonomy by securing access to raw materials and increasing its influence in the region.[13] Although redirecting its trade with these smaller countries was not economically efficient, it did increase Germany's political leverage. Germany would offer very favorable terms to these small states so as to reorient and deepen these trade relations. As these small states became more dependent on trade with Germany, their options of "exit" became increasingly costly. But because these same trade relations played a much smaller role in the much larger German economy, the potential costs of disruption were asymmetrical, and the dependent trade relationship also created political dependence. Germany used its own internal market as a tool of state power, enhancing its political autonomy by using trade and economic dependence to develop asymmetrical power relationships.

In weighing the degree to which it is willing to become dependent on other states, a state must consider the larger trade-offs. In an relatively open world economy, becoming dependent on other states is part of a larger set of mutual dependences. States *A, B,* and *C* are mutually dependent on each other at some level. This mutual dependence is, after all, what the theories of specialization and comparative advantage—discussed in Chapter 2—tell us is so rewarding to states. An open system of trade, money, and finance creates efficiency gains that leave all the states better off than if they simply remained antarkic national economies. So a state contemplating expanding its exposure to the world economy must calculate the trade-offs between the absolute economic gains from trade and the losses it produces in terms of autonomy. A state that cares about its security in a world of anarchy will be attentive to this trade-off: it will want to achieve all the economic gains it can, because this is part of what creates the national basis of its power position, but it will also be willing to forego some of those economic gains if they create dependency vulnerabilities.

Seek Relative and Absolute Gains

Finally, a third implication for states operating within an anarchic system is that they will care about their *relative standing* in the system.[14] A state cannot rely fully on the promises of other states; in the final analysis it must act to protect itself from the possibility of domination by other states. The ultimate insurance that a state has in looking after its own security is its own power capabilities. Power is relative: when one state gains more of it, other states lose some. In this competition for security, states will care about their relative position in the world economy. If state *A* is growing faster than state *B,* state *A* is gaining in underlying power resources. If at all possible, states would like to be growing faster, getting wealthier, and becoming technologically more advanced than other states. When security is at stake, and the possibility of war or domination looms, states will care a great deal about not just doing well economically, but doing better than the states that potentially threaten them.

This attention to relative standing has been sharpened in the contrast between *relative* and *absolute gains.* In making choices about economic relations with other states, states can think about the payoffs in one of two ways. One way is to simply make choices that give the state the most economic gains in absolute terms; this is the logic of the neoclassical theory of trade. If policy *X* leads to 20 units of economic gain for my state, and policy *Y* leads to 10 units of gain for my state, the choice is obvious: in maximizing my state's absolute economic gains, I will choose policy *X.* But in an insecure and dangerous world, conditions may exist that prompt a state to calculate its interests in terms of relative gains instead of absolute ones. If policy *X* gives my state 20 units but also gives the other state 40 units of economic gains, we both gain but the other state gains more. If policy *Y* gives me 10 units of gain but gives the other state 5 units of gain, my absolute gains are less but my relative gains are greater in comparison to those of the other state. If my state's goal is to look after its relative power position, then it may be rational for my state to pursue relative gains over absolute gains. A recent study of American attitudes toward Japan reveals this relative gains logic at work: a majority of the Americans polled in a survey responded that they would rather gain less overall if they could nonetheless gain more than the Japanese.[15]

The specific conditions in which a state finds itself will likely shape the incentives to pursue relative gains. A state worries about the distribution of gains within an economic relationship for one ultimate reason: the risk of war. The possibility—however distant—that a state's trading partner might someday be a grave and dangerous adversary is what the state calculates in terms of relative gains. But if this eventuality is utterly remote—if the costs of war are huge and the possible gains from war are tiny—the larger returns based on calculations of absolute gains will probably win out. Furthermore, if the specific realm of economic gains is not related to the ultimate determination of war or war potential, this too might tip the calculations in favor of absolute gains. Finally, the number and variety of states operating within the trade relationship can also alter the calculation: the more actors involved in the transactions, the harder it is for a state to track the outcomes and to estimate war-threatening possibilities.[16]

State-Building, War, and Markets

As we have just seen, states are profoundly ambivalent about world markets. They are both attracted to and threatened by economic openness, for with openness they face the prospect of both great gains and great losses. An open world economy can stimulate trade and investment that fuel economic growth, raise living standards, and create a wealth base from which the state can extract resources to pursue its geopolitical goals. But it can also undermine domestic industry, destabilize employment, and leave the society dependent on an external world it cannot control. Between these dangers and opportunities, states have made choices over the centuries about how to operate within the larger international system.

The deep logic of states in their relations with markets has been captured by the historian Charles Tilly, who has studied the critical moments in early-modern European history when capitalism and state formation were both beginning to take shape.[17] At this early moment in European history, states were just emerging, attempting to build themselves up—in sum, they were engaged in "state-building." This process inevitably involved protracted wars with neighboring would-be state-builders. But state-building and war-making are expensive propositions, so state leaders needed to find ways to extract resources from the people in their territories. As Tilly notes, "power holders' pursuit of war involved them willy-nilly in the extraction of resources for war making from the populations over which they had control and in the promotion of capital accumulation by those who could help them borrow and buy."[18] The smaller the political area and the less commercial the society, the more difficult it was to extract enough resources to pursue war and state-building. Taxes on land, for example, were more difficult to collect than taxes on trade, particularly where large flows of trade came into seaports or other easily monitored checkpoints. In early-modern Europe, state-building and war-making went hand in hand, and both required increasingly sophisticated techniques of taxation and fiscal management. State-builders also realized that their success hinged on the prosperity of the commercial societies they controlled: they had an incentive to make the economy and market society thrive. Wealth and power were inextricably linked.

In Europe of the early-modern era, state competition, technological change, and the increasing size of states and scale of war fueled the transformation in the relationship between states and the economy. In the years between 1400 and 1700, rulers mostly contracted with mercenary troops and relied heavily on capitalists within their region for loans and the collection of taxes. After 1700 and into the present era, states created mass armies and navies, with soldiers drawn increasingly from their own populations, the military establishments became formally part of the state, and the administrative organs of the state became directly responsible for the fiscal management of the national territory.

What resulted was an evolution in the mode of extraction that states employed to raise funds and support the military and the state's expanding activities. In traditional, nonmonetized societies, the state relied mainly on the forced extraction of tribute from those within the state's territorial reach. As societies became more commercial and monetized, the ease with which the state could monitor and extract funds increased. In more commercial societies, taxation could shift from tribute, rents, and tolls at strategic ports to customs taxes and, ultimately, income taxes. As Tilly notes, "taxes on flows, stocks, and especially income . . . yield a high return for a given amount of effort at collection, and adapt more readily than tribute or rents to alterations in state policy. A state attempting to collect exactly the same amount from the same tax in a less commercialized economy faces greater resistance, collects less efficiently, and therefore builds a larger apparatus of control in the process."[19] States with societies at higher levels of commercialization and capital intensiveness could extract resources more efficiently, and those at lower levels of commercialization were at a competitive disadvantage and required a larger and more coercive state apparatus.

In the seventeenth century, for example, Holland was the most commercialized state in Europe and was able to raise funds for its military through public credit and taxation on flows of goods. "An intensely commercial economy permitted the seventeenth-century Dutch state to follow a path that the neighboring Prussians found barred and that the English, newly blessed with a Dutch king, borrowed in the 1690s. By adopting Dutch fiscal techniques, the English managed to reduce their previous dependence on Dutch bankers, and eventually to best the Dutch at war."[20] For less commercialized states, the resources needed for war were still primarily lodged in the agricultural countryside, controlled by semi-autonomous land barons, and the state was forced to use more inefficient and coercive mechanisms of ex-traction, including expropriation, cooptation, conscription, and heavy-handed taxation.

In this strategic situation, the fundamental problem for state leaders was that capitalists and traders were mobile: they are inherently transnational, capable of moving across (or around within) territorial units. States, on the other hand, are territorial: their reach is confined to their own national frontiers. But capitalists and traders are also vulnerable. Because their property and assets can be seized, they need protection and property rights. At the dawn of capitalism in the sixteenth century, would-be state leaders struggled with this dilemma. Tilly likens it to the protection rackets of organized crime: states offered footloose capitalists protection, property rights, and rules in exchange for commitments by capitalists to locate their productive activities within the territorial sphere of the state. Capitalists and traders would get protection and states would get the creation of wealth within their territory—a portion of which they could extract for the ongoing tasks of state building.

The economists Douglass North and Robert Thomas have taken this logic one step further.[21] They see states in an ongoing strategic competition with other states, and believe that the successful and secure states will be those that are able to encourage a rising economy and find efficient ways to extract resources from that economy without stifling growth. Because capitalists are mobile and search out the most congenial and profitable places to produce and trade, states find themselves competing with each other to attract and retain productive capital and enterprise within their borders. Successful states will create a safe and secure political setting for mobile capital. Interstate economic competition creates incentives to provide stable property rights and predictable and institutionalized limits on the coercive and arbitrary role of the state within the economy. But interstate geostrategic competition creates incentives to extract resources from this society, so the state must find indirect and tolerable mechanisms to raise resources for its strategic goals.

For North and Thomas, the interstate competition between states is what created the incentives for states to develop domestic systems of property rights. In turn, it was the establishment of these property rights that allowed capitalists and entrepreneurs to capture the bulk of the profits from their own growth-generating activities and innovations. North and Thomas argue that this historical development—the establishment of property rights—allowed for the emergence of sustained economic growth. A virtuous developmental circle was established: state-building, war-making, and capitalist accumulation went together; modern warfare and large standing armies necessitated the creation of centralized bureaucratic states, and these states generated rising demands for taxes and resources, which in turn brought states into alliances with capitalists and commercial society. As European princes and kings turned their regimes into centralized bureaucratic states, they became increasingly dependent on and indebted to bourgeois bankers and producers, who in turn relied on the state to enforce property rights and maintain stable political rule.

This logic allows us to appreciate variations in how states viewed and developed their own economies and governments. Where interstate competition was intense and capitalists and traders highly mobile, states should have had the greatest incentives to establish rules and institutions that harmonized with market capitalism and efficient mechanisms of extraction. Where competition was less fierce and productive assets less mobile, states should have been less likely to refrain from heavy-handed and intrusive intervention and control of the domestic economy, because penalties were fewer.

 PRIMARY DOCUMENT 4.2

Economy and Government

> It is not by the intermeddling . . . of the omniscient and omnipotent State, but by the prudence and energy of the people, that England has hitherto been carried forward in civilisation; and it is to the same prudence and the same energy that we now look with comfort and good hope. Our rulers will best promote the improvement of the nation by strictly confining themselves to their own legitimate duties, by leaving capital to find its most lucrative course, commodities their fair price, industry and intelligence their natural reward, idleness and folly their natural punishment, by maintaining peace, by defending property, by diminishing the price of law, and by observing strict economy in every department of state. Let the government do this: People will assuredly do the rest.

Source: Lord Macaulay, "Southey's colloquies on society" (1930), in *Critical and Historical Essays Contributed to the Edinburgh Review* (New York: Armstrong and Sons, 1880), p. 121.

Core Principle

In a laissez-faire arrangement between state, society, and economy, the government agrees not to interfere in the economic endeavors of the people, and in turn, those endeavors benefit the state.

States had to adjust to and compete for mobile capital from the very beginning of the European state-building enterprise. An international market for securities emerged first in Amsterdam in the seventeenth century. Trade and banking groups operated throughout Europe and the Mediterranean world beginning in the sixteenth century. The Welsers of Augsberg, who had banking operations in Europe and the Mediterranean, opened a branch in Venezuela in 1528. The Fuggers owned mines in central Europe and the Alps, and along with associates in Venice were the dominant financial concern in Antwerp, the most important financial center at the time. They had branches in Portugal, Spain, Chile, Fiume, and Dubrovnik (the last two located in what is today Croatia), and they had agents in India and China by the end of the sixteenth century.[22]

In the early modern era, as political scientist Stephen Krasner argues, "rulers could not secure the revenue that they needed to fight wars from domestic sources, and they were, therefore, compelled to borrow internationally, often at high interest rates that prompted periodic defaults."[23] During the eighteenth century, Great Britain could raise only about 10 percent of its revenues through domestic taxation, and France about 5 percent. As the struggle to establish domestic fiscal systems unfolded, European rulers were

 PRIMARY DOCUMENT 4.3

Autonomy, Historically

"A domestic market is to be greatly preferred to a foreign one because it is in the primary nature of things far more to be relied upon. It is the primary object of the policy of nations to be able to supply themselves with subsistence from their own soils; and manufacturing nations as far as circumstances permit, endeavor to produce from the same source the raw materials necessary for their own fabrics."

Source: Alexander Hamilton, "Report of the Secretary of the Treasury on the Subject of Manufacturers made the 5th of December 1791" (Washington, D.C.: R. C. Weightman, 1809), pp. 24–25.

Core Principle

Government play an active role promoting and protecting the national economy because only a productive economy can provide the tax revenues necessary for state-building and war-making.

forced into borrowing internationally.[24] It was only in the nineteenth century, as Tilly notes, that European states began to develop the types of fiscal systems that could more fully fund state-building and war-making. At the same time, states differed in their ability to maneuver within a competitive state system that required access to international credit. Some states, such as Great Britain, were able to raise funds relatively easily from foreign banks, whereas other states were less successful. The reliability of the state itself—the credibility of its financial commitments—was a critical determinant of its fiscal capacity and ultimately its military success.[25]

This focus on the early experiences of European state-building shows the dual logic of states. States have had a huge interest in encouraging dynamic economic growth within their national territories, so as to build the wealth base necessary to wage war and compete with other states. Interstate competition was a powerful incentive to get states to muster national economic growth and find ways to direct it and use it for wider international purposes. From their earliest moments, states have wanted the economy to lay golden eggs, so they could take a few of those eggs for their own purposes. The historical trick has been to play the game right: to encourage egg production and to pursue egg extraction, but do so without threatening the goose's ability to lay the eggs.

Hegemony and Economic Openness

At rare moments in world history, a state has emerged with enough power to decisively shape the international economy. When a state is big enough—with a wide range of economic, political, technological, and military capabilities—it has the incentives and ability to actually create and manage the world political economy. The United Kingdom in the mid-nineteenth century and the United States after World War II are the two great cases where a so-called **hegemonic state** has emerged with sufficient power and opportunity to open and organize world markets. In these situations, the hegemonic state is in a position to think about its interests in a long-term and expansive way: it need not just *react* to the world economy but can actually use its hegemonic position to *create* rules and institutions that open up the world economy. The hegemonic state has the power and interest to organize the world economy as a whole.

The Theory of Hegemonic Stability

This perspective on state power and the world economy has become known as *hegemonic stability theory*. According to this argument, the openness and stability of the world economy depends on the presence of a hegemonic power that, acting in its own enlightened self-interest, plays the role of organizer and supervisor of the world economy. In the most simple formulation, as put forth by political scientist Robert Keohane, the theory holds that "hegemonic structures of power, dominated by a single country, are most conducive to the development of strong international regimes whose rules are relatively precise and well obeyed. . . . [T]he decline of hegemonic structures of power can be expected to presage a decline in the corresponding international economic regimes."[26] The hegemonic state uses its superordinate position to establish the rules and institutions of the system and keeps it stable and open; when the hegemonic state declines, the stability and openness of the system decline as well.

The importance of a dominant state in providing world economic leadership was first stressed by political scientist Charles Kindleberger in his study of the Great Depression. In exploring the collapse of the world economy after 1929, Kindleberger looked at a variety of potential causes, such as specific government policies and long-term shifts in economics and technology, but he ultimately focused on leadership. In his view, the United Kingdom was unable and the United States was unwilling to take measures to ensure openness and stability in the world economy during this interwar moment of crisis. The United Kingdom was no longer the leading world power by the late 1920s, and the United States, although newly powerful, had not fully recognized its increasing importance and leadership responsibilities. According to Kindleberger, the hegemonic state can exercise leadership during a crisis by keeping its domestic market open to trade in goods from distressed countries, providing international financing and liquidity, and pursuing macroeconomic policies aimed at counteracting negative economic trends.[27] In 1929, the United States failed to recognize its special leadership role and pursued instead its own narrow, short-term interests—caving in, along with the other major world powers, to protectionist interests and competitive devaluations of currencies. Rather than attempt to counteract the collapse of world markets, the United States made the situation worse by erecting the infamous Smoot-Hawley tariff, one of the most protectionist bills in American history.

In Kindleberger's view, leadership involves more than simply the wielding of power: the leading state must have some recognition of its special responsibilities for the management of the world economy. The leading state must be able to use its domestic market to stabilize the larger international economy, and it must be able to resist domestic pressures to look out for its citizens' own interests. Leadership requires a reformulation of the leading state's understanding of its interests and capacities. Elites must develop a conception of the state's larger role and conceive of its interests in a farsighted and dynamic way. The state may forgo some short-term gains by resisting protection and restrictive policies, but its actions in fact serve the country's larger, long-term interests. The United States in the 1930s was not yet imbued with this understanding of its role.

Tracing the rise and decline of British and American hegemony in the nineteenth and twentieth century reveals the relationship between hegemony and the openness and stability of the world trading system. The two great moments of openness in the world economy—in the mid-nineteenth century and the post-1945 era—coincide with the rise of British and American hegemony, respectively. In the nineteenth century, the United Kingdom became the world's leading military and economic power, and it actively sought to use its power to create and maintain a relatively open world economy. As political scientist Robert Gilpin points out, "with the political triumph of the middle class, committed to the ideology of liberalism, Great Britain used its influence to usher in the age of free trade. The example of British economic success, the general acceptance of liberal ideals among the major economic powers, and the recognized benefits of trade encouraged states to negotiate tariff reductions and to open their borders to the world market."[28] In 1846, the British government took the dramatic and unilateral step of repealing its infamous Corn Laws, thereby lowering its protective tariffs in agriculture. This decision was part of a more general British movement toward free trade. At the same time, the United Kingdom pressured its European partners to reciprocate. It negotiated the so-called Cobden-Chevalier trade treaty with France, agreeing to French political and economic dominance in northern Italy in exchange for French tariff reductions. The United Kingdom also opened its domestic markets to industrial and agricultural goods from continental Europe and North America, stimulating the political coalitions advocating free trade in Germany and the United States. It also exercised leadership through example as the most advanced industrialized country of the day, demonstrating that economic gains could be achieved through tariff reductions and open markets. The result was a mid-nineteenth-century movement toward an open world economy.

As hegemonic stability theory would predict, as British hegemony declined, the system of open world markets also began to unravel. British power peaked in the 1870s, and in the decades that followed European countries and the United States moved away from free trade. The correlation was not tight or absolute: there was some revival of trade in the decades before World War I and the United Kingdom itself remained committed to open trade, the gold standard, and unfettered capital movements into the 1930s. But its capacities to manage the system and ensure openness had diminished by the turn of the century, and the system ultimately reflected this shift.[29]

In the 1940s, a new hegemonic power emerged, and again the world economy was reopened. As we shall discuss in Chapter 5, the United States played a decisive role in reopening and reorganizing the world economy after World War II. As hegemonic stability theory would expect, the United States had both the capacities and the incentives to construct a relatively open world economy. As a result, the trade barriers and restrictions of the interwar period were slowly reduced. A set of new international institutions was created, at the urging of the United States, to facilitate and manage the newly open economic system; these became known as the Bretton Woods institutions. The United States used the full complement of its powers—military, political, economic, and ideological—to push the world in the direction of openness. Moreover, unlike the British era, the American hegemonic era entailed a much more systematic use of institutions and explicit multilateral rules to establish and maintain economic openness.

Fifty years later, the postwar world economy remains relatively open, and the United States remains in a hegemonic position. Until the world experiences a decline in American hegemony, it will not be possible to draw definitive conclusions about the role of hegemony in the current system. Hegemony may ultimately not be necessary in order to maintain an open world economy.[30] The density of institutions and the spread of societal interests committed to a world economy may be sufficient to keep that system open—at least in the absence of a crisis, when Kindleberger's leadership responsibilities may indeed be needed. Despite the possibility of self-sustaining openness in the current world system, however, a dominant state wielding an ideology of free trade and backed with material capabilities may still be necessary, at least in the creation of an open economic system.

Why Is a Hegemon Needed?

But if all states benefit from an open economic system, why is leadership or hegemony necessary? One answer is that states do not always see or act upon the logic of free trade; they have a variety of competing goals, including political stability and security, so their choices about trade can become embedded in a larger and more complicated set of calculations. A leading state with a clear interest in free trade and with few worries about stability and security will be a more forceful proponent of an open system—and it will have the resources to seek its realization.

Another answer is hinted at in Kindleberger's analysis of the Great Depression: an open trade system is a public or collective good. A public good is something—like a lighthouse in a harbor, for example—that, once provided, cannot be denied to anyone and whose consumption by one does not diminish its consumption by others. But because each individual can "consume" the good without paying for it, the good will tend to be underproduced. Everyone benefits from the public good but no one has the economic incentive of profit to produce it, unless someone has an interest in paying a disproportionate share for its provision, or unless an actor—such as a government—can find a way to tax everyone for its provision.

If the system of open trade is in some sense a public good, the importance of a leader or hegemon for its creation and operation is understandable. The principles of nondiscrimination and most-favored-nation treatment are aspects of the contemporary world trade system that arguably are public goods. The management of an efficient international monetary system, with stable exchange rates, is also potentially a public good. States may benefit from the presence of these stable and open rules, but they do not have a direct incentive to provide them. After all, small and secondary states do not have the resources to provide such international public goods themselves, and there are severe limits on the ability of a group of small states to actively cooperate to pay for the provision of such goods. The provision of the good after all—at least in an anarchic world of states—involves more than simply a tax on states; it requires the active monitoring and enforcement of multilateral rules and practices. Moreover, at moments of crisis when the world economy contracts, the actions of the biggest states matter most. If all states have a short-term incentive to protect against imports when markets collapse or to manipulate exchange rates to gain a trade advantage, any crisis will be exacerbated and everybody will be worse off.

If there is a public-good aspect to an open world economy, then the role of a leading or hegemonic state may be critical. As Kindleberger argues, if a state is sufficiently large, it could very well identify its own individual interest with the interest of the larger world economy. It, too, could "free ride" and suffer the consequences when states, each acting according to its short-term interests, together move the system toward closure. But a leading or hegemonic state, when it conceives of its interests in a sufficiently expansive way, has the incentive and the capacity to provide the public good. Even if it is unable to "tax" other states, the hegemonic state will still be better off over the long term by providing the public good.[31]

If creating and sustaining an open world economy requires a powerful or hegemonic state, the leadership that that state provides has many elements: economic, military, political, and ideological. Gilpin argues that all these aspects of hegemony were present in both the British and American eras. The hegemon must actively use its material capabilities to get other states to move toward openness. But equally important is the more indirect use of the hegemon's own economy: using access to its internal market as a positive inducement for other states to liberalize and participate within an open system. Likewise, the promulgation of a liberal ideology of free trade has also accompanied the two great eras of world economic openness. Because the construction of a legitimate world economy—one that is mutually acceptable to all states that participate in it—is desirable, the hegemonic state will have incentives not to act too coercively or arbitrarily. For the hegemon, achieving this legitimacy may entail making compromises on the terms of free trade and openness and taking steps to reassure other states that it will not gain disproportionately from the arrangements.

International Institutions

In the past century, international institutions have increasingly become part of the operation of the world economy. International institutions have been devised by states as mechanisms to accomplish a variety of goals, and the "institutional strategies" that states have used have evolved over history. Institutions can be used to extend the power and reach of leading or hegemonic states. They can be used to solve joint problems and to make participating states better off. And international institutions can be reflections

➤ **TIMELINE 4.1**

Turning Points in the Postwar Global Political Economy

1944	Bretton Woods conference is convened
1946	International Monetary Fund and World Bank become operational
1947	General Agreement on Tariffs and Trade (GATT) is signed in Geneva
1948	Foreign Assistance Act is passed, creating the Marshall Plan
1951	European Coal and Steel Community is formed
1957	Treaty of Rome is signed, creating the European Economic Community (EEC)
1971	"Nixon Shocks": United States leaves the gold standard; Bretton Woods regime ends
1973	EEC expands membership for the first time Organization of Petroleum Exporting Countries sparks oil crisis
1982	Mexico announces inability to pay interest on foreign loans; Brazil follows; debt crisis begins
1986	Single European Act is signed
1989	Communism collapses
1991	Maastricht treaty is signed, allowing for European economic and monetary union
1994	Uruguay round of GATT is concluded; World Trade Organization is created
1999	Euro is introduced

of more widely shared ideas and beliefs on the part of leaders across a range of states about how the world economy, and international relations more generally, should be organized.

The leading view of international institutions—*neoliberal institutional-ism*—sees institutions as "solutions" to interstate problems. In a world of self-interested states, cooperation can provide benefits that leave all states better off, but social dilemmas stand in the way and encourage cheating. The key focus of neoliberal institutional theory is the way in which institutions provide information to states and reduce the incentives for cheating.[32] Neoliberal theory sees institutions as agreements or contracts between actors that reduce uncertainty, lower transaction costs, and solve collective-action problems. Institutions provide information, enforcement mechanisms, and other devices that allow states to realize joint gains. Institutions are explained in terms of the problems they solve; they are constructs that can be traced back to the actions of self-interested individuals or groups. For example, the World Trade Organization (WTO)—established in 1995 to replace the General Agreement on Tariffs and Trade (GATT), one of the Bretton Woods institutions—provides an elaborate set of rules and procedures through which trade disputes are to be settled. Through the WTO, trade conflicts are dampened and contained by inserting them into an agreed-upon institutionalized settlement process.

In general terms, neoliberal theories see institutions as having a variety of international functions and impacts; they serve in various ways to facilitate cooperation and alter the ways in which states identify and pursue their interests.[33] Liberal theories have also identified and stressed the importance of institutions that serve as foundational agreements or constitutional contracts among states—what political scientist Oran Young described as "sets of rights and rules that are expected to govern [states'] subsequent interactions."[34]

Another way that institutions can matter is in providing mechanisms and processes for conflict resolution. When states create and operate within international institutions, it is claimed, the scope and severity of their conflicts can be reduced. The reasons supporting this claim involve a series of arguments about the relationships between states, interests, and the logic of dispute resolution. But fundamentally, when states agree to operate within international institutions, they are in effect creating a political process that shapes, constrains, and channels state actions in desirable ways. Interstate institutions establish a political process that helps to contain conflict by creating mechanisms that can move the dispute toward some sort of mutually acceptable resolution.

At the heart of the American political tradition is the view that institutions can serve to overcome and integrate diverse and competing interests: state, region, ethnicity, class, and religion. American constitutionalism is infused with the belief that state power can be restrained and rights and protections of individuals ensured through the many institutional devices and procedures that they specify. The separation of powers, checks and balances, and other devices of the balanced Constitution were advanced as ways to ensure limits on power. These theories of institutional balance, separation, oversight, and judicial review have an intellectual lineage that traces back through the Baron de Montesquieu and John Locke all the way to Aristotle.

By specializing functional roles and dispersing political authority, the concentration of power and the possibility of tyranny are prevented.[35] In this way, institutional design can help define and ensure the durability of desirable political order.

It is this deeply held view that has made U.S. officials so inclined to build and promote international institutions. Indeed, the historical record of such U.S. support is striking. When the United States has had an opportunity to organize international relations—such as after the two world wars—it has been unusually eager to establish regimes and multilateral institutions.[36] After 1919 it pursued the League of Nations, and after 1945 it championed a flood of institutions with different purposes, functions, and scope. The American architects of postwar order are justly famous for their efforts to institutionalize just about everything: security, monetary relations, trade, development assistance, peacekeeping, and dispute resolution.[37] When one compares and contrasts the era of British hegemony with that of American pre-eminence, one of the first things to note is that the American era is much more institutionalized.[38]

Institutions can go beyond these liberal purposes to play a more direct role in power management and control. The U.S. interest in institutionalizing international relations after World War II was driven by a variety of factors. But it mattered that the United States was in an unprecedented power position after the war. The sheer asymmetry of power relations between the United States and its potential postwar partners made institutions an attractive way to reassure Europe and Japan that the Americans would neither dominate nor abandon them, and a functioning political process, made possible by the wide array of institutions, was useful in legitimating the postwar hegemony of the United States.[39] Likewise, the industrialized great powers at the midpoint of the twentieth century were much more complex and interdependent than their counterparts had been in the early nineteenth century, so there was a lot more human activity to organize than before. The political calculus and social purpose of states had evolved, and these changed circumstances were reflected in the functional imperatives of the 1940s.[40]

States operating within international institutions can dampen conflict and mitigate anarchy in several specific ways. Two types of general institutional "effects" are most important: institutions constrain, and institutions socialize. Institutions constrain state behavior in that the rules and roles that institutions prescribe create incentives and costs that channel states in particular directions. Violating the rules creates direct costs by provoking responses

from others (such as sanctions or retaliation). Constraints may also be manifest because of the "sunk costs" invested in an institution, which make it relatively more expensive to start from scratch and create a new institution.
International institutions are not unlike domestic institutions: they create a
"political landscape" that provides advantages, constraints, obstacles, and
opportunities for actors who inhabit them. Properly engineered, they can
bias state actions toward the desired rules and roles.

International institutions can also socialize states by influencing the ways
in which states think about their interests. In becoming socialized to accept
certain ways of thinking, as political scientist Martha Finnemore argued,
states "internalize the roles and rules as scripts to which they conform, not
out of conscious choice, but because they understand these behaviors to be
appropriate."[41] In other words, the interests and preferences of states are not
completely fixed, and institutions can play a role in cultivating certain foreign
and domestic policy orientations. States might initially agree to operate in an
international institution because of the manipulation of incentives by the
hegemon, but after a while, through a complex process of socialization, the
rules and values of the institution may come to be embraced by the state as
right and proper.[42]

In pushing for the establishment of an array of postwar international institutions, U.S. officials hoped that the postwar institutions would "rub off"
on the other states that agreed to join. In creating the United Nations, officials worked under the assumption that the establishment of mechanisms
for dispute resolution would channel conflicts in nonviolent directions. In
creating GATT, officials also anticipated that economic conflicts could
be trapped and diffused in a framework of rules, standards, and dispute-
resolution procedures. In establishing the Marshall Plan for aiding postwar
Europe, U.S. officials insisted that the Europeans create a joint recipient institution that would force them to work together in allocating funds; the
Americans hoped that, as a result, a habit of cooperation would emerge.

Both these ways in which institutions matter echo the American political
tradition. The notion of institutional constraints is implicit in republican political theory, wherein the Constitution, the separation of powers, and the institutional layers and limits on authority inhibit the aggrandizement of power.
The belief that institutions can socialize is also an extension of the classical
liberal belief that the political system is not simply a mechanical process
where preferences are aggregated, but a system where persuasion and justifi-
cation matter as well.

Conclusion

States are the formal ruling organizations of countries, and they look both outward at the international system and inward at their own society. In the modern era, states are uniquely privileged organizations. They alone can claim a monopoly on rule and on the use of force within their own territorial domains. They lay exclusive claims to juridical, fiscal, and political authority. International organizations and regional associations and unions can effectively increase and limit state capacity, but they are not able to raise armies or collect taxes. States remain territorially sovereign and legally empowered to act on behalf of their societies.

The underlying anarchy of the state system creates both constraints and opportunities for states operating in the wider world economy. The result is a decidedly ambivalent relationship between state and market. The anarchy and competition of the international state system gives states reasons both to foster and to thwart the market. States need markets because the market economy is the fundamental location where wealth is created. States care about wealth creation because wealth is a key source of state power and because the well-being of the state, over the long term, depends on the well-being of the society of which it is a part. This chapter has explored the various ways in which this basic organizational reality of politics shapes the way states support and limit the wider world of markets.

World markets and the politics of states, in turn, shape and constrain each other. National economies give states a power base but can also undermine states or force changes in national policies. At the same time, governments and states are critical actors in creating the rules and institutions that support world markets. Governments are the gatekeepers between the national economy and the world economy. They establish and maintain the macroeconomic framework—making choices about interest rates, exchange rates, and fiscal policy, which in turn influence the rates of economic growth, inflation, and unemployment. More generally, the rise of world markets has required governments to make systematic commitments to the opening of their domestic economies to inward and outward trade and investment.

International institutions, devised by states as mechanisms to accomplish a variety of goals, have evolved over the centuries. To agree to operate within a multilateral institution is to accept restraints and obligations on government policy in return for the anticipated cooperation of other states. Institutional agreements can facilitate economic exchange by creating mechanisms that allow states to share the gains and costs of openness. They can be used to solve joint problems that leave states mutually better off. International institutions can also play a role in a more general way in binding and constraining states. Finally, international institutions can be reflections of ideas and beliefs more widely shared across states about how the world economy—and international relations more generally—should be organized.

Notes

[1]Theda Skocpol, "Bringing the State Back In: Strategies of Analysis in Current Research," in Peter Evans, Dietrich Rueschemeyer, and Theda Skocpol, eds., *Bringing the State Back In* (New York: Cambridge University Press, 1985), p. 7. Economist Douglass North usefully defines the state as "an organization with a comparative advantage in violence, extending over a geographic area whose boundaries are determined by its power to tax constituents." See Douglass C. North, *Structure and Change in Economic History* (New York: W. W. Norton & Co., 1981), p. 21.

[2]We are making simplifying assumptions here about the state and society similar to the simplifying assumptions of economic theory; these assumptions can be relaxed when exploring political economy in the real world.

[3]On variations in the capacities of states and distinctions between "strong" and "weak" states, see Stephen D. Krasner, *Defending the National Interest: Raw Materials Investments and U.S. Foreign Policy* (Princeton: Princeton University Press, 1978); and Michael Mastanduno, David Lake, and G. John Ikenberry, "Toward a Realist Theory of State Action," *International Studies Quarterly* 33 (December 1989), pp. 457–74.

[4]Peter J. Katzenstein, ed., *Between Power and Plenty* (Madison: University of Wisconsin Press, 1978); John Zysman, *Governments, Markets, and Growth: Financial Systems and the Politics of Industrial Change* (Ithaca: Cornell University Press, 1983); and Jeff Hart, *Rival Capitalism: International Competitiveness in the United States, Japan, and Western Europe* (Ithaca: Cornell University Press, 1992).

[5]For an evocative—and pessimistic—portrait of Russian society in the 1990s, see Jeffrey Taylor, "Russia Is Finished," *Atlantic Monthly,* May 2001.

[6]For the classic statement of the problem of anarchy, see Kenneth Waltz, *Theory of International Politics* (New York: Random House, 1979).

[7]See Stephen D. Krasner, *Sovereignty: Organized Hypocrisy* (Princeton: Princeton University Press, 1999).

[8]For good surveys of the political economy implications of realist theory, see Jonathan Kirshner, "The Political Economy of Realism," in Ethan Kapstein and Michael Mastanduno, eds., *Unipolar Politics: Realism and State Strategies after the Cold War* (New York: Columbia University Press, 1998); Joe Grieco, "Anarchy and the Limits of Cooperation," *International Organization* 42, no. 3 (Summer 1988); and Robert Gilpin, *The Political Economy of International Relations* (Princeton: Princeton University Press, 1987).

[9]Kenneth Waltz draws out this implication in "The Myth of National Interdependence," in Charles Kindleberger, ed., *The International Corporation* (Cambridge: MIT Press, 1970).

[10]For a discussion of sensitivity and vulnerability dependence, see Robert Keohane and Joseph Nye, *Power and Interdependence* (Boston: Little, Brown, 1977).

[11]See Peter J. Katzenstein, *Small States in the World Economy* (Ithaca: Cornell University Press, 1989).

[12]On the promotion of trade dependence as a tool of state power, see the classic statement by Albert Hirschman, *National Power and the Structure of Foreign Trade* (1945; reprint Berkeley: University of California Press, 1980).

[13]For a good discussion of Hirschman, see Kirshner, "The Political Economy of Realism."

[14]For a survey of arguments and debates about relative and absolute gains, see David Baldwin, ed., *Neorealism and Neoliberalism: The Contemporary Debate* (New York: Columbia University Press, 1993).

[15]Michael Mastanduno, "Do Relative Gains Matter? America's Response to Japanese Industrial Policy," *International Security* 16 (Summer 1991), pp. 73–113.

[16]For arguments that modify and extend the relative-absolute gains logic, see articles in Baldwin, ed., *Neorealism and Neoliberalism.*

[17]Charles Tilly, "War Making and State Making as Organized Crime," in Evans, Rueschemeyer, and Skocpol, eds., *Bringing the State Back In.*

[18]Tilly, "War Making and State Making," p. 172.

[19]Charles Tilly, *Coercion, Capital, and European States: AD 990–1990* (Cambridge: Blackwell, 1990), p. 89.

[20]Tilly, *Coercion, Capital, and European States,* p. 90.

[21]Douglass C. North and Robert Paul Thomas, *The Rise of the Western World: A New Economic History* (Cambridge: Cambridge University Press, 1973).

[22]Fernand Braudel, *Civilization and Capitalism: 15th–18th Century,* Vol. 2, *The Wheels of Commerce* (New York: Harper and Row, 1982), pp. 186–87.

[23]Stephen Krasner, "Globalization: Content and Discontent," unpublished paper, 1998, pp. 8–9.

[24]See John Brewer, *The Sinews of Power: War, Money and the English State, 1688–1783* (New York: Knopf, 1989).

[25]See Douglas North and Barry Weingast, "Constitutions and Commitment: The Evolution of Institutions Governing Public Choice in Seventeenth-Century England," *Journal of Economic History* (1989), pp. 803–32.

[26]Robert Keohane, "The Theory of Hegemonic Stability and Changes in International Economic Regimes, 1967–1977," in Ole Holsti, Randolph M. Siverson, and Alexander L. George, eds., *Change in the International System* (Boulder: Westview Press, 1980), p. 132.

[27]Charles P. Kindleberger, *The World in Depression, 1929–1939* (Berkeley: University of California Press, 1973), esp. p. 247.

[28]Robert Gilpin, *The Political Economy of International Relations* (Princeton: Princeton University Press, 1987), p. 73.

[29]For an important version of the hegemonic argument, see Stephen Krasner, "State Power and the Structure of International Trade," *World Politics* 28 (1976), pp. 17–47.

[30]See Robert Keohane, *After Hegemony: Cooperation and Discord in the World Political Economy* (Princeton: Princeton University Press, 1984).

[31]For a good survey of the literature on hegemonic stability theory and the current state of the theoretical debate, see David A. Lake, "Leadership, Hegemony, and the International Econ-

omy: Naked Emperor or Tattered Monarch with Potential?" *International Studies Quarterly* 37 (1996), pp. 459–89.

[32]Robert Keohane, *After Hegemony*; and Lisa Martin, *Coercive Cooperation: Explaining Multilateral Economic Sanctions* (Princeton: Princeton University Press, 1992).

[33]For a recent survey, see Lisa Martin, "An Institutionalist View: International Institutions and State Strategies," in T.V. Paul and John A. Hall, eds., *International Order and the Future of World Politics* (New York: Cambridge University Press, 1999). The liberal literature on international institutions and regimes is large. See Stephen Krasner, ed., *International Regimes* (Ithaca: Cornell University Press, 1981); Steph Haggard and Beth Simmons, "Theories of International Regimes," *International Organization*, 41 (1987), pp. 491–517; and Volker Rittberger, ed., *Regime Theory and International Relations* (Oxford: Oxford University Press, 1995).

[34]Oran Young, "Political Leadership and Regime Formation: On the Development of Institutions in International Society," *International Organization* 45, no. 3 (Summer 1991), p. 282. See also Oran Young, *International Cooperation: Building Regimes for Natural Resources and the Environment* (Ithaca: Cornell University Press, 1989). The concept of constitutional contract is discussed in James M. Buchanan, *The Limits of Liberty* (Chicago: University of Chicago Press, 1975), esp. Chapter 5.

[35]See Melvin Richter, *The Political Theory of Montesquieu* (Cambridge: Cambridge University Press, 1977).

[36]Of course, the United States has also been assiduous in ensuring that there are limits and escape clauses in the binding effects of institutions.

[37]On the postwar surge in institution building, see Craig Murphy, *International Organization and Industrial Change* (New York: Oxford University Press, 1994.)

[38]For comparisons of American and British hegemony, see Robert Gilpin, *U.S. Power and the Multinational Corporation: The Political Economy of Foreign Direct Investment* (New York: Basic Books, 1975); and David Lake, "British and American Hegemony Compared: Lessons for the Current Era of Decline," in Michael Fry, ed., *History, the White House, and the Kremlin: Statesmen as Historians* (New York: Columbia University Press, 1991), pp. 106–22.

[39]These arguments are made in G. John Ikenberry, *After Victory: Institutions, Strategic Restraint, and the Rebuilding of Order after Major War* (Princeton: Princeton University Press, 2001).

[40]See John G. Ruggie, *Winning the Peace: America and World Order in the New Era* (New York: Columbia University Press, 1996).

[41]Martha Finnemore, *National Interests in International Society* (Ithaca: Cornell University Press, 1996), p. 29.

[42]See G. John Ikenberry and Charles Kupchan, "Socialization and Hegemonic Power," *International Organization* (Summer 1990).

Chapter 5

State Power and the Promotion of National Interests through Economic Integration

---

OBJECTIVES

- Understand the geopolitical goals that underlie the open world economic system, using U.S. economic hegemony following World War II as a case study.
- Explore the results of U.S. grand strategy after World War II, including social welfare protection, European integration, and the opening of the Japanese market. Compare these goals to U.S. aims and actions after the Cold War.
- Understand how the expansion of market relations serves the strategic interests of the leading state by creating a hospitable environment for trade, economic ties that reduce power-balancing and strategic rivalries, and an international focus that thwarts nationalism.

Introduction

The world economy bears the imprint of powerful states. At various historical junctures, such as after great wars and other upheavals in international relations, leading states have been presented with unusual opportunities to shape the basic organization and rules of regional and global markets. The United Kingdom after the Napoleonic wars of the early nineteenth century and the United States after World War II are the most dramatic and far-reaching examples of major states that have had the power and opportunity to build and manage the world economy. But the economic goals that these leading states pursued have been closely tied to their more general political and security goals and their ambitions in the creation of international political order. Powerful states—when opportunities arise—tend to promote a particular international economic order as a way to achieve their more general political-strategic interests.

This chapter examines the ways in which great powers use markets—particularly through the expansion of economic openness and integration—as a tool of security policy and a means to ensure international order. It will focus on the policies and agreements pursued by the United States with Europe and Japan after World War II and on the ways in which American political and strategic goals were pursued through the organization and extension of market relations. In today's post–Cold War era, similar patterns can be discerned in U.S. policy. As we saw in Chapter 4, power and markets are intimately connected and states both promote and manipulate markets in pursuit of their national interests, even as markets themselves shape and constrain state policies. This logic was seen on a grand scale after World War II, when the United States emerged as a hegemonic power. U.S. power was put at the service of creating a relatively open world economy, but this was because an open world economy would in turn benefit the United States—its state, its society, and its national security.

The expansion of world market relations—and increased economic interdependence—can serve the political and strategic interests of a leading state in a variety of ways. First, a leading state may calculate, quite simply, that an open world economy increases the nation's access to markets, technology, and resources, thereby fostering greater domestic economic growth and wealth and, ultimately, enhancing national security and state power. This basic logic informed the American proposals for rebuilding the world economy after 1945. The United States emerged from the war as the most advanced and productive economy in the world. Its leading industries were well positioned for global competition. An open world economy—organized around nondiscriminatory, multilateral rules—was an obvious national interest. U.S. policy-makers concerned with national economic advancement were drawn to a postwar agenda that reduced trade barriers and promoted global multilateral economic openness.

A second political-strategic interest that might prompt a leading state to pursue market openness and integration is the opportunity to influence the political and economic orientations of other states and regions. A world economy divided into closed and rival regional blocs may be contrary to the economic and security interests of the leading state. During World War II, the government officials who were planning U.S. policies for after the war agreed that the United States could not remain a viable great power yet still be isolated within the Western Hemisphere. The U.S. economy would need to integrate itself into a wider, pan-regional world economy. The war itself was in part a struggle over precisely this matter. German and Japanese military aggression had been aimed at the creation of exclusive regional blocs in Europe and Asia, respectively. The U.S. economy would thrive best in a world without blocs, and its status as a leading great power depended on economic openness. World economic integration was a necessary condition for the U.S. economy to prosper, and open markets would prevent the return of 1930s-style economic blocs.

Third, the promotion of open and integrated markets can also serve the goal of creating close-knit or binding economic ties that help reduce strategic rivalry and the need to balance power. This might be called "strategic interdependence," wherein the leading state purposely tries to entangle itself and the other great powers in each other's economy. In its postwar policies toward Japan and Western Europe, the United States sought to foster stronger economic relations as a way to reduce the possibility that these states would become its great-power rivals. As the Cold War began to emerge, the United States was increasingly interested in stimulating economic growth in Japan and Europe, and it was willing to forego full reciprocity in trade liberalization in order to see Japan's and Europe's economic prospects improve. But the United States also sought to influence the global pattern of trade and investment—particularly with regard to Japan—in a way that would tie these states more closely to the U.S. economy. The United States wanted to bring noncommunist Asia and Western Europe into the American-led "free world," and the promotion of economic linkages was part of this strategy.

Strategic interdependence was also pursued within Europe. The solution to the "German problem" after World War II was to economically integrate the allied zones of occupied Germany within the wider Western European economy. The celebrated European Coal and Steel Community, which created joint French-German ownership of basic war industries, embodied this strategic goal. Economic integration can create mutual dependencies that make autonomous and destabilizing security competition more difficult. The same logic reappeared more recently during the process of German unification, when, to mollify other countries' concerns about the potential strength of a reunited German state, Germany agreed to tie itself even more fully to Europe through monetary union.

Finally, a leading state may promote economic openness and integration so as to promote the more general political evolution of states and international relations. U.S. officials who embrace liberal beliefs about politics and economics had long anticipated that expanding world trade and investment would indirectly promote and reward movement by states toward liberal democracy—and a world of democratic states would reduce security threats and allow the United States to more fully realize its international goals. Trade and investment strengthen the private sector within an economy, empowering civil society as a counterweight to a strong state, and create vested interests within a country in favor of pluralistic political order and stable and continuous relations between states. This was the view most forcefully made by the U.S. secretary of state, Cordell Hull, during World War II. Free and open trade would not just stimulate economic growth but would also strengthen democratic regimes around the world and make war less likely. In Hull's words, "when trade crosses borders, soldiers don't."

We will explore these basic logics of grand strategy and economic openness and integration as they were pursued by the United States and other great powers in the post–World War II era and are pursued even today. What these episodes reveal is that the postwar construction of an open multilateral world economy was facilitated by American political and strategic goals that incorporated market tools and economic integration as part of the conduct of great-power politics and postwar order-building.

Market Openness and American Postwar Grand Strategy

The construction of an open world economic order in the aftermath of World War II remains one of the remarkable accomplishments of the twentieth century. Agreements reached by the United States and the United Kingdom during the war and ratified in Bretton Woods, New Hampshire, in 1944 marked a decisive move toward openness—a move that was a bit astonishing, given the ravages and dislocations wrought by the war, and given the competing postwar interests. After the war, additional agreements were reached between the United States, the countries of Europe, and Japan that further solidified the open and multilateral character of the postwar world economy. By 1948 the Cold War was a reality and additional compromises were struck between the United States and its partners that intensified economic cooperation and facilitated the integration of Germany and Japan into the multilateral order. The Marshall Plan in Europe and the 1951 security pact between the United States and Japan helped cement these ties. By the beginning of the 1950s, a open world economy was in full sway; trade and investment across regions expanded rapidly as a result of tariff liberalization, a stable exchange-rate system, and a postwar economic boom.

The Economic Blocs of the 1930s

American plans for an open postwar world economy were made at the height of the war, and the dominant view among policy thinkers was that the postwar economy must overcome the destructive economic policies that had characterized the 1930s. In the view of most U.S. officials, World War II was the result of a decade of economic fragmentation, trade protectionism, and regional conflict among the great powers. President Harry Truman gave voice to this view in a speech at Baylor University in March 1947 (see Primary Document 5.1).

Around the world in the 1930s, the great powers were moving toward exclusive and antagonistic economic blocs. Germany pursued a series of bilateral trade agreements with eastern European countries in order to consolidate its own economic and political sphere of influence in the region. When Nazi Germany began its military campaign to conquer Europe, it envisioned a postwar continent that would be organized around and controlled by the Third Reich.[1] Japan pursued an even more overt campaign to create what it called a "greater East Asian co-prosperity sphere." The Japanese military carried out an aggressively expansionist policy beginning in the early 1930s in Manchuria and northern China, and eventually spread its reach into Southeast Asia. This territorial expansion and military buildup reflected the growing influence of the Japanese military and the "imperial way" over the country's civilian government.[2] Japanese grand strategy was based on the view that the country's security and economic prosperity could best be provided through the direct and exclusive imperial control of raw materials and markets within its region. As in Germany, the prevailing view in Japan held that Japan's status as a great power rested on the orchestration of military power, resource and economic autonomy, and regional territorial control.

PRIMARY DOCUMENT 5.1

Truman on Trade and World Peace

At this particular time, the whole world is concentrating much of its thought and energy on attaining the objectives of peace and freedom. These objectives are bound up completely with a third objective—reestablishment of world trade. In fact the three—peace, freedom, and world trade—are inseparable. The grave lessons of the past have proved it.

Economic conflict is not spectacular—at least in the early stages. But it is always serious. One nation may take action in behalf of its own producers, without notifying other nations, or consulting them, or even considering how they may be affected. It may cut down its purchases of another country's goods, by raising its tariffs or imposing an embargo or a system of quotas on imports. And when it does this, some producer, in the other country, will find the door to his market suddenly slammed and bolted in his face. Or a nation may subsidize its exports, selling its goods abroad below their cost. When this is done, a producer in some other country will find his market flooded with goods that have been dumped. In either case, the producer gets angry, just as you or I would get angry if such a thing were done to us. Profits disappear; workers are dismissed. The producer feels that he has been wronged, without warning and without reason. He appeals to his government for action. His government retaliates, and another round of tariff boosts, embargoes, quotas, and subsidies is under way. This is economic war. In such a war nobody wins.

Certainly, nobody won the last economic war. As each battle of the economic war of the thirties was fought, the inevitable tragic result became more and more apparent. From the tariff policy of Hawley and Smoot, the world went on to Ottawa and the system of imperial preferences, from Ottawa to the kind of elaborate and detailed restrictions adopted by Nazi Germany. Nations strangled normal trade and discriminated against their neighbors, all around the world.

President Harry Truman gave this speech at Baylor University in Waco, Texas, on March 6, 1947.

Source: "Address on Foreign Economic Policy, Delivered at Baylor University, March 6, 1947," *Public Papers of the President of the United States: Harry S. Truman, 1947* (Washington, D.C.: U.S. Government Printing Office, 1963), pp. 167–72.

Core Principle

President Truman's belief that free trade was an inseparable part of a peaceful world informed the work of the American architects of the postwar world order.

In a less obvious or aggressive way, the United Kingdom also was pursuing a strategy of discriminatory economic cooperation with its partners in the British Commonwealth, a nonterritorial economic bloc that gave preferences to current and former British colonies. An economic grouping was organized beginning in 1933 among the Commonwealth countries, facilitating trade while creating barriers to exchange with countries that did not use the British currency, the pound sterling. By the end of the 1930s, the world had effectively been carved up into relatively insular economic blocs, antagonistic groupings that U.S. officials believed were at least partly responsible for the onset of war.[3]

U.S. Interests and Open Markets

American strategic thinkers began their debates about economic insularity versus openness in the 1930s, as they witnessed the collapse of the world economy and the emergence of German and Japanese regional blocs and the British imperial preference system. The question these thinkers pondered was whether the United States could remain as a great industrial power within the confines of the Western Hemisphere. What were the minimum geographical requirements for the country's economic and military viability? For all practical purposes this question had been answered by the time the United States entered the war. An economic bloc in the Western Hemisphere would not be sufficient; the United States must have security of markets and access to raw materials in Asia and Europe, as well. The culmination of this debate and the most forceful statement of the new consensus was presented in political scientist Nicholas John Spykman's 1942 book *America's Strategy in World Politics*.[4] If the rimlands of Europe and Asia became dominated by one or several hostile imperial powers, the security implications for the United States would be catastrophic, Spykman concluded. To remain a great power, the United States could not allow itself "merely to be a buffer state between the mighty empires of Germany and Japan."[5] It had to seek openness, access, and balance in Europe and Asia. A similar conclusion was reached during the war by experts involved in a study group at an influential New York organization, the Council on Foreign Relations. This study group's concern was the necessary size of the "grand area"—i.e., the core world regions on which the United States depended for economic viability.[6]

This view that the United States needed access to Asian and European markets and resources—and therefore could not let a potential adversary control the Eurasian landmass—was also embraced by postwar defense planners. As the war was coming to an end, U.S. defense officials began to see that the country's security interests required the building of an elaborate system of "forward" bases—that is, bases in Asia and Europe for the U.S. military. Hemispheric defense would be inadequate.[7] Defense officials also saw access to Asian and European raw materials, and keeping those materials out of the hands of a prospective enemy, as a U.S. security interest. The historian Melvin Leffler notes that "[Secretary of War Henry] Stimson, [Undersecretary of War Robert] Patterson, [Assistant Secretary of War John] McCloy, and Assistant Secretary [of War] Howard C. Peterson agreed with [Secretary of the Navy James] Forrestal that long-term American prosperity required open markets, unhindered access to raw materials, and the rehabilitation of much—if not all—of Eurasia along liberal capitalist lines".[8] Indeed, the forward base systems were partly justified because they could assure access to raw materials and deny such resources to an adversary. Some defense studies went further and argued that postwar threats to Eurasian access and openness were more social and economic than military: economic turmoil and political upheaval were the real threats to American security, for they invited the subversion of liberal democratic societies and Western-oriented governments. A study conducted by the Central Intelligence Agency concluded in mid-1947, "The greatest danger to the security of the United States is the possibility of economic collapse in Western Europe and the consequent accession to power of Communist elements."[9] Socioeconomic stability, political pluralism, access to resources and markets, and American security interests were all tied together.

American strategic planners began with the question of how the United States could sustain itself as a great power within a world of encroaching economic blocs and drew the conclusion that an open world economy, organized around a multipolar array of democratic and capitalist states, was essential to the country's postwar national interest. A desirable international order would need to be defined by more than military capacity and power balances; the United States would need to be surrounded by a pluralistic and accessible economic and political environment. These considerations led directly to support for an open, multilateral postwar world economy.

Another group of American officials—State Department officials who were concerned primarily with the political organization of postwar order—similarly defined the national interest in terms of the building of an open world economy. The most forceful advocate of this position was Secretary of

State Hull. Throughout the Franklin Roosevelt presidency, Hull and other State Department officials consistently maintained that an open international trading system was central to U.S. economic and security interests and fundamental to the maintenance of postwar peace. Hull agreed with the widespread view that the bilateralism and economic blocs of the 1930s were the root causes of world political instability and war. Charged with responsibility for commercial policy, the State Department championed tariff reductions, most prominently in the 1934 Reciprocal Trade Agreement Act and the 1938 U.S.-British trade agreement. Trade officials at the State Department saw liberal trade as a core U.S. interest that reached back to the Open Door policy of the 1890s.[10] In the early years of the war, this liberal economic vision dominated American thinking about the future world order and became the initial opening position as the United States engaged the United Kingdom and other states on the shape of the postwar international order.

These officials used classic liberal arguments to make their case. To begin with, the United States would emerge from the war with the largest and most competitive economy, and so an open economic order would obviously be in the country's national economic interests. But they also argued that an open system was an essential element of a stable world political order: it would discourage the type of ruinous economic competition, protectionism, and discriminatory blocs that had contributed to the Depression and to the war. Free trade and open markets would also reward and reinforce democratic government around the world, undercutting strong states and military dictatorships that threatened world peace. Finally, and just as important, this State Department vision of openness—a sort of "economic one-worldism"—was expected to lead to an international order in which American "hands-on" management would be modest. The system would, in effect, govern itself. The postwar order, organized around free trade, would be open and peaceful, and the United States would not need to directly manage its operation.

These views dominated American thinking about postwar order. U.S. security and peaceful relations among the great powers were impossible in a world of closed and exclusive economic regions. The challengers to an open multilateral order occupied almost every corner of the advanced industrialized world. Germany and Japan each had pursued a dangerous path into the modern industrial age that combined authoritarian capitalism with military dictatorship and coercive regional autarky. But the British Commonwealth and its imperial preference system was also a challenge to an open order. The hastily drafted **Atlantic Charter** drawn up by Roosevelt and British prime minister Winston Churchill in 1941 was an American effort to ensure

The Atlantic Charter, August 14, 1941

First, their countries seek no aggrandizement, territorial or other;

Second, they desire to see no territorial changes that do not accord with the freely expressed wishes of the people concerned;

Third, they respect the right of all peoples to choose the form of government under which they live; and they wish to see sovereign rights and self-government restored to those who have been forcibly deprived of them;

Fourth, they will endeavor, with due respect for their existing obligations, to further the enjoyment by all States, great or small, victor or vanquished, of access, on equal terms, to the trade and to the raw materials of the world which are needed for their economic prosperity;

Fifth, they desire to bring about the fullest collaboration between all nations in the economic field with the object of securing, for all, improved labor standards, economic advancement and social security;

Sixth, after the final destruction of the Nazi tyranny, they hope to see established a peace which will afford to all nations the means of dwelling in safety within their own boundaries, which will afford assurance that all the men in all the lands may live out their lives in freedom from fear and want;

Seventh, such a peace should enable all men to traverse the high seas and oceans without hindrance;

Eighth, they believe that all of the nations of the world, for realistic as well as spiritual reasons, must come to the abandonment of the use of force. Since no future peace can be maintained if land, sea or air armaments continue to be employed by nations which threaten, or may threaten, aggression outside of their frontiers, they believe, pending the establishment of a wider and permanent system of general security, that the disarmament of such nations is essential. They will likewise aid and encourage all other practicable measures which will lighten for peace-loving peoples the crushing burden of armaments.

August 1941, President Franklin D. Roosevelt and Prime Minister Winston S. Churchill met on board a ship in a bay off the coast of Newfoundland, Canada, to compose this set of guiding principles that they hoped would guide international relations and the world economy after the war.

> ### Core Principle
>
> The principles of free trade, equal access for countries to the raw materials of the world, and international economic collaboration to advance labor standards, employment security, and social welfare were enshrined in the institutions established after World War II to guide the international political economy.

that the United Kingdom signed on to these liberal democratic war aims (see Primary Document 5.2). This joint statement of principles affirmed free trade, equal access for countries to the raw materials of the world, and international collaboration in the economic field so as to advance labor standards, employment security, and social welfare.[11] Roosevelt and Churchill were intent on telling the world that they had learned the lessons of the interwar years—and those lessons were fundamentally about the proper organization of the Western world economy. Not just the enemies of the United States, but also its friends, had to be reformed and integrated.

Roosevelt wanted to use the Atlantic Charter as a way to extract from the British a pledge not to use the war for purposes of territorial or economic imperialism. In doing so, Roosevelt was attempting at least in part to prevent a repeat of what he strongly felt hurt peace efforts after World War I: Allied intrigues and secret understandings pursued without U.S. knowledge that had the effect of undermining President Woodrow Wilson's Fourteen Points. But Roosevelt was also seeking to reach agreement with the United Kingdom on war aims at an early moment when the United States was in a strong position. This, too, was a lesson that Roosevelt and other U.S. officials had learned from Wilson's experience.

Roosevelt's aim with the Atlantic Charter was to begin the process of locking the European democracies into an open postwar international order. The charter itself and the principles behind it attracted broad support in the United States. John Foster Dulles, a prominent Republican foreign policy expert, applauded the Atlantic Charter and its emphasis on a postwar world that allowed for "growth without imperialism," supported by "an international body dedicated to the general welfare" and the establishment of "procedures within each country" to ensure movement toward economic openness.[12] During the 1944 presidential election campaign, the Republican Party's committee on postwar foreign policy reaffirmed its commitment to a "stabilized interdependent world," urging U.S. participation after the war in cooperation with other states to prevent military aggression, expand international trade, and secure monetary and economic stability.[13]

From these various wartime perspectives, U.S. officials articulated a common position. At the heart of the country's postwar grand strategy would be a systematic effort to open markets and integrate regions. The national interest necessitated the expansion and integration of the world economy. This was a view that united leading domestic business interests, liberal internationalists, and geopolitical strategists. How this goal would be achieved, however, remained highly contested at home and abroad—requiring political bargains both with European partners and within American society.

Open Markets and Social Bargains

The initial American vision of postwar order championed by the State Department was quite simple: a multilateral system of free trade. But U.S. policy evolved during the four years between the Atlantic Charter and the actual postwar arrangements, as the United States maneuvered to reach agreement with the British and other European countries and cope with unfolding economic and political disarray. The Europeans were interested less in securing an open postwar economy than in providing safeguards and protections against postwar economic dislocations and unemployment. The United States eventually moved toward a compromise settlement. Rather than a simple system of free trade, the industrialized countries would establish a managed order organized around a set of multilateral institutions (see Essential Economics 5.1) and a social bargain that sought to balance openness with domestic welfare and stability.[14]

During the war, the idea of an open world economy was one thing that liberal visionaries and hard-nosed national security strategists could agree upon. This goal united American postwar planners and was the seminal inspiration for the work of the conference on postwar economic cooperation that was held in Bretton Woods, New Hampshire, in July 1944.[15] In his farewell remarks to that conference, Secretary of the Treasury Henry Morgenthau asserted that the agreements that had been reached marked the end of economic nationalism, by which he meant not that countries would give up pursuit of their national interests, but that trade blocs and economic spheres of influence would not be the vehicles through which to do so.

ESSENTIAL ECONOMICS 5.1

Institutions and the World Economy

The **International Moretary Fund** (IMF) is headquartered in Washington, D.C. It has 183 member states and a large professional staff. The IMF was created to supervise the operation of the monetary system and provide short-term financing to member countries facing balance-of-payment difficulties. The IMF's lending resources come primarily from financial contributions from member countries; the amount of these contributions is determined by the member's economic size. IMF decisions are made by weighting voting, with votes reflecting the member's financial contribution, so the United States, Japan, and the major European countries have a leading voice in IMF policy. As of early 2001, 91 member states were recipients of about $65 billion in outstanding IMF credits.

The **World Bank** (officially named the International Bank for Reconstruction and Development) is headquartered in Washington, D.C., with 183 member states and 10,000 professional staff members. It supports long-term investment projects in developing countries. The Bank obtains financial resources for its lending programs by borrowing on world capital markets and by receiving contributions from donor countries. Poverty reduction and the facilitation of sustainable economic development are its core goals. The World Bank makes its key decisions on the basis of weighted voting, giving the United States, Japan, and the major European countries a dominant influence. By the year 2001 the bank had outstanding loans to or other development programs in more than 100 countries, and it disbursed approximately $17.3 billion in new loans during its 2001 fiscal year.

The **World Trade Organization** (WTO) is headquartered in Geneva, Switzerland, with 142 members and a large professional staff. Its mission is the promotion of an open world trading system through the reduction of trade barriers and the provision of rules and mechanisms to settle trade disputes. The forerunner of the WTO was the General Agreements on Tariffs and Trade (GATT), created in 1948 as an interim step designed to facilitate "freer and fairer" trade. Through a series of "multilateral trade rounds" over the decades, GATT dramatically reduced tariffs. In 1995 GATT was replaced by the WTO, which has more responsibilities and powers than did its predecessor.

Core Principle

The Bretton Woods agreements led to the formation of several important institutions that facilitate the openness and stability of the world economy.

Yet American ideas for a multilateral free trade order had few enthusiastic proponents in Europe. The United Kingdom and France were not convinced of the intrinsic virtues of an unregulated open trading system, and various political factions in both countries maintained their prewar ambitions to hold on to their declining imperial possessions and spheres of influence. Beyond the desire to retain their imperial holdings, the Europeans also worried about postwar depression and the protection of their fragile economies. These concerns made them weary of the Americans' stark proposals for an open world trading system and led them to favor instead a more regulated, compensatory system.[16]

British and American differences were exposed as early as the summer of 1941, when the celebrated economist John Maynard Keynes, working for the British government, traveled to Washington, D.C., to begin negotiations over postwar economic plans. These negotiations were triggered by disagreements over Article VII of the U.S.-British Lend-Lease agreement, which set forth the terms for postwar settlement of mutual aid obligations. (The Lend-Lease agreement itself set out the terms of America's massive military aid program to the United Kingdom.) The article stipulated that neither country would seek to restrict trade and both would take measures to reduce trade barriers and eliminate preferential tariffs. American politicians wanted to make sure, after helping to ensure the United Kingdom's survival, that U.S. businesses would not be shut out of British Commonwealth markets. State Department officials presented their ideas on postwar free trade, and Keynes found them hopelessly inadequate. To Keynes—and the British government— American ideas for an open postwar world economy entailed a return to the nineteenth-century system whereby open markets and the gold standard exposed national economies to abrupt and painful swings and contractions. The discussions revealed sharply different views on the virtues of an open trading system. The State Department saw such a system as an absolute necessity and a matter of principle, whereas Keynes and his colleagues viewed it as an attempt to rebuild what they considered a harmful and long outdated laissez-faire trade system—or what Keynes called "the lunatic proposals of Mr. Hull."[17]

Movement toward a compromise came only later, after the two governments shifted their negotiations away from trade to monetary order and discovered a more tractable set of issues. Keynes came to the view that perhaps an agreement could be reached with the United States for a monetary order that would be expansionary, one that could keep the trading system open but still safeguard against depression.[18] What followed was a flurry of monetary planning in both countries, with Treasury Department economist Harry Dexter White leading U.S. planning. Both the British and the American plans sought to eliminate foreign-exchange controls and restrictive financial practices, and to provide rules for changes in rates of exchange. The Keynes plan was more ambitious and included provisions for a new international currency and obligations on countries that enjoyed balance-of-payments surpluses to extend credit to countries suffering balance-of-payments deficits. The White plan restricted the obligations of creditor countries and proposed more modest resources to be used to respond to balance-of-payments crises.[19] The two plans provided the framework for the negotiations that were held throughout 1943 and up to the Bretton Woods conference in July 1944. Many of the compromises leaned in the direction of the American plan—most important, the limitation on creditor-country liability—but the plans shared a vision of managed open economic order that would attempt to give governments the tools and resources to manage imbalances without resort to policies that could bring on deflation and high levels of unemployment.

The agreement between British and American monetary planners was particularly important because it served to transcend the stalemate over the postwar trade system. Once agreement was reached in this area, the State Department found its old-style trade proposals of secondary significance in the emerging postwar settlement. The "embedded liberal" ideas of the Anglo-American deal on monetary order paved the way for broader agreement on postwar relations among the industrialized countries.[20]

The Anglo-American monetary agreement also resonated within the wider circles of British and American politics. The **Bretton Woods agreements** allowed political leaders to envisage a postwar economic order in which multiple and otherwise competing political objectives could be combined. The alternatives from the past—of the nineteenth century and of the interwar period—posed options that were politically too stark. Outside the narrow transatlantic community of economists and policy experts, politicians were looking for options that could steer a middle course.

This search for a middle course between bilateralism and laissez-faire was clearly on the minds of the British. After a conversation with John Foster Dulles (who was at the time a corporate lawyer in New York City), the British ambassador to the United States, Lord Halifax, cabled the British Foreign Office in October 1942:

The most interesting point on the economic side of the discussion was Mr. Dulles' exposition of the Cordell Hull School of free trade, and the place which it had in the plans of the Administration. I said to him that I thought that we did not clearly understand what the significance of the Hull policies was. There was a feeling in some quarters here that we were faced with two alternatives, either we must revert to a completely 19th century system of laissez-faire, or else we must safeguard our balance of payments position by developing a bilateral system of trade with those countries whose natural markets we were. It seemed to me that neither of these courses would work, the first was clearly impossible, the second might be disastrous. I asked Mr. Dulles whether there might be some middle course which would take account of our special difficulties and which at the same time would satisfy Mr. Cordell Hull on the question of discrimination, preferences, etc.[21]

The Bretton Woods agreements were important because they served as a basis on which to build broader coalitions around a relatively open and managed order. They presented a middle path that generated support from both the conservative free-traders and the new enthusiasts of economic planning. Both groups agreed that simply lowering barriers to trade and capital movements was not enough. The leading industrialized states had to actively supervise and govern the system. Institutions, rules, and active involvement of governments were necessary. Another lesson that had been drawn from the 1930s was the fear of economic contagion, wherein unwise or untoward policies pursued by one country threaten the stability of others. As Roosevelt said at the opening of the Bretton Woods conference, "the economic health of every country is a proper matter of concern to all its neighbors, near and far."[22]

But the settlement also allowed governments to deliver on the new promises of the welfare state, pursuing expansionary macroeconomic policies and protecting social welfare. Since the late nineteenth century, the United States and European countries had been slowly developing domestic policies and institutions that would provide more protections for workers. The great economic turmoil of the 1930s was particularly critical in pushing Western governments to take greater responsibility for managing unemployment and social security. In the decades after World War II, these governments expanded their role in the domestic economy and built modern welfare programs (see Essential Economics 5.2). In the nineteenth century, governments were not held responsible for unemployment and economic dislocation among their citizens, but by the time that the United States and the United Kingdom began to negotiate the rules and arrangements for the post–World War II economic order, political leaders were increasingly aware that employment stability and social security were critical tasks of government. An unfettered free trade system might create greater economic growth but it would also increase domestic economic instability and risk sharp swings in employment. In this context, British and American leaders had incentives to search for a postwar economic order that would both provide the benefits of openness and allow for some social protections.

More generally, the emphasis on creating an order that provided economic openness and stability was, as seen earlier, a central objective of American postwar planners. Liberal free traders came to support this goal by recognizing the new necessity of a managed capitalist order that could give governments the ability to pursue economic growth and stable employment. Security officials came to this view by recognizing that the greatest security threats to Europe (and, indirectly, to the United States) came from inside these societies, through economic crisis and political disarray.[23]

In seeking agreement on postwar economic relations, the United States moved in the direction of the United Kingdom and the rest of Europe. The British were instrumental in lobbying and gaining the support of the agencies of the U.S. government that were most congenial with their aims. The result was a system that was more or less open, provided institutions to manage this openness, but also offered enough loopholes to allow governments to protect their weak economies. The United States won the agreement it had hoped for, and the Europeans secured commitments, mechanisms, and obligations institutionalized in the postwar order.

Promoting European Integration

The country's postwar strategic interests also led the United States to promote European political and economic integration, which at least indirectly provided further support for an open and integrated world economy. By 1947 it had become clear that the Bretton Woods agreements would not be sufficient to get Europe on its feet and revive the world economy. The United Kingdom and the rest of Europe had been much more weakened by the war than U.S. officials had realized, and this meant that the United States would need to play a more direct role—and spend much more money—in rebuilding Europe than they initially expected. At the same time, relations with the Soviet Union quickly deteriorated, providing additional incentives for the United States to assist Europe and to build more intensive economic and se-

ESSENTIAL ECONOMICS 5.2

Government Spending as a Percentage of GNP

	WEST GERMANY	SWEDEN	UNITED KINGDOM	UNITED STATES
1940	12[a]	12	23[b]	18
1960	15	24	30	27
1980	43	57	42	33

[a]1935   [b]1938

Source: Edwin S. Mills, *The Burden of Government* (Stanford, CA: Hoover Institution Press, 1986), p. 12.

> *Core Principle*
>
> In the postwar decades, the welfare revolution swept through the advanced industrialized world. Middle-class and working-class people experienced a expanded range of welfare services. Expanded government spending as a share of GNP, shown in this table, reflects that transformation.

curity relations. The Cold War served to draw the United States into a more active leadership of the world economy bolstered U.S. support for European integration, and strengthened U.S. determination to build transatlantic political and security institutions that in turn supported economic openness.

U.S. support for a unified Europe emerged as early as 1947, as troubles with the Soviet Union grew and the vision of "one world" order began to fade. As officials in the State Department rethought relations with Western Europe and the Soviet Union, a new policy emphasis emerged, concerned with the establishment of a strong and economically integrated Europe— what some officials came to call a "third force" in postwar order. The policy shift was not to a bipolar or spheres-of-influence approach with a direct and ongoing U.S. military and economic presence in Europe; instead, the aim was to build Europe into an independent center of military and economic power and thereby to overcome the problem of postwar German power by integrating it into a wider, unified Europe.

U.S. officials championed the idea of a united Europe initially as the best way to strengthen the political and economic foundations of the postwar European states. Their emphasis was not on directly confronting Soviet activities in Western Europe but on repairing the war-ravaged economic, political, and social institutions that made communist inroads possible in Europe. An American effort to aid Europe would best be conducted not by directly fighting communism but by restoring European growth and living standards. State Department officials, for example, supported the creation of a multilateral clearing system in Western Europe that would encourage the reduction of trade barriers and eventually evolve into a customs union.[24] They hoped to encourage the rise of a united and economically integrated Europe standing on its own apart from the Soviet sphere and the United States. "By insisting on a joint approach," the State Department official George Kennan later wrote, "we hoped to force the Europeans to think like Europeans, and not like nationalists, in this approach to the economic problems of the continent."[25]

A unified Europe was also seen by U.S. officials as the best mechanism for deterring the revival of German militarism. Kennan argued in a 1949 paper that U.S. officials saw "no answer to [the] German problem within [a] sovereign national framework. [The] Continuation of historical process within this framework will almost inevitably lead to [a] repetition of [the] post-Versailles sequence of developments. . . . [The] only answer is some form of European union which would give young Germans [a] wider horzon. . . ."[26] As early as 1947, Dulles was arguing that the economic unification of Europe would generate "economic forces operating upon Germans" that were "centrifugal and not centripetal"—"natural forces which will turn the inhabitants of Germany's state toward their outer neighbors" in a cooperative direction. Through an integrated European economy, including the internationalization of the Ruhr Valley (the German industrial heartland), Germany "could not again make war even if it wanted to."[27] Likewise, the U.S. high commissioner for Germany, John McCloy, argued that a "united Europe" would be an "imaginative and creative policy" that would "link Western Germany more firmly into the West and make the Germans believe their destiny lies this way."[28] If Germany was to be bound to Europe, Europe itself would need to be sufficiently unified and integrated to serve as an anchor.

Encouraging European unity also appealed to the State Department officials working directly on European recovery. In their view, the best way to get Europe back on its feet was by encouraging a strong and economically integrated Europe. They also wanted to increase the Western orientation of European leaders and to prevent a political drift to the left or the right. This goal could be achieved, they believed, not just by ensuring economic recovery but also by creating political objectives to fill the postwar ideological and moral vacuum. As one May 1947 document argued, "the only possible ideological content of such a program was European unity."[29] Other officials who were concerned primarily with an open postwar trading system were alarmed by the economic distress in Europe and saw U.S. aid and European unity as necessary steps to bring Western Europe back into a stable and open system.[30] These views helped push the Truman administration to announce the Marshall Plan, which brought massive amounts of American economic aid to Europe. The plan itself would be administered in a way to promote European unity.[31] The idea of a united Europe would provide the ideological bulwark for European political and economic construction. But disputes between the British and the French over the extent of supranational political authority and economic integration, as well as European unwillingness to establish an independent security order, left the early proposals for a European "third force" unfulfilled.

U.S. support for European unification unfolded as the Cold War became a reality and Europe and the United States bargained over the shape of the postwar order. In the first years after the war, U.S. officials were eager for the restarting of European economic growth, which was important both as a hedge against political instability and support for communism and as a necessary step in the building of an open world economy. But to get growth in Europe, German industrial production and trade ties with the continent needed to be restarted. This need, in turn, raised the question of how to reintegrate and reconstruct Germany without risking the revival of militarism and aggression. As conflict with the Soviet Union intensified, the rebuilding of the western zones of Germany became all the more important, and at each step, the answer was to bind Germany to the rest of Western Europe. But in accepting this solution to the "German problem," the other states in Europe insisted that the United States play a direct role in guaranteeing their security. Thus the reconstruction and integration of Germany and the U.S. security commitment to Europe went together.

The United Kingdom and France both favored establishing direct security ties with the United States over making Europe into a "third force." The United States, however, argued that any U.S. security commitment would have to be preceded by a Europe-wide security arrangement. The Brussels Treaty among the Western European states provided such an arrangement and thus set the stage for the North Atlantic Treaty (which created the North Atlantic Treaty Organization, or NATO) a year later.[32] But even this watershed agreement by the United States to make a solemn security commitment to Europe was seen by State Department officials as a way to bolster the Europeans' confidence and willingness to unify. In this sense, U.S.

security support might best be seen as a continuation of the logic that was embodied in the Marshall Plan: the United States was encouraging the Europeans to build pan-regional political and economic institutions that would make Europe a more stable and peaceful pillar of world order.

Apart from containing the Soviet Union and rehabilitating Germany, the United States supported European integration because it would connect all the great powers of Europe together, thereby undercutting nationalism and strategic competition. Regional integration would not only make Germany safe for Europe, it would also make Europe safe for the world. The Marshall Plan reflected this American line of thinking, as did the Truman administration's support for the Brussels Pact, the European Defense Community, and the Schuman Plan.[33] In the negotiations over the North Atlantic Treaty in 1948, U.S. officials made clear to the Europeans that a security commitment from the United States hinged on European movement toward integration. One State Department official remarked that the United States would not "rebuild a fire-trap."[34] Congressional support for the Marshall Plan was also premised, at least in part, not just on transferring dollars to Europe but also on encouraging integrative political institutions and habits.[35]

The various elements of the settlement among the North Atlantic countries fit together. The Marshall Plan and NATO were part of a larger institutional package. As historian Lloyd Gardner argues, "each formed part of a whole. Together they were designed to 'mold the military character' of the Atlantic nations, prevent the balkanization of European defense systems, create an internal market large enough to sustain capitalism in Western Europe, and lock in Germany on the Western side of the Iron Curtain."[36] NATO was a security alliance, but it was also embraced as a device to help organize political and economic relations within the Atlantic area. The resulting European and Atlantic orders facilitated economic revival in Europe and expanding trade and investment between the two regions. U.S. political and strategic interests continued to drive U.S. policies toward the construction of a world economy, but the bargains and institutional frameworks needed to make economic openness possible became increasingly elaborate and multilayered.

MAP 5.1

The Japanese Economic Bloc in East Asia, 1875–1939

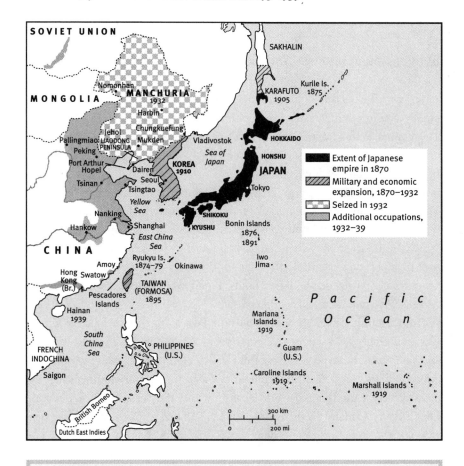

Core Principle

American foreign policy after World War II tried to prevent a recurrence of the Japanese expansionism and regionalism that had marked the preceding seven decades. As this map shows, between 1875 and 1939, Japan constructed an empire that dominated large portions of eastern Asia. U.S. postwar policy—especially after 1948—focused on integrating Japan into the world economy.

Recasting Wartime Foes as Economic and Strategic Partners

Bringing Japan into the World Economy

American officials traced the cause of war in Asia to Japan's forced establishment of a closed and restrictive economic bloc in East Asia (see Map 5.1). The United States hoped after the war to eradicate Japanese militarism and regional domination and restore Nationalist China as a great power. As the Nationalist Chinese slowly lost their hold on the mainland to their communist opposition, however, the United States shifted its strategy back to Japan. The occupation of Japan initially focused on introducing democracy and market reform to the country, but as the Cold War took hold in Asia after 1948, the U.S. emphasis shifted to policies that fostered economic growth and political stability. Still, throughout the early postwar years, American economic goals served the larger political and strategic objective of integrating East Asia into an open world economy.

American diplomats disagreed on how best to deal with Japan after the war. Some officials thought that militarism was only weakly rooted in Japan and therefore favored a relatively mild policy of eradicating militarism in the armed forces, implementing constitutional reform, and reintegrating the country into a multilateral world economy. But the actual U.S. occupation force, led by General Douglas MacArthur, pursued a much more aggressive campaign to demilitarize and democratize Japanese politics and society and implant principles and institutions that mirrored American values.[37] The economic reform program focused on dissolving the *zaibatsu*, the highly concentrated financial and industrial combines that dominated the Japanese economy. In the American view, such giant industrial structures were directly behind both German and Japanese militarism and stood in the way of individual rights and liberties. The U.S. occupation's attack on such structures, part of a broader Truman administration campaign to liberalize postwar economic institutions around the world, aimed to remove the economic sources of dictatorship and military aggression.[38]

In these early years, the U.S. occupation did little to promote the integration of Japan into the world economy. Democratization and economic reform were pursued even as the domestic economy itself deteriorated. As late as

1947, industrial production and per capita income were still at only half of their prewar levels. The occupation forces also retained existing curbs on foreign trade and actually imposed more restrictions. The Cold War came later to Asia than to Europe, and regional or global strategic objectives were less influential in the conduct of occupation policy in Japan than they were in Germany and the rest of Europe.[39]

The big shift in U.S. policy occurred after 1948. The failure of economic reform in Japan, worries about political instability, the victory of the Communists in China, and the growing strategic importance of Japan all contributed to a new policy orientation stressing economic growth and incorporation into the world economy. The State Department led the way in 1948 in stressing the strategic importance of Japan in the region and placing East Asia within the wider global context of the containment of communist influence. Kennan and other policy planners urged the relaxation of war reparations, the easing of controls over political and economic institutions, and an end to efforts at industrial and financial reform. In their view, the aggressive U.S. reconstruction of Japanese politics and society was not working and was risking political upheaval that could bring communists into power. The new emphasis of U.S. policy encouraged economic growth and built the foundations for an ongoing U.S.-Japanese security partnership.

In the ensuing years, Japan was brought into the American security and economic orbit. The United States took the lead in helping Japan find new commercial relations and sources of raw materials in Southeast Asia to substitute for the loss of the Chinese and Korean markets.[40] Japan and Germany were now twin junior partners of the United States, stripped of their military capacities and reorganized as engines of world economic growth. Containment in Asia was based on the growth and integration of Japan in the wider, noncommunist Asian regional economy—what Secretary of State Dean Acheson called the "great crescent," referring to the countries arrayed from Japan through Southeast Asia to India. Historian Bruce Cumings captured the logic behind this policy: "In East Asia, American planners envisioned a regional economy driven by revived Japanese industry, with assured continental access to markets and raw materials for its exports."[41] This strategy would link threatened noncommunist states along the crescent, create strong economic links between the United States and Japan, and lessen the importance of the remaining European colonial holdings in the area. The United States would actively aid Japan in re-establishing a regional economic sphere of influence in Asia, allowing Japan to prosper and play a regional leadership role within the larger U.S. postwar order. Japanese economic growth, the expansion of regional and world markets, and the fighting of the Cold War went together.

The solidification of a strategic partnership between Tokyo and Washington drove U.S. policy after the fall of China to the Communists. Japanese officials arrived in San Francisco in September 1951 to sign a peace treaty with 48 countries, and, during that same visit, Japan signed a bilateral security pact with the United States, thereby anchoring the American security order in East Asia. Only after the security partnership took shape did the economic integration of Japan into the world economy begin. Throughout the last years of the Truman administration and into the Eisenhower administration, U.S. officials identified Japanese economic success with their country's regional strategic interests. Unusual steps would be taken to boost Japan's economy and foreign trade: "The entry of Japanese goods into the United States should be facilitated," argued a National Security Council document in 1952. The United States was urged to "utilize Japan . . . as a source of supply on a commercial basis for equipment and supplies procured by U.S. armed forces or under United States aid programs for other countries."[42] Similar policies continued into the 1950s. The United States was willing to forego fully reciprocal trade relations if it meant that Japan's economy would be bolstered and lead to the growth and stabilization of noncommunist Asia.

It was only later that Japan was fully incorporated into the multilateral economic order. Despite American backing, Japan did not gain equal status in GATT from the European states until the late 1950s.[43] Even more so than in Europe, the Cold War containment strategy *in East Asia* drove the methods and terms by which the United States sought to expand and integrate markets. The bilateral security partnership with Japan—and later, a larger array of bilateral partnerships in the region—created incentives and a political framework in which the United States could stimulate economic growth and market relations. The United States identified its own national interest with the rising economic fortunes of its new allies. The Bretton Woods model of economic openness was supplemented, and to some extent replaced, by a world economy situated within regional security institutions and Cold War political partnerships.

Germany and European Economic Integration

Political and security objectives underlay the push for regional economic integration in Europe throughout the postwar era. Many Europeans—and the United States as well—strongly believed that economic and political integration were essential to prevent future war on the continent. This solution was seen to be particularly relevant to the relationship between Germany and France, which had been the central great-power antagonists in three European wars in less than a century. Economic integration and the construction of a regional political order were also seen by many as a way to safeguard postwar capitalism and democracy in Western Europe and ensure a stable role for the Federal Republic of Germany (FRG, or West Germany) after 1949. When the Cold War ended 50 years later and Germany was poised for reunification, European leaders again emphasized economic and political integration as a means to shield the region from a new era of German dominance.

France's promotion of economic integration with Germany stood at the heart of its own postwar security policy in Western Europe. French leaders, of course, had few strategic options. As it had after World War I, France again initially pursued a policy aimed at undermining the ability of Germany to rebuild its industrial and military capabilities. Reparations, disarmament, and permanent Allied occupation of German industrial areas were elements of this balance-of-power strategy. But it soon became impossible to sustain such a policy: the onset of the Cold War, the necessities of economic integration to French revival, and pressures from allies all forced the French to search for an alternative security strategy. Tying Germany down in a web of European and transatlantic economic and security institutions emerged as the necessary solution to the problem of postwar European order.

This strategy of economic and political integration also appealed to the leaders of the new West German republic, including its first chancellor, Konrad Adenauer. By agreeing to bind itself to a regional economic organization and the Atlantic alliance, the FRG could create the more stable environment it needed to foster domestic economic growth and the consolidation of democracy. West Germany's willingness to tie itself to its neighbors allayed fears within Europe of a resurgence of German militarism and aggression. West Germany would not reconstruct itself as a traditional great power; it would be enmeshed in a web of regional economic and security ties that would institutionally restrain West German power. With these safeguards, a reconstructed and strong West Germany would be acceptable within Eu-

➤ **TIMELINE 5.1**

Milestones on the Road to European Integration

1951	Treaty of Paris establishes the European Coal and Steel Community
1957	Treaties of Rome establish the European Economic Community (EEC) and the European Atomic Energy Community
1962	Common Agricultural Policy is launched
1968	European customs union is completed
1970	European political cooperation (foreign policy coordination) is launched
1973	Denmark, Ireland, and the United Kingdom join the EEC
1975	European Council is launched
1979	European Monetary System is launched
1981	Greece joins the EEC
1986	Single European Act launches the single-market program, extending EEC competence in environmental policy, economic and social cohesion, research and technology policy, and social policy
1986	Spain and Portugal join the EEC
1989	European Commission responsibility is extended to competition policy
1992	Maastricht treaty forms the European Union (EU) on the road to transforming European political cooperation into the common foreign and security policy, and launches intergovernmental cooperation on justice and home affairs
1995	Austria, Finland, and Sweden join the EU
1997	Treaty of Amsterdam extends EU competence over certain aspects of justice and home affairs and sets a target date for completion of "an area of freedom, security, and justice"
1998	European Central Bank is inaugurated in Frankfurt, Germany
1999	Common monetary policy and single currency (the euro) are launched in 11 countries
2002	Euro becomes legal tender

rope, and that strong country would become increasingly important as the Cold War heated up.

This strategy of binding West Germany to Europe and creating an integrated European order unfolded in several steps (see Timeline 5.1). The European Coal and Steel Community (ECSC), proposed by French foreign minister Robert Schuman in May 1950 and established in 1951, was the earliest milestone in this strategy. Under this plan, six countries—the FRG, France, Italy, Belgium, the Netherlands, and Luxembourg—agreed to put their coal and steel industries under supranational control. The short-term goal of this measure was to phase out the Allied control of the West German coal and steel sectors, which had been managed by the International Ruhr Authority since the war's end. But the longer-term goal was to tie postwar West German industrial capacity to a wider European institutional structure. As political scientist Michael J. Baun notes, "through the ECSC, the integration of a rebuilding Germany into the Western community of democratic states could begin, and German industrial power could be harnessed to the anti-Soviet cause."[44] West Germany's heavy industries—the core of its warmaking capacity—were reconstructed in a European-controlled enterprise. Rather than balance against Germany or destroy its industrial base, France and Western Europe moved instead to bind West Germany to the wider regional order.[45]

Just months after Schuman announced his plan for the ECSC, the French government came forward with a plan for a European defense community (EDC). This plan called for the integration of national defense forces and the creation of a European army under a unified command. The initiative embodied the same logic as that for the ECSC: France and other European countries realized that West German rearmament was increasingly inevitable under the strains of a mounting Cold War. In recent months, the Soviet Union had successfully tested an atomic bomb and North Korea had invaded the South. The EDC was proposed to ensure that West German rearmament took place within a European institutional framework, thereby making it less destabilizing or threatening to neighboring states. In the end, the EDC was never implemented and the French General Assembly voted it down in August 1954. But an institutional framework was established with the signing of the North Atlantic Treaty in 1948 and its subsequent evolution to include the permanent stationing of U.S. troops in Europe, multinational forces, and an integrated military command structure. As noted earlier, this NATO framework provided the necessary binding assurances and commitments between Europe and the United States to allow West German military rebuilding to proceed.

European economic integration took a decisive step forward in June 1955 when the six members of the ECSC met in Messina, Italy, and agreed to establish a common market through the elimination of all tariff barriers between them and the creation of a customs union for trade with nonmembers. This meeting was the basis of the 1957 Treaty of Rome that established the European Economic Community (EEC). A tripartite institutional structure was put in place that built on the ECSC model; the EEC comprised an executive commission (the European Commission), a council of ministers, and a legislative assembly. The basic technique of economic integration that was pursued for most of the EEC's first two decades was "negative integration," which involved the creation of tighter economic links between member countries through the elimination of barriers to the movement of goods across national borders. Apart from the common external trade policy, the new economic organization did not pursue a significant "positive" integration strategy, which would have involved forming common economic policies and building supranational institutions.[46] The Common Agricultural Policy, established in 1964 and entailing subsidies and a common external tariff on agricultural products, is a significant exception to this lack of a positive integration strategy.

In the years that followed, the underlying logic of European integration—involving the stabilization of Franco-German relations—remained in the background as the member states maneuvered for advantage and negotiated over the terms of EEC enlargement (see Map 5.2). By 1968, the transition to the Common Market was complete. In 1973 the United Kingdom joined the EEC after more than a decade of resistance by France. The following year, the members created the European Council to provide an intergovernmental mechanism for more direct and ongoing direction of EEC affairs by the heads of government. But during the 1970s the momentum of European economic integration was lost, for the strategic goals that prompted the early economic links had already been achieved.

It really was only in the late 1980s that ambitious new goals of European integration were articulated. In 1985 the European Commission president, Jacques Delors, announced plans for the 1992 single-market initiative, which would complete the long-term goal of an open internal European market. This new effort to root out barriers to trade and investment was driven by a variety of factors, including the growing recognition by many European leaders that the ability of Europe to keep up with the expanding and leading-

MAP 5.2

Expansion of the European Economic Community/European Union, 1951–95

Members
Fast-track applicants
Other applicants
Not yet invited to negotiate
1951 Date of joining/*application**

Source: Robert Cottrell, "My Continent Right or Wrong," *Economist*, October 29, 1999, available at www.economist.com/surveys/PrinterFriendly.cfm?Story ID=325726&CFID=108954&CFTOKEN=1628528.

Core Principle

Over the decades, western Europe has both expanded and deepened its economic and political cooperation and integration. This map shows the expanding membership of the European Union, as well as its possible expansion to include countries in eastern and central Europe and the Mediterranean region in the years ahead.

edge economies of Asia and North America was being hampered by government controls and divergent national regulations.[47] The major states of Europe also increasingly shared the view that their national economic goals could be achieved only through greater regional and international integration and cooperation. French president François Mitterrand and West German chancellor Helmut Kohl rekindled the Franco-German collaborative spirit of the previous generation in discovering that their own national interests could best be advanced though a common economic agenda.

Soon after the single-market initiative was underway, European leaders took the next step and announced plans to move toward monetary union. Some officials believed that transaction costs related to currency exchange posed a significant barrier to greater regional trade and investment flows, and as such a joint monetary policy and, eventually, a common currency were necessary to complement the single-market vision. Others supported monetary union because it would provide the necessary underpinning for a great political union. Yet another source of support came from European countries that were increasingly feeling the economic and monetary dominance of West Germany.[48] The French were particularly sensitive to this matter, and their support for monetary union was in part driven by their interest in weakening German monetary hegemony and transferring some measure of monetary control from the Bundesbank to European institutions. With responsibility for monetary policy-making moved to a European-wide organization, the French government would be able to strengthen its own voice over Europe's direction.[49] This view was shared by most of the other European countries; monetary union would give governments a role in monetary decision-making that would otherwise be pursued unilaterally by West Germany.

The issue of German economic dominance of Europe became even more pronounced with the end of the Cold War and the prospective reunification of West Germany and East Germany. After the Berlin Wall fell in November 1989 and the East German regime collapsed, Chancellor Kohl called for early reunification but also sought to make clear that a united Germany would remain squarely within the EEC and the NATO alliance. Again, in a fashion similar to the reintegration politics of the early 1950s, Germany sought to reassure its neighbors by agreeing to integrate itself further into the regional economic and political order.

The broad thrust of German policy was to reassure its neighbors—both east and west—that a unified and inevitably more powerful Germany would be deeply enmeshed in wider regional institutions.[50] West German Foreign Minister Hans-Dietrich Genscher articulated this basic German view in a

January 1990 speech: "We want to place the process of German unification in the context of [European] integration, . . . the West-East partnership for stability, the construction of the common European house and the creation of a peaceful European order from the Atlantic to the Urals."[51] Genscher and other German leaders did not always mention NATO in these statements, which worried U.S. officials in the early months of the unification debate, but their basic message was clear: to gain agreement on unification, Germany was prepared to further bind itself to its neighbors.

The United States supported German unification more enthusiastically than did France or the United Kingdom, and it tried to rally allied support by extracting assurances from West Germany about the wider institutional arrangements in which unification would occur. The overriding American goal throughout these months was to ensure that a unified Germany would remain firmly embedded in the NATO alliance. During late 1989, the United States began articulating a policy that linked German unification to assurances about Germany's continued commitment to European and Atlantic institutions. President George H.W. Bush presented this view as U.S. policy at a NATO meeting in Brussels on December 4, 1989, and later stated it in public: "Unification should occur in the context of Germany's continued commitment to NATO and an increasingly integrated European Community, and with due regard for the legal role and responsibilities of the Allied powers."[52] The NATO alliance and European economic integration would bind Germany to Europe, and the United States would ensure agreement by adding its own security commitment.

President Mitterrand was cautious about German unification but his emphasis was on the need to deepen European integration and West Germany's ties to the European Community (EC). In a letter to President Bush on November 27, 1989, Mitterrand argued, "Each of our governments is very aware of the role that the EC can and must play in the definition of a new European equilibrium, as soon as the EC has reinforced its own cohesion."[53] Soon thereafter, in a meeting with Genscher, Mitterrand again linked German unification to progress toward a more integrated Europe. In a meeting between Mitterrand and Bush on St. Martin in the Caribbean on December 16, the French leader again affirmed his view that German unification must be linked to developments in NATO and the EC Arms control, EC integration, European monetary union, and U.S. cooperation with Europe must all be addressed together in order to create a new Europe of which German unification would be a part. "Otherwise," warned Mitterrand, "we will be back in 1913 and we could lose everything."[54] The linkage between

German unification and European union was explicit. In March 1990, Kohl proposed an accelerated plan for European integration but also signaled Germany's readiness to embark on ambitious steps toward greater European integration, including a willingness to begin negotiations on the terms of European political union. Kohl was already a supporter of greater European integration, but the willingness of the German leader to move quickly with an ambitious plan for European monetary and political union was tied to his own agenda for German unity.[55]

At each stage in the development of European unity, the great powers were engineering the expansion of economic ties as a way to advance wider political and strategic interests. Expanded market interdependence was a tool to enhance political stability by solving security dilemmas and tying the great powers together. Economic integration and regional institutional structures played a critical role in reassuring France and the other European states that a reconstructed and more powerful Germany could be a cooperative and stable force on the continent.

Conclusion

Powerful states with leading economies have an overwhelming interest in promoting an open world economy. The United Kingdom in the nineteenth century and the United States in the twentieth century were hegemonic states on the cutting edge of the technological revolution in production and transportation, and both identified their own well-being with the construction of a global market order. As the most productive and competitive economies in their time, the United Kingdom and the United States used their considerable military and political power to push other countries toward market openness. After World War II, a direct connection was identified between U.S. economic prosperity—along with the wealth and power that prosperity would generate—and the openness of the world economic order. The United States had emerged as the most powerful state in the world, but that power would have been less complete or of shorter duration if the United States had not sought to open markets and integrate the global economy.

There were additional reasons why U.S. political and strategic interests were advanced by open and integrated world markets. One important impulse in the U.S. embrace of economic openness was the view that economic nationalism and regional blocs were a major source of conflict in the 1930s and a cause of the war. Exclusive economic spheres not only harmed American economic interests, they also directly threatened American security interests by generating conflict among the great powers. As one scholar argued, "The American intention was to lessen the economic importance of political boundaries and enhance security of all states by giving every state equal opportunity for access to markets and raw materials and thereby to defuse the issue that had led to the economic struggles of the 1930s."[56] Economic interdependence and American security were tightly linked.

Another element in the U.S. embrace of openness was the view that linked economies would reduce power-balancing and strategic rivalry among the great powers. If Germany and Japan were integrated into the U.S. economic orbit, they would be less likely to become security rivals again. As the Cold War unfolded, the institutional structures that were created to bind Japan and Germany to the West were made increasingly elaborate, and, ultimately, security alliances provided the key to binding the states together. But security and economic ties reinforced each other. Germany's reconstruction and return to sovereign statehood hinged on the strength of its economic ties to France and the EC and its security ties with the United States. The same was true after the Cold War as Germany emerged as the dominant state in Europe.

These considerations make it clear that the opening of the world economy after World War II was given critical support by the system of security cooperation triggered by the Cold War. Indeed, the postwar multilateral world economy is in fundamental respects a creature of the Cold War. The Soviet threat fostered cohesion among the capitalist democracies and provided the "political glue" that held the world economy together. The U.S. military guarantee to Europe and Asia provided national security reasons for Japan and the Western democracies to open their markets. Free trade was a way to cement the alliance, and the alliance in turn facilitated the settlement of economic disputes. The export-oriented development strategies of Japan and the smaller countries of East and Southeast Asia depended on the willingness of the United States to accept their imports and to live with huge trade deficits; alliance ties with Japan, South Korea, and other Southeast Asian countries made this politically more tolerable. Economists and liberal visionaries have long made a compelling case for free trade and open markets, but it was only when political leaders and security officials could also do so that the world actually moved in that direction.

Finally, expectations of more diffuse and long-term effects also inform the strategic embrace of integration and open markets. It has been a staple of U.S. thinking about foreign policy that the spread of trade and investment into the nondemocratic world would stimulate and reinforce the economic and political forces pushing for political change. An expanding market society acts as a counterweight to strong, autocratic states and encourages the rise of a middle class that favors democratic institutions. This belief was at the center of the Clinton administration's policy toward China and its support for integrating China into the world economy. In the wake of the deal between the two countries over Chinese entry into the World Trade Organization, a reporter commented, "For a president who talks constantly these days about harnessing the forces of economic globalization, the agreement to integrate China into the global trading system marked the culmination of [President Bill] Clinton's single biggest imprint on American foreign policy: the use of American economic power for strategic ends. That is what this agreement is all about, locking in China's commitment to economic reforms and with it, he is betting, a further opening of Chinese society."[57] To promote economic interdependence is to allow the grand forces of economic change to move countries around the world in the direction of the United States. Trade and investment are a solvent for authoritarian politics. To the extent that an expanding world economy stimulates the rise of democracy around the world, U.S. security and political interests are advanced.

Notes

[1]On German regional economic ambitions, see John Gerard Ruggie, "Multilateralism: The Anatomy of an Institution," in John Gerard Ruggie, ed., *Multilateralism Matters* (New York: Columbia University Press, 1994), pp. 8–14.

[2]See James Crowley, *Japan's Quest for Autonomy: National Security and Foreign Policy, 1930–1939* (Princeton: Princeton University Press, 1966).

[3]For arguments that the great midcentury struggle was between a open capitalist order and various regional, autarkic challengers, see Bruce Cumings, "The Seventy Years' Crisis and the Logic of Trilateralism in the New World Order," *World Policy Journal* (Spring 1991); and Charles Maier, "The Two Postwar Eras and the Conditions for Stability in Twentieth-Century Western Europe," in Charles Maier, *In Search of Stability: Explorations in Historical Political Economy* (New York: Cambridge University Press, 1987).

[4]Nicholas John Spykman, *America's Strategy in the World: The United States and the Balance of Power* (New York: Harcourt, Brace, 1942).

[5]Spykman, *America's Strategy in World Politics*, p. 195.

[6]See Council on Foreign Relations, "Methods of Economic Collaboration: The Role of the

Grand Area in American Foreign Economic Policy," in *Studies of American Interests in the War and Peace,* July 24, 1941, E-B34 (New York: Council on Foreign Relations, 1941).

[7]See Melvyn P. Leffler, "The American Conception of National Security and the Beginning of the Cold War, 1945–48," *American Historical Review* 48 (1984), pp. 349–56.

[8]Leffler, "The American Conception of National Security," p. 358.

[9]Central Intelligence Agency, "Review of the World Situation as It Relates to the Security of the United States," September 26, 1947, quoted in Leffler, "The American Conception of National Security," p. 364.

[10]On the State Department's commitment to a postwar open trading system, see Lloyd Gardner, *Economic Aspects of New Deal Diplomacy* (Madison: University of Wisconsin Press, 1964); and Richard Gardner, *Sterling-Dollar Diplomacy: The Origins and the Prospects of Our International Economic Order* (New York: McGraw Hill, 1969).

[11]Churchill insisted that the charter did not mandate the dismantlement of the British empire and its system of trade preferences, and only the last minute sidestepping of this controversial issue ensured agreement. See Lloyd C. Gardner, "The Atlantic Charter: Idea and Reality, 1942–1945," in Douglas Brinkley and David R. Facey-Crowther, eds., *The Atlantic Charter* (London: Macmillan, 1994), pp. 45–81.

[12]John Foster Dulles, "Peace without Platitudes," *Fortune* 25 (January 1942): 42–43.

[13]See Andrew Williams, *Failed Imagination? New World Orders of the Twentieth Century* (New York: Manchester University Press, 1998), pp. 98–100.

[14]This section draws on G. John Ikenberry, "A World Economy Restored: Expert Consensus and the Anglo-American Postwar Settlement," *International Organization* 46 (Winter 1991–92).

[15]This argument is made in Robert A. Pollard, *Economic Security and the Origins of the Cold War, 1945–1950* (New York: Columbia University Press, 1985).

[16]On Anglo-American disagreements over the nature of the postwar order, see Randall Bennett Woods, *A Changing of the Guard: Anglo-American Relations, 1941–1946* (Chapel Hill: University of North Carolina Press, 1990). The strongest claims about American and European differences over postwar political economy are made by Fred Block, *The Origins of International Economic Disorder* (Berkeley: University of California Press, 1977), pp. 70–122.

[17]R. F. Harrod, *The Life of John Maynard Keynes* (London: Macmillan, 1951), p. 512.

[18]Alfred E. Eckes, Jr., *Search for Solvency: Bretton Woods and the International Monetary System, 1944–71* (Austin: University of Texas Press, 1975), p. 65.

[19]The White plan is published in "Memorandum by the Secretary of the Treasury [Morgenthau] to President Roosevelt," May 15, 1942, *Foreign Relations of the United States [FRUS], 1942,* Vol. 1 (Washington, D.C.: U.S. Government Printing Office, 1959), pp. 171–90.

[20]For a discussion of "embedded liberalism," see John G. Ruggie, "International Regimes, Transactions, and Change: Embedded Liberalism in the Postwar Economic Order," in Stephen D. Krasner, ed., *International Regimes* (Ithaca: Cornell University Press, 1983); and John G. Ruggie, "Embedded Liberalism Revisited: Institutions and Progress in International Economic Relations," in Emmanuel Adler and Beverly Crawford, eds., *Progress in Postwar International Relations* (New York: Columbia University Press, 1991).

[21]Dispatch from Ambassador Halifax to the Foreign Office, October 21(?), 1942, FO371/31513 (Public Records Office, Foreign Office Files, Kew, United Kingdom).

[22]Franklin Roosevelt, "Opening Message to the Bretton Woods Conference," Bretton Woods, N.H., July 1, 1944, quoted in the *New York Times,* July 2, 1944, p. 14.

[23]For a discussion of the domestic pressures for a stable postwar economy, see Robert Griffith, "Forging America's Postwar Order: Domestic Politics and Political Economy in the Age of Truman," in Michael J. Lacey, ed., *The Truman Presidency* (Washington, D.C.: Woodrow Wilson Center Press, 1989), pp. 57–88. On the wide appeal of growth-oriented policies and institutions and their role in facilitated agreement within the West, see Charles Maier, "The Politics of Productivity," in Peter J. Katzenstein, ed., *Between Power and Plenty: The Foreign Economic Policies of Advanced Industrial States* (Madison: University of Wisconsin Press, 1978).

[24]Ernst H. Van Der Beugel, *From Marshall Plan to Atlantic Partnership* (Amsterdam: Elsevier, 1966), p. 43.

[25]George Kennan, *Memoirs: 1925–1950* (Boston: Little, Brown, 1967), p. 337.

[26]"Question of European Union," Policy Planning Staff paper quoted in Klaus Schwabe, "The United States and European Integration: 1947–1957," in Clemens Wurm, ed., *Western Europe and Germany, 1945–1960* (New York: Oxford University Press, 1995), p. 133.

[27]Ronald W. Pruessen, *John Foster Dulles: The Road to Power* (New York: Free Press, 1982), Chapter 12.

[28]Thomas A. Schwartz, *America's Germany: John J. McCloy and the Federal Republic of Germany* (Cambridge: Harvard University Press, 1991), p. 95.

[29]Quoted in Van Der Beugel, *From Marshall Plan to Atlantic Partnership*, p. 45.

[30]See "The European Situation," Memorandum by the Under Secretary of State for Economic Affairs, *FRUS, 1947*, Vol. 3, pp. 230–320.

[31]For the argument that European cooperation and unity—perhaps even an "economic federation"—was an integral part of the European Recovery Program, see "Summary of Discussion on Problems on Relief, Rehabilitation and Reconstruction of Europe," May 29, 1947, *FRUS, 1947*, Vol. 3, p. 235. See also Michael Hogan, "European Integration and the Marshall Plan," in Stanley Hoffman and Charles Maier, eds., *The Marshall Plan: A Retrospective* (Boulder: Westview Pr, 1984); and Michael Hogan, *The Marshall Plan: America, Britain, and the Reconstruction of Western Europe, 1947–1952* (New York: Cambridge University Press, 1987).

[32]The Brussels Treaty, signed on March 17, 1948, by the United Kingdom, France, the Netherlands, Belgium, and Luxembourg, bound these countries to protect each other from aggression. This European grouping later came to be called the Western European Union.

[33]The European Defense Community was a failed effort to build a Europe-wide security organization. The Schuman Plan—also called the European Coal and Steel Community—was launched in 1950 as the first major effort to unify Europe and bind Germany to the rest of the continent through cross-national integration of heavy industry.

[34]"Minutes of the Fourth Meeting of the Washington Exploratory Talks on Security," July 8, 1948, *FRUS, 1948*, Vol. 3, pp. 163–69.

[35]See Van Der Beugel, *From Marshall Plan to Atlantic Partnership*; and Geir Lundestad, *"Empire" by Integration: The United States and European Integration, 1945–1997* (New York: Oxford University Press, 1998).

[36]Lloyd Gardner, *A Covenant with Power: American and World Order from Wilson to Reagan* (New York: Oxford University Press, 1984), p. 81.

[37]For the definitive account of the American occupation of Japan, see John Dower, *Embracing Defeat: Japan in the Wake of World War II* (New York: W. W. Norton & Co., 1999).

[38]See Robert Pollard, *Economic Security and the Origins of the Cold War, 1945–1950* (New York: Columbia University Press, 1985), pp. 174–79.

[39]Pollard, *Economic Security and the Origins of the Cold War*, pp. 178–79.

[40]Michael Schaller, "Securing the Great Crescent: Occupied Japan and the Origins of Containment in Southeast Asia," *Journal of American History* 69 (September 1982), pp. 392–414.

[41]Bruce Cumings, "Japan's Position in the World System," in Andrew Gordon, ed., *Postwar Japan as History* (Berkeley: University of California Press, 1993), p. 38.

[42]Quoted in Stuart Auerbach, "The Ironies That Built Japan Inc.," *Washington Post,* July 18, 1993, A1.

[43]Pollard, *Economic Security and the Origins of the Cold War*, p. 187.

[44]Michael J. Baun, *An Imperfect Union: The Maastricht Treaty and the New Politics of European Integration* (Boulder: Westview, 1996), p. 12.

[45]French support for the ECSC was also driven by more practical and immediate commercial goals, such as gaining access to cheap German coal as an input to its steel production. The actual political and economic achievements of the ECSC are also widely questioned. See John Gillingham, *Coal, Steel, and the Rebirth of Europe, 1945–1955: The Germans and French from the Ruhr Conflict to Economic Community* (Cambridge: Cambridge University Press, 1991); Alan S. Milward, *The Reconstruction of Western Europe, 1945–1951* (Berkeley: University of California Press, 1984); Alan S. Milward, *The European Rescue of the Nation-State* (London: Routledge, 1993); and Andrew Moravcsik, *The Choice for Europe: Social Purpose and State Power from Messina to Maastricht* (Ithaca: Cornell University Press, 1998), Chapter 2.

[46]On positive and negative integration, see John Pinder, "Positive Integration and Negative Integration: Some Problems of Economic Union in the EEC," *The World Today* 24 (1968), pp. 88–110.

[47]See Wayne Sandholtz and John Zysman, "1992: Recasting the European Bargain," *World Politics* 42, no. 1 (October 1989), pp. 95–128; Andrew Moravcsik, "Negotiating the Single European Act: National Interests and Conventional Statecraft in the European Community," *International Organization* 45, no. 1 (Winter 1991), pp. 19–56; and David R. Cameron, "The 1992 Initiative: Causes and Consequences," in Alberta Sbragia, ed., *Euro-Politics* (Washington, D.C.: Brookings Institution, 1992), pp. 23–74.

[48]See Loukas Tsoukalis, *The New European Economy: The Politics and Economics of Integration* (New York: Oxford University Press, 1991).

[49]This argument is made in Joseph M. Grieco, "State Interests and Institutional Rule Trajectories: A Neorealist Interpretation of the Maastricht Treaty and European Economic and Monetary Union," *Security Studies* 5, no. 3 (Spring 1996); and Joseph M. Grieco, "The Maastricht Treaty, Economic and Monetary Union and the Neo-Realist Research Programme," *Review of International Studies* 21 (1995), pp. 21–40.

[50]On Chancellor Kohl's ambition of tying Germany to Europe and the Atlantic alliance so as to reassure neighboring countries, see Elizabeth Pond, *The Rebirth of Europe* (Washington, D.C.: Brookings Institution, 1999), pp. 39–40.

[51]"German Unity within the European Framework," Speech by Foreign Minister Hans-Dietrich Genscher at a conference at the Tutzing Protestant Academy, January 31, 1990, quoted in Robert Hutchins, *American Diplomacy and the End of the Cold War: An Insider's Account of U.S. Policy in Europe, 1989–1992* (Baltimore: Johns Hopkins University Press; and Washington, D.C.: Woodrow Wilson Center Press, 1997), p. 120.

[52]George H. W. Bush, "The President's News Conference in Brussels," December 4, 1989,

in *Public Papers of President George Bush: 1989* (Washington, D.C.: Government Printing Office, 1990), Vol. 2, p. 1648.

[53]Quoted in Philip Zelikow and Condoleezza Rice, *Germany Unified and Europe Transformed: A Study in Statecraft* (Cambridge: Harvard University Press, 1995), p. 116.

[54]George H. W. Bush and Brent Scowcroft, *A World Transformed* (New York: Knopf, 1998), p. 201.

[55]Hutchins, *American Diplomacy and the End of the Cold War,* p. 118.

[56]Robert Gilpin, "Economic Interdependence and National Security in Historical Perspective," in Klaus Knorr and Frank N. Trager, eds., *Economic Issues and National Security* (Lawrence: Regents Press of Kansas, 1977), p. 55.

[57]David E. Sanger, "A Deal That America Just Can't Refuse," *New York Times,* November 16, 1999, p. A1.

Chapter 6

State Power and the Promotion of National Interests through Economic Sanctions and Incentives

OBJECTIVES

- Understand the different kinds of economic sanctions and incentives that are available to states, as well as the different purposes for which states impose or extend them.
- Identify and explore the conditions under which economic sanctions and economic incentives are more or less likely to be successful.
- Understand the problems associated with the use of either sanctions or incentives, and why countries often turn to them in spite of those problems.

Introduction

We discussed in Chapter 5 the overall strategy pursued by the United States after World War II to build a more open international economy in part to rehabilitate Germany and Japan economically, to channel their politics in a democratic direction, and to bring them into a broader diplomatic coalition directed toward the containment of Soviet expansionism. In that instance of remarkably successful grand strategy, the United States formulated and implemented a long-term economic program (an open world economy) in support of a long-term political-strategic objective (a robust democratic coalition arranged against Soviet imperialism).

States also use economic policy instruments that are more immediate in their effects in order to achieve relatively short-term political-strategic objectives. After the September 11, 2001, terrorist attacks, for example, the United States assembled an international coalition directed against Osama bin Laden, his al Qaeda terrorist network, and the Taliban ruling authority that had harbored bin Laden and al Qaeda in Afghanistan. The United States needed Pakistan to be a part of that coalition. In order to secure Pakistani support, the U.S. government removed the economic sanctions it had imposed against Pakistan when that country and India had tested nuclear devices in 1998, and the United States also provided Pakistan financial aid and debt relief worth about $1 billion. In other words, to get Pakistan's cooperation in the fight against international terrorism, the United States essentially bribed the Pakistani government.

This chapter looks closely at the use of economic actions as instruments of diplomatic-military strategy. It looks in particular at two classes of such economic instruments: economic sanctions and economic incentives. An ***economic sanction*** is a threatened or actual interruption of economic ties by an initiator state against a target state for the purpose of forcing the target to meet a specific political demand of the initiator. An ***economic incentive*** is a promised or actual extension by an initiator state of an economic benefit to a target in exchange for compliance by the target with a political demand of the initiator.

Economic sanctions and incentives are controversial policy instruments. It is unclear, for example, whether they are more likely to help or to hinder efforts by an initiating country to influence a target country. We will discuss in this chapter the many types of economic sanctions and incentives from which an initiator state may choose in seeking to influence a target state. We will also discuss the many reasons why sanctions and incentives may have limited success in changing the behavior of a target. We will also discuss why, in spite of their many drawbacks, economic sanctions and incentives are often used by initiating states as instruments of foreign policy. We will find that such measures often provide policy leaders with the opportunity to advance national interests, especially when the use of military force is considered too costly. Thus, we can expect that economic sanctions and incentives will likely be an important but contested component of the foreign policies of states for many years to come.

Economic Sanctions as an Instrument
of Foreign Policy

Bases for Analysis

As already noted, an economic sanction is a threatened or actual interruption by an initiator state of economic relationships with a target state for the purpose of forcing the target to meet a specific political demand of the initiator.[1] Sanctions can be analyzed along four dimensions: the types of economic relationships that are put at risk by the initiator, the number of initiator states, the directness with which the economic ties between the initiator and target are interrupted, and the initiator's political objectives.

Types of Economic Relations Put at Risk

In choosing between the various types of sanctions, countries can focus their actions on trade with another country or on financial relations with that country.

TRADE SANCTIONS

Several types of policy instruments are available to an initiator who chooses to impede the target's commercial relations. First, the initiator may try to impose a ***blockade*** against the target, seeking to stop all commerce between the target and the outside world, if necessary by the use of force. For example, Germany used submarine warfare to blockade the United Kingdom during both World War I and World War II, and its attacks on U.S. shipping in pursuit of that blockade led the United States to declare war on Germany in April 1917.

The initiator may instead seek to impose an ***embargo*** against the target, in which case the initiator seeks to prohibit some or all of its own exports to the target but does not interfere with financial contacts between its residents and the target and does not interfere with economic ties between the target and third countries. For example, after the Soviet Union invaded Afghanistan in December 1979, the United States imposed a partial embargo by cancelling several contracts for large sales of U.S. grain to the Soviet Union (which at the time was suffering from a string of poor harvests).[2] In the same vein, in an effort to undermine Nicaragua's leftist Sandinista government, the United States imposed a full trade embargo on that country in May 1985, but, at least officially, did not prohibit U.S. financial dealings in Nicaragua.[3]

Third, the initiator might attempt to impose a **boycott** against the target, thereby prohibiting some or all imports from the target.[4] An initiator that imposes an embargo against a country often imposes a boycott against it as well. For example, since the early 1960s, when Fidel Castro came to power in Cuba, the United States has maintained both a full-scope trade embargo and a full-scope boycott against that country.

Finally, the initiator might elect to impose a sanction that consists of the revocation of **most-favored-nation (MFN) status.** Most-favored-nation status is a term under the World Trade Organization (WTO) whereby member states extend to one another unconditionally the same treatment with regard to imports that they extend to the nation that is their "most-favored" partner, thus greatly facilitating access to their home markets. Nonmembers of the WTO, however, are not automatically accorded MFN status; they have to negotiate it separately with each of their trading partners. Thus, the extension of MFN by one country to another can be a major incentive, and, by denying equal access to its market, the revocation of MFN by one country from another can be a major sanction. The United States, for example, each year from 1989 to 1994 threatened not to renew MFN status for China unless it improved its human rights behavior following the massacre at Beijing's Tiananmen Square in June 1989.[5]

FINANCIAL SANCTIONS

A second category of sanctions available to an initiator concerns financial relationships. For instance, an initiator might undertake **currency attacks** against a target to weaken its exchange rate. The United States chose this option during the Suez crisis of 1956, selling British pounds as a way of pressuring the United Kingdom to terminate its efforts with France and Israel to seize the Suez Canal by force and thereby to topple the Egyptian government of Gamal Abdel Nasser.[6]

Second, an initiator might impose a **freeze on financial assets,** or a denial to residents of the target country of access to financial assets they hold in the initiating country. For example, in 1979, in response to the seizure of U.S. diplomats and the U.S. embassy in Tehran, the United States government denied Iranians access to $12 billion in financial assets that they held in the United States.[7] Similarly, the United States in the early 1990s sought to pressure the authoritarian Haitian government to accept a democratic re-

PRIMARY DOCUMENT 6.1

Unilateral Economic Sanctions: The United States and Burma

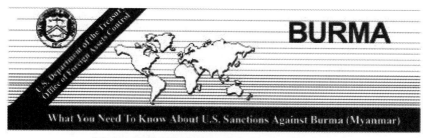

An overview of the Burmese Sanctions Regulations
Title 31 Part 537 of the U.S. Code of Federal Regulations

■ **INTRODUCTION** - On May 20, 1997, in response to the Burmese Government's large scale repression of and violence against the Democratic opposition, President Clinton issued Executive Order No. 13047 declaring a national emergency with respect to Burma. The order, issued under the authority § 570(b) of the Foreign Operations, Export Financing and Related Programs Appropriations Act, 1997 (Public Law 104-208) (the "Act") and the International Emergency Economic Powers Act (50 U.S.C. 1701-1706)("IEEPA"), prohibits new investment in Burma by U.S. persons, and their facilitation of new investment in Burma by foreign persons. The summary which follows is intended as a broad overview of the Regulations.

Criminal penalties for violating the Burmese Sanctions Regulations range up to 10 years in jail, $500,000 in corporate, and $250,000 in individual fines. In addition, civil penalties of up to $11,000 per violation may be imposed administratively.

Some examples of prohibited new investment are as follows:

✔ A U.S. company wishes to build a new factory in Burma where its products will be produced. This is likely to involve an agreement for the development of industrial, commercial, and human resources located in Burma and is prohibited.

✔ A U.S. contractor has been asked by a foreign oil company to be the general contractor for its oil exploration project in Burma. The U.S. company would not only supervise the sub-contractors, but also guarantee their performance. This activity is considered new investment and is prohibited.

✔ A U.S. sub-contractor has been asked to perform a service for the general contractor in the previous example, but will have no supervisory functions. The sub-contractor is merely providing a service and its activities in Burma are not prohibited (see "**General Exemptions**" below).

✔ A U.S. company has been asked by a European company to provide ongoing technical support for its factory in Burma. The contract calls for the U.S. company to be paid a percentage of the profits generated by the Burmese factory. This is a prohibited new investment in Burma.

This excerpt from U.S. regulations banning new U.S. foreign direct investment in Burma is taken from the U.S. Treasury's Web site. It indicates that, in response to human rights violations of the Burmese government, the United States government, as of May 1997, has banned new foreign direct investment by U.S. residents and firms in that country.

Source: U.S. Department of Treasury, Office of Foreign Assets, "Sanctions Programs Summary," Available at www.treas.gov/ofac/.

Core Principle

Countries use economic sanctions to try to influence the behavior of other countries when normal diplomatic means are unavailable or unsuccessful.

placement by freezing financial assets in the United States owned by the Haitian government and by a number of wealthy Haitians who had been supporting the authoritarian regime.[8]

A third type of financial sanction consists of **bans on private bank lending and foreign direct investment**. For example, in 1986, in an effort to pressure the South African government to abandon its policy of apartheid, the U.S. Congress passed legislation that forbade American banks from extending loans to South Africa and banned most new private direct investments there by U.S. enterprises.[9] Similarly, in 1995 the Clinton administration forbade U.S. oil firms from making investments that would help develop Iran's oil resources.[10] As shown in Primary Document 6.1, in 1997 the Clinton administration also banned new U.S. foreign direct investment in Burma (Myanmar) in response to human rights abuses by the Burmese military government.

Finally, an initiator may elect to employ as a sanction the denial of bilateral or multilateral economic assistance to a target. In 1982, for example, the United States forced the World Bank and the Inter-American Development Bank to stop making loans to Nicaragua's leftist government.[11] Similarly, after India and Pakistan tested nuclear weapons in 1998, the United States, Germany, and Japan temporarily froze their aid programs for those countries, and the United States indicated it would vote against major new loans for them by the International Monetary Fund (IMF) and the World Bank.

Number and Coordination of Initiators

Initiators may employ economic sanctions either on their own or in conjunction with other states. **Unilateral sanctions** are imposed by an initiator against a target without the initiator's asking other countries to join it in the sanctioning. (It may, however, ask other countries not to assist the target in evading the impact of the unilateral sanctions.) Two examples of unilateral economic sanctions programs are the U.S. grain embargo imposed against the Soviet Union in 1980 and the progressively tougher economic sanctions the United States has imposed against Iran since the mid-1980s to try to compel it to cease its support for international terrorism.

As an alternative to the imposition of unilateral sanctions, states sometimes work together to employ sanctions against a target, in which case they are pursuing a strategy of **multilateral sanctions.** For example, as can be observed in Primary Document 6.2, the United Nations (UN) Security Council imposed an economic blockade against Iraq after the latter invaded

Multilateral Economic Sanctions: The United Nations and Iraq

Acting under Chapter VII of the Charter,

1. *Determines* that Iraq so far has failed to comply with paragraph 2 of resolution 660 (1990) and has usurped the authority of the legitimate Government of Kuwait;

2. *Decides*, as a consequence, to take the following measures to secure compliance of Iraq with paragraph 2 of resolution 660 (1990) and to restore the authority of the legitimate Government of Kuwait;

3. *Decides* that all State shall prevent:

(*a*) The import into their territories of all commodities and products originating in Iraq or Kuwait exported therefrom after the date of the preset resolution;

(*b*) Any activities by their nationals or in their territories which would promote or are calculated to promote the export or trans-shipment of any commodities or products from Iraq or Kuwait; and any dealings by their nationals or their flag vessels or in their territories in any commodities or products originating in Iraq or Kuwait and exported therefrom after the date of the present resolution, including in particular any transfer of funds to Iraq or Kuwait for the purposes of such activities or dealings;

(*c*) The sale or supply by their nationals or from their territories or using their flag vessels of any commodities or products, including weapons or any other military equipment, whether or not originating in their territories but not including supplies intended strictly for medical purposes, and, in humanitarian circumstances, foodstuffs, to any person or body in Iraq or Kuwait or to any person or body for the purposes of any business carried on in or operated from Iraq or Kuwait, and any activities by their nationals or in their territories which promote or are calculated to promote such sale or supply of such commodities or products;

4. *Decides* that all States shall not make available to the Government of Iraq, or to any commercial, industrial or public utility undertaking in Iraq or Kuwait, any funds or any other financial or economic resources and shall prevent their nationals and any persons within their territories from removing from their territories or otherwise making available to that Government or to any such undertaking any such funds or resources and from remitting any other funds to persons or bodies within Iraq or Kuwait, except payments exclusively for strictly medical or humanitarian purposes and, in humanitarian circumstances, foodstuffs;

Iraq invaded and occupied Kuwait on August 2, 1990. Four days later, in an effort to coerce Iraq's withdrawal from Kuwait, the United Nations Security Council adopted UN Security Council Resolution 661, which imposed comprehensive economic sanctions against Iraq. The sanctions were not sufficient to induce a withdrawal: that required massive military operations by the United States, the United Kingdom, and a number of other countries in early 1991.

Source: U.N. Security Council, Resolution 661, August 6, 1990, available at http://www.un.org/Docs/scres/1990/661e.pdf.

Kuwait in August 1990. Similarly, when the United States and its allies won the Persian Gulf War against Iraq in February 1991, the UN Security Council agreed to maintain an embargo and a boycott against Iraq (except, later, for the sale of a limited amount of oil under UN supervision for the purpose of importing food and medical supplies) in order to compel it to accede to a number of conditions, most notably to stop its efforts to acquire chemical, biological, and nuclear weapons.

The Target Country: Primary vs. Secondary Sanctions

We can further analyze economic sanctions on the basis of whether they are imposed by the initiator directly or indirectly against the target. *Primary sanctions* are those in which the initiator seeks directly to interrupt bilateral economic ties between itself and the target, and thereby directly to impose costs on the target. For example, the U.S. grain embargo against the Soviet Union in 1980 was a primary sanction, for it was the Soviet Union that was denied full access to U.S. grain.

The alternative to primary sanctions are *secondary sanctions*, through which the initiator seeks to impose economic penalties against third countries as a way of forcing them to curtail their economic transactions with, and thus indirectly to hurt, the target country. For example, the Helms-Burton Act, which President Bill Clinton signed into law in March 1996, threatens to impede the U.S. operations of foreign firms if they use or purchase U.S.-owned assets that were previously nationalized by the Castro government in Cuba. The act allows U.S. private citizens who believe their confiscated properties in Cuba have been acquired by foreign firms to sue those firms in U.S. courts, and it authorizes the U.S. government to forbid entry into the United States by foreign corporate executives who are employed by those firms, as well as their families.[12]

The Initiator's Political Objectives

We can also analyze sanctions in terms of the political objectives of the initiating country. At least three such political objectives can be identified. First, states often use sanctions for the purpose of *deterrence*—that is, they use the threat of economic sanctions to persuade a target not to undertake some action it appears to be contemplating.[13] A recent example of an (ultimately unsuccessful) attempt to use the threat of economic sanctions for the purposes of deterrence can be observed in South Asia: in the spring of 1998, the United States explicitly warned India and Pakistan that it would impose economic sanctions if they tested nuclear devices, which first India and then Pakistan did, triggering in turn the application of limited U.S. economic sanctions.[14]

Second, an initiator may turn to sanctions for the purpose of *coercion*—that is, an initiator threatens to or actually does impose sanctions against a target country in an effort to persuade the latter to stop some action it has already commenced. For example, the United States imposed progressively harsher economic sanctions against Libya from the 1970s to the 1990s to coerce that country to cease its sponsorship of international terrorism.

Third, initiators may use sanctions in order to signal their intentions and resolve. In other words, initiators sometimes use economic sanctions for the purposes of *signaling* that some behavior of the target country is unacceptable, and that additional, more violent actions might follow if the target country does not adjust its behavior. Hence, when the United States and its UN partners imposed comprehensive economic sanctions against Iraq after it invaded Kuwait in 1990, they hoped to communicate to Saddam Hussein the view that the Kuwaiti takeover was unacceptable, and that they might ultimately turn to military options to force it out of Kuwait.

The Efficacy of Economic Sanctions

Research on economic sanctions indicates that they generally do not help the initiator change the behavior of the target, and that this low policy efficacy has many different causes.

Success Rates for Economic Sanctions

Essential Economics 6.1 provides an overview of the frequency with which countries have applied economic sanctions during most of the twentieth

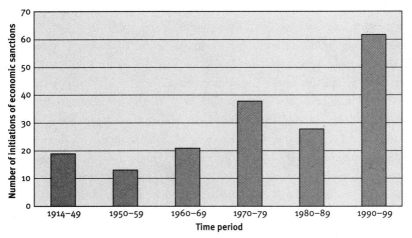

⊹ **ESSENTIAL ECONOMICS 6.1**

Use of Economic Sanctions, 1914–99

Source: Gary Hufbauer and Barbara Oegg, "Economic Sanctions: A Primer for Journalists," *The Quill*, January–February 1999, Figure 1.

Core Principle

Economic sanctions have been used with increasing frequency, especially since the early 1990s.

---

century. During the full period, sanctions were imposed on 181 occasions, and, as can be observed in the figure, the frequency with which sanctions were employed increased modestly over most of the century but increased sharply during the 1990s.

A key question relating to economic sanctions is whether they help initiators achieve their policy goals in regard to targets. One key study found that between 1914 and 1990 economic sanctions helped the initiator country attain its policy goals in about 34 percent of the instances in which sanctions were imposed.[15] However, other analysis suggests that sanctions are much less likely to be successful, perhaps having as little as a 5 percent chance of helping the initiator influence the target.[16] In two other recent analyses studying sanctions through 1990, sanctions were found to have been effective only 30 percent of the time. Furthermore, although sanctions assisted the initiator achieve its goals in 50 percent of the instances in which sanctions were employed between 1914 and 1945, this success rate decreased to 44 percent for the period between 1945 and 1969 and declined to 26 percent for the period between 1970 and 1989. In the most recent period, 1990–99, the rate at which sanctions achieved their goals was similar to that of the 1970s and 1980s.[17]

One critique of early sanctions studies is that they fail to take into account the fact that in many instances in which the initiator was successful, it had used not just economic sanctions but other instruments as well, including military force; this finding calls into question which instrument brought about the change in the target's behavior. Other scholars studying the same issue have suggested that, when target behavior has been made to change, it has been the application of military force by the initiator, and not economic sanctions, that most often has been responsible for bringing about the change.[18] Moreover, economic sanctions have been found to be most likely to induce a change in the target's behavior when the general relationship between the initiator and the target is positive and friendly, and least likely to be successful when the initiator's relationship with the target is generally negative and hostile.[19] These findings suggest that economic sanctions are most useful when they are least needed as a way of promoting national interests, and least effective when they are most required as an instrument of foreign policy.

Influences on the Effectiveness of Economic Sanctions

At least five conditions influence the effectiveness of economic sanctions: the possibility of pre-emptive moves by the target, the availability of alternative suppliers, the target's capacity to insulate its domestic supporters from the effects of sanctions, balances of initiator-target resolve, and unintended consequences. As we will see below, each of these conditions often works in favor of the target and against the initiator.

First, a target that is unable to prepare itself for sanctions is more likely to suffer from their imposition than one that anticipates their imposition and takes countermeasures aimed at mitigating their impact. For example, the Libyan government, recognizing in December 1991 that the United States, the United Kingdom, and France were moving toward sanctions to force it to hand over Libyan intelligence officials implicated in the bombings of Pan Am flight 103 in December 1988 and French UTA flight 772 in September 1989, began to move its short-term financial assets out of France and the United Kingdom and to place them in financial institutions in Switzerland

and the Persian Gulf States. Libya performed similar operations to shield its financial assets abroad and to stockpile imported goods when the UN sought to enhance international economic sanctions against it in December 1993.[20]

Second, if the initiator is the target's sole supplier of an economic benefit that can be withheld through sanctions, then the target is much more likely to suffer from the imposition of the sanctions, and thus it would have a much greater incentive to comply with the initiator's demands. On the other hand, if there are multiple suppliers of the benefit, then the failure of an initiator to foster or force those alternative suppliers to cooperate in a sanctions effort makes the goal of the initiator vastly more difficult if not impossible to achieve.[21] The Carter administration hampered the effectiveness of its own grain embargo against the Soviet Union in 1980 by allowing the sale of 8 million metric tons of U.S. grain whose delivery had previously been guaranteed in a U.S.-Soviet long-term agreement signed in 1975. The Soviet Union also turned to other grain-producing countries, especially Argentina, Canada, and Australia. As a result, although U.S. grain sales to the Soviet Union declined from 19.4 million metric tons in 1979 to about 11 million tons during the embargo period of January 1980–April 1981, grain sales by other countries to the Soviet Union increased from 5.6 million tons to 29.5 million tons, and whereas total Soviet grain imports averaged about 2 million tons per month during 1979, they averaged 2.5 million tons per month during the embargo period.[22]

Third, if the domestic supporters of the government of a target country would be seriously hurt by sanctions, then that government would have a particularly strong incentive to comply with the initiator's demands and thereby to avoid the domestic political costs of those sanctions. However, sanctions are most often applied against authoritarian governments, which often can use their power to ensure that members of their country's elite are least hurt by the sanctions and to shift the burdens associated with the sanctions onto the less powerful (and invariably poorer) elements of the population.[23] As one foreign policy analyst wrote about the U.S. sanctions against the Haitian military regime in 1991, "enough supplies of goods and fuel reached Haiti for the richest sectors of society to survive relatively unscathed. At the same time, the sanctions pushed the large mass of Haitian poor even closer to or below the subsistence level."[24] Initiators might hope that members of the target country's public would respond to their hardships by overthrowing the authoritarian regime, yet the type of authoritarian state that most often attracts economic sanctions—the Soviet Union, North Korea, Cuba, Iran, and Iraq, for instance—also knows very well how to squelch any manifestation of domestic discontent and thus can short-circuit the pathway from sanctions to mass dissatisfaction to an overthrow of the target regime.

Fourth, the success of sanctions can hinge on the relative strength of each side's resolve. An initiator government hopes that it will impose such high economic costs on the target through the imposition of sanctions that it will break the will of the target to resist its political demands. But economic sanctions can instead strengthen the target's determination to defy the initiator. Much of the risk here depends on the target's understanding of the initiator's intentions. Targets that have generally friendly relations with an initiator are likely to comply because they do not fear that compliance will lead to yet additional demands; targets that have generally poor relations with initiators may decide that they must resist today's sanctions lest they face more demands tomorrow.[25] Furthermore, the target might view sanctions as a signal not of the initiator's strong resolve, but of its lack of resolve. Rather than believe that sanctions are a signal of worse to come, the target may conclude that they are a sign of an initiator's reluctance to do more (such as take military action) to get the target to adjust its behavior. The initiator's resolve may also be weakened by *"sanctions fatigue."*[26] Citizens of the initiator country, or even the policy-makers themselves, may come to believe that the sanctions are failing, are hurting innocent civilians, and ought to be abandoned. This tendency toward sanctions fatigue has undermined the UN sanctions regime against Iraq imposed following the Persian Gulf War.[27]

Finally, the imposition of sanctions often brings unintended negative consequences. From the viewpoint of the initiator, the application of economic sanctions may have at least two such deleterious consequences. First, sanctions might precipitate undesired target behavior by increasing rather than decreasing the probability that the target will undertake or continue behavior deemed undersirable by the initiator. For example, the United States froze Japanese financial assets in July 1941 in response to Japan's occupation of Indochina. This financial sanction (to some degree unintentionally) had the effect of halting all shipments of U.S. oil to Japan after July, which in turn contributed materially to Japan's decision to launch a war against the United States.[28] Similarly, the United States in 1997 and 1998 sought to deter Pakistan from testing its nuclear weapons by, among other things, imposing restrictions on both economic aid and conventional (non-nuclear) military assistance. Some analysts have suggested that this cutoff of conventional military aid "actually may have increased Pakistan's reliance on a nuclear option, both because the sanctions cut off Islamabad's access to U.S. weaponry and because they dramatically weakened Pakistan's confidence in its traditional relationship with Washington."[29] In the same vein, when the Clinton administration threatened in early 1994 not to renew China's MFN status unless the Chinese government improved its treatment of political dissidents, the Chinese government reacted by arresting a number of additional dissidents.[30]

Second, although the initiator may hope that sanctions will isolate the target, often they instead isolate the initiator. For example, the Reagan administration in June 1982 sought to compel the United Kingdom, France, Germany, and Italy to stop a gas-pipeline project with the Soviet Union by announcing that, on the basis of U.S. law, no U.S.-owned subsidiary in Europe, nor any European-based firm with operations in the United States, could participate in the project. The Europeans bitterly resented this effort by the United States to stop the project by claiming that its laws and regulations applied to firms in Europe. They were also aware that the U.S. administration in April 1981 had ended the U.S. grain embargo against the Soviet Union; thus, the Reagan administration's actions seemed to them to be hypocritical. The result was a serious diplomatic dispute during the summer of 1982 that pitted an increasingly isolated United States against a highly united Western Europe.[31] Ultimately, the United States relented in its efforts to stop the pipeline. Similarly, after President Clinton signed the Helms-Burton Act into law in March 1996, the European Union (EU) threatened to take the United States to the WTO and to challenge the international legality of the act, Canada threatened legal action under the terms of the North American Free Trade Agreement, and the Inter-American Juridical Committee, an advisory body of the Organization of American States, ruled that the act violated international law. In U.S.-EU agreements announced in April 1997 and May 1998, the Clinton administration promised to continue to issue waivers, as a result of which the U.S. government effectively did not implement Helms-Burton. The George W. Bush administration has continued this policy of nonimplementation.[32]

The Utility of Economic Sanctions

Given the problems with economic sanctions, why do initiators rely on them so often? We can identify at least four reasons for this persisting reliance on sanctions: their relative utility compared to other policy instruments, their capacity for partial and indirect success, their effect on the target's power-projection capacity (as opposed to its intentions), and their efficacy as a signaling instrument.

Economic Sanctions as a Least-Bad Policy Option

When we evaluate sanctions efforts, we need to ask how U.S. policymakers might reasonably have evaluated the likely costs and benefits of sanctions compared to other options, including the option of doing nothing.[33] For example, the United States has not succeeded in bringing about the downfall of the Castro regime in Cuba through the use of sanctions and has sustained both economic and diplomatic costs in maintaining those sanctions for four decades. As an alternative, the United States might have used direct military force to try to dislodge Castro. However, an early indirect U.S. application of force against Castro's regime—the 1961 Bay of Pigs invasion—may well have contributed to the Soviet decision in the autumn of 1962 to place nuclear-tipped ballistic missiles on the island, which in turn instigated the most serious U.S.-Soviet crisis during the entire Cold War. The resolution of the October 1962 Cuban missile crisis included a U.S. commitment to the Soviet Union not to use force to overthrow the Castro regime, and therefore any U.S. application of force after 1962 would quite possibly have brought the United States into direct military conflict with the Soviet Union.

Similarly, the United States either before or after 1962 might have simply accepted the Castro regime and normalized relations with it. This action, however, might have sent a signal that countries in Latin America could also have anti-American revolutions, could become allies with the United States' arch-rival in world politics, and could even become the base of operations for that rival's military forces against the United States, all at little or no cost. Again, from the viewpoint of U.S. policy-makers, normalization of relations with Cuba would have entailed very high costs to U.S. interests. It is in that context, one in which military force would have been prohibitively expensive and diplomacy alone would have entailed serious setbacks, that economic sanctions seemed to be the least problematic—or "least bad"—option available to U.S. policy-makers.

Economic Sanctions as a Path to Partial or Indirect Success

Although economic sanctions may not by themselves induce full compliance by the target with the demands of the initiator, they may help the initiator partially attain its goals. For example, although U.S. threats of economic sanctions have had little impact on China's human rights practices, the United States has attained significant success in using the application of selected economic sanctions to affect China's policies regarding the sale of missiles and other sensitive military equipment to countries in the Middle East. China began in the 1980s to see the Middle East as a market for cruise missiles and ballistic missiles: during that decade it sold cruise missiles to Iran and ballistic missiles to Saudi Arabia. China also arranged a sale of ballistic missiles to Syria, but the United States used limited economic sanctions in 1991 and 1992 to induce China to cancel that sale and has apparently persuaded China not to pursue further the Middle East market for this category of weapons.[34]

Sometimes, what would appear to be a rather modest economic sanctions program—one that, in fact, appears to have no direct impact on the target— may actually have powerful secondary effects that *are* harmful to the target. For example, in 1983 the U.S. Congress mandated that the United States had to vote against the granting of any new loans by the IMF to South Africa. From the viewpoint of international banks, the loss of U.S. support for IMF help to South Africa meant that an important "safety net" for their investments had been removed. When domestic violence increased in South Africa in 1984 and 1985, and general business conditions began to deteriorate, international banks, although they legally could do business in the country, viewed the U.S. requirement to vote against IMF loans to South Africa as a source of uncertainty as to whether their investments in that country were safe, and as a matter of precaution they began to decline to make new loans and even began to withdraw funds from the country. That cutoff in private capital created truly serious economic problems for the apartheid government.[35] Thus, although the U.S. economic sanctions in 1983 by themselves certainly did not bring about the end of apartheid in South Africa in the early 1990s, they did have a large impact at a critical juncture in the mid-1980s, when they contributed to the flight of international investors from South Africa, which in turn undermined the economic foundations of the white-dominated regime.

Economic Sanctions as an Inhibitor of Growth in the Target's Power

Although sanctions may not induce a near-term shift in the target's behavior, they can, in two ways, constrain the growth of its military power and its capacity to achieve its goals. First, sanctions can impair the target's economic growth, which forms an essential component of its overall power. As we discussed in Chapter 2, international economic integration provides important opportunities for a country to accelerate its rate of national economic growth. Following that line of reasoning, the imposition of sanctions could reduce the growth of a country's power potential by constraining its rate of economic growth. The strategy of seeking to weaken a target country's economy and thus its capacity to project power can be observed in U.S. sanctions policy toward Cuba since 1962, its sanctions on Iran since the mid-1980s (especially the 1995 U.S. ban on participation by U.S. firms in Iran's oil and gas industries), and the UN sanctions against Iraq since 1990.

Second, economic sanctions can deny external sources of war potential to the target. An initiator may seek to limit the transfer to the target country of the specific goods or technology that might augment the target country's military capability. For example, during the Cold War the United States worked with its industrialized democratic partners through a group called the "Coordinating Committee," or Cocom, to limit the sale of military-related goods and technology to the Soviet Union and its communist satellites.[36]

It is often difficult to estimate the impact of these two strategies in particular sanctions cases, because the comparison that needs to be made is between the amount of power the target was in fact able to amass in the presence of economic sanctions, and the amount of power the target might have accumulated if the sanctions had not been in place.[37] Arguments based on such counterfactual comparisons are impossible to prove. Yet sometimes evidence does exist that economic denial has constrained the growth of the target's military power. For example, U.S. sanctions caused private and foreign official creditors to be restrained in their lending to Iran in the early to mid-1990s. This cutoff in foreign credit to Iran, together with national economic policy errors and a decline in international oil prices, sharply curtailed that country's financial capacity to import military hardware. Iranian weapons imports in the 1990s were much lower than what the Iranian government had earlier announced it would buy during that period: for example, whereas Iran had ordered between 1,000 and 1,500 tanks between 1989 and 1996, it had taken delivery of only 184 of them by the mid-1990s. Furthermore, Iran has been much less able to acquire military power that could be used in the strategically important Persian Gulf, such as mines, missile boats, and what would have been its third submarine, than would have been the case had sanctions not been in effect.[38] In the same vein, although UN economic sanctions have not changed Saddam Hussein's aggressive intentions, they have probably reduced his capacity to initiate war.[39]

Economic Sanctions as Political Signals

As noted earlier, initiators turn to economic sanctions to communicate their foreign interests and resolve. Sanctions provide the opportunity for initiators to so communicate to both foreign and domestic audiences, and thus sanctions are attractive to initiators in spite of their drawbacks, because they have three desirable signaling properties.

First, sanctions may act as a costly signal to the target. In his study of sanctions, Baldwin points out that, although President Franklin Roosevelt, in his 1937 "Quarantine Speech," warned Japan about its aggression in China, the Roosevelt administration did not back up this warning with economic sanctions, leading Japan (and Germany) to believe that Washington's words were not worthy of serious attention: they were merely "cheap talk."[40] Baldwin suggests that if an initiator wants to credibly signal its disapproval to a target, but is not yet willing to commit military force, then it must communicate that it is willing to impose some level of costs not just on the target, but on itself as well, to reduce the chances that the target will achieve its objectives. The very costliness of the sanctions to the initiator—in terms of forgone economic benefits, domestic criticism, and possibly international controversy—may persuade the target that the initiator really does mean whatever signal of warning or disapproval it is articulating.[41]

Second, sanctions may serve as a consistent signal to foreign audiences. Economic sanctions may provide initiators with an ability to communicate consistency in their preferences both to targets and to third parties. Baldwin has pointed out that the importance of so communicating consistency can be appreciated by asking how the world would have reacted if the Carter administration had not taken some form of strong action, like the grain embargo, in response to the Soviet invasion of Afghanistan in December 1979. The whole point of U.S. foreign policy since 1945 had been to contain the Soviet Union and to make it less likely that the Soviet government could conclude that the use of military force would advance its interests around the world. Going forward with the U.S.-Soviet grain trade as though nothing had happened "would have sent a signal to the Soviets and other countries, but not the signal that the Carter administration wanted sent!"[42] Of course, as we discussed earlier, the Carter administration's decision to permit the sale and shipment of a large amount of grain already promised to the Soviet Union undermined the consistency of the signal that the Carter administration was trying to send to the Soviets and to U.S. grain-producing allies. In the same vein, the inconsistency of the Reagan administration's policy in

1981 and 1982 regarding economic relations with the Soviet Union—that is, telling the West Europeans to stop their pipeline project with the Soviet Union, while simultaneously ending the U.S. grain embargo—surely undermined the U.S. stance in the eyes of both its friends and its adversaries.[43]

Finally, sanctions may serve as a signal of resolve and consistency to domestic constituencies in the initiator country. Economic sanctions provide an opportunity for an initiator government to communicate foreign policy consistency to its domestic audience. Since the mid-1980s, for example, the United States has maintained at great cost a formidable military force in the Persian Gulf region in order to contain Iraq and Iran and thereby to assure Western and Japanese access to the huge oil resources in the region. It would seem inconsistent and odd if, on the one hand, the United States maintained such forces directed against those two countries while, on the other hand, it conducted business as usual with those countries. Maintaining economic sanctions against them allows the U.S. government to claim that its policies with regard to Iran and Iraq are consistent and mutually reinforcing, and thereby to avoid deterioration in domestic support for its policies in the region.

Economic Incentives as an Instrument of Foreign Policy

Bases for Analysis

As noted at the beginning of this chapter, an ***economic incentive*** is a promised or actual extension by an initiator state of an economic benefit to a target in exchange for compliance by the target with a political demand of the initiator.[44] The most important ways in which to analyze incentives are in terms of the directness and character of the benefits transferred, and the political objectives of the initiator.

Directness in Transferring Economic Benefits

An initiator, especially a powerful initiator such as the United States, has at its disposal at least three different classes of incentives: granting of direct transfers of economic benefits to the target, granting the target access to the initiator's markets, and granting the target access to international economic institutions controlled by the initiator.

INCENTIVES BASED ON DIRECT TRANSFERS OF BENEFITS

The most obvious form of incentive that an initiator can offer a target is the transfer of some form of tangible economic benefit. Such direct benefits come in three forms, the first of which involves direct transfers of goods. For example, in January 1990, and in the context of extreme economic decay in the Soviet Union, the Soviet government sent the West German government a request for food aid; the West German government immediately arranged for the shipment of meat and dairy products worth 220 million deutsche marks. The context of this direct transfer was a discussion the previous June between Soviet president Mikhail Gorbachev and West German chancellor Helmut Kohl, as a result of which Kohl concluded that if Germany provided aid to the Soviet Union, the latter might accept German reunification.[45]

Second, states often use financial subsidies as economic incentives. For example, in January 1631, in the midst of the Thirty Years' War, the Catholic Austrian-Spanish Habsburg empire appeared poised to defeat the Protestant princes and thus not only restore Catholicism to all of Europe, but also make the Habsburgs the political hegemon of the continent. However, the French royal government, under the direction of Cardinal Richelieu, negotiated a treaty with the Protestant Swedish king, Gustavus Adolphus, as a result of which France agreed to fund in significant measure an expansion of Swedish military operations against the Habsburgs in Germany (the Swedes had commenced low-level operations in 1630). France had been supporting the Dutch Protestants against the Habsburgs since 1624 and would soon be supporting several German princes so that they too might resist the Habsburgs.[46]

Third, states often employ preferential lending arrangements as economic incentives. Initiators often seek to influence targets by extending loans to them on terms that are vastly superior to what the target might find on the open market, if indeed the target would be able to obtain any private credit at all. For example, in May 1990, in response to a Soviet request for financial credits, and as a part of West Germany's strategy to secure the withdrawal of Soviet troops from eastern Germany, a personal aide to Chancellor Kohl undertook a secret mission to Moscow with the presidents of two major German banks; there Kohl brokered (and guaranteed the payment on) loans from the banks to the Soviet government worth 5 billion deutsche marks. The total compensation package of subsidies and preferential financial credits that the Germans extended to the Soviets to persuade them to leave eastern Germany came to 87 billion deutsche marks.[47]

INCENTIVES BASED ON ACCESS TO THE TARGET'S MARKETS

Rather than offering subsidies or financial incentives to a target government, initiators may offer indirect incentives to targets by allowing them the opportunity to sell products in the initiator's home market, or by allowing them to purchase goods made by initiator-country producers. An example of such an access-based economic incentive was discussed earlier in connection with sanctions—namely, the extension of MFN status. As we noted in our discussion of sanctions, the extension by an initiator of MFN status to a target not currently enjoying it can be a major incentive. The United States, during its efforts in the 1960s and early 1970s to pursue détente with the Soviet Union, sought to use MFN status as a key incentive to encourage good Soviet international behavior. Moreover, the United States, seeking to make China a partner in its struggle with the Soviet Union, gradually relaxed during the 1970s many of the trade restrictions it had imposed on that country when the Communist Party came to power there in 1949, and it extended MFN status to China in early 1980. The United States since then made the continued extension of MFN status to China a centerpiece of its engagement strategy toward that country; now that China has been admitted to the WTO, it automatically and unconditionally receives MFN treatment from the United States.

Just as being granted the opportunity to sell goods in an initiator's market can be an incentive, so too can be the opportunity to buy goods from suppliers in the initiator country. This opportunity is usually provided in terms of a relaxation of export restrictions previously imposed on a target. During the early 1980s, for example, the United States promoted a strategic alignment with China against the Soviet Union in part by relaxing most U.S. official restrictions on American sales of military technology to China while largely maintaining these restrictions on the Soviet Union. This U.S. policy in favor of China was initiated by the Carter administration in April 1980 and was brought most fully into effect by the Reagan administration in May 1983 when it announced that, when it came to technology exports, China would be treated no differently than were the most trusted U.S. trading partners.[48]

INCENTIVES BASED ON ACCESS TO INTERNATIONAL INSTITUTIONS

The United States, Japan, and Germany, by virtue of their economic power, control the world's key multilateral and regional economic institutions, including the IMF, the World Bank, the WTO, and the EU. Hence, these powerful states can offer admission to these important institutions, or aid provided by them, as incentives for targets' good behavior. The United States, for example, as part of its opening to China in 1971, permitted China to join the IMF and the World Bank. This membership has benefited China enormously: as of June 2000, China was the second-largest recipient of all loans that the World Bank had made since it started operations in the late 1940s, and China was the single largest recipient of outstanding or newly approved World Bank loans.[49] In a similar vein, after the United States and its allies defeated Yugoslavia in the war for Kosovo in 2000, which brought about the fall of then-president Slobodan Milosevic and his replacement by a democratic government led by President Vojislav Kostunica, the United States together with its EU partners arranged for the extension of a $1.3 billion multilateral aid package to the new Yugoslav government in exchange for its extradition of Milosevic to the Netherlands to stand trial for war crimes and crimes against humanity.[50]

The Initiator's Political Objectives

States use economic incentives to affect the preferences and behavior of actual or potential partners, and of actual or potential adversaries.

ECONOMIC INCENTIVES AND POLITICAL PARTNERS

Initiators often turn to economic incentives in order to forge strategic alignments. During the 1930s, for example, Nazi Germany put into place a range of economic arrangements whereby Romania, Hungary, and Bulgaria disproportionately gained from their trade with Germany and thereby became dependent on that country and ultimately allied with it during World War II.[51] The United States, as noted previously, extended incentives to China in the 1970s and early 1980s in order to forge an informal alignment with it against the Soviet Union. Similarly, because Iran was the chief rival of the United States in the Middle East during the 1980s, the U.S. government supported Iraq in its decade-long war with Iran in a number of ways, including extending to Iraq loans of $500 million so it could import U.S. agricultural products, and permitting $500 million in sales of U.S. goods that could be used either for civilian or for military purposes.[52]

Second, states often employ economic incentives in order to attract military allies. All of the main European powers, for instance, used financial inducements to attract allies in the years leading up to World War I. In 1887, when deterioration in Russian-German political relations led German chancellor Otto von Bismarck to reduce Russian access to the German bond market, the French government, eager to win Russia as a potential ally against Germany, stepped in and arranged loans to Russia between 1888 and 1890 totaling 3 billion francs; France had its alliance with Russia by 1894.[53] Similarly, increasingly fearful of Nazi Germany in the mid- to late 1930s, the British government sought to increase the likelihood that the highly isolationist United States would come to its rescue. In those years, as we saw in Chapter 5, the United Kingdom had a trading bloc in place with its British Commonwealth partners (including such agricultural giants as Canada, Australia, and New Zealand). The operation of this bloc severely restricted access by U.S. producers to the important British market. To build goodwill with the United States, and especially with the agricultural American Midwest, the British government offered in 1937 a trade agreement, mutually agreed upon in November 1938, that opened the British market to U.S. exports, including, most notably, some agricultural products.[54]

Third, states employ economic incentives in order to sustain wartime allies. As noted above, Cardinal Richelieu provided subsidies to Sweden in 1631, just after it entered the Thirty Years' War; this subsidy was renewed in 1633. In 1635–36, when, in the face of new Habsburg military victories, the German Protestant princes began to move toward a separate peace with the Habsburg emperor and thus appeared ready to leave the Swedish forces isolated, Cardinal Richelieu renewed French aid to Sweden so that it could carry on as a French ally.[55] In the same vein, with passage in 1941 of the Lend-Lease agreement, the United States, prior to and during its participation in World War II, provided $50 billion in equipment and other economic assistance to its wartime allies. About $31 billion of the total went to the United Kingdom and other countries in the British Commonwealth, and over $11 billion went to the Soviet Union.

Finally, states sometimes employ economic incentives in order to deny potential partners to adversaries. For example, after World War II, it appeared that economically desperate Western European countries such as France and Italy might turn to local communist parties for political leadership, which would have tilted the balance of world power in favor of the Soviet Union. To prevent that, as we noted in Chapter 5, the United States intervened and re-invigorated Western Europe through the Marshall Plan, which provided about $12 billion to the countries in that region between 1948 and 1951.

➤ **TIMELINE 6.1**

The Application of Economic Incentives: The United States and North Korea, December 1985–October 1994

December 1985	North Korea signs the Nuclear Nonproliferation Treaty (NPT), signaling cooperation with Western-backed arms-control initiatives
May 1992	North Korea signals United States that it will leave the NPT unless incentives are offered: namely, a nuclear reactor and nuclear fuel. North Korea realizes that the United States will likely value its continued cooperation.
June 1992	North Korea tells United States directly that incentives relating to nuclear reactor and fuel are required to keep it in the NPT
March 1993	North Korea threatens to withdraw from the NPT, which would give it freedom to produce nuclear weapons
June 1994	U.S.–North Korean militarized crisis ensues
Summer 1994	Both sides realize that de-escalating tensions will require a U.S. concession to some of North Korea's nuclear demands and a North Korean commitment to use those nuclear capabilities within the NPT
October 1994	U.S. and North Korea sign "Agreed Framework," under which North Korea stays in NPT and receives nuclear reactors in return

ECONOMIC INCENTIVES AND POLITICAL ADVERSARIES: THE CASE OF NORTH KOREA

States often use economic incentives to prevent a deeply conflictual relationship from becoming violent or to bring about an amelioration of tensions with a current adversary. A key example of an incentive applied for the purpose of keeping an adversary at bay concerns the United States and North Korea. The highlights of this case are presented in Timeline 6.1.[56]

In the mid-1980s, and notwithstanding its signing in December 1985 of the nuclear Nonproliferation Treaty (NPT), North Korea appeared to be expanding its nuclear program by building two new nuclear power plants that, despite their supposed intended use for energy generation, could allow North Korea to build many nuclear weapons. Years of difficult exchanges over these plants ended with a threat in March 1993 from North Korea that it would renounce its adherence to the NPT. This announcement led to a crisis in June 1994 during which the United States and North Korea stepped

Except from the U.S.–North Korean "Agreed Framework," October 1994

Delegations of the governments of the United States of America (U.S.) and the Democratic People's Republic of Korea (DPRK) held talks in Geneva from September 23 to October 21, 1994, to negotiate an overall resolution of the nuclear issue on the Korean Peninsula.

Both sides reaffirmed the importance of attaining the objectives contained in the August 12, 1994 Agreed Statement between the U.S. and the DPRK and upholding the principles of the June 11, 1993 Joint Statement of the U.S. and the DPRK to achieve peace and security on a nuclear-free Korean peninsula. The U.S. and the DPRK decided to take the following actions for the resolution of the nuclear issue:

I. Both sides will cooperate to relace the DPRK's graphite-moderated reactors and related facilities with light-water reactor (LWR) power plants.

> 1) In accordance with the October 20, 1994 letter of assurance from the U.S. President, the U.S. will undertake to make arrangements for the provision to the DPRK of a LWR project with a total generating capacity of approximately 2,000 MW(e) by a target date of 2003.

- The U.S. will organize under its leadership an international consortium to finance and supply the LWR project to be provided to the DPRK. The U.S., representing the international consortium, will serve as the principal point of contact with the DPRK for the LWR project.
- The U.S., representing the consortium, will make best efforts to secure the conclusion of a supply contract with the DPRK within six months of the date of this Document for the provision of the LWR project. Contract talks will begin as soon as possible after the date of this Document.
- As necessary, the U.S. and the DPRK will conclude a bilateral agreement for cooperation in the field of peaceful uses of nuclear energy.

> 2) In accordance with the October 20, 1994 letter of assurance from the U.S. President, the U.S. representing the consortium, will make arrangements to offset the energy foregone due to the freeze of the DPRK's graphite-moderated reactors and related facilities, pending completion of the first LWR unit.

- Alternative energy will be provided in the form of heavy oil for heating and electricity production.
- Deliveries of heavy oil will begin within three months of the date of this Document and will reach a rate of 500,000 tons annually, in accordance with an agreed schedule of deliveries.

3) Upon receipt of U.S. assurances for the provision of LWR's and for arrangements for interim energy alternatives, the DPRK will freeze its graphite-moderated reactors and related facilities and will eventually dismantle these reactors and related facilities.

- The freeze on the DPRK's graphite-moderated reactors and related facilities will be fully implemented within one month of the date of this Document. During this one-month period, and throughout the freeze, the International Atomic Energy Agency (IAEA), will be allowed to monitor this freeze, and the DPRK will provide full cooperation to the IAEA for this purpose.
- Dismantlement of the DPRK's graphite-moderated reactors and related facilities will be completed when the LWR project is completed.
- The U.S. and the DPRK will cooperate in finding a method to store safely the spent fuel from the 5 MW(e) experimental reactor during the construction of the LWR project, and to dispose of the fuel in a safe manner that does not involve reprocessing in the DPRK.

With this agreement, the United States offered to arrange for the construction of two nuclear reactors in North Korea in exchange for a commitment by the latter that it would freeze its nuclear weapons program.

Source: "Agreed Framework between the United States of America and the Democratic People's Republic of Korea," October 21, 1994, posted by Arms Control Association at www.armscontrol.org/documents/af.asp.

Core Principle

In some instances, economic incentives can be more effective than sanctions in influencing the behavior of a target state.

to the brink of war. In October 1994, however, the United States and North Korea drew up an "Agreed Framework" that resolved the major concerns of both sides (see Primary Document 6.3).

In the Agreed Framework, North Korea promised to remain in the NPT, to not build nuclear weapons or the facilities needed to produce them, and to bring its nuclear facilities under the international supervision required by the NPT. The United States, for its part, agreed to arrange for the construction of two nuclear power plants in North Korea (plants that were not suitable to support a weapons program) and to provide funding (roughly $50–$60 million per year) for heavy fuel oil imports while the two plants were being built. The costs of the two power plants, about

$5 billion, would be covered largely by South Korea and to some extent by Japan.

As noted earlier, states sometimes employ economic incentives not simply to control the dangers of conflict-prone relationships but to move current adversaries in the direction of amicability. This was the intention of President Richard Nixon and National Security Adviser Henry Kissinger as they pursued détente with the Soviet Union in the early 1970s.[57] The economic incentives that helped constitute the détente strategy included the opportunity for the Soviets to buy U.S. grain and selected technology-intensive capital goods, official U.S. credits to make those purchases possible, and MFN status. The United States hoped that, in return, the Soviets would cooperate on arms control and other measures to reduce the risk of nuclear war, continue to help stabilize the political-military order in Europe, exercise restraint in their efforts to promote communism in the developing world, and encourage North Vietnam to accept a peace treaty with the United States.

This détente strategy unraveled between 1973 and 1975. In 1973, when it granted the Soviet Union MFN status, the U.S. Congress attached conditions regarding Soviet emigration policies (conditions that were unacceptable to the Soviets); the Soviet Union and the United States experienced a significant diplomatic and even military crisis in the midst of the October 1973 Arab-Israeli War; and U.S. hopes that détente would translate into mutual restraint in the developing world were dashed beginning in 1975 as both the United States and the Soviet Union competed for influence in Angola's civil war. The Carter administration tried to revitalize détente in the late 1970s, but when the Soviets invaded Afghanistan in December 1979, a second Cold War commenced; it ended only with the nonviolent demise of the Soviet Union in the late 1980s.

The Efficacy of Economic Incentives

The breakdown of U.S.-Soviet détente raises the key question of whether and under what conditions incentive-based strategies are likely to be successful, and whether incentives or sanctions are more likely to advance an initiator's interests with a target.

The Comparative Efficacy of Incentives and Sanctions

In our discussion so far, we have seen examples of both the success and the failure of economic incentives: U.S.-Soviet détente made only limited progress, but France was successful in wooing Russia prior to World War I, and Germany was successful in speeding the withdrawal of Soviet troops from the eastern part of the country after reunification.

More systematic analyses of the effectiveness of incentives seem to indicate that incentives have a good chance of being effective, and that they are more likely than sanctions to be successful in helping an initiator achieve its policy goals. Several studies support this conclusion. One study of 32 instances from the 1850s to the 1990s in which Germany applied either sanctions or incentives found that incentives helped Germany achieve its policy goals in 22 of 24 applications, while each of the 8 applications by Germany of sanctions was unsuccessful.[58] Another researcher, in a study comparing voting by countries in the United Nations with IMF lending to those countries between 1985 and 1994, has found that, the more a country's UN votes converged with those of the United States, the more likely it was to receive IMF loans.[59] A similar study found that, as a country's UN votes between 1984 and 1993 converged with those of the United States on matters that the latter considered important, the more bilateral aid the voting country received from the United States.[60] Yet another study of voting found that, from the early 1970s to the early 1990s, the more closely a country's UN votes matched the votes of the United States or other major donors, the more bilateral aid it received from those donors.[61] Finally, scholars have found that the United States was unsuccessful in its effort in the late 1980s to withhold bilateral aid to compel countries to cast their votes in the UN in a manner consistent with U.S. preferences.[62] This last finding, in conjunction with the finding that extensions of bilateral aid are often associated with favorable recipient UN voting patterns, suggests that incentives are more efficacious than sanctions in advancing an initiator's interests with a target.

However, scholars have emphasized that the data linking UN voting to external assistance should be interpreted with great care. For example, although it is possible to interpret the UN voting–bilateral aid link in the manner suggested above (namely, that donors use aid to purchase UN votes), there is also a good chance that the recipients are voting not to obtain aid but because they already share strong interests with the donor, including military alliance ties, and that the aid flow reflects this larger framework of shared interests and cooperation, not a tit-for-tat economic incentive. Still, further statistical analyses indicate that, if there is an alignment between donors and potential recipients that manifests itself in a convergence in their voting at the UN, this produces an increase in bilateral aid going to the recipients.[63] This result suggests that the inducement process is not simply one in which the United States tells a potential recipient that if it votes one way, it will receive more aid, but rather that there is a more indirect process by which the United States and the recipient become friendlier, the United States rewards that friendship with more aid, and this process reflects itself as well as a convergence in U.S.-donor voting patterns.

Influences on the Effectiveness of Economic Incentives

Several conditions regarding the target, the initiator, and the combination of the two may contribute to the likelihood of the initiator's success in using economic incentives as a tool of foreign policy.

TARGET CHARACTERISTICS

A country facing dire economic problems may be more receptive to incentives and amenable to the conditions attached to them.[64] The Soviet Union by the 1970s, for example, was unable to feed its population or exploit its own natural resources (especially oil). As a result, the offer of U.S. grain and oil-extraction technology must have been very appealing to the Soviets and must have made détente very attractive to them. Likewise, the Soviet Union in 1990 was facing food shortages and was bankrupt; these conditions surely made the offer of German assistance all the more appealing and the link to Soviet withdrawal from eastern Germany all the more palatable. North Korea, too, has been facing serious food shortages and even mass starvation for many years, making the offer of U.S. aid very attractive and forgoing (at least for the moment) a nuclear weapons program seem worthwhile.

Moreover, a target country that is already predisposed to good relations with the initiator is more likely to respond to incentives in the manner desired by the initiator. For example, the Roosevelt administration recognized by the late 1930s that Nazi Germany was a serious threat, and Roosevelt was as a consequence highly open to the British offer to negotiate a trade agreement in 1937 and 1938. Thus, the British government had an ally in the Roosevelt administration in trying to prepare the United States for war with Germany, and this common interest likely greatly facilitated the negotiation of the agreement by the two governments and the presentation of it by the Roosevelt administration to Congress and the American public. Similarly, the Soviet government under Leonid Brezhnev wanted U.S. recognition of the status quo in Eastern and Central Europe, including the status of Berlin, and this dovetailed closely with the U.S. objective to use détente to remove the possibility that disputes about that city could, as they did in the 1940s,

1950s, and even the early 1960s, bring the two countries to a point of serious confrontation. When the economic incentive to achieve détente was offered by the United States in the form of grain and technology sales, these mutual interests further eased the process of agreement.

INITIATOR CONDITIONS

Three conditions relating to the initiator are likely to influence its capacity to use economic incentives to exercise influence over a target: its control over the flow of benefits to the target, its capacity to coordinate with other suppliers of the benefit, and its ability to threaten credibly that the target will be sanctioned if it does not accept the incentives and political conditions attached to them.

An initiator that has strong control over the benefits of interest to the target is much more likely to find that extension of such benefits will bring about changes in the target's behavior. U.S. policy-makers and observers believed during the 1970s that, as the supplier of the most advanced computers and oil-and-gas extraction equipment in the world, the United States could use access to those technologies as a basis for influencing Soviet behavior.[65] The United States was reluctant to provide aid to the Soviet government during the late 1980s because it feared that the Soviets might thereby become reinvigorated or might use the aid to continue to help regimes unfriendly to the United States, such as Cuba.[66] Hence, in 1990, no other major country was offering the Soviet Union the level of assistance that Germany was, in return for which it wanted the Soviets out of eastern Germany.

If the initiator does not have strong control because there are alternative suppliers of the benefits of interest to the target, then the capacity of the initiator to coordinate with those alternative suppliers is likely to influence strongly the impact of incentives.[67] For example, the United States was moderately successful during much of the Cold War in coordinating with Japan and the countries of Western Europe on the matter of transfers of technology to the Soviet Union, and this coordination made the prospect of enhanced access to those technologies a meaningful element of the U.S. offer of détente in the early 1970s. Of course, if the initiator is unable to coordinate with other suppliers on incentives or sanctions, both lose their value. For example, as the UN sanctions regime against Iraq was increasingly violated during the late 1990s, U.S. promises to bring about a formal relaxation of the sanctions if that country complied with its commitments not to build weapons of mass destruction must have had less and less appeal to the Iraqi leadership.

Finally, an initiator is more likely to be successful with incentives if it also has sanctions at its disposal; in other words, the initiator may be most successful when it can make offers that cannot be refused. One comprehensive study of sanctions has suggested that an initiator is most likely to be successful in its application of economic incentives when it also persuades the target that it will use serious sanctions if its incentives are not accepted in exchange for an adjustment in the target's behavior. For example, the North Korean government in 1994 may have accepted the combination of incentives and obligations associated with the Agreed Framework in part because it understood that the alternative was U.S. sanctions and, ultimately, the possibility of U.S. military force being used against it. In contrast, the absence of credible sanctions may have hobbled the EU's attempted engagement of Iran in the early 1990s.[68]

INITIATOR-TARGET INTERACTIVE CONDITIONS: THE QUESTION OF DOMESTIC INSTITUTIONS

Some scholars have proposed that domestic institutional arrangements in both the initiator and the target country can affect the likelihood of success of economic incentives. These scholars have suggested that targets with strong authoritarian leaders often are good candidates for incentives, since their leaders can deliver on promised changes in the country's foreign policy behavior in exchange for whatever incentives are being offered to the country. Thus the success of the U.S. incentive aimed at winning détente with the Soviet Union under Leonid Brezhnev: enjoying strong control over Soviet foreign policy in the late 1960s and early 1970s, Brezhnev could force the changes in Soviet foreign policy that the United States wanted. In contrast, Iran's semidemocratic system of government severely hampered the EU's efforts to engage that country.[69]

Other scholars, however, have suggested that a democratic country such as the United States is most likely to be successful in the use of incentives when its targets are other democracies, for democracies find it easier to reach agreements that include incentives and, more important, verify one another's compliance with those agreements. One study of the 68 cases between 1950 and 1992 in which the United States employed economic and military aid as an inducement to bring about a political concession by a target revealed that the United States was successful in 25 of 38 attempts (or

66 percent of the time) when the target was nondemocratic, whereas it was successful in 26 of 30 attempts (or 87 percent of the time) when the target was democratic.[70] In this view, then incentives, seem especially efficacious when the target is a democracy.

The Risks of Economic Incentives

The risks associated with the use of economic incentives may be appreciated by focusing on their effects on targets, their effects on initiators themselves, and, finally, their implications for third parties.

Effects on the Target

The availability of incentives might encourage a target, in order to be offered those incentives, to pursue exactly the policy stance that runs contrary to the interests of the initiator, in a variation on extortion.[71] Not too long after North Korea signed the NPT in December 1985, it may have been looking for a way to get the United States to compensate it for not pursuing its nuclear program. The North Korean government understood that the United States was deeply concerned about North Korean compliance with the NPT, given the impact that noncompliance would have on the vitality of the NPT itself. However, "what Pyongyang's leadership may have had more difficulty determining was how to get Washington's attention and what price America would be willing to pay for North Korea's compliance. Thus, Pyongyang embarked on a series of calculated risks to identify the depth of U.S. concern and the size of America's pocketbook."[72] In May 1992, when Hans Blix, the director of the International Atomic Energy Agency (the international institution that is responsible for monitoring compliance with the NPT), visited North Korea in the context of growing evidence that that country was violating the treaty, North Korean officials told him that "they would forfeit their nuclear weapons program in exchange for help in obtaining new light-water nuclear reactors and fuel." North Korean officials "repeated this proposal to U.S. diplomats in Beijing on June 1."[73] Thus, North Korea was apparently pursuing its nuclear weapons program not just to have nuclear weapons, but for the explicit purpose of being offered and receiving compensation from the United States for not completing the program. As we saw earlier in the end, the United States offered nuclear reactors and oil.

In addition to opening opportunities for extortion, incentives may also produce, for the initiator, a more formidable adversary down the road. The most important contemporary example of the use of incentives involves the United States and China.[74] The United States has numerous conflicts of interest with a China that is increasingly powerful and, on occasion, seriously belligerent. China has threatened repeatedly to use major force to prevent the independence of Taiwan.[75] In addition, it has claimed ownership of the potentially oil-rich Spratly Islands and other parts of the South China Sea and has applied low levels of force in support of those claims.[76] Moreover, China has sold nuclear weapons technology and missiles to Pakistan and has come close to sales of nuclear technology to Iran.[77]

In response, the United States is pursuing a strategy of engaging China in political and particularly in economic affairs. It has offered China valuable economic incentives, such as supporting Chinese membership in the WTO and not trying to block the selection of Beijing as the host city for the 2008 Olympic Games. The long-term goal of this engagement is to encourage China to accept the contemporary international order, and to prompt economic modernization in that country, which in turn will push China toward democracy and the peacefulness that democracy might engender.

The problem with this strategy is that while it might bring about a more democratic and peaceful China, it almost certainly *is* producing a more potent China. China has enjoyed, by virtue of economic integration with the United State, what economist Albert Hirschman termed the "supply effect"[78]: it has attained access to U.S. goods, including powerful computers and sophisticated machine tools, that directly or indirectly enhance its military power. It remains to be seen, however, whether this economic enmeshment will generate a high level of what Hirschman further termed the "influence effect"—namely, that by virtue of enjoying the benefits of trading with the United States, China will wish not to forgo that trade and will therefore be open to U.S. influence. In the meantime, the United States is buying insurance against a revisionist China by strengthening its alliances with Japan and other countries in the region, and by developing new weapons capabilities.

Effects on the Initiator: Vested Interests and the K-Street Syndrome

The fostering of trade between two countries generates "vested interests" in one or both: it fosters the development of domestic interest groups that have a stronger commitment to the trading relationship than does the country as a whole.[79] We have seen the development of such vested interests in the

United States as it has engaged China. For several years, U.S. multinational enterprises, often employing one of the many lobbying firms located on K Street in Washington, D.C., vigorously pressed the U.S. government to grant the necessary annual renewal of MFN status for China so that they could promote their businesses in that country. They also mobilized in support of permanent MFN status for China in the 2000 public debate that ended in a congressional vote in favor of granting China that status by virtue of its accession to the WTO.

What might then be termed "K-Street Syndrome"—political activism by vested interests in favor of economic contacts with a foreign country made possible by a strategy of engagement—is most likely to advance the policy preferences of the initiator if the syndrome operates in the target.[80] If the target country has an authoritarian government, however, as in the case of China, domestic interest groups in the target country, although they may develop a preference for good relations with the initiator as a result of the latter's strategy of economic engagement, will not have the ability to make their government take heed of that preference. The United Kingdom found itself in precisely these circumstances in 1914. The British government at that time considered itself constrained by domestic business and financial groups with a stake in Germany, and thus it hesitated to be too explicit in warning Germany that the United Kingdom would intervene militarily if Germany invaded Belgium. In contrast, the autocratic German government of Kaiser Wilhelm was unresponsive to its own export-oriented business interests, which wanted peace with the United Kingdom and the rest of Europe, and the German government also recognized that the British government was constrained by British vested interests. This combination of German governmental unresponsiveness to vested interests at home and its expectations that the British government was hobbled by vested interests emboldened the German government, and thus contributed to the outbreak of the war.[81]

Effects on Innocent Third Parties: The Problem of the Diversion of Resources

The use by initiators of bilateral and multilateral economic aid as incentives may produce an economically inefficient distribution of such assistance around the world.[82] One-third of all U.S. bilateral assistance, for example, goes to Egypt and Israel, not because these countries practice particularly meritorious economic policies or are especially needy, but because the United States uses the assistance to keep those two countries from fighting one another and to keep them both committed to the U.S. sponsored peace process in the Middle East. Similarly, Japan, which traditionally has used foreign aid to spur its own economic relations with recipient countries, has begun instead to use its foreign assistance to promote nuclear nonproliferation. That is a worthy goal, but to the extent that Japan uses aid to prevent nuclear proliferation, it moves further away from a donor strategy based on the needs of many, many deserving countries.[83]

The Utility of Economic Incentives

Given these many problems with the use of economic incentives, why do initiator countries continually use incentives to solve foreign policy problems? For one thing, as noted earlier, they may in fact work to promote the initiator's interests. Furthermore, the net benefits of incentives often exceed those of the alternatives. For example, the United States might have responded in 1993 and 1994 to North Korea's threat to withdraw from the NPT with economic sanctions, but Washington had already restricted all U.S. economic contacts with that country, and therefore any additional economic sanctions would have needed to be imposed by other countries at the behest of the United States. Yet neither China, nor Japan, nor South Korea, the three of which are North Korea's main economic contacts, was willing to impose economic sanctions.[84] The United States might have launched a military strike against North Korea's main nuclear facility at Yongbyon and did, in fact, approach South Korea, Japan, and China about this option during the most dangerous moments of the crisis in 1994. Again, these countries demurred.[85] If the crisis had ended in a full-scale ground war, it would have been monstrous in character: the commander of U.S. forces in Korea estimated that such a war would have generated 80,000 to 100,000 U.S. soldiers killed, and economic losses to all participants in the range of $1 trillion.[86] Compared to those costs, it is very hard to criticize the decision of the United States to put off the day of reckoning by offering North Korea a few hundred million dollars for the fuel oil, and $5 billion, provided by other countries, for the two nuclear reactors.

Conclusion

Economic sanctions and economic incentives are instruments used by an initiator against a target to achieve political ends. Initiators use economic sanctions to impose costs on targets that do not comply with the initiator's demands, with the goal of forcing those targets to comply. Initiators use economic incentives as rewards for a target's complying with the initiator's political demands, thereby enticing targets to adjust their behavior. Hence, both sanctions and incentives are examples of the frequent use by states of economic means to achieve political ends, and as such they are important examples of how, from the viewpoint of states, economics and politics are tightly integrated in the international system.

Neither economic sanctions nor economic incentives provide an easy or sure means by which an initiator can attain immediate political results. However, notwithstanding the difficulties in using either type of policy instrument, they may work in whole or in part; they may have direct or indirect benefits; and they may constitute the least-bad option available to an initiating country, especially if military force is prohibitively expensive. For these reasons, we may expect that economic sanctions and economic incentives will remain a significant part of the diplomacy of states for many years to come.

Notes

[1]The definitive study of economic sanctions and foreign policy is David Baldwin, *Economic Statecraft* (Princeton: Princeton University Press, 1985).

[2]Robert L. Parlberg, *Food Trade and Foreign Policy: India, the Soviet Union, and the United States* (Ithaca: Cornell University Press, 1985), pp. 170–212.

[3]Kenneth R. Rodman, "Sanctions at Bay? Hegemonic Decline, Multinational Corporations, and U.S. Economic Sanctions since the Pipeline Case," *International Organization* 49 (Winter 1995), p. 114.

[4]This distinction between trade embargos and trade boycotts draws from Baldwin, *Economic Statecraft*, p. 41. Baldwin notes that the term "embargo" is often used to refer to a prohibition on all trade, both exports and imports.

[5]Robert S. Ross, "China," in Richard N. Haass, ed., *Economic Sanctions and American Diplomacy* (New York: Council on Foreign Relations Press, 1998), especially pp. 21–28.

[6]Jonathan Kirshner, *Currency and Coercion: The Political Economy of International Monetary Power* (Ithaca: Cornell University Press, 1995), pp. 63–82.

[7]Baldwin, *Economic Statecraft*, pp. 251–61.

[8]Gideon Rose, "Haiti," in Haass, ed., *Economic Sanctions*, pp. 60 and 65.

[9]Rodman, "Sanctions at Bay?," p. 127.

[10]See Patrick Clawson, "Iran," in Haass, ed., *Economic Sanctions*, p. 87.

[11]Rodman, "Sanctions at Bay?," p. 119.

[12]For a helpful overview of the Helms-Burton Act, see Stefaan Smis and Kim van der Borght, "The E.U.-U.S. Compromise on the Helms-Burton and D'Amato Acts," *American Journal of International Law* 93 (January 1999), pp. 227–36.

[13]This discussion of the objectives of economic sanctions follows Richard N. Haass, "Introduction" and "Conclusion," in Haass, ed., *Economic Sanctions*. Haass specifies punishment as a fourth possible objective of the initiating country. However, insofar as either prospective or actual punishment is necessary for sanctions to meet the objectives of deterrence, coercion, or signaling, it is very difficult to observe instances in which punishment is a unique objective of the initiator.

[14]Haass notes the India case in "Conclusion," p. 200.

[15]See Gary Clyde Hufbauer, Jeffrey Schott, and Kimberly Ann Elliot, *Economic Sanctions Reconsidered: History and Current Policy*, 2 vols., 2d ed. (Washington, D.C.: Institute for International Economics, 1990). For additional analysis suggesting that economic sanctions can be effective, see Elizabeth S. Rogers, "Using Economic Sanctions to Control Regional Conflicts," *Security Studies* 5 (Summer 1996), pp. 43–72.

[16]Robert Pape, "Why Economic Sanctions Do Not Work," *International Security* 22 (Fall 1997), pp. 90–136. For a useful debate on this matter, see Kimberly Ann Elliott, "The Sanctions Glass: Half Full or Completely Empty?" *International Security* 23 (Summer 1998), pp. 50–65; and Pape, "Why Economic Sanctions *Still* Do Not Work," *International Security* 23 (Summer 1998), pp. 66–77.

[17]See Kimberly Ann Elliott and Gary Clyde Hufbauer, "Same Song, Same Refrain? Economic Sanctions in the 1990's," *American Economic Review* 89 (May 1999), Table 1, p. 404, as well as their discussion at p. 404. Also see Gary Clyde Hufbauer and Barbara Oegg, "Economic Sanctions: A Primer for Journalists," *The Quill*, January–February 1999, Table 1.

[18]T. Clifton Morgan and Valerie Schwebach, "Fools Suffer Gladly: The Use of Economic Sanctions in International Crises," *International Studies Quarterly* 41 (1997), pp. 27–50.

[19]Daniel W. Drezner, "Conflict Expectations and the Paradox of Economic Coercion," *International Studies Quarterly* 42 (December 1998), pp. 709–31.

[20]Gideon Rose, "Libya," in Haass, ed., *Economic Sanctions*, pp. 136–37.

[21]On the importance of cooperation among suppliers in the imposition of sanctions, see Michael Mastanduno, *Economic Containment: COCOM and the Politics of East-West Trade* (Ithaca: Cornell University Press, 1992); and Lisa L. Martin, *Coercive Cooperation: Explaining Multilateral Economic Sanctions* (Princeton: Princeton University Press, 1992).

[22]These figures are from Parlberg, *Food Trade and Foreign Policy*, p. 195.

[23]Haass, "Conclusion," p. 203.

[24]Rose, "Haiti," p. 63.

[25]Daniel W. Drezner, *The Sanctions Paradox: Economic Statecraft and International Relations* (Cambridge: Cambridge University Press, 1999).

[26]Haass, "Conclusion," p. 205.

[27]John M. Goshko, "U.S. Seeks to Alter Iraq 'Oil for Food' Program," *Washington Post*, January 15, 1999, p. A24; and "U.S. Suggests Letting Iraq Sell Unlimited Amount of Oil," *Baltimore Sun*, January 15, 1999, p. 16A.

[28]See Scott D. Sagan, "From Deterrence to Coercion to War: The Road to Pearl Harbor," in Alexander L. George and William E. Simons, eds., *The Limits of Coercive Diplomacy*, 2nd ed. (Boulder: Westview Press, 1994), especially pp. 67–74.

[29]Haass, "Conclusion," pp. 198, 201.

[30]Ross, "China," p. 17.

[31]See Bruce W. Jentleson, *Pipeline Politics: The Complex Political Economy of East-West Energy Trade* (Ithaca: Cornell University Press, 1986), pp. 172–214.

[32]See Smis and van der Borght, "E.U.-U.S. Compromise," pp. 228–29, 231–34; Wayne S. Smith, "Our Dysfunctional Cuban Embargo," *Orbis* 42 (Fall 1998), pp. 533–45; and Christopher Marquis, "Bush Forgoes Trying to Bar Cuba Deals by Foreigners," *New York Times,* July 17, 2001, p. 8.

[33]See Baldwin, *Economic Statecraft,* especially pp. 121, 118–28, and, on the particular case of U.S. sanctions against Cuba, 174–89.

[34]See Ross, "China," pp. 21–26. Ross points out (pp. 22–24) that China did transfer ballistic missiles to Pakistan in 1992, in retaliation for U.S. sales of advanced fighter aircraft to Taiwan; however, under U.S. pressure, again in the form of selected economic sanctions, the Chinese appear not to have allowed the Pakistanis to deploy the missiles as of 1998.

[35]Rodman, "Sanctions at Bay?" pp 127–29.

[36]See Mastanduno, *Economic Containment.*

[37]On the importance of counterfactual reasoning when assessing economic sanctions, see Baldwin, *Economic Sanctions,* p. 22.

[38]Clawson, "Iran," p. 95.

[39]Eric Melby, "Iraq," in Haass, ed., *Economic Sanctions,* p. 120. For a similar argument regarding U.S. economic sanctions on Cuba, see Baldwin, *Economic Statecraft,* p. 180.

[40]Baldwin, *Economic Statecraft,* pp. 170–71.

[41]Baldwin, *Economic Statecraft,* p. 107.

[42]Baldwin, *Economic Statecraft,* p. 273.

[43]Baldwin, *Economic Statecraft,* pp. 280–81. See also Jentleson, *Pipeline Politics,* p. 196.

[44]Path-finding studies in the use of economic incentives in world politics include Jacob Viner, "International Finance and Balance of Power Diplomacy, 1880–1914," *Southwestern Political and Social Science Quarterly* 9 (June 1928), pp. 407–51; Albert O. Hirschman, *National Power and the Structure of Foreign Trade* (Berkeley: University of California Press, 1945); and David A. Baldwin, "The Power of Positive Sanctions," *World Politics* 24 (October 1971), pp. 19–38. Important recent works include Eileen M. Crumm, "The Value of Economic Incentives in International Politics," *Journal of Peace Research* 32 (August 1995), pp. 313–30; William J. Long, *Economic Incentives and Bilateral Cooperation* (Ann Arbor: University of Michigan Press, 1986), p. 54; David Cortright, ed., *The Price of Peace: Incentives and International Conflict Prevention* (Lanham: Rowman & Littlefield, 1997); Thomas Bernauer and Dieter Ruloff, eds., *The Politics of Positive Incentives and Arms Control* (Columbia: University of South Carolina Press, 1999); Richard N. Haass and Meghan L. O'Sullivan, eds., *Honey and Vinegar: Incentives, Sanctions, and Foreign Policy* (Washington, D.C.: Brookings Institution Press, 2000); and the summary of the preceding book in Richard N. Haass and Meghan L. O'Sullivan, "Terms of Engagement: Alternatives to Punitive Policies," *Survival* 42 (Summer 2000), pp. 113–35.

[45]See Randall Newnham, "The Price of German Unity: The Role of Economic Aid in the German-Soviet Negotiations," *German Studies Review* 22 (October 1999), p. 429.

[46]Geoffrey Roberts, *The Thirty Years' War,* 2d ed. (London: Routledge, 1997), pp. 63, 111–12.

[47]The financial package is detailed in Newnham, "Price of German Unity," pp. 429–31, 440–41.

[48]Long, *Economic Incentives,* p. 54. The United States also sought in the mid- to late 1970s

to use a strategy of relaxing technology-export restrictions to induce Soviet cooperative behavior. See Samuel P. Huntington, "Trade, Technology, and Leverage: Economic Diplomacy," *Foreign Policy*, No. 32 (1978), pp. 63–80.

[49]See World Bank, *Annual Report: 2000*, Appendix 13, available at www.worldbank.org/html/extpb/annrep/pdf/appndx/wb_a13.pdf.

[50]See Judy Dempsey and Gordon Cramb, "Donors Pledge $1 Billion as Yugoslav Tensions Deepen," *Financial Times*, June 29, 2001, available at news.ft.com/ft/gx.cgi/ftc?pagename= View&c=Article&cid=FT3JIEFAK OC&live=true&tagid=ZZZAFZAVA0C&subheading=europe.

[51]This is the thesis developed by Hirschman, *National Power*. For a recent analysis of the operation of the German preferential arrangements, see Kirshner, *Currency and Coercion*, pp. 121–36.

[52]Kenneth I. Juster, "The United States and Iraq: Perils of Engagement," in Haass and O'Sullivan, eds., *Honey and Vinegar*, pp. 54–55. Also see Bruce W. Jentleson, *With Friends Like These: Reagan, Bush, and Saddam, 1982–1990* (New York: W. W. Norton & Co., 1994).

[53]Viner, "Finance and Balance of Power Diplomacy," pp. 410–11. Once a good political relationship is established, partners may also be favorably disposed toward a deepening of their economic ties, since doing so creates militarily stronger allies. See Joanne Gowa, *Allies, Adversaries, and International Trade* (Princeton: Princeton University Press, 1994).

[54]Lars S. Skalnes, "Grand Strategy and Foreign Economic Policy: British Grand Strategy in the 1930s," *World Politics* 50 (1998), especially pp. 598–99.

[55]Roberts, *Thirty Years' War*, p. 133.

[56]Superb overviews of the U.S.–North Korea case are provided by Amy E. Smithson, "North Korea: A Case in Progress," in Bernauer and Ruloff, eds., *Politics of Positive Incentives*, pp. 73–110; Scott Snyder, "North Korea's Nuclear Program: The Role of Incentives in Preventing Deadly Conflict," in Cortright, ed., *Price of Peace*, pp. 55–81; and Leon V. Sigal, "The United States and North Korea: Cooperative Security on the Agreed Framework," in Haass and O'Sullivan, eds., *Honey and Vinegar*, pp. 70–94.

[57]See James M. Goldgeier, "The United States and the Soviet Union: Lessons of Détente," in Haass and O'Sullivan, eds., *Honey and Vinegar*, pp. 120–36; and, for a comprehensive review of détente and its aftermath, see Raymond L. Garthoff, *Détente and Confrontation: American-Soviet Relations from Nixon to Reagan*, rev. ed. (Washington, D.C.: Brookings Institution Press, 1994).

[58]Randall Newnham, "More Flies with Honey: Positive Economic Linkage in German *Ostpolitik* from Bismarck to Kohl," *International Studies Quarterly* 44 (March 2000), especially p. 90.

[59]Strom Thacker, "The High Politics of IMF Lending," *World Politics* 52 (October 1999): 38–75, especially p. 59.

[60]T. Y. Wang, "U.S. Foreign Aid and UN Voting: An Analysis of Important Issues," *International Studies Quarterly* 43 (March 1999), pp. 199–210.

[61]Alberto Alesina and David Dollar, "Who Gives Foreign Aid to Whom and Why," *Journal of Economic Growth* 5 (March 2000), pp. 46–47. Other scholars also have found that the United States has been especially prone to use bilateral aid as a way of helping military allies; however, they do not direct their research to the question of whether the United States has used bilateral aid as a way of attracting allies. See Peter J. Schraeder, Steven W. Hook, and Bruce Taylor, "Clarifying the Foreign Aid Puzzle: A Comparison of American, Japanese, French, and Swedish

Aid Flows," *World Politics* 50 (1998), pp. 294–323. For a comprehensive political analysis of the foreign assistance of several important donors, including the United States, see Steven W. Hook, *National Interest and Foreign Aid* (Boulder: Lynne Rienner, 1995).

[62]Charles W. Kegley, Jr., and Steven W. Hook, "U.S. Foreign Aid and U.N. Voting: Did Reagan's Linkage Strategy Buy Deference or Defiance?" *International Studies Quarterly* 35 (September 1991), pp. 295–312.

[63]Alesina and Dollar, "Who Gives Foreign Aid," pp. 46–47.

[64]See Richard N. Haass and Meghan L. O'Sullivan, "Conclusion," in Haass and O'Sullivan, eds., *Honey and Vinegar*, pp. 164–65.

[65]For the view that the United States had a strong bargaining position by virtue of its control over best-technology oil-extraction equipment, see Huntington, "Trade, Technology, and Leverage," p. 73.

[66]Daniel W. Drezner, "The Trouble with Carrots," in Jean-Marc F. Blanchard, Edward D. Mansfield, and Norrin M. Ripsman, eds., *Power and the Purse: Economic Statecraft, Interdependence, and National Security* (London: Frank Cass, 2000), p. 201.

[67]Haass and O'Sullivan, "Terms of Engagement," p. 123; and Haass and O'Sullivan, "Conclusion," p. 176.

[68]Haass and O'Sullivan, "Terms of Engagement," pp. 122–23; also see Haass and O'Sullivan, "Conclusion," pp. 174–75.

[69]Haass and O'Sullivan, "Terms of Engagement," p. 118; and Haass and O'Sullivan, "Conclusion," pp. 162–64.

[70]Drezner, "The Trouble with Carrots," p. 206.

[71]On this problem, see Thomas Bernauer and Dieter Ruloff, "Introduction and Analytical Framework," in Bernauer and Ruloff, eds., *Politics of Positive Incentives*, pp. 29–30.

[72]Smithson, "North Korea," p. 76.

[73]Smithson, "North Korea," p. 79.

[74]See Robert Lee Suettinger, "The United States and China: Tough Engagement," in Haass and O'Sullivan, eds., *Honey and Vinegar*, pp. 12–32; and Paul A. Papayoanou and Scott L. Kastner, "Sleeping with the (Potential) Enemy: Assessing the U.S. Policy of Engagement with China," in Blanchard, Mansfield, and Ripsman, eds., *Power and the Purse*, pp. 157–87.

[75]See Robert S. Ross, "The 1995–96 Taiwan Strait Confrontation: Coercion, Credibility, and the Use of Force," *International Security* 25 (Fall 2000), pp. 87–123.

[76]See Gerald Segal, "East Asia and the 'Constrainment' of China," *International Security* 20 (Spring 1996), especially pp. 116–23. Robert Ross, who finds that China is generally pursuing a cautious foreign policy, has suggested that the exception is China's assertive policy regarding the Spratly Islands. See Ross, "Beijing as a Conservative Power," *Foreign Affairs* 76 (March–April 1997), pp. 41–42.

[77]See J. Mohan Malik, "China and the Nuclear Non-Proliferation Regime," *Contemporary Southeast Asia* 22 (December 2000); and Ross, "China," pp. 21–28. It should be noted that Ross argues that China became more cautious about making arms sales to Middle Eastern countries after 1988.

[78]Hirschman, *National Power*, pp. 14–40.

[79]Hirschman, *National Power*, pp. 28–29.

[80]The idea of the "K-Street Syndrome" is inspired by Peter Stone's reporting on U.S. busi-

ness lobbying on behalf of MFN for China. See Peter H. Stone, "K Street Musters for the Middle Kingdom," *National Journal,* March 25, 2000.

[81]Paul A. Papayoanou, "Interdependence, Institutions, and the Balance of Power," *International Security* 20 (Spring 1996), pp. 42–76.

[82]A potential second problem with incentives and third parties concerns demonstration effects—that is, the initiator's extension of an incentive to one target to persuade the latter not to undertake some action might encourage other countries to undertake, or to threaten to undertake, that same action, so that they too may enjoy the incentive. The possible operation of this problem is noted in Haass and O'Sullivan, "Terms of Engagement," p. 115.

[83]William J. Long, "Nonproliferation as a Goal of Japanese Foreign Assistance," *Asian Survey* 39 (March–April 1999). For the alternative view that Japanese aid policy is still driven mostly by commercial considerations, see Steven W. Hook and Guang Zhang, "Japan's Aid Policy since the Cold War: Rhetoric and Reality," *Asian Survey* 38 (November 1998).

[84]See Sigal, "The United States and North Korea," pp. 73–75, 79–80.

[85]Sigal, "The United States and North Korea," p. 79.

[86]Drezner, "The Trouble with Carrots," p. 215.

Chapter 7

Economic Globalization and Political Backlash

Introduction

OBJECTIVES
- Develop a firm grasp of the meaning and chief characteristics of economic globalization.
- Identify and discuss important technological and political sources of globalization in the contemporary world economy.
- Estimate the extent to which individuals and countries are living in a new political-economic environment as a result of economic globalization.
- Examine the new concerns that globalization creates in national communities.

During the 1990s, a new phrase came into usage in discussions of the world economy: *economic globalization*. This term describes the possibility that the current international economy, comprising a network of economic ties binding otherwise relatively discrete national economies, may be transforming itself into a single, worldwide economy, one in which national economies are no longer autonomous social arrangements.

Economic globalization is a highly controversial matter. For one thing, observers disagree about the historical meaning of contemporary economic globalization. Put most bluntly, is our world of irreversible global economic integration new, or have we been here before? This question is important for two reasons, the first of which concerns the likely effects of contemporary globalization. For some observers, present-day globalization is a uniquely potent force for peace among nations. Others, however, point out that economic globalization today is no greater than that which occurred during what is often termed the "Golden Era" of world economic integration between roughly 1880 and 1914, an era that ended with World War I. If today's economic globalization is on a uniquely high trajectory, then the failure of economic integration in the past to prevent war need not reduce our confidence in the capacity of the current globalization to mitigate the risk of future war; however, if today's level of integration is not qualitatively greater than that of earlier times, then we need to be more cautious in relying on economic integration to produce peace tomorrow. Determining whether contemporary economic globalization is or is not historically unique is an important matter from the viewpoint of estimating the prospects for war and peace among nations.

Second, whether today's globalization has historical precedent can tell us much about the potential reversibility of contemporary economic globalization. If today's more optimistic observers are correct that contemporary global integration reflects powerful new technological and economic forces, then we might conclude that globalization has now become self-generating and is an unstoppable and irreversible force. And yet, during the Golden Era, it was thought that the fruits of economic integration were "normal, certain, and permanent" (see Primary Document 7.1). Perhaps, today's skeptics would suggest, we are not living in a wholly novel world of interdependence but instead are just now reattaining the level of economic integration that was achieved in 1914. If that is correct, then we need to be aware that present-day levels of globalization can, in principle, be reversed, just as occurred after 1914. We would need to live with, and guard against, the risk that, just as earlier economic globalization unraveled into economic nationalism, so too the current era might unwind, perhaps ending, as occurred in the 1930s, in mutually antagonistic regional trade blocs. We could not be confident that economic globalization is self-generating simply by virtue of technology and economics; we would need instead to recognize that other, political conditions must be satisfied both nationally and internationally in order that globalization may operate.

The historical standing of contemporary world economic integration, then, is the first main axis of controversy about economic globalization. The

PRIMARY DOCUMENT 7.1

John Maynard Keynes on the Golden Era of Economic Integration

What an extraordinary episode in the economic progress of man that age was which came to an end in August, 1914. . . . The inhabitant of London could order by phone, sipping his morning tea in bed, the various products of the whole earth, in such quantity as he might see fit, and reasonably expect their early delivery upon his doorstep; he could at the same moment and by the same means adventure his wealth in the natural resources and new enterprises of any quarter of the world, and share, without exertion or even trouble, in their prospective fruits and advantages; or he could decide to couple the security of his fortunes with the good faith of the townspeople of any substantial municipality in any continent that fancy or information might recommend. He could secure forthwith, if he wished, cheap and comfortable means of transit to any country or climate without passport or other formality, could despatch his servant to the neighboring office of a bank for such supply of the precious metals as might seem convenient, and could then proceed abroad to foreign quarters, without knowledge of their religion, language, or customs, bearing coined wealth upon his person, and would consider himself greatly aggrieved and much surprised at the least interference. But, most important of all, he regarded this state of affairs as normal, certain, and permanent, except in the direction of further improvement, and any deviation from it as aberrant, scandalous, and avoidable. The projects and politics of militarism and imperialism, of racial and cultural rivalries, of monopolies, restrictions, and exclusion, which were to play the serpent to this paradise, were little more than the amusements of his daily newspaper, and appeared to exercise almost no influence at all on the ordinary course of social and economic life, the internationalization of which was nearly complete in practice.

Source: John Maynard Keynes, *The Economic Consequences of the Peace* (New York: Harcourt, Brace and Howe, 1920), pp. 10–12.

Core Principle

Economic integration during the Golden Era allowed many individuals to have access to new goods, services, financial assets, and travel. However, contemporary economic globalization is not necessarily natural, inevitable, or irreversible, for the first era of such integration, which Keynes points out seemed to have no end, was in fact destroyed by war and was followed by a process of international economic disintegration that lasted for more than three decades.

second great axis of contention surrounding economic globalization involves its desirability. Whatever its historical precedents, should we warmly welcome or fervently fear today's trends? Economic globalization is a process that, in the eyes of some, provides humankind with new possibilities for the most efficient and intelligent employment of the world's resources; it provides for a greater diversity of experiences for more and more persons, either through employment or travel abroad or through consumption of new goods and services; and, as noted above, it is a potent force for peace among nations. To others, however, economic globalization is fostering an uncontrolled and unsustainable exploitation of the world's natural resources; it is producing economic and social inequality both within and among nations; it helps a relatively narrow global elite at the expense of the world's poor; and it injects new risks and new forms of instability in economic and political relations between countries.

The stakes, then, in the debates about economic globalization are tremendous. They raise in stark terms the questions of whether we should be optimistic or pessimistic about the future, of whether we should anticipate a world of peace and greater material abundance for more and more people, or one in which ecological disasters proliferate and tensions seethe both within and among nations. Perhaps the state itself will be supplanted as the principal focus of political action and loyalty in a globalized world economy: would such a development be good or bad for the majority of the world's peoples? Few things about the world economy, then, are as important as understanding the historical standing of contemporary economic globalization and its meaning for individuals and societies. It is to those matters that we direct our attention in this chapter.

Contemporary Economic Globalization in Historical Perspective

*"**Economic Globalization**"* refers to the growing integration since World War II of the national economies of most of the advanced industrialized countries of the world and of an increasing number of developing nations, to the degree that we may be witnessing the emergence and operation of a single, worldwide economy. This enhanced integration of world economic activity consists of increased cross-border flows of a greater variety of goods and services, more extensive cross-border flows of short-term and long-term cap-

ital, and an increasingly dense and complex network of transnational production involving multinational enterprises as well as independent suppliers.

As we discussed in Chapter 1, the world enjoyed an initial "Golden Era" of economic integration from the 1870s to the outbreak of World War I in 1914. This Golden Era was followed by an attempt at reconstitution of world economic integration during the 1920s, and a truly sharp decay in such integration from the 1930s to the end of the 1940s. Since the 1950s, the world has witnessed a tremendous expansion in the scope and intensity of cross-border economic integration. But are we living in a truly new era of global economic integration?[1]

The Globalization of Trade

As we noted in Essential Economics 1.1 in Chapter 1 (page 61), international trade has been growing much faster than total world economic activity. In a nutshell, whereas merchandise exports were more than 19 times greater in 1999 than they had been in 1950, total world economic activity was somewhat more than 6 times greater in 1999 than in 1950. As we also noted in Essential Economics 1.3 in Chapter 1 (page 81), the United States has certainly participated in the growing integration of national economies with the international trading system: U.S. exports and imports equaled less than 10 percent of the country's **gross national product** (GNP) in the early 1950s but had grown to almost 25 percent of U.S. GNP by the end of the 1990s.

The general historical trend regarding economic globalization that we sketched in Chapter 1—of growth of world economic integration up to 1914, then collapse in the face of World War I, the Great Depression, and World War II, and then recovery and possibly achievement of a new level of economic integration—can be observed in Essential Economics 7.1. It presents information on ratios of merchandise exports to **gross domestic product** (GDP) worldwide and in the seven main industrialized countries, as we did in Essential Economics 1.2 (page 7); however, whereas Essential Economics 1.2 covers only the time period from 1950 to 1998, Essential Economics 7.1 covers a much longer period, from 1870 to 1998.

At least two observations can be made in connection to Essential Economics 7.1. First, we can clearly see in the GDP figures for the entire world the rise, decline, and rejuvenation of trade integration. That is, during the Golden Era, from 1870 to 1913, trade as a ratio of world GDP rose from roughly 5 percent to 8 percent. Trade then collapsed, so that in 1950 trade

⁎ ESSENTIAL ECONOMICS 7.1

Exports' Contribution to National Economies, 1870–1998

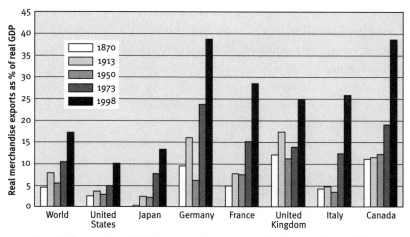

Note: Both exports and GDP are based on 1990 constant international dollars.

Source: Angus Maddison, *The World Economy: A Millennial Perspective* (Paris: Organization for Economic Cooperation and Development, 2001), Table F-5, p. 363, and, for Italy and Canada, Table A1-b, p. 184, and Table F-2, p. 361.

Core Principle

The world has experienced two great periods of economic integration, the first from 1870 to 1913 and the second from 1945 to the present. Between 1914 and 1945, by contrast, the international economy disintegrated.

---

as a ratio of world GDP had slipped back to 5.5 percent. Since then, trade has enjoyed a marked resurgence, so that even by 1973 the trade-GDP ratio for the world had exceeded the Golden Era's high, and by the end of the 1990s it reached a bit more than 17 percent. Second, the level of exports relative to GDP in each of the seven largest industrialized countries was greater at the end of the 1990s than it was during the Golden Era. We can therefore infer that the world economy, and its main national constituents, are more integrated today than at any prior time in modern history.[2]

Beyond this overview of how trade contributes to GDP, at least four other attributes of contemporary trading relationships reinforce the view that present-day international economic integration has attained a more intense level than was achieved even in the Golden Era.

Surge in Merchandise Trade

Economists point out that the fastest-growing sector of the economies of the advanced countries in recent decades has been services, which until quite recently have not been highly integrated into world trade. Instead, until recently, most trade has consisted of cross-national flows of merchandise such as manufactured goods, mining products, and agricultural goods. Thus, one helpful way to estimate the importance of trade across time is to compare over time the ratio of the level of merchandise trade of a country to its overall national merchandise production.[3]

This way of thinking about changes in the historical importance of trade is pursued in Essential Economics 7.2, which reports on merchandise trade (measured as the average of merchandise exports and imports) relative to national merchandise value-added (the value of goods beyond raw materials) in the years from 1890 to 1990. As with the data shown in Essential Economics 7.1, we find in Essential Economics 7.2 that, with the exception of the United Kingdom and Japan, merchandise trade has become a more prominent component of total domestic merchandise value-added for the advanced countries, even when compared to the pre–World War I period, again suggesting that trade integration has become more important for many of the key countries of the world.

Growing Trade in Services

Commerce in services has been growing very rapidly in the current period of globalization, as well. In the case of the United States, for example, exports of services constituted about 29 percent of all U.S. exports in 1998, compared to 17 percent in 1960 and only 2 percent in 1900.[4] Hence, it is not just in the goods-producing sectors that we are observing enhanced globalization, but also increasingly in the faster-growing service sectors as well.

Merchandise Trade and Globally Integrated "Value-Added Chains"

International commerce in recent years has often consisted of intra-industry trade, as we noted in Chapter 2, or of intra-firm trade (sales from one firm to another of intermediate goods that will serve as inputs for a final product). These activities "slice up the value-added chain"—that is, firms increasingly draw on both in-house and independent suppliers on a worldwide basis for manufactured inputs and components, thereby tying more closely together

ESSENTIAL ECONOMICS 7.2

Merchandise Trade and Domestic Merchandise Value-Added, Major Industrial Countries, 1890–1990

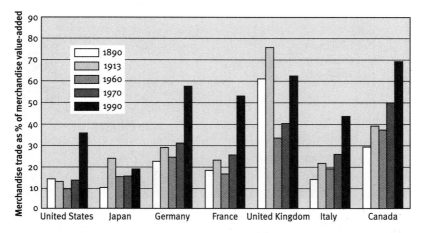

Source: Robert C. Feenstra, "Integration of Trade and Disintegration of Production in the Global Economy," *Journal of Economic Perspectives* 12 (Fall 1998), p. 35.

Core Principle

Merchandise trade has become more prominent in advanced industrialized countries, suggesting increasing economic integration.

---

the national manufacturing systems of different countries.[5] Although imported inputs made up about 6 percent of all intermediate goods purchased in the United States in 1972, this figure rose to about 14 percent in 1990.[6] By the late 1990s, about 60 percent of the value of the hardware of personal computers consisted of imported components.[7]

Integration of the Newly Industrialized Countries

Finally, Essential Economics 7.3 shows that certain fast-growing newly industrializing countries—in particular, South Korea, Taiwan, Malaysia, Singapore, Hong Kong (now a part of China), and, more recently, China itself—have become important exporters to the world market. The implications of their success is discussed below and in chapter 8.

Developing Countries' Share of World Merchandise Exports, 1985–95

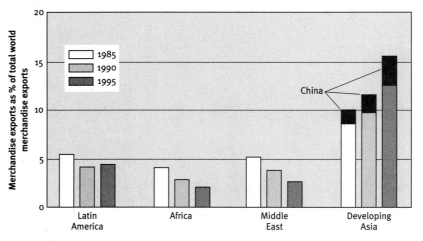

Source: World Trade Organization, "Participation of Developing Countries in World Trade: Overview of Major Trends and Underlying Factors" (Geneva: WTO, 1996), p. 8, available at www.wto.org/english/tratop_e/devel_e/w15.htm.

Core Principle

Newly developing countries show important signs of increasing economic integration. The rapid industrialization of many East and Southeast Asian countries has quickly developed the region and integrated it more closely into the global economy. In particular, South Korea, Taiwan, Malaysia, Singapore, Hong Kong (now a part of China), and, more recently, mainland China itself, have spearheaded this new growth.

Capital Markets and Contemporary Global Economic Integration

The second major form of economic activity in which globalization can be observed in the contemporary world system is in the integration of capital markets. We see such growth in capital-market integration with respect to foreign-exchange transactions and, more important, from the viewpoint of long-term capital-market integration, cross-national movements of foreign direct investment.

MAP 7.1

A Modern Multinational Enterprise: Motorola

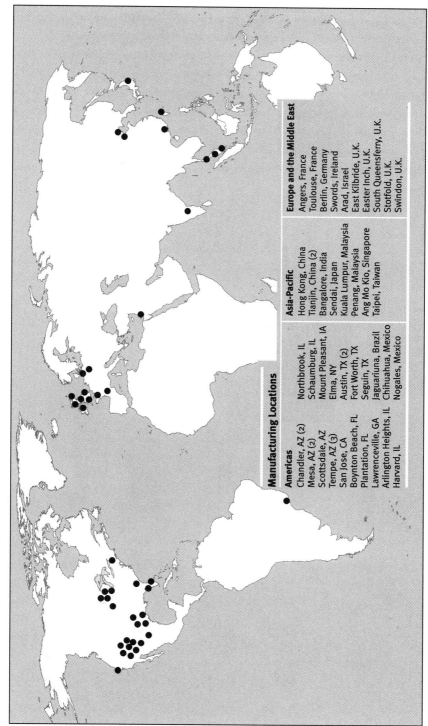

Manufacturing Locations

Americas

Chandler, AZ (2)	Northbrook, IL
Mesa, AZ (2)	Schaumburg, IL
Scottsdale, AZ	Mount Pleasant, IA
Tempe, AZ (3)	Elma, NY
San Jose, CA	Austin, TX (2)
Boynton Beach, FL	Fort Worth, TX
Plantation, FL	Seguin, TX
Lawrenceville, GA	Jaguariuna, Brazil
Arlington Heights, IL	Chihuahua, Mexico
Harvard, IL	Nogales, Mexico

Asia-Pacific

Hong Kong, China
Tianjin, China (2)
Bangalore, India
Sendai, Japan
Kuala Lumpur, Malaysia
Penang, Malaysia
Ang Mo Kio, Singapore
Taipei, Taiwan

Europe and the Middle East

Angers, France
Toulouse, France
Berlin, Germany
Swords, Ireland
Arad, Israel
East Kilbride, U.K.
Easter Inch, U.K.
South Queensferry, U.K.
Stotfold, U.K.
Swindon, U.K.

Motorola is an important example of the modern multinational enterprise. As the map shows, Motorola in 2000 had manufacturing facilities in fourteen different countries. It should also be noted that, of Motorola's total sales of about $38 billion in 2000, 58 percent resulted from its international sales operations.

Source: It's About People and the Planet: 2000 Global Corporate Citizenship Report (Schaumburg, IL: Motorola, 2001), p. 8, available at www.motorola.com/EHS/environment/reports/2000report.pdf.

Foreign-Exchange Transactions

The volume of foreign-exchange transactions, often undertaken for the purposes of very short-term investments, totaled about $1.5 trillion per day during April 1998, up from about $600 billion per day during April 1989.[8] In fact, foreign-exchange transactions for the purposes of investment now dwarf such transactions for the purposes of international trade in goods and services. Compared to the $1.5 trillion per day in foreign-exchange transactions that took place during April 1998 for all purposes, the value of global exports of goods and services alone during 1997 was about $25 billion per trading day.[9]

⋇ **ESSENTIAL ECONOMICS 7.4**

Foreign Direct Investment and Gross Fixed Capital Formation, 1980–97

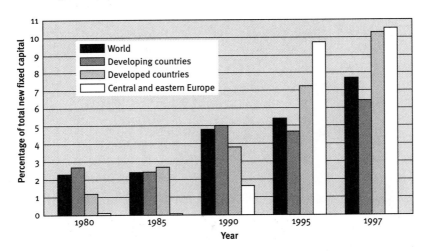

Source: United Nations Conference on Trade and Development (UNCTAD), *World Investment Report: 1999* (Geneva: UNCTAD, 1999), p. 12.

Core Principle

Foreign direct investment has become a key source of capital formation in all major groups of countries.

Foreign Direct Investments: The Multinational Enterprise

Globalization in finance has been important not just with respect to short-term investments, but also with respect to very long-term capital movements—namely, *foreign direct investment (FDI).* Such FDI is undertaken typically by *multinational enterprises (MNEs),* which are firms that have two main characteristics:[10] first, to varying degrees, they have significant operations not just in the countries in which they are headquartered, but also in other countries; and second, multinational enterprises seek, and to varying degrees achieve, the formulation and implementation of *global strategies,* in which they seek to view the world not as a collection of individual national markets, but as a single, integrated global market. Map 7.1 shows these two characteristics for one very prominent multinational enterprise: Motorola.

FDI plays an increasingly significant role in fueling the world economy. As can be observed in Essential Economics 7.4, FDI inflows undertaken by MNEs and others paid for about 8 percent of the world's new fixed capital in 1997, up from 5 percent in 1990 and about 2 percent in 1980. For developing countries the growth in importance of FDI has been even more dramatic: FDI made up about 1 percent of new capital investment in those countries in 1980, 4 percent in 1990, and over 10 percent in 1997.

U.S. Integration with World Capital Markets

Just as we found in the discussion centering around Essential Economics 1.3—that the U.S. economy has become more tightly integrated with the international trading system—so too have its financial linkages with foreign capital markets become much more complex. Total cross-border capital inflows and outflows for the United States equaled about 2 percent of U.S. GNP during the 1960s, but they equaled about 14 percent of U.S. GNP during the mid- to late 1990s.[11] A particularly important and growing form of American financial participation abroad has been that of foreign direct investment: the value of U.S. foreign direct investment abroad was equal to about 6–7 percent of U.S. GNP from 1914 to 1960, whereas the value of such investments by the mid-1990s was equal to a full 20 percent of U.S. GNP.[12]

Contemporary Capital Market Integration in Historical Perspective

As we noted earlier, some signs indicate that the international financial system is more integrated today than it was during the Golden Era, but the evidence is not as conclusive in this matter as it is with respect to trade. In this section we will examine two measures of international capital market integration within and across time periods: the first focuses on the financial flows that take place to accommodate deficits and surpluses in the current accounts of countries; the second looks at what often motivates financial operations across countries—their different interest rates.

Capital Market Integration and Current Account Balances

To evaluate a country's level of international financial integration, economists often examine the ratio of the absolute value of the country's current-account balance to its gross domestic product.[13] What does this ratio show us? As we discussed in Chapter 3, if a country experiences a current account surplus, the surplus is accommodated by the acquisition by the country's residents of foreign financial assets, and therefore an outflow of capital; if a country experiences a current account deficit, the deficit is accommodated through the sale by the country's residents of financial assets to foreigners, and therefore an inflow of foreign capital. The absolute value of a country's current account balance thus provides insight into the magnitude of its participation in international capital markets as either a source or a recipient of such capital. Furthermore, taking the average of this measure for a group of countries during a particular period of time sheds light on the level of overall global capital integration that was in effect during that period, thereby making comparisons of global capital integration across time also possible.

Essential Economics 7.5 presents estimates, drawn from work by economists Maurice Obstfeld and Alan Taylor; of such averages for 12 advanced countries over five-year spans between 1870 and 1996. As can be observed in the figure, current account balances averaged a bit more than 3 percent of GDP in the 1890–1913 period, dropped on average to only a bit more than 1 percent during the Great Depression, and recovered only to somewhat more than 2 percent by the late 1980s and mid-1990s.[14] It would appear, then, on the basis of the information in Essential Economics 7.5, that the contemporary international capital market still has some way to go before it reaches the level of integration that was attained during the Golden Era.

✳ ESSENTIAL ECONOMICS 7.5

Estimated Extent of International Capital Flows, 1870–1996

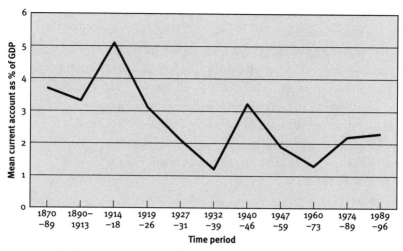

Note: Absolute value of current account balance is used to calculate percentages.

Source: Maurice Obstfeld and Alan M. Taylor, "The Great Depression as a Watershed: International Capital Mobility over the Long Run," in Michael D. Bordo, Claudia Goldin, and Eugene N. White, eds., *The Defining Moment: The Great Depression and the American Economy in the Twentieth Century* (Chicago: University of Chicago Press, 1998), Table 11.1, p. 359.

> *Core Principle*
>
> **W**hen measured using capital flows relative to national income, the financial integration of the 1990s has still not reached the level of integration achieved among the advanced countries from 1870 to 1913.

Capital Market Integration and Cross-National Interest Rates

Although a focus on current account balances suggests that the world today is not as integrated from a financial viewpoint as it was prior to World War I, by using an alternative measure of capital market integration—one that focuses on cross-national differences in interest rates—the case can be made that we may already have experienced in recent years not just a return to pre–World War I levels of capital market integration, but a new, higher level of such integration.

Obstfeld and Taylor have suggested that an important indicator of capital market integration is the degree of cross-national dispersion of rates of return for a given class of financial assets. The first fact to keep in mind in looking at this measure is that interest payments for a financial instrument are usually fixed at the time the instrument is issued. For example, when the U.S. government issues a five-year Treasury bond, it promises to pay a fixed number of dollars in interest each year to the bond holder. The second fact to keep in mind is that one element of the overall capital market is the market for debt instruments, such as U.S. Treasury bonds, and the prices for these instruments rise and fall in response to their supply and demand. Thus, the current return on U.S. five-year Treasury bonds at any given moment is measured by dividing the fixed interest payment per year for the bond by the current market price for that bond. For example, if the interest payment is $150 and the current price for a bond is $950, then the return is 5.26 percent.

Let us now imagine that the capital markets of the United States and the United Kingdom are tightly integrated: residents in each country can easily purchase the other country's currency and its financial instruments. Let us also imagine that, for some reason, the return on the five-year U.S. Treasury bond, previously about equal to the five-year U.K. bond's return, suddenly becomes lower than the return on the U.K. government bond. In response, and assuming that there have been no changes in investor expectations about future exchange rates, investors in both the United States and the United Kingdom, seeing that the U.K. bond is offering a higher return, will tend to sell off their five-year U.S. bonds and buy five-year U.K. bonds. The effect will be a reduction in the price of the U.S. bond and an increase in its return, as well as an increase in the price of the U.K. bond and a decrease in its return. Quite soon, the returns on U.S. and U.K. bonds would once again be about equal, ending the incentive for investors to sell additional U.S. bonds in favor of U.K. bonds. Hence, to the extent that the two markets are integrated, we should see smaller rather than larger differences, or divergences, in the rates of return for comparable financial instruments in the two markets.

Keeping this background in mind, look at Essential Economics 7.6, which shows changes in the average level of dispersion (as measured by the standard deviation) in returns on comparable debt instruments among ten countries during five-years time periods beginning in the 1870s and ending in the mid-1990s.[15] As the figure shows, the standardized level of dispersion in returns was about 3.4 percentage points in the years prior to the outbreak of World War I. The dispersion in returns jumped dramatically during that war

☆ **ESSENTIAL ECONOMICS 7.6**

Worldwide Variation in Interest Rates, 1870–1996

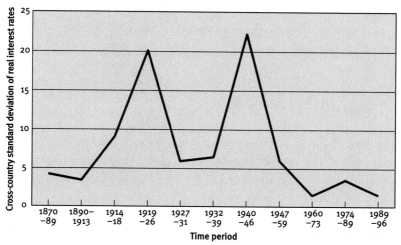

Source: Obstfeld and Taylor, "The Great Depression as a Watershed," Table 11.3, p. 366.

Core Principle

When measured using inter-nation variation in interest rates, recent capital-
market integration may have surpassed that of the Golden Era.

---

and shortly thereafter; it showed signs of declining during the late 1920s
but again jumped during the Great Depression and especially in the context
of World War II. Most important, the standardized level of dispersion in returns has decreased markedly in recent years, and during the 1989–96 period it was 1.7 percentage points—substantially lower than it was during the
Golden Era. This fact suggests that there has been a marked integration of
capital markets in recent years, and that we are perhaps now living in a period of capital market integration that is at least equal to, and perhaps greater
than, the first period of intense economic globalization.[16]

The Sources of Globalization

Contemporary global economic integration has been prompted by both technological developments and political conditions within and among the major trading countries of the world.

Technology and Globalization

Technology, or the state of knowledge used in production, is clearly an important part of the story of the increasing globalization of the present-day world economy. At least three types of technological change are tightening the linkages across national economies. First, continuing improvements in transportation technology have reduced the costs of international exchanges of goods, services, and technology itself. In the first era of globalization the most important advances in transportation centered around sea transport; these advances reduced transportation costs for goods by perhaps as much as 50 percent between 1870 and 1913.[17] It appears that ocean-shipping costs continued to decrease during the early years after World War II but then leveled off by the early 1960s. However, remarkable advances in air-transport technology have dramatically reduced air-freight costs, by perhaps as much as 80 percent between the mid-1950s and the late 1990s. As a consequence, whereas only about 9 percent of all U.S. imports arrived by air in 1974, about 19 percent did so in 1996.[18]

Second, and perhaps even more important than cost-cutting improvements in transportation technology, advances in communications and computing technology have created new opportunities today for both trade and cross-national financial transactions. For example, an average long-distance, three-minute telephone call in 1930 cost the equivalent of $293 in 1998 dollars, but by 1998 such a call cost only 36 cents.[19] Computers, too, while becoming vastly more powerful, have grown less and less expensive throughout the past few decades.

Third, MNEs have learned how to employ these advances in transportation, communications, and computing technologies in order to become more active in the world economy. Managers in MNEs have learned how to use cheaper telecommunications, increasingly powerful computers, and, during the past decade, the Internet to coordinate the operations of their subsidiaries and their independent suppliers across national borders and even around the world. Moreover, financial firms have learned to employ the new telecommunications and computing technologies to develop, price, and trade new international financial products, such as currency options, and to identify and monitor new and profitable investment opportunities in foreign markets. Thus, the interaction between improved communications and computing technology, on the one hand, and advances in knowledge regarding management and investment, on the other, may be the most important technical driver of modern globalization.[20]

Political Sources of Economic Globalization

Technological advances by themselves have not been sufficient to bring about the movement toward globalization but instead have facilitated such integration because national and international political conditions have created an environment conducive to greater international economic interconnections. At least four such political factors have contributed to the national and international foundations for contemporary economic globalization.

As we discussed in Chapter 5, since World War II, many national governments have undertaken multilateral (and, in some cases, unilateral) steps to reduce tariffs and other barriers to trade. As a result of successive rounds of multilateral negotiations under the auspices of the General Agreement on Tariffs and Trade (GATT), now the World Trade Organization (WTO), the average tariff on industrial products charged by the advanced countries has dropped from 40 percent to 4 percent. Similarly, in recent years the industrialized nations and an increasing number of developing countries and former socialist countries have unilaterally and jointly removed capital controls, thus permitting enhanced cross-border flows of capital for investment purposes.[21]

Furthermore, when trade conflicts have developed and financial crises have erupted, governments have worked together through GATT, the WTO, the International Monetary Fund (IMF), and more informal gatherings such as the Group of Seven (G-7) process linking the major industrialized countries to contain and to manage the possible harmful effects of such conflicts and crises. These collaborative efforts by countries to pursue commercial conflict and financial crisis-management have helped prevent serious retreats from economic integration, and they have contributed to the general trend toward a more open world economy.

Although governments of the advanced industrialized countries have taken the lead in global economic liberalization, they have also constructed international agreements facilitating trade and financial integration in such a way as to permit temporary departures from such integration, and they have put into place national systems of social insurance that essentially limit the risks and actual economic losses that individuals and groups must bear as a result of such liberalization. This combination of foreign and domestic policies on the part of the most industrialized countries since World War II, crafted to pursue managed and progressive liberalization with domestic social insurance, has been called the "embedded liberalism" compromise. At its core is a national political commitment by governments to economic liberalization abroad, but with a commitment as well by governments to compensate those at home who have been left behind or harmed by such liberalization.[22] This willingness to accept some protectionism has encouraged more countries to participate in the liberalization of the world economy.

Finally, just as embedded liberalism has been the domestic political foundation for national economic liberalization by the advanced countries, American power has been the international political foundation for such global economic integration. American power has provided military security to Japan and the Western European nations and thus has allayed the security fears of those countries and permitted them greater leeway in their efforts to work together and with others on behalf of globalization. American power has also been the foundation of the GATT/WTO and IMF regimes, and the United States has been the major exponent of liberalization in those regimes and in their efforts to manage international economic conflicts and crises.[23]

The Consequences of Economic Globalization

In recent years, students of contemporary economic globalization have investigated the possible effects of economic globalization on world peace, on national economic welfare, on national economic policy independence, and on national cultural autonomy.

Economic Globalization and World Peace

In a thoughtful and provocative book titled *The Lexus and the Olive Tree*, Thomas Friedman, the journalist and foreign affairs columnist for the *New York Times*, has put forward what he terms the "Golden Arches Theory of

Conflict Prevention." Friedman observes that, as of the time he was writing in the late 1990s, no two countries had gone to war with each other after they had each hosted a branch of the McDonald's fast-food franchise. He uses this humorous observation to articulate a serious proposition: "Today's globalization system significantly raises the costs of countries using war as a means to pursue honor, react to fears or advance their interests."[24] Friedman is careful to point out that he does not believe that contemporary economic globalization absolutely ends the risk of war, and he recognizes that commentators in earlier periods mistakenly believed that international economic integration had obviated the danger of war. However, he does emphasize that he thinks that contemporary globalization is different at least in degree from that of earlier periods: "The bottom line is this: If in the previous era of globalization nations in the system thought twice before trying to solve problems through warfare, in this era of globalization they will think about it three times."[25]

Thus, one possible consequence of increases in economic globalization might be decreases in the danger of war. The argument in favor of this proposition begins with the point that as economic interconnections between two countries increase, each country achieves greater welfare, and therefore each country develops a progressively greater stake in the continuation and intensification of interconnections with its partner. The second step in the argument is that, because war would lead to a breakage of their mutually profitable and beneficial economic contacts, partners have a progressively stronger incentive not to permit any particular political or diplomatic disagreement to escalate to military conflict. In general, then, as economic interdependence between two countries increases, each nation's incentives to manage and resolve disputes without going to war also go up, with the result being a lower overall danger of war as the world experiences intensified economic globalization.

Yet an alternative view about the general effects of growing economic interdependence on the prospects for war and peace holds that globalization increases the points of contact between two countries and therefore the number of potential disagreements between them, and thereby actually *increases* the risk that conflicts might develop between the two countries.[26] In addition, as we discussed in Chapters 2 and 6, countries can grow faster through participation in the international economy, and they can attain through such participation a wider range of goods that have a direct or indirect bearing on their military power (as when they buy weapons or the technology on which moderns weapons are based). With such international economic participation, states can acquire greater military power and thereby become more confident that they can settle disputes with others through the use of military force.[27] Thus, according to this second perspective, the general effect of growing economic interdependence may be to increase, not decrease, the risk of war.

Finally, a third perspective on economic interdependence and war argues that growing economic interdependence may reduce an already low risk of war between democracies, but it has no depressive effect and may even have an exacerbating effect on the risks of war between two nondemocracies or between democratic and authoritarian states.[28] According to this perspective, two key assumptions of the interdependence-peace thesis are that governments are responsive to the desires of their citizens for the economic benefits generated by globalization and interdependence, and that they will be held accountable by those citizens if they become involved in foreign adventures and thus put those economic benefits in jeopardy. Such responsiveness and accountability may be true of governments in democracies, but not in authoritarian states. Indeed, as we discussed in Chapter 6 in the case of Germany, the United Kingdom, and the outbreak of World War I, authoritarian states, believing that democratic governments fear the loss of the benefits of economic interdependence, might react to growing interdependence with democracies by becoming more and not less aggressive toward them, in the belief that the democracies might be willing to make concessions rather than forgo the benefits of economic contacts.

Economic Globalization and National Economic Welfare

In the discussion so far, we have explored the manner in which economic globalization might affect political relationships between nations; now we turn our attention to the ways in which globalization might be affecting economic relationships *within* countries.

Economic Globalization and the Risk of External Shocks

In very general terms, economic globalization is introducing new and profoundly powerful sources of change in the economies, societies, and perhaps even the cultures of nations. One key result of this closer interconnectedness seems to be a growing sense of anxiety on the part of many individuals and even national communities that they cannot comprehend, let alone participate in the management of, these new motors of change. As Friedman has suggested, "the defining anxiety in globalization is fear of rapid change from an enemy you can't see, touch or feel—a sense that your job, community or workplace can be changed at any moment by anonymous economic and technological forces that are anything but stable."[29]

This conjunction of rapid economic globalization, externally induced shocks and change, and anxiety about the capacity of the former to bring about the latter is illustrated perhaps most dramatically in the area of international finance, and specifically by the problem of short-term capital flows, financial crises, and the cross-national spread of such crises among what are often previously very successful economies. The 1990s witnessed a number of cases of financial crisis contagion, and we will review some of these when we discuss in Chapter 8 the challenges of enhanced international financial integration for developing countries.

However, it should be emphasized that cross-national transmissions of financial crises have not been restricted to emerging-market economies alone. For example, when the currencies of Italy and France came under attack in 1992 after they and other European Union countries set a path for economic and monetary union (EMU), Sweden's currency also came under pressure even though Sweden had not proposed to join EMU and indeed was not a member of the European Union!

Similarly, in the context of financial turbulence in East Asia, Latin America, and Russia during 1997 and 1998 (turbulence that we will describe in detail in Chapter 8), emerging markets around the world collapsed, and international investors generally decided to undertake a "flight to quality"— that is, they began to favor only the safest of investments issued by the most creditworthy issuers, such as notes and bonds issued by the German and U.S. governments. However, a number of unregulated U.S. and European investment enterprises—so-called hedge funds—had earlier gambled that just the opposite would occur. They had assumed that, as the Europeans coalesced around a single interest-rate structure with their entry into EMU, less creditworthy financial instruments, such as Italian government bonds, would experience greater demand and thereby go up in price, and demand for traditionally more creditworthy instruments, such as German bonds, would remain stable or even decline, with an associated drop in price. For one U.S. hedge fund, Long Term Capital Management (LTCM), the result of this incorrect assumption was catastrophic investment losses: its total capital base contracted from about $4.1 billion at the beginning of August 1998 to about $600 million toward the end of September. However, these losses had ramifications well beyond the offices of LTCM: a number of U.S. and European banks had invested in LTCM, and because of its losses, combined with other losses these banks had sustained as a result of having invested in emerging markets, they were threatening to sharply curtail their national and international lending, which would then exacerbate the sharp declines in financial markets that by then had spread from the emerging markets to the stock markets of the advanced countries.[30] To prevent such a credit squeeze and the potential for a serious additional shock to world financial markets, the Federal Reserve Bank of New York began an effort on September 18, 1998, to organize a financial rescue of LTCM, an effort that resulted in an injection of $3.5 billion in new capital into LTCM by 14 large U.S. banks and other financial institutions.[31] In the aftermath of the crisis, U.S. Federal Reserve Board chair Alan Greenspan said it had been necessary to coordinate the LTCM rescue because, in a reference to the Asian and Russian financial crises, "financial market participants were already unsettled by recent global events," and "had the failure of LTCM triggered the seizing up of markets, substantial damage could have been inflicted on many market participants, including some not directly involved with the firm, and could have potentially impaired the economies of many nations, including [the United States]."[32] The Federal Reserve Bank had prevented this outcome, but, among the many lessons to be learned, one that is clearly important for American students of international political economy is that financial crises in seemingly far-off countries can eventually come to the United States.

Economic Globalization and National Economic Independence

The advanced industrialized countries have also faced new challenges to their capacities to pursue a wide range of economic policies as a result of economic globalization, especially as trade has increased and multinational enterprises have expanded the scope and intensity of their global operations.

GLOBALIZATION AND THE QUESTION OF GROWING INCOME INEQUALITY

Globalization appears to be bringing about social dislocations in the advanced countries in two distinct patterns: high levels of employment but growing income inequality in the United States (and to some degree in the United Kingdom), and greater unemployment but avoidance of increases in income inequality in most of Western Europe.[33] Between the early 1970s and the early 1990s, while globalization of the U.S. economy was gathering force, the real wages of U.S. workers without a high school degree declined by almost 25 percent, and the discrepancy between the wages of more highly paid U.S. workers (those in the 90th percentile of the distribution) and those of lesser-paid workers (those in the 10th percentile) also increased by about 25 percent between 1970 and 1992.[34] At the same time, while the U.S. unemployment rate fell to about 4 percent at the end of the 1990s, unemployment rates in Western Europe remained stubbornly above 10 percent.[35]

In relating these trends to globalization, critics have suggested that trade, and in particular trade with low-wage emerging economies such as Mexico or China or Thailand, by itself directly causes reductions in the demand for labor in the industrialized countries. They suggest further that modern trade flows, in a manner that would be consistent with expectations of the Stolper-Samuelson theorem discussed in Chapter 2, bring about income inequality in the United States, for there wages and other labor conditions are less controlled by the government, and so a trade-induced decrease in demand for unskilled labor translates into lower wages for such workers, not lower employment among them. At the same time, a trade-induced reduction in demand for unskilled labor in Europe produces higher unemployment, for there governments impose a number of fixed labor costs on employers and restrictions on firings of workers already employed, and therefore a decrease in demand for labor generates a reduction not in wages offered but in the number of new hirings.

Economists have emphasized that this one-to-one association between trade integration and the labor market does not hold; instead, they have suggested that the bulk of the downward shift in demand for unskilled labor is due to advances in technology that substitute skilled for unskilled labor. They have suggested further that the direct impact of trade may account for only about 10 percent, or at the very most 20 percent, of the reduction in the demand for labor during the past two decades and the associated deterioration in the relative earnings of unskilled labor.[36]

However, increases in foreign competition through trade integration might be an important spur for companies to undertake technological innovation, and thus trade might be having an important indirect effect on the reduction of demand for unskilled labor by way of its contribution to technological innovation in the advanced countries.[37] Moreover, technological innovations in the advanced countries, such as faster and cheaper communications, permit international outsourcing, which in turn may reduce the demand for labor in the advanced countries.[38]

Furthermore, even if trade integration does not by itself account for the full reduction in the demand for unskilled workers, such integration might be contributing in part to other deleterious trends for those workers. For example, the increased ease of international outsourcing by U.S. firms for inputs may be increasing the degree to which a small change in labor costs at home will cause U.S. firms to substitute foreign for local suppliers of intermediate products. Given that American unskilled workers recognize that increases in their wages will lead to an increasingly severe reduction in demand for their services, such workers will be less able to press for better wages, will need to pay for a larger share of their fringe benefits, and will experience greater volatility in their earnings.[39] Hence, increases in trade integration may play substantial both direct and indirect roles in eroding the real earnings of unskilled workers in the industrialized countries.

ECONOMIC GLOBALIZATION AND THE "GOLDEN STRAITJACKET"

But globalization may do more than affect income inequality; it might also place what Friedman has called a "golden straitjacket" on governments. In order to enjoy the benefits of globalization, governments may believe that they are constrained in their freedom to use fiscal or monetary or social policy to ameliorate the problems faced by unskilled workers. For example, if a government seeks to increase corporate taxes levied for the purpose of providing supplementary income to unskilled workers hurt by foreign competition, firms might simply shift a greater proportion of their corporate activities and reported revenues to lower-tax, more business-friendly countries. Thus the government policy would lead to decreased tax revenues and less resources to assist unskilled workers.

ECONOMIC GLOBALIZATION AND THE "RACE TO THE BOTTOM"

Economic globalization might also cause the advanced countries to abandon their commitments to the compromise of embedded liberalism, the cornerstone of the post–World War II era of economic cooperation and liberalization both within and among the advanced industrialized states. That is, in order to be "friendly" to footloose multinational enterprises and prevent them from relocating to low-wage, low-standard developing countries, governments in the rich countries may undertake a "race to the bottom" with respect to their policies on the environment and those that more immediately affect the welfare of workers. Hence, workers in industrialized countries might be faced with reduced real wages, higher insecurity about future earnings, and few policy safeguards in areas such as government-mandated worker-safety standards and conditions. At the same time, national communities in the developed and the developing worlds might experience serious

Nongovernmental Organizations and the Critique of Globalization

GLOBAL ENVIRONMENTAL ISSUES
Attacking the Root Causes of Environmental Destruction

Global Environmental Issues

Trade, Investment and
the Environment

International Finance and
the Environment

Corporate Accountability
and the Environment

Back to FOE Home

Deforestation: Who's Behind the Destruction?

Only one fifth of the Earth's original forest cover remains in large, relatively undisturbed areas like Brazil's Amazon, and this is threatened every day by pressures from human activity like unsustainable natural resource extraction. Extractive industries similarly threaten already damaged forests, like those of Madagascar, whose fragmented nature and high number of unique species make them conservation priorities. Companies exploiting the resources of these forests are often backed by large, publicly-funded institutions like the World Bank and the US Overseas Private Investment Corporation. And many times they reap the benefits of forests made vulnerable by macroeconomics—as a condition for its financial support, the International Monetary Fund often requires countries not only to increase their exports of natural resources, but to cut their spending on government programs designed to protect the environment. Brazil's government recently proposed to cut its environmental spending by two-thirds in order to meet targets set by the IMF.

Source: www.foe.org/international/envissues/.

Core Principle

Nongovernmental organizations have made very effective use of the World Wide Web in their advocacy efforts directed against economic globalization. In this selection, taken from the Web site maintained by the Friends of the Earth, the NGO argues that deforestation is a serious problem and is in significant measure caused by the operations of private firms, and that the practices of the U.S. government as well as the World Bank and the International Monetary Fund are exacerbating the problem.

---

environmental degradation as a result of economic globalization (see Primary Document 7.2).

Furthermore, as noted earlier, there may be grounds to suggest that international economic integration may be constraining rises in the wages of some societal segments in the advanced countries. However, to date there is little evidence that a race to the bottom in environmental and labor regulations has occurred in the developed countries as they have deepened their economic integration with developing nations.[40] Indeed, as we discuss in the next chapter, the evidence seems to indicate that MNEs prefer higher-standard countries for their operations.

Economic Globalization and National Cultural Autonomy

Friedman and other close observers of globalization have highlighted a third major challenge to countries that are participating in the process of closer world economic integration: namely, striking a balance between their interest in enjoying the benefits derived from their greater integration with the world and their desire to retain their own languages, their own literatures, their own modern media, and other characteristics of their distinctive way of life—that is, their own cultures. Many countries, both developed and developing, are distressed that American culture appears to be the basis for the emerging new global culture being generated by globalization. According to Friedman, "globalization has a distinctly American face: It wears Mickey Mouse ears, it eats Big Macs, it drinks Coke or Pepsi and it does its computing on an IBM or Apple laptop, using Windows 98, with an Intel Pentium II processor and a network link from Cisco Systems."[41]

AMERICAN CINEMA AND THE FRENCH BACKLASH

We can observe both the growing influence of American culture and the backlash it generates even in other advanced societies in the case of France and its deep-seated concerns about American-made films. During the late 1990s, U.S.-made films attracted between 70 percent and 80 percent of total box-office receipts in the European Union (EU) countries; in France itself American films won about 60 percent of the theater-going market.[42] As we shall see in a moment, the French government has responded to what it sees as U.S. dominance of world film-making and of the European film market with a highly developed policy of protection against U.S. film imports and a policy that promotes French film-makers. Moreover, the French have succeeded in enlisting the support of their EU partners in pursuing the goal of limiting U.S. domination of the European film and television industries.

However, before we examine France's policies together with those of its EU partners, it may be useful to consider the rationale for those policies. The French government has argued that American market dominance in cultural products such as films and television shows is, in the first place, the result not of superior American film-making or television production, but of unfair and predatory American business practices. In particular, the French have argued that the United States' near monopoly in world media arises from the fact that American film and television studios are able to use the earnings they derive from the huge U.S. market as a basis for the production of flashy films and shows and, perhaps more important, as the basis for out-advertising all other competitors in foreign markets. Thus, many members of the French political and cultural elite argue, U.S. audiovisual producers have come to dominate foreign markets even if American media products lack artistic or cultural or moral value.

The French also argue that, whatever might be the sources of American success in the film and TV industry, the French government has the right and indeed the duty to intervene and limit the exposure of its population to U.S.-origin media products that have a significant cultural component. There are two grounds for this view. First, American films and TV (and, indeed, pop music), for many members of the French cultural elite in and out of government, are often not just artistically without value, they are intrinsically bad from a cultural and moral viewpoint: they are trite in their materialism and they are corrupting in their glorification of violence. Second, even if U.S. films and other media are not intrinsically bad, the French population's exposure to them may in the long term undermine the authenticity of the French culture and its bedrock, the French language. As the *Economist* noted in a report on France's Ministry of Culture in 1998, "the ministry's officials are convinced that a rising tide of American popular culture is swamping France," and for the officials in the ministry and for the French cultural elite the issue is not just a matter of who watches which films, but rather "that Hollywood is a Trojan horse bringing with it Disneyland Paris, fast-food chains and free advertising for American products from clothes to rock music."[43] Hence, according to this view, in order to preserve a key public good for both France and the world—namely, the French culture—the French government has an obligation to support the French film arts and to limit France's exposure to U.S. films and TV shows, even if many French people want to see them and even if these U.S. media products have no immediate negative impact on the French population. The alternative, in this line of thinking, is to witness the slow, inexorable contamination of French language with Americanisms, and the steady, inevitable Americanized corruption of French, and indeed European, culture.

AMERICAN PRINT MEDIA AND CANADIAN CONCERNS ABOUT CULTURAL AUTHENTICITY

Americans might react to French concerns and arguments about the dangers posed by the special economic and cultural role of the United States in contemporary globalization by suggesting that they simply reflect France's dissatisfaction with its status as a former great power. Yet similar expressions of concern can be found in other countries with very different histories from that of France. In Canada, for example, about 95 percent of all films that are shown are foreign, most of which are American-made, and 80 percent of the magazines distributed and read are also foreign, and again most of these originate in the United States.[44] Thus there has been a long-standing national conversation in Canada about the problems and indeed possible threats that close economic integration with the United States poses for the development and maintenance of a unique (English-) Canadian cultural identity.[45] As we shall see in the next sector, Canada has sought to protect its cultural industries even as it has sought to integrate its economy more closely with the U.S. economy, even to the point of becoming embroiled in an international legal dispute with the United States. In sum, concerns are widespread and may be growing that the Americanization of national cultures around the world may be an integral part, but also an unwelcome consequence, of the intensified globalization of the world economy.

National Reactions to Economic Globalization

To date, nations have pursued mostly unilateral responses to their enhanced integration with the world economy, and for the most part these policies have sought to embrace the new opportunities afforded by economic globalization. In some instances, however, countries have imposed unilateral constraints on external linkages or installed temporary pauses on their further integration into the world economy. In addition, in a number of areas, countries have sought to formulate collaborative responses to the challenges posed by economic globalization. Some of these cooperative endeavors among countries, as we shall see, aim at limiting the manner in which the countries so cooperating relate to the larger global economy. Other collaborative responses seek not to limit economic globalization but to shape it in such a way as to be somewhat less turbulent and less impervious to the social, economic, and political conditions and preferences of the countries that are participating in the globalization process.

Unilateral Responses to Economic Globalization

For the most part, countries have accepted that, in order to achieve the great benefits afforded by enhanced integration with the world economy, they

TIMELINE 7.1

Major Anti-globalization Demonstrations, 1994–2001

July 1994	Washington, D.C.: Annual meetings of IMF/World Bank
November–December 1999	Seattle: WTO ministerial meeting
September 2000	Prague: Annual meetings of IMF/World Bank
April 2001	Quebec City: Summit of the Americas
July 2001	Genoa: Group of Seven Summit

need to adapt to the constraints that such integration imposes on their freedom of choice. We will focus on how developing countries are affected by this issue in Chapter 8. Most of the advanced countries, however, have embraced globalization and are adapting to its requirements. Nevertheless, the advanced countries, too, show signs of backlash against globalization: these signs include mass demonstrations undertaken in the context of global economic meetings, modest governmental restrictions on global integration, "globalization fatigue" in the United States and Europe, and occasional U.S. policy unilateralism to fix the terms of globalization to meet American preferences.

Rise of Mass Protests against Globalization

One key sign of widespread social anxiety about economic globalization is the recent spate of mass protests, chronicled in Timeline 7.1, against globalization. These protests have occurred mostly in the advanced countries and have taken place alongside what used to be low-visibility international meetings on trade and finance.

As can be seen in the timeline, large street protests erupted in Washington in July 1994 during ceremonies marking the 50th anniversary of the founding of the IMF and the World Bank. However, the mass movement against globalization seized the world's attention most spectacularly in Seattle in late November and early December 1999. There, protests that drew 40,000 persons and brought about the arrests of about 600 individuals, disrupted a meeting of the WTO members' trade ministers, and appeared to contribute to the failure at that ministerial meeting to launch a new round of multilateral trade negotiations. (The launching had in fact been aborted well

before the meeting due to disputes between the United States and the EU
and between the developed and the developing countries.)[46] This debacle
was followed by additional protests against economic globalization in Prague
in September 2000, during the annual meeting of the IMF and the World
Bank. During those demonstrations, at least 100 protesters and police officers were injured.[47] More antiglobalization demonstrations took place in
Quebec City in April 2001, during the third Summit of the Americas, at
which 34 countries were laying the groundwork for the negotiation of the
Free Trade Agreement of the Americas. During these protests, involving
some 25,000 people, at least 130 people were arrested and several dozen
protesters and police officers were injured.[48] And then, in July 2001, came
Genoa, where some 200,000 people protested against globalization during
the G-7 annual summit; 280 protesters were arrested, 231 protesters and police officers were injured, and one protester was shot and killed by police.[49]

Modest National Restrictions on Global Integration

Governments, recognizing their citizens' increased anxieties about globalization, are taking modest steps to protect elements of their national economies
as they generally become more tightly connected to the global economy. We
have already noted the concerns expressed in France and Canada about imports of American cultural products: movies in the case of France and both
films and magazines in the case of Canada. France has responded to its worries about U.S. domination of the French movie and TV markets with a
range of unilateral measures and collaborative strategies (collaborative strategies will be discussed in the last section of this chapter). The French government has for years continued to maintain a quota on the import of U.S.
films into France, it prevents some American cable channels (including the
Cartoon Network) from being carried by French cable providers, and it has
required that radio stations that broadcast popular music ensure that 40 percent of that music be French. The French government also imposes a special tax on gross movie-theater receipts, producing a tax revenue of about
$150 million per year during the mid-1990s, which is then used together
with other government fiscal programs to subsidize the French film industry.[50]

In the same vein, the Canadian government has sought to protect the
Canadian magazine industry against its American competitors as a matter of
cultural security. Canada in 1995 sought to impose a special 80 percent
excise tax on advertising that was being placed on "split-run" magazines—that

is, foreign-origin magazines with local Canadian content and advertising added to them. At the time the tax was imposed, there was only one such "split-run" magazine: Time-Warner's *Sports Illustrated*. Canada's purpose in imposing the tax was to offset a structural advantage that would be enjoyed by American magazine producers who might undertake such split-run Canadian editions: U.S.-based magazines, because they largely if not entirely cover their production costs by virtue of their huge American subscription bases, would be able to sell space to Canadian advertisers for their Canadian runs at very low rates, and thereby would be able to lure a lot of Canadian advertisers who otherwise might have chosen to buy (more expensive) space in Canadian magazines. The result would be a reduction in support for Canadian magazines of all kinds, and thereby greater pressure on the maintenance of a unique Canadian culture. The United States challenged Canada's split-run tax (and related measures) under the auspices of the WTO dispute-settlement procedures and won its case in July 1997. Canada agreed to remove the split-run tax, but it has continued to express concerns that this practice might seriously harm Canada's independent magazine industry and thus the Canadian culture.[51]

Signs of American and European "Globalization Fatigue"

Elements of U.S. trade policy may reflect "globalization fatigue"—that is, a reaction to concerns about globalization that takes the form not of restricting existing international economic contacts, but of temporarily pausing the pursuit of higher levels of globalization.[52] For example, the decision of the U.S. Congress in 1997 not to grant President Bill Clinton the authority to negotiate the incorporation of Chile into the North American Free Trade Agreement may have been driven by a number of purely domestic political circumstances, but it also seemed to reflect a general wariness in Congress about the political utility of further trade liberalization in the wake of congressional passage of NAFTA in 1993 and the WTO accord of 1994. Even by mid-2001, President George W. Bush did not have, and seemed reluctant to press for, a congressionally authorized mandate for a new multilateral effort under the auspices of the WTO to promote world liberalization of trade.

In the same vein, official European concerns and reluctance at the end of the 1990s about further liberalization of trade in agricultural products, including genetically modified products, may be indicative of a political calculation by the EU members' governments that their respective home publics are not just worried about the health and safety issues surrounding such products, but are uneasy at the prospect of undertaking a big new push toward further trade liberalization and economic globalization. This fatigue regarding liberalization at the global level might be especially worrisome for the Western Europeans in light of their already ambitious regional agenda, which includes both EMU and the extension of EU membership to a number of former socialist countries in eastern and central Europe.

Accepting Globalization on One's Own Terms

Finally, we sometimes see efforts by the world's most powerful nations—particularly the United States—to impose conditions on the way in which they will interact with other nations in the new globalized economy. For example, the United States succeeded in the early 1990s in imposing changes in the manner in which Mexican and other foreign fishing firms could harvest tuna if they wanted access to the American market. The goal of the United States was to force foreign fishing fleets to use fishing nets that would reduce the number of dolphins unintentionally killed as the tuna were harvested, and to make the foreign fishing nets and techniques as dolphin-friendly as those required of American fishing fleets.[53] (It should be noted that the United States succeeded in imposing these changes in fishing techniques even though Mexico won a GATT case against the United States on the issue.) In the same vein, the United States has forced oil tankers registered under the flags of its trading partners to be equipped in such a way as to make intentional oil spills less likely.[54]

Similarly, in an effort to reduce the risk of bank failures in the face of more integrated world capital markets, the United States, after striking a bilateral deal with the United Kingdom, essentially compelled other major banking countries to impose on banks headquartered in their national jurisdictions U.S.-preferred minimum standards for capital reserves.[55] Finally, the United States and, in some instances, the member states of the EU have made the extension by them of preferential trading arrangements to developing countries conditioned on improved worker rights and working conditions in those countries.[56]

Collaborative Responses to Globalization

In addition to the unilateral measures just described, countries seek to use collaborative approaches to the problems posed by economic globalization.

Collaboration as a Shield

Some collaborative efforts seek to limit the exposure of countries to the forces of globalization. For example, as part of its protection of French culture, in 1989 the French government persuaded its partners in what was then the European Economic Community (now the EU) to put into place a quota system for the importation of audiovisual products. According to a 1989 European Community directive, all European TV channels were required to have a minimum of 50 percent European-content programming (France, as noted earlier, pursues a higher, 60 percent European-content level for French broadcasting, and 40 percent of the total must be of French origin). Moreover, the French government was successful in persuading its EU partners to reject U.S. efforts at the end of the GATT-sponsored Uruguay round of trade negotiations in 1994 to liberalize trade in the motion-picture industry.[57]

Similarly, the United States and, to some degree, its EU partners, have sought in recent years to link worker rights and working conditions to trade liberalization under the auspices of GATT and its successor, the WTO.[58] To date the United States has been modest both in its diplomatic goals and its achievements in this area. At the end of the Uruguay round in 1994, for example, it called for acknowledgment of the substantive linkage between the issues of trade and labor. Together with the EU, the United States also pressed its trading partners at the controversial Seattle WTO ministerial meeting in 1999 to agree to establish a working party on labor issues that would be jointly managed by the WTO and the International Labor Organization (ILO). Both efforts met with little success and contributed in some measure to the failure of the Seattle meeting to lay the groundwork for the inauguration of a new multilateral WTO trade round.

The problem, from the viewpoint of such developing countries as Brazil and especially India, is that this U.S.-EU interest in talking about labor standards in the framework of trade liberalization is patently protectionist. Indeed, what the emerging countries most fear is that the U.S. government will introduce onto the WTO-ILO agenda an issue that has been promoted in Washington for many years by American labor unions and nongovernmental organizations concerned about foreign labor standards and practices: the idea of including some form of *social clause* in future WTO trade-liberalization agreements. Such a clause would permit WTO members to withdraw trade concessions and perhaps even impose trade sanctions against WTO partners that were found not to be faithfully implementing core international labor standards as posited in a number of ILO conventions.

From the viewpoint of many developing countries, the social-clause route would entail an unfair imposition of foreign standards on their domestic labor systems, with a possible resulting loss in comparative advantage. Equally unacceptable, it would also constitute a serious and, from their viewpoint, unwarranted infringement on the sovereign rights of these countries to address their labor problems in ways that acknowledge their less-developed status. In the end, from the perspective of developing countries, a social clause would allow developed countries to pursue under the auspices of the WTO, protectionism *against* them rather than liberalization *with* them.

Collaboration and the Management of Globalization

While the European Community's broadcasting directive and the U.S. interest in worker rights might be viewed as collaborative efforts to restrict globalization, other collaborative efforts seem quite clearly not to have this intent. They seem aimed at managing globalization without curtailing it. For example, in the wake of the Asian, Russian, and Brazilian financial crises at the end of the 1990s, the United States, Europe, and Japan worked with their partners in the IMF to develop new policy mechanisms aimed at reducing the incidence and severity of such crises in the future. This IMF-based effort at developing a "new international financial architecture" recommended in October 1998 a number of steps directed toward mitigating the risk and severity of currency and financial crises. Among the proposals, the IMF partners urged emerging-market governments to provide more information on a timely basis about their national economic circumstances (such as their total foreign liabilities and foreign-currency reserve levels), and to develop stronger regulatory institutions for their banking sectors. The IMF members also urged private creditors from the industrialized countries to develop new lending practices whereby they would work together to forestall panicked selling of emerging-market assets in the face of temporary market turbulence. Finally, they proposed a number of collaborative actions that the IMF members might undertake to be better prepared to limit financial crises and their contagion in the future.[59]

Conclusion

Economic globalization is among the most powerful forces shaping our contemporary world. It is affecting in profound ways what we consume, how and where we conduct business, how we marshal and employ savings, and how we communicate with one another. It is changing the structure of many societies, creating vast new opportunities for some and wrenching, terrifying dislocations for others.

Although globalization is making it easier for individuals to become more aware of cultures in far-off lands, it may also be creating for some individuals a sense of loss of their long-held values and ways of life. Globalization makes autarky more and more costly and less and less plausible for a nation in the modern world, but it also creates tighter and tighter constraints on the autonomy of those national communities that choose to participate in the global economy. Indeed, contemporary globalization draws into sharp relief the age-old tension that market society presents to its participants: freer markets present opportunities for new growth, new achievement, new wealth, new consumption, and higher welfare, but they also raise new risks for booms and busts, intensify the problem of greater efficiency co-existing with greater inequality, and give new weight to the question of whether the choice in favor of markets and international intercourse might undermine a community's sense of cultural coherence and social solidarity.

Whether and how societies in both the industrialized nations and the emerging-market countries manage the tensions that are produced by intensified economic interactions will surely determine the scope and sustainability of economic globalization, and thus the shape and texture of the social world in which we will live in the years to come.

Notes

[1]On the question of the relative level of current global integration, see Paul Krugman, "Growing World Trade: Causes and Consequences," *Brookings Papers on Economic Activity* 1 (1995), p. 3; for other helpful discussions that place contemporary globalization in historical perspective, see International Monetary Fund (IMF), *World Economic Outlook, May 1997: A Survey by the Staff of the International Monetary Fund* (Washington, D.C.: IMF, May 1997), pp. 112–16, available at www.imf.org/external/pubs/WEOMAY/Weocon.htm; Douglas A. Irwin, "The United States in a New Global Economy? A Century's Perspective," *American Economic Review* 86 (May 1996), pp. 41–46; Dani Rodrik, *Has Globalization Gone Too Far?* (Washington,

D.C.: Institute for International Economics, 1997), pp. 7–9; Richard E. Baldwin and Philippe Martin, "Two Waves of Globalization: Superficial Similarities, Fundamental Differences," National Bureau of Economic Research (NBER) working paper series, 6904 (January 1999), available at www.nber.org/papers/w6904; and Michael D. Bordo, Barry Eichengreen, and Douglas A. Irwin, "Is Globalization Today Really Different Than Globalization a Hundred Years Ago?" NBER working paper 7195 (June 1999), p. 6, available at www.nber.org/papers/w7195.

[2]Angus Maddison, who compiled the data presented in Essential Economics 7.1, has cautioned that, because export prices have increased over time at a slower rate than overall prices in most countries, the export-GDP ratios are lower when expressed in constant prices in the earlier years than they are when expressed in current prices. See Angus Maddison, *The World Economy: A Millennial Perspective* (Paris: Organization for Economic Corporation and Development, 2001), p. 363. However, in a separate study Maddison, by looking at arithmetic averages of the export-GDP ratios of 12 European industrialized countries, suggests that, in general, trade integration when measured in current prices does appear to be higher in recent years than it was during the Golden Era. See Angus Maddison, "The Nature and Functioning of European Capitalism: A Historical and Comparative Perspective," *BNL Quarterly Review*, No. 203 (December 1997), p. 471.

[3]On the utility of focusing on the ratio of merchandise exports to merchandise value-added as an indicator of trade integration, see Robert C. Feenstra, "Integration of Trade and Disintegration of Production in the Global Economy," *Journal of Economic Perspectives* 12 (Fall 1998), pp. 33–35; Irwin, "United States in a New Global Economy?" p. 42; Bordo, Eichengreen, and Irwin, "Globalization Today," p. 7; and Nicholas Crafts, *Globalization and Growth in the Twentieth Century*, IMF working paper WP/00/44 (March 2000), p. 26, available at www.imf.org/external/pubs/ft/wp/2000/wp0044.pdf.

[4]Council of Economic Advisers (CEA), *Economic Report of the President 2000* (Washington, DC: U.S. Government Printing Office, 2000), p. 203; also see Bordo, Eichengreen, and Irwin, "Globalization Today," pp. 10–11.

[5]Krugman, "Growing World Trade," p. 5.

[6]Feenstra, "Integration of Trade," p. 37.

[7]CEA, *Economic Report of the President 2000*, p. 205.

[8]CEA, *Economic Report of the President 2000*, p. 205.

[9]CEA, *Economic Report of the President 1999* (Washington, DC: U.S. Government Printing Office, 1999), p. 224.

[10]For important discussions of the structures and operations of multinational enterprises, see Michael E. Porter, *The Competitive Advantage of Nations* (New York: Free Press, 1998); and Paul Doremus, William Keller, Louis Pauly, and Simon Reich, *The Myth of the Global Corporation* (Princeton: Princeton University Press, 1998).

[11]CEA, *Economic Report of the President 2000*, p. 206.

[12]Bordo, Eichengreen, and Irwin, "Globalization Today," p. 62.

[13]For a helpful discussion of the economic rationale for this measure, see Maurice Obstfeld and Alan M. Taylor, "The Great Depression as a Watershed: International Capital Mobility over the Long Run," in Michael D. Bordo, Claudia Goldin, and Eugene N. White, *The Defining Moment: The Great Depression and the American Economy in the Twentieth Century* (Chicago: University of Chicago Press, 1998), p. 357.

[14]For additional discussion of this finding, see Obstfeld and Taylor, "International Global

Mobility over the Long Run," p. 358. See also Maurice Obstfeld, "The Global Capital Market: Benefactor or Menace?" *Journal of Economic Perspectives* 12 (Fall 1998), pp. 11–12; also see IMF, *World Economic Outlook, May 1997,* p. 114.

[15]The ten countries covered by the Obstfeld and Taylor data set are Australia, Belgium, Canada, France, Germany, Italy, the Netherlands, Sweden, the United Kingdom, and the United States. In a few instances, one or another country is not included in a period. For a discussion of their data procedures and their results, see Obstfeld and Taylor, "International Capital Mobility," pp. 363–66. For a comparable graphical analysis of changes in the dispersion of real returns, see IMF, *World Economic Outlook, May 1997,* pp. 14–115.

[16]For similar assessments, see Obstfeld and Taylor, "International Capital Mobility," pp. 363–64; and IMF, *World Economic Outlook, May 1997,* pp. 115–16.

[17]Bordo, Eichengreen, and Irwin, "Globalization Today," p. 16.

[18]CEA, *Economic Report of the President 2000,* p. 209; and Bordo, Eichengreen, and Irwin, "Globalization Today," p. 17.

[19]CEA, *Economic Report of the President 2000,* pp. 209–10.

[20]On the manner in which MNEs have learned how to use advanced technology to manage their worldwide business operations, see Wolfgang H. Reinicke, *Global Public Policy: Governing without Government?* (Washington: Brookings Institution Press, 1998), pp. 15–18.

[21]CEA, *Economic Report of the President 2000,* p. 212.

[22]John Gerard Ruggie, "International Regimes, Transactions, and Change: Embedded Liberalism in the Postwar Economic Order," in Stephen Krasner, ed., *International Regimes* (Ithaca: Cornell University Press, 1983), pp. 195–232.

[23]See Kenneth N. Waltz, *Theory of International Politics* (Reading: Addison-Wesley, 1979), pp. 70–71.

[24]Thomas L. Friedman, *The Lexus and the Olive Tree* (New York: Farrar, Straus and Giroux, 1999), p. 197; also see pp. 195–96.

[25]Friedman, *Lexus and Oliver Tree,* p. 198. For empirical evidence in support of the view that growing economic interdependence, see John Oneal and Bruce Russett, "The Classical Liberals Were Right: Democracy, Interdependence, and Conflict, 1950–1985," *International Studies Quarterly* 41 (June 1997), pp. 267–94; and John Oneal and Bruce Russett, "Assessing the Liberal Peace with Alternative Specifications: Trade Still Reduces Conflict," *Journal of Peace Research* 36 (July 1999). For a comprehensive scholarly treatment of this subject, see Bruce Russett and John Oneal, *Triangulating Peace: Democracy, Interdependence, and International Organizations* (New York: W. W. Norton & Co., 2001).

[26]See, for example, Kenneth N. Waltz, "The Myth of National Interdependence," in Charles P. Kindleberger, ed., *The International Corporation: A Symposium* (Cambridge: MIT Press 1970), pp. 205–23; Kenneth W. Waltz, "Globalization and Governance," *PS: Political Science & Politics* 32 (December 1999); and Katherine Barbieri, "Economic Interdependence: A Path to Peace or a Source of Interstate Conflict?" *Journal of Peace Research* 33 (February 1996), pp. 29–50.

[27]Albert O. Hirschman, *National Power and the Structure of Foreign Trade* (Berkeley: University of California Press, 1945), p. 14.

[28]Christopher Gelpi and Joseph M. Grieco, "Democracy, Trade, and the Nature of the Liberal Peace," paper delivered at the annual meeting of the American Political Science Association, San Francisco, CA, September 2001, available at www.duke.edu/~/gelpi/liberalpeace.doc.

[29]Friedman, *Lexus and Olive Tree*, p. 11.

[30]I. Jeanne Dugan, "More Losses Reported in Fund Collapse," *Washington Post*, September 26, 1998, p. C1.

[31]See "Statement by William J. McDonough, President, Federal Reserve Bank of New York," Committee on Banking and Financial Services, U.S. House of Representatives, October 1, 1998, available at www.house.gov/financialservices/3399mcdo.htm. Also see William Lewis, Richard Waters, and Tracy Corrigan, "$3.5bn Bail-Out for Hedge Fund," *Financial Times*, September 4, 1998, p. 1.

[32]See "Statement by Alan Greenspan, Chairman, Board of Governors of the Federal Reserve System," Committee on Banking and Financial Services, U.S. House of Representatives, October 1, 1998, p. 1, available at www.house.gov/financialservices/10198gre.htm.

[33]For a theoretical analysis of this differential response of Europe and America to economic globalization, see Krugman, "Growing World Trade," pp. 14–19.

[34]Baldwin and Martin, "Two Waves of Globalization," p. 20.

[35]International Monetary Fund, *World Economic Outlook, October 1999* (Washington, DC: IMF, 1999), p. 72, available at www.imf.org/external/pubs/ft/weo/1999/02/index.htm.

[36]Baldwin and Martin, "Two Waves of Globalization," p. 21.

[37]Rodrik, *Has Globalization Gone Too Far?* p. 17.

[38]Feenstra, "Integration of Trade," pp. 41–42.

[39]Rodrik, *Has Globalization Gone Too Far?* pp. 16–25.

[40]Daniel W. Drezner, "Bottom Feeders," *Foreign Policy*, No. 122 (November–December 2000), pp. 64–70.

[41]Friedman, *Lexus and Olive Tree*, pp. 233, 309.

[42]Tyler Cowen, "French Kiss-Off, *Reason* 30 (July 1998), p. 1. See also Mel van Elteren, "GATT and Beyond: World Trade, the Arts, and American Popular Culture in Western Europe," *Journal of American Culture* 19 (Fall 1996), pp. 59–73; and Bill Grantham, "America the Menace: France's Feud with Hollywood," *World Policy Journal* 15 (Summer 1998).

[43]"Culture Wars," *Economist*, September 12, 1998, p. 1.

[44]"Culture Wars," p. 2.

[45]For a helpful overview, see William Watson, *Globalization and the Meaning of Canadian Life* (Toronto: University of Toronto Press, 1998).

[46]"The Non-Governmental Order," *Economist*, December 11, 1999; and "The Siege of Seattle," *Financial Times*, December 13, 1999.

[47]See "Bloody Riots Outside IMF Summit in Prague," United Press International Newswire, September 27, 2000; and "Prague Riots a Turning Point for IMF Meetings," United Press International newswire, September 29, 2000.

[48]See "A Cautious Yes to Pan-American Trade," *Economist*, April 28, 1991; and "Smoke Signals: Tear Gas, Protest, and Trade Differences Filled the Air in Quebec City," *Time International*, April 30, 2001.

[49]See James Blitz, "Italy Defends Genoa Police Operation," *Financial Times*, July 23, 2001; and "Italy Under Fire for Police Behavior at G8," Reuters newswire, July 26, 2001.

[50]Cowen, "French Kiss-Off," pp. 6–8; and van Elteren, "GATT and Beyond," p. 1.

[51]See World Trade Organization, "Canada—Certain Measures Concerning Periodicals: Report of the Panel," WTO Document WT/DS31/R, available at www.wto.org; Marci McDonald,

"Menacing Magazines," *Maclean's*, March 24, 1997; and John Urquhart and Bhushan Bahree, "WTO Orders Canada to Drop Magazine Rule," *Wall Street Journal*, July 1, 1997, p. B8.

[52]I. M. Destler, a long-time student of U.S. trade politics, suggested at the end of the 1990s that U.S. trade policy was "on hold." See T. M. Destler, "Trade Policy at a Cross Roads," *Brookings Review* (Winter 1999), pp. 26–30.

[53]Thomas E. Skilton, "GATT and the Environment in Conflict: The Tuna-Dolphin Dispute and the Quest for an International Conservation Strategy," *Cornell International Law Journal* 26 (1993): 455–94.

[54]Ronald Mitchell, "Intentional Oil Pollution of the Oceans," in Peter M. Haas, Robert O. Keohane, and Marc A. Levy, eds., *Institutions for the Earth: Sources of Effective International Environmental Protection* (Cambridge: MIT Press, 1993), pp. 183–247.

[55]Ethan B. Kapstein, "Between Power and Purpose: Central Bankers and the Politics of Regulatory Convergence," in *International Organization* 46 (Winter 1992; special issue edited by Peter M. Haas), pp. 265–88.

[56]Virginia A. Leary, "Workers' Rights and International Trade: The Social Clause," in Jagdish Bhagwati and Robert E. Hudec, eds., *Fair Trade and Harmonization: Prerequisites for Free Trade?* Vol. 2, *Legal Analysis* (Cambridge: MIT Press, 1996), pp. 210–14.

[57]See van Elteren, "GATT and Beyond," pp. 1–2.

[58]See Leary, "Workers' Rights and International Trade"; and Eddy Lee, "Globalization and Labor Standards: A Review of Issues," *International Labor Review* 136 (1997).

[59]For a helpful overview of these and other proposals relating to the construction of a "new international financial architecture," see CEA, *Economic Report of the President 1999*, pp. 267–305.

Chapter 8

Developing Nations and the World Economy

Introduction

OBJECTIVES

- Develop an appreciation for the great variation among developing countries in terms of the achievement of economic progress during the past half-century.
- Understand the wide range of international economic linkages that exist between developing and transitional economies and the international economy, focusing on trade, investment, and official assistance.
- Explore the key policy controversies that surround each type of linkage between developing countries and the world economy.

During much of the Cold War, from the early 1950s through the early 1980s, observers of world affairs often spoke of three distinct groups of nations on the international scene: the "First World" was composed of the advanced industrialized democracies; the "Second World" comprised the Soviet Union and its communist "satellite" states in Eastern Europe, as well as Cuba, China, North Korea, and North Vietnam; and the "Third World" consisted of the countries that had attained independence only after World War II (in particular, the new states in Asia and Africa) and those that had been independent for some time but were still relatively poor (including the nations of Central and South America, most of the Middle Eastern countries, Turkey, and Iran).

The military intervention by the Soviet Union in Czechoslovakia in 1968, the armed clashes between the Soviet Union and China in 1969, and the strategic rapprochement between China and the United States in the early 1970s shattered any lingering sense of a distinct, unified communist world, and the collapse of the Warsaw Pact in 1989 and of the Soviet Union itself in 1991 definitively ended the Second World. Most of the countries that used to be a part of the communist world are now at various stages of transition to market economies; almost all are busily seeking to become integrated into the world economy. These states are often viewed as one type of developing country.

The Third World, or, in today's terminology, the "developing world" and its "emerging economies," has experienced equally dramatic change during the last three decades. Some formerly developing countries, particularly South Korea, Singapore, and Taiwan, have effectively attained First World standards of national economic activity and per capita income. Other developing nations, most notably China, but also such countries as Thailand and Malaysia, have enjoyed remarkable rates of economic growth and may in time converge economically with the industrialized countries. Still others, many of which are in Latin America, have grown economically in absolute terms in recent decades, but have not made any relative progress in terms of per capita income. Finally, a distressing number of developing countries (heavily concentrated in Africa) have actually experienced declines in real economic growth on a per capita basis and have in recent decades fallen further behind the developed world in the economic domain.

Why do we see this spectacular success in much of East Asia, stagnation in large parts in Latin America, and actual economic deterioration throughout wide swaths of sub-Saharan Africa? What can be done to improve the prospects of the hundreds of millions of people who, this very day, live without adequate food or shelter, and without hope that their children will lead a better life? Are there opportunities associated with the international economy that can help poor countries become richer, or are there operations associated with it that typically keep down those who are on the lower economic rungs of the international community? Do international economic institutions such as the World Bank and the International Monetary Fund (IMF), which are supposed to help developing countries, actually hurt their prospects for sustained economic growth and social and political progress?

These are the questions that we address in this chapter. We will see that, from both a practical and a moral viewpoint, few questions are as important—or as controversial.

Economic Experiences Among Developing Countries

To gain a sense of the remarkable diversity of economic experiences among groups of developing countries, look at Essential Economics 8.1, which reports levels of per capita income for different groups of countries in 1970, 1985, and 1998. These per capita income levels are expressed in dollars and employ *purchasing-power-parity* **(PPP)** conversion rates to permit us to compare the capacity of individuals in different countries to purchase a similar basket of goods. Also reported in the figure are the average growth rates in income per capita enjoyed by countries in various groupings between 1970 and 1998. These figures show that, although developing countries in East Asia surged economically during the latter three decades of the twentieth century, countries in South Asia moved forward very slowly, those in the Americas and the Middle East and Europe basically stood still, and those in Africa suffered a serious negative trend in real economic growth.

Following the lead of a recent report published by the IMF, we can also obtain a sense of the tremendous diversity of historical experiences of different groups of developing countries in the world economy by examining the degree to which these different groups, as well as particular countries, have converged with what the IMF has termed the "leading country" in the world economy during a particular period of time. Essential Economics 8.2 provides such a perspective on economic convergence from 1870 to 2000. For the purposes of comparison, the United Kingdom is classified as the leading country in the world economy in 1870 and 1900, and the United States is designated as the leading country thereafter.

Several key points can be derived from Essential Economics 8.2. First, the greatest economic success story in modern history is that of Japan, whose gross domestic product (GDP) per capita went from one-fourth of that of the United States in 1913 to three-quarters of the U.S. level in 2000. Second, China is a country that is now on the move: after experiencing relative decline from 1870 to 1950, and after making almost no relative progress for more than two decades, China's per capita income between 1973 and 2000 surged from about 7 percent to 23 percent of that of the United States.

Per Capita Income, Developed and Developing Countries, 1970–98

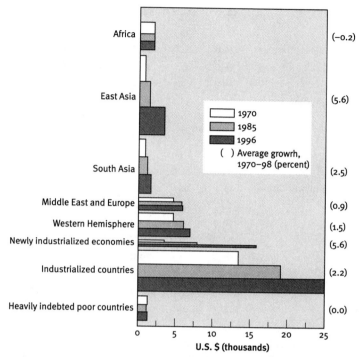

Notes: Figures use purchasing-power-parity conversion rates. Thickness of the bars varies by the population of the regional or country grouping.

Source: International Monetary Fund, *World Economic Outlook May 2000* (Washington, DC: IMF, May 2001), p. 113, available at www.imf.org/external/pubs/ft/weo/2000/01/pdf/chapter4.pdf.

Core Principle

Economic growth varies across the developing world. As can be observed in this figure, although developing countries in East Asia surged economically during the latter three decades of the twentieth century, countries in South Asia moved forward very slowly, those in the Americas, the Middle East, and Europe basically stood still, and those in Africa suffered a serious downward trend in real economic growth.

✳ ESSENTIAL ECONOMICS 8.2

GDP Per Capita as a Percentage of Leading Country's GDP, 1870–2000

	1870	1900	1913	1950	1973	2000
Western Europe	64.7	67.3	69.8	53.5	74.0	74.1
Areas of recent European settlement	74.8	87.6	98.7	96.7	96.8	96.5
Southern Europe (including Turkey)	34.0	34.2	33.0	21.1	36.2	36.1
Eastern Europe	33.3	29.9	31.9	27.5	34.6	15.5
Eastern Europe (excluding Soviet Union/Russia)	35.9	35.1	38.2	23.9	30.9	13.3
Soviet Union/Russia	31.4	26.5	28.0	29.6	36.5	16.6
Latin America	23.3	23.4	27.1	26.0	26.4	20.1
Asia	17.8	14.8	14.0	8.0	10.8	15.9
Asia (excluding Japan and China)	19.0	14.4	13.7	7.8	8.6	8.3
Japan	22.7	24.7	25.1	19.6	66.3	75.6
China	16.0	14.2	13.0	6.4	7.1	23.0
Africa	14.7	10.9	10.8	8.7	7.9	4.8
World	27.4	27.5	29.0	22.3	24.8	21.9
GDP per capita						
United Kingdom	3,263	4,593	5,032	6,847	11,992	19,704
United States	2,457	4,096	5,307	9,573	16,607	27,272

Notes: Leading country is the United Kingdom for 1870–1900, the United States for 1913–2000. "Areas of recent European settlement" is the IMF designation for Australia, Canada, New Zealand, and the United States. GDP per capita is given in 1990 purchasing-power-parity dollars.

Sources: International Monetary Fund, *World Economic Outlook May 2000* (Washington, DC: IMF, 2000), p. 160, available at www.imf.org/external/pubs/ft/weo/2000/01/pdf/chapter4.pdf. The IMF reports that the data up to 1973 are from Angus Maddison, *Monitoring the World Economy 1820–1992* (Paris: Organization for Economic Cooperation and Development, 1995).

Core Principle

In the past 50 years, most East Asian countries have made notable progress toward converging industrialized nations, while Latin America and Africa have lagged further behind.

MAP 8.1

Relationship between per capita income and Individual Life Expectancy, 1999

(a) GNP per capita, 1999

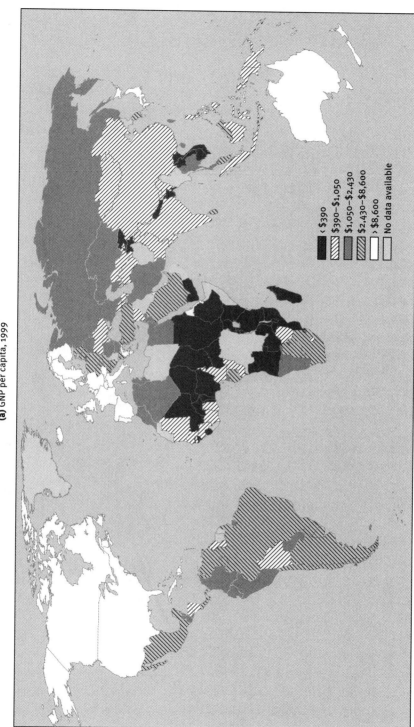

Note: Per capita GNP is expressed in current dollars using the World Bank Atlas method.

Source: World Bank, *World Development Indicators 2001*, CD-ROM (Washington, DC: World Bank, 2001).

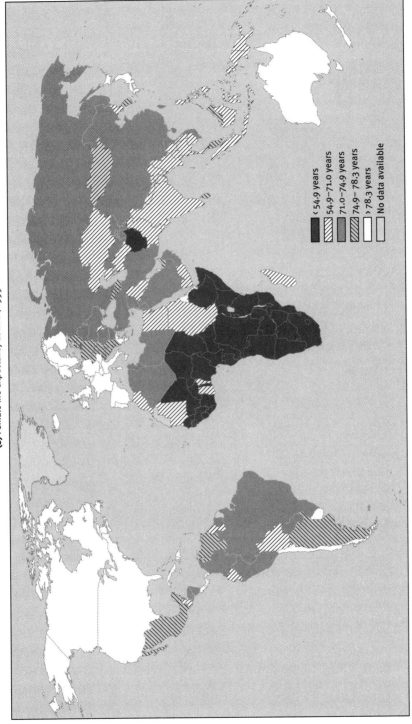

(b) Female life expectancy at birth, 1999

< 54.9 years

54.9–71.0 years

71.0–74.9 years

74.9–78.3 years

> 78.3 years

No data available

Core Principle

A country's level of economic activity is likely to be a strong determinant of the basic welfare and life opportunities of the country's residents, including the opportunity to enjoy an extended lifetime. These maps show a strong correlation between per capita GNP, presented in panel (a), and the life expectancy of females in those countries, presented in panel (b).

Third, the countries of Latin America made only a small gain in relative per capita income between 1870 and 1913, after which they essentially stood still economically for 60 years; since 1973 Latin American nations have experienced a decline in income relative to that of the United States. Fourth, we can see in the table the slow, steady relative decline of the former Soviet Union and its Eastern European satellite states during the last quarter of the twentieth century, a decline that contributed to the collapse of the Soviet empire. Fifth, African countries in 1950 were, on average, not very far behind China relative to U.S. per capita income. Yet, whereas China has made gains relative to the United States in recent years, per capita incomes in the nations of Africa have fallen further behind, dropping on average from about 9 percent of the U.S. per capita income level in 1950, to about 8 percent in 1973, to about 5 percent in 2000.

In sum, judging from both Essential Economics 8.1 and 8.2, over the past 50 years, many East Asian countries have made remarkable progress in converging economically with the advanced industrialized nations, and in some cases have actually done so, and China has been making serious progress in catching up with the industrialized world. Countries in Latin America have essentially stood still economically or have even fallen behind. Finally, the bulk of the African states have experienced serious, sustained declines in terms of both absolute economic activity and relative economic performance. Fabulous success and tragic failure are then the hallmarks of different countries in the developing world, with profound implications for the residents of those countries. One of the most serious implications of low per capita income is a markedly reduced life expectancy, particularly for women. Map 8.1 illustrates this extraordinarily close relationship between national income per capita and life expectancy of females. Understanding the sources of the former in order to reverse the latter constitutes both a practical and a moral imperative for all of us, and it is in search of that understanding that we now direct our efforts.

Developing Nations and International Trade

Does international trade help or hamper the growth prospects of developing countries? To address that question, it is first necessary to appreciate the diversity in experiences of major groups of developing countries.

Developing Country Experiences with Trade

The diversity of developing country experiences in the international trading system can be observed in Essential Economics 8.3, which provides information on the origins and magnitudes of exports by countries and groups of countries in different parts of the world during the second half of the twentieth century. Once more we can see the rise of East Asia since World War II: although the countries in that region originated, as a group, only about 15 percent of total world exports as late as 1973, they were the source of more than one-fourth of all exports by the end of the 1990s. Especially spectacular has been the performance of what the World Trade Organization (WTO) calls the "six East Asian traders" (Hong Kong, Malaysia, South Korea, Singapore, Taiwan, and Thailand): their combined share of world exports jumped from a little more than 3 percent to 10 percent in only 26 years! The countries of Latin America have gradually lost world market share in exports. Moving to Eastern Europe, as with their share of leading-country income, the trade performance of the then-socialist countries stagnated and then steadily lost ground during the 1970s and 1980s. The countries of Africa, again, present the most disturbing performance record: although they were the source of 6 percent to 7 percent of world exports from the late 1940s through the early 1960s, their share had dropped to the range of 2 percent by the end of the 1990s.

In the preceding section we observed that although several countries in East Asia have made great progress in achieving increases in per capita income, many in Latin America have stood still while many in Africa, and especially in sub-saharan Africa, have suffered declines. Now we are observing that this domestic economic performance closely matches the external commercial performance of these countries, raising the key question of whether trade plays a role in fostering national economic growth.

✳ ESSENTIAL ECONOMICS 8.3

Value of World Exports and Share of World Exports, 1948–99

	1948	1953	1963	1973	1983	1993	1999
Value							
World	58.0	83.0	157.0	578.0	1,835.0	3,639.0	5,473.0
Share							
World	100.0	100.0	100.0	100.0	100.0	100.0	100.0
North America	27.5	24.6	19.4	17.2	15.4	16.8	17.1
Latin America	12.3	10.5	7.0	4.7	5.8	4.4	5.4
Western Europe	31.0	34.9	41.0	44.8	39.0	43.7	43.0
Central and Eastern Europe and former Soviet Union	6.0	8.2	11.0	8.9	9.5	2.9	3.9
Africa	7.4	6.5	5.7	4.8	4.4	2.5	2.0
Middle East	2.1	2.1	3.3	4.5	6.8	3.4	3.1
Asia	13.8	13.2	12.6	15.0	19.1	26.3	25.5
Japan	0.4	1.5	3.5	6.4	8.0	10.0	7.7
China	0.9	1.4	1.3	1.0	1.2	2.5	3.6
Australia and New Zealand	3.7	3.2	2.4	2.1	1.4	1.5	1.3
Six East Asian traders	3.0	2.6	2.4	3.4	5.8	9.7	10.0
Other Asia	5.8	4.5	3.1	2.1	2.7	2.6	3.0
GATT/WTO Members	60.4	68.7	72.8	81.8	76.0	86.9	89.7

Note: Export values are in billions of U.S. dollars. All other figures are percentages of total world exports.

Source: World Trade Organization, *International Trade Statistics 2000* (Geneva: WTO, 2000), p. 28, available at www.wto.org/english/res_e/statis_e/stats2000_e.pdf.

Core Principle

The diversity of developing nations' experiences can be observed in the magnitudes of their exports. East Asian countries have experienced the most growth in the past 50 years whereas Latin American trade has stagnated and Africa's share of world exports has declined.

Policies and Ideas about Trade and Development

Does trade openness produce economic development and does autarky impede development? Since World War II, academic debates and policy efforts by developing countries have moved through at least four phases on this question.

The 1940s and 1950s: Export Pessimism and Import-Substituting Industrialization

In the decade after World War II, many developing-country governments, professional economists, and developed-country governments came to the view that trade integration was hampering the growth prospects of many developing nations.[1] Most of the newly independent nations of Asia and Africa, and to a large extent the more established but still relatively poor nations of Latin America, possessed a comparative advantage in primary products, such as oil, copper and other minerals, and cotton and other unprocessed agricultural products. But by midcentury, seeking to fuel growth by exporting such goods in exchange for consumer or capital goods seemed to be infeasible on a number of grounds. First, as a consequence of technological innovations that either made more efficient use of primary products or yielded substitutes for them, demand in the developed countries for primary products was growing very slowly, and primary-product prices appeared to be facing a long, downward trend. Second, prices for manufactured exports from developed countries appeared to be on an upward trajectory. Third, given this "export pessimism," developing countries were experiencing a deterioration in their terms of trade with developed countries and needed as a result to export larger and larger volumes of their primary goods to obtain a given volume of developed-country manufactured goods. Fourth, analysts and governments believed that the *infant-industry argument* (introduced in Chapter 2) might hold true for developing countries: because established foreign producers had such massive advantages against any new domestic entrant in a developing country, continuing openness to trade on the part of developing countries meant that otherwise potentially successful domestic producers would not try to enter the market, thus denying the country important mechanisms for growth.

Given this line of analysis, by the mid-1950s, many developing countries sought to implement a strategy of *import-substituting industrialization (ISI)*. According to this strategy, a developing-country government would temporarily restrict imports of manufactured goods, subsidize local private and state-owned firms that were or could become local producers of such goods, and, by so compelling a substitution of local for foreign products, promote the rapid industrialization and long-term growth of the country. The goal of this strategy was, after a period of such protection, to make national producers competitive with foreign suppliers at least in some lines of production, and therefore in time to use the protection of such local firms and reintegrate the country into the world economy on more favorable terms.

The 1960s and 1970s: The Failure of ISI and the Emergence of the Export-Led Growth Strategy

Many developing countries, including Brazil, Mexico, India, Egypt, and Turkey, sought to implement ISI strategies during the 1950s, 1960s, and even the 1970s. These countries might have had grounds to believe that their domestic markets were sufficiently large that, if national firms were protected for some period of time, they might someday be able to stand against international competitors. Quite interestingly, however, a number of small countries also sought to implement ISI strategies, including some that would become in later years the great export machines of the developing world, such as South Korea and even Taiwan.

For some years after their initiation, ISI strategies appeared to deliver good rates of national economic growth for several of the countries noted above. However, enjoying as they did protection from international competition, as well as subsidized credit and privileged access to foreign exchange, local firms in these countries had little incentive to become efficient producers; instead they became increasingly inefficient. Hence, after a few good years characterized by a burst of industrial activity behind the new import restrictions, many of these countries found that their national growth rates began to stagnate. Furthermore, because local producers were voracious users of foreign exchange, these countries soon faced serious balance-of-payments problems.

In response to these problems, Taiwan in the late 1950s, and South Korea in the early 1960s (the latter under some pressure from the United States) turned away from import substitution and moved toward a strategy of *export-led growth (ELG)*. Through such a strategy, import restrictions and other policy-induced biases in favor of production solely for the local market were reduced, and in fact producers oriented to export markets came to be favored by preferential access to credit and foreign exchange. Singapore, which entertained ideas of pursuing an ISI strategy while it was part of the newly independent Malaysia, realized after its formal merger with Malaysia failed in 1965 that as an independent city-state it could not pursue ISI, and instead it turned to ELG. Hong Kong, as a British colony, never considered ISI to be feasible and moved rapidly after World War II toward ELG. Hence, by the mid-1960s, the four "Asian tigers" (Taiwan, South Korea, Singapore, and Hong Kong) were all committed to ELG and began to achieve the growth in both exports and national income depicted in Essential Economics 8.1 and 8.2. By the 1970s, these countries had been joined in the pursuit of ELG by such countries as Thailand, Malaysia, and, most notably, China; by the 1980s it was clear that East Asia was enjoying an economic miracle of growth and development.

The 1980s to the Present: The "Washington Consensus" and New Thoughts about Trade

Brazil, Mexico, Turkey, and India persisted with ISI through the 1970s. Yet Turkey, facing extremely serious balance-of-payments problems arising from the incapacity of its ISI-based economy to adjust to the two major oil crises of the 1970s, shifted course in 1980 and began to pursue a strategy of ELG. Brazil and Mexico also faced increasingly serious debt problems during the 1970s and early 1980s, and both turned to a more open economic strategy in the late 1980s and early 1990s. India, also experiencing persistent payments problems, finally turned toward domestic and external liberalization in 1991.

Thus, by the late 1980s and early 1990s, these large developing countries seemed to be adhering to what came to be called the ***Washington consensus,*** a new view about development that was being pressed by the U.S. government and by the major international financial institutions, the IMF and the World Bank (both of which are headquartered in Washington, D.C.).[2] In general terms, the Washington consensus advocated that, to achieve sustainable growth, countries should pursue macroeconomic stability, rely on private enterprise rather than state-owned firms, and reduce barriers to trade and investment and thus allow international market forces to direct the country to the most efficient employment of its human and natural resources.

By the close of the 1990s, the Washington consensus appeared to be widely accepted in the international development community as the best overall approach to sustained rapid growth.[3] However, a few voices have been raised in recent years at least about the validity of an unvarnished or unqualified free-market approach to development, including unqualified free trade. The most sophisticated critique of such an approach to development has been put forward by economist Dani Rodrik, who has suggested, among other things, that the statistical literature that links trade openness to national economic growth may be seriously flawed. He has also suggested, by virtue of his own statistical analysis, that the removal of trade restrictions does not explain the variations in economic growth among many developing countries during the 1990s, once we take into account their initial income levels, government spending, and inflation rates. Third, Rodrik has emphasized that the experiences of the East Asian success stories, and especially the movement by Taiwan and South Korea to ELG in the early 1960s, may not be readily applicable to the still-struggling developing countries of today. Taiwan and South Korea, he reminds us, have enjoyed substantial U.S. financial support since World War II and could in turn use those resources to construct world-class economic infrastructures; the countries of sub-Saharan Africa enjoy no similar level of support today. In addition, he has noted, Taiwan and especially South Korea remained less than fully open after they abandoned ISI for ELG; they could do so because they were bound by fewer restraints arising from their membership in the General Agreement on Tariffs and Trade (GATT) and the IMF than is the case for African or Latin American countries today. Hence, Rodrik warns, although trade openness may be necessary for growth, it is not likely to be the *only* thing necessary, and thus an unqualified move to freer trade may not by itself spur faster rates of growth in the least-developed countries.[4]

It should be noted, however, that numerous high-quality studies do find a strong positive relationship between trade and economic development.[5] Moreover, top trade economists, professional staff members at key international economic institutions including the World Bank and the IMF, and officials in important developed-country governments are in fact aware that freer trade may be necessary but not sufficient to bring about economic development.[6] These observers and practitioners have emphasized that trade integration is an important and even critical element of an efficacious, sustainable development strategy, but it needs to be supplemented with macroeconomic stability, market-friendly domestic governmental institutions (including an effective and predictable legal system), and a favorable international environment. We will return to this emerging understanding of the conditions needed for growth in the concluding section of this chapter.

⋇ ESSENTIAL ECONOMICS 8.4

Total Long-Term Financial Flows to Developing Countries, 1970–99

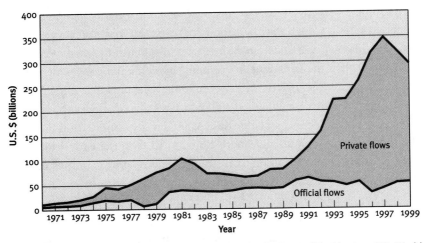

Source: World Bank, *Global Development Finance*, CD-ROM, (Washington, DC: World Bank, 2000), data series DT.NFA.OFFT.CD (official flows) and DT.NFA.DLXF.CD (private flows).

Core Principle

Long-term financial flows to developing countries increased dramatically in the 1990s. Private rather than governmental sources have been the main driver of this increase, but flows from both private and official sources have been inconsistent on a year-to-year basis.

Developing Countries and International Finance

Crucial to the analysis of the experiences of developing countries is an examination of the role of international financial flows in their economic development. Although financial flows are an important source of the investment needed to fuel economic growth, they can also be sources of trouble for developing countries, leading to crises and dependencies that may instead hinder growth. The discussion that follows analyzes trends in financial flows to developing countries, focusing on the different sources and types of financial flows that move to developing nations.

Financial Flows to Developing Countries

Developing countries face different benefits and challenges by virtue of whether they are the recipients of long-term or short-term inflows of foreign capital. **Long-term financial flows,** as defined by the World Bank, are forms of capital that are intended to be available to residents and entities in the recipient countries for a period of one year or more. **Short-term financial flows,** by contrast, are designed to last less than a year. For example, imagine a loan that a bank might extend to a borrower in a foreign country: a long-term bank loan would include repayment terms requiring full repayment of the loan over a period greater than one year; a short-term bank loan would require full repayment within one year or less.

Essential Economics 8.4 summarizes the total flow of long-term financial resources to developing countries between 1970 and 1999. This figure shows, first of all, that although total long-term financial flows remained less than $50 billion per year during most of the 1970s, and exceeded $100 billion on an annual basis only once during the 1980s, they increased dramatically during the 1990s, reaching almost $350 billion in 1997. Second, private rather than governmental sources of capital have been central to the growth of long-term financial flows to developing countries in recent years: during the second half of the 1990s, private flows constituted four-fifths or more of total annual long-term flows to developing nations; official sources of long-term financing contributed little if at all to the dramatic total growth shown in the figure. Third, both private and official-source flows to developing countries can vary greatly from year to year: most notably, in just the three years between 1997 and 1999, the period during which there were severe financial crises in Asia, Latin America, and Russia, total private flows to developing countries dropped from $304 billion to less than $240 billion.

PRIVATE LONG-TERM CAPITAL FLOWS

Although we touched on the subject of financial instruments in our discussion of international finance in Chapter 3, it will be helpful to our discussion here to have a more complete understanding of the four main categories of long-term international private financial flows, all of which are relevant to developing countries. The first such category is **foreign direct investment,** which, according to the World Bank, consists of investments "made to acquire a lasting management interest (usually of [at least] 10 percent of voting stock) in an enterprise operating in a country other than that of the investor (defined according to residency), the investor's purpose being

✳ **ESSENTIAL ECONOMICS 8.5**

Private Long-Term Financial Flows to Developing Countries, 1970–99

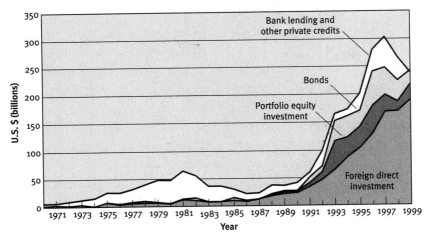

Source: World Bank, *Global Development Finance*, CD-ROM, data series BX.KLT.DINV.CD.DT (FDI), BX.PEF.TOTL.CD.DT (portfolio investment), DT.NFL.PNGB.CD and DT.NFL.PBND.CD (bonds), and DT.NFL.PNGC.CD, DT.NFL.PCBK.CD, and DT.NFL.PROP.CD (bank lending and other private credits).

Core Principle

The flows of four types of long-term capital to developing nations show that all types of investment have increased, especially in the 1990s.

---

an effective voice in the management of the enterprise."[7] When an investor acquires an ownership interest in a foreign firm, usually by buying common stock shares issued by the firm or traded in a local stock market, but does not acquire a stake sufficiently large to exercise control over the firm's operations, the investor is making a ***portfolio equity investment,*** the second category of private financial flows. The third category is that of ***portfolio bond investments,*** wherein an investor from one country purchases a bond that is issued by an entity in another country. As we discussed in Chapters 3 and 7, a bond is a debt instrument: the bond's issuer (which could be a national or subnational government or agency, or a private or publicly owned enterprise) sells the instrument for cash and promises to repay the initial loan amount (the principal) by some predetermined maturity date, and also agrees to pay a mutually agreed-upon sum of money (interest) each quarter or year until

✳ ESSENTIAL ECONOMICS 8.6

Private Long-Term Financial Flows to Developing Countries, 1970–99

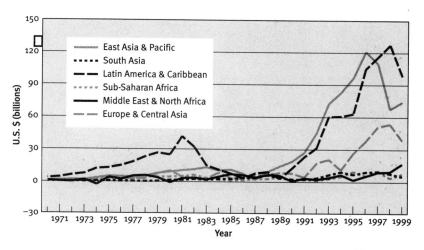

Source: World Bank, *Global Development Finance*, CD-ROM, data series DT.NFA.PRVT.CD.

Core Principle

Different regions of developing nations have experienced different levels of long-term financial flows.

---

the bond's maturity date. Being a class of long-term financing, bonds mature, or become due for full or final payment of principal, after a period of one year or more. The principal on government-issued bonds is guaranteed by the government of the country where the bonds originated; private enterprise bonds are not guaranteed. Finally, the class of flows characterized as *long-term commercial bank lending and trade-related credits* includes loans by private banks to entities in a foreign country, or the extension of a credit by some other private entity for the purpose of facilitating the payment of an export from that entity to a foreign country, with repayment for either type of loan due some time after one year.

Essential Economics 8.5 illustrates the magnitude of the flows of these four types of private long-term capital to developing countries during the past three decades. The graph shows us, first, that portfolio equity became an important type of private capital inflow for developing countries only in the 1990s. Second, although foreign direct investment and commercial

⋇ **ESSENTIAL ECONOMICS 8.7**

Foreign Direct Investment Flows to Developing Countries, 1970–99

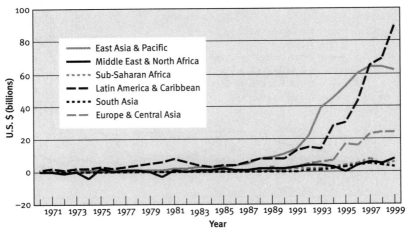

Source: World Bank, *Global Development Finance*, CD-ROM, data series BX.KLT.DINV.CD.DT.

Core Principle

Growth is correlated to foreign direct investment. Regions lagging in growth, such as sub-Saharan Africa, also lag in foreign direct investment, whereas more prosperous developing regions, such as Asia, attract foreign direct investment.

---

banking flows were roughly equal in size during the 1980s and made up the bulk of long-term capital flows during the 1970s and 1980s, by the 1990s foreign direct investment was far and away the most important private source of resources for developing countries. Third, the decline in private flows to developing countries at the end of the 1990s was due largely to decreases in portfolio equity flows (which recovered somewhat at the end of the decade) and portfolio bond flows (which did not so recover). Commercial bank lending and other trade credits compensated for the drop in portfolio flows in the crisis year of 1997 (as did loans from official sources), but these, too, contracted in 1998 and became sharply negative in 1999. In contrast, foreign direct investment flows increased from 1996 to 1997 and then held remarkably steady during the crisis years of 1997 and 1998.

Essential Economics 8.6 shows the same private long-term foreign finan-

✳ ESSENTIAL ECONOMICS 8.8

Official Finance Flows to Developing Countries, 1970–99

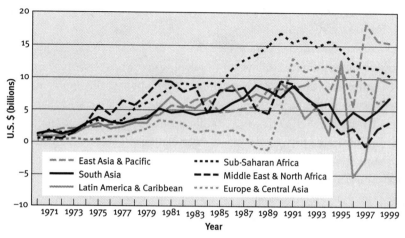

Source: World Bank, *Global Development Finance*, CD-ROM, data series DT.NFA.OFFT.CD.

Core Principle

Official financial flows to developing nations have increased dramatically; Southeast Asia and Latin America have especially benefited from them. Wide swings in official yearly flows to developing regions, however, can imperil development.

---

cial flows to developing countries, but this figure separates them not by type of capital but by destination. As this figure shows, the nations of South Asia, the Middle East and North Africa, and sub-Saharan Africa have not benefited from the large increases in overall long-term private capital inflows during the 1990s; instead, the countries in Latin America and East Asia received the bulk of these new private inflows. By comparing Essential Economics 8.6 with the data presented in Essential Economics 8.1, we can see that the three regions that did not experience strong inflows of private flows had weak track records in development during the past three decades; the one developing region that did receive substantial long-term private capital flows, East Asia, enjoyed tremendous success. However, receiving foreign capital does not automatically translate into strong growth, for Latin America attracted roughly as much private long-term capital as did East Asia during the three decades shown, but it did not experience a similar rate of growth in per capita income. Essential Economics 8.6 also underscores how volatile these flows of private long-term capital can be for developing countries: note the tremendously sharp drop in such flows to Latin America and especially East Asia between 1996 and 1998.

We saw in Essential Economics 8.5 the prominence of foreign direct investment in total financial flows to developing countries. Essential Economics 8.7 gives us a glimpse of the regional distribution of this most important form of capital flow to developing nations. Here, again, we find that the regions that lagged in growth—the Middle East and North Africa, South Asia, and sub-Saharan Africa—also failed to attract substantial foreign direct investment. East Asia was a major recipient of such investments, but so was Latin America, which, as we have already seen, failed to achieve strong increases in per capita income. Thus foreign direct investment, too, is part of the pathway to development, but by itself it does not guarantee strong economic growth.

OFFICIAL CAPITAL FLOWS

Essential Economics 8.8 presents information on the distribution of official capital flows (except for short-term credits provided by the IMF, which will be discussed later in this chapter) to developing countries in various regions of the world. We can see from this figure that Latin America and especially East Asia have been important beneficiaries of official flows; indeed, in recent years China and Indonesia have been among the biggest recipients of World Bank loans. Also notice that year-to-year variations in regional disbursements of official flows are very high and appear to have increased dramatically during the 1990s, a matter to which we will return later in our discussion of possible risks for developing countries as they participate in the international financial system.

PRIVATE SHORT-TERM FINANCIAL FLOWS

To this point we have discussed long-term capital flows to developing countries from both private and official sources. There is, however, one last form of capital that flows to developing (and among developed) countries, namely, private short-term investments. Such investments are clouded with great uncertainties; however, it appears that they originate largely with banks and other private financial institutions, as well as with multinational enterprises. A short-term investment, as we noted earlier, requires repayment within one year or less. We offered a hypothetical example of such an invest-

⁎ ESSENTIAL ECONOMICS 8.9

Private Short-Term Financial Flows to Developing Countries, 1972–99

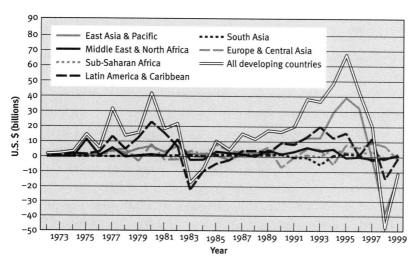

Source: World Bank, *Global Development Finance*, CD-ROM, data series DT.NFL.DSTC.CD.

> *Core Principle*
>
> **S**hort-term capital flows to developing countries expanded and then contracted sharply in the 1990s, contributing to a number of financial crises.

ment in Chapter 3, when we suggested that an American bank might extend a loan of U.S. dollars to a Mexican bank, with both principal and interest to be repaid in dollars after 90 days. After 90 days, the U.S. bank might or might not renew the loan.

Essential Economics 8.9 presents an overview of such short-term private capital flows to developing countries. The figure indicates that such short-term capital flows to developing countries first surged and then contracted sharply during the 1990s. Moreover—and here we see a powerful source of the financial crises that took place during the second half of the 1990s—East Asia and Latin America each experienced stunning reversals in private short-term capital inflows between 1996 and 1998. East Asia, for example, enjoyed inflows of private short-term capital in the amounts of about $40 billion and $32 billion in 1995 and 1996, respectively, but experienced outflows of such capital (meaning that payments on and liquidations of old loans exceeded receipts of new loans) in the amounts of about $1 billion in 1997 and almost $40 billion in 1998.

Policy Issues Regarding Private Capital Flows to Developing Countries

As suggested in the preceding section, foreign capital flows to developing countries can have significant policy ramifications, as they did in the East Asian and Latin American financial crises of the late 1990s. In analyzing these policy issues, recall from the discussion so far that private foreign investments can take many forms, including short-term investments, commercial bank loans and other trade-related credits, portfolio bond or equity investments, and foreign direct investments. From the viewpoint of policy-making in a developing country, we can make a distinction between foreign direct investments and the other categories of investments just listed. The basis for this distinction concerns the ease of exit by investors and the level of direct presence of the foreign investors in the host country's economy. All the other categories of investments listed can normally be liquidated (that is, sold or not renewed) quite readily and often represent short-term commitments by investors; foreign direct investments, on the other hand, are usually less readily liquidated and normally entail a longer-term commitment by the investor to the recipient country. Moreover, portfolio investors and bank lenders remain one step removed from the host economy; foreign direct investors, by virtue of their management interest in foreign firms, usually are more closely integrated into the host country's economy.

PRIVATE SHORT-TERM FLOWS AND THE RISK OF FINANCIAL-CRISIS CONTAGION

The massive shifts shown in Essential Economics 8.9 were not just year-to-year fluctuations; during the 1990s, there were a number of instances in which a country that was highly favored with liquid inflows (and, in particular, short-term loans) one week witnessed massive outflows the very next week. Such massive shifts in capital-account transactions can create serious difficulties for macroeconomic stability and growth in a developing country. Indeed, they contributed to the balance-of-payments and foreign-exchange crises that occurred in the 1990s in Mexico (discussed in Chapter 3) and other countries in Latin America, in Russia, and, most spectacularly, in East Asia.[8] Moreover, short-term and other liquid flows played a key role in an international financial problem that emerged prominently during the 1990s: *financial-crisis contagion,* which occurs when one developing country goes into a crisis due to a sudden reversal of liquid capital flows, and then

> **TIMELINE 8.1**

The International Financial-Crisis Contagion, 1997–99

1997

January–May	Thai baht comes under pressure
May 15	Thailand introduces capital controls
July 2	Thailand allows the baht to float
July 11	Philippines allows the peso to float
August 14	Indonesia allows the rupiah to float
August 20	IMF announces international financial rescue package for Thailand
September 1	Malaysia introduces capital controls
October 14	Taiwan allows the new Taiwan dollar to float
October	Stock markets in United States and Europe suffer major declines
November 15	IMF announces financial rescue package for Indonesia
November 20	South Korea allows the won to float
December 3	IMF announces international financial rescue package for South Korea

1998

April–May	World commodity prices, including price of oil, decline sharply
May	Violence breaks out in Indonesia surrounding economic collapse
August 17	Russia defaults on foreign debts, devalues the ruble
August 25	IMF announces new financial rescue package for Indonesia

1999

January 13	Brazil allows the real to float

other developing countries, which may or may not have had comparable policy or business conditions, also experience rapid outflows of such foreign capital and all the instabilities unleashed by those outflows.[9]

A vivid example of financial-crisis contagion occurred in 1994–95, when the collapse of the Mexican peso, discussed in Chapter 3, was followed by outflows of capital from a number of countries in Latin America, which in turn induced a sharp contraction in economic activity in that region. The world witnessed an even more dramatic instance of financial crisis contagion, however, between 1997 and 1999, when, as is chronicled in Timeline 8.1, a financial crisis developed in Asia and then spread beyond that region to Eastern Europe and Latin America.[10]

In July 1997, after several months of large outflows of foreign short-term capital, massive drops in Thailand's equity and foreign-exchange markets, and the unsuccessful imposition of capital controls, the Thai government ceased its attempts to maintain its currency peg and elected to allow the Thai baht to float. Similar crises then suddenly and surprisingly erupted in the Philippines, Indonesia, and Malaysia, and all of these countries were ultimately compelled to abandon their own pegged exchange-rate systems during the summer and fall of 1997. Taiwan, even though it had a much stronger economy, also experienced a run on its currency, the new Taiwan (NT) dollar, and a serious decline in its stock markets, and was compelled in October to allow the NT dollar to float. The contagion then spread to Hong Kong, and then to South Korea, which was forced to abandon its exchange-rate peg in November and to seek support from the IMF in December.

As short-term foreign capital ceased to be available to these East and Southeast Asian countries, they were forced, in the manner outlined in Chapter 3, to increase interest rates in an attempt to defend their currencies; their economies promptly contracted, and thus their demand for raw-material imports was sharply curtailed. As a consequence, Russia, a major exporter of oil, became a target of currency sales. By mid-August 1998 the ruble had collapsed and the Russian government effectively defaulted on its short-term debts to domestic and foreign creditors. This default, in turn, led to a sharp decline in investor confidence in all emerging markets, including those in Latin America, even though governments in that region had been following vastly more prudent economic policies than had Russia. By January 1999, the Brazilian government was forced to announce an austerity program and an official devaluation of the Brazilian real.

Thus, during 1997–99, several important developing and transitional-market economies, after enjoying in most cases several years of tremendous capital inflows of all types and rapid economic growth, experienced rapid short-term capital outflows, currency crises, and wrenching contractions of their national economies. The costs of the crisis were grave. For example, Argentina's GDP contracted by 5 percent in the wake of the Mexican financial crisis, and its unemployment rate increased from about 11 percent in 1994 to almost 18 percent in 1995 and 1996. In South Korea, unemployment rose from about 3 percent or less in 1996 and 1997 to over 6 percent in 1998 and

1999; in Indonesia, numerous riots broke out, many lives were lost, and the percentage of the population living in poverty jumped from about 11 percent in 1997 to almost 20 percent in 1998.[11]

By the end of the 1990s, most of the countries that had experienced these great financial crises were enjoying strong recoveries. Still, both for residents and for observers, these crises left in their wake new levels of anxiety about the benefits and risks of financial globalization. Foreign investors suddenly appeared to constitute an uncoordinated and unmanageable "electronic herd" running about the world: they might suddenly and inexplicably turn against an otherwise healthy emerging economy simply because it shared an economic label with a country toward which investor sentiment turned sour.[12]

Notwithstanding the trauma that many developing countries have experienced as a result of financial-crisis contagion, for the most part these countries have continued to believe that the benefits of integration greatly outweigh the risks. For example, Argentina, which in the early 1990s had pursued liberalization and had established a currency board to fight inflation and assure foreign investors of the stability of the Argentine peso, did not reverse course when it was hit by a financial crisis emanating from the Mexican financial collapse of 1994–95 (but purely domestic factors brought about a collapse of the Argentine currency and currency board in early 2002).[13] Such Asian countries as South Korea, Thailand, the Philippines, and to some degree Indonesia continued to adhere at the end of the 1990s and the beginning of the new century to the requirements of globalization.

Yet, in other important instances, countries that otherwise have been huge beneficiaries of economic integration have nevertheless elected to undertake policies to limit their exposure to highly liquid foreign-capital inflows. For example, Chile, a key example of successful economic liberalization in the 1980s, was sufficiently worried at the outset of the 1990s about potentially destabilizing short-term capital inflows that it imposed partial controls on such inflows in 1991.[14] Malaysia, in the midst of the 1997–98 Asian financial crisis, and after attempting many orthodox responses (such as raising interest rates), imposed emergency capital controls in September 1998. The fact that both Chile and Malaysia largely avoided the turmoil that Thailand, South Korea, and especially Indonesia experienced during the Asian financial crisis has led some analysts to suggest that the more restrictive strategy used by Chile and Malaysia might be appropriate for other developing countries.[15] At the least, the financial crises of the 1990s have led many to the conclusion that increased openness by developing countries to international capital markets should occur in conjunction with the building of—or, even better, after the building of—reasonably well functioning national banking and equity systems, so that these countries are less vulnerable to external financial shocks.[16]

FOREIGN DIRECT INVESTMENT AND MULTINATIONAL ENTERPRISES

Academic and policy debates about foreign direct investments in developing countries, usually undertaken by large multinational enterprises (MNEs), have gone through several phases. In the immediate postwar years, most foreign direct investments in developing countries were undertaken by MNEs in the areas of natural resources and extractive industries. Many developing-country governments believed that foreign direct investments in general limited growth in a host country, and thus many sought to encourage manufacturing MNEs to establish local production facilities as a part of their import-substituting industrialization strategies. However, as ISI increasingly seemed not to be working in several important developing countries (such as Brazil), economic theorists began to develop a "dependency" critique of the impact of MNEs on developing countries.[17]

The dependency approach suggested that economic integration in general, and openness to MNEs in particular, doomed developing countries to relative backwardness. Given the way that MNEs structured their worldwide operations, the argument suggested, high-value activities were being clustered in the "core" industrial countries, with progressively less-valuable activities taking place in the "semi-periphery" and "periphery" of developing nations. Both business and government elites in the noncore developing countries collaborated with this arrangement, it was believed, because they aspired to the consumption patterns in the core and thus accepted the core's hegemony. Thus, for some critics, such as Fernando Henrique Cardoso (who would later become presidents of Brazil), the task was somehow to promote an alternative, more statist program of economic policy in developing countries.

In contrast, scholars in what may be termed the "bargaining school" suggested that developing-country elites did have an incentive to improve the terms of their countries' relations with MNEs and did have the capacity to bring this about. Business scholar Raymond Vernon, for example, suggested that host-country governments would want to show their respective home publics that they had not become pawns of foreign investors, and thus they would pressure MNEs to improve their contributions to national economic development. Moreover, Vernon argued, while MNEs often held the major bargaining chips (such as technology) before they entered a country and thus could drive a hard bargain with the host government, once they had acquired assets in the country, those assets became hostages to the goodwill of the host government, and therefore the latter could force the MNEs to tilt the balance of benefits in favor of the host country.[18]

By the mid-1980s, however, as the ISI strategy came into disfavor, strong state controls over both national and foreign economic agents were seen to be highly ineffective. Moreover, the countries in East and Southeast Asia, who had attracted MNEs as part of their export-oriented strategies, provided clear evidence that MNEs could vitally assist in export-based industrialization: for example, MNEs helped such successful integrators as Malaysia and Thailand become a part of "global commodity chains" linking developing-country producers to advanced-country consumers.[19] Thus, during the 1980s and into the 1990s, many developing-country governments liberalized their policies on foreign direct investment.

By the late 1990s, most developing-country governments and outside observers viewed MNEs as potent generators of growth for developing countries and as valuable links to the global economy. Most amazingly, Cardoso, the leading dependency writer in the world during the 1960s, worked hard as president of Brazil in the 1990s to adjust Brazilian policy in such a way as to attract rather than to shun or control MNEs. Yet academic observers have continued their useful discussion about the degree to which foreign firms might help spur growth in developing nations. By encouraging the operations of MNEs in their countries, for example, developing countries could increase the likelihood of (but could not guarantee) improving their economies by joining global commodity chains. Yet skepticism has been expressed that MNEs will ever invest the necessary resources to upgrade skills and capabilities within most developing countries, thus limiting greatly the benefits those countries might otherwise enjoy from incorporation into global production systems.[20]

MNEs have also been at the center of the critique of globalization that has been articulated by a number of labor-rights, human-rights, and environmental activists.[21] These critics charge that many MNEs enter developing countries in order to exploit their cheap labor and abundant natural resources.[22] MNEs, these enties also argue, seek through their entry into developing economies to escape the stronger worker-health and safety standards enforced in the developed nations, and in so doing they tolerate or even create inhumane workplace conditions in those foreign facilities. Third, critics of MNEs have alleged that these firms, wanting to reduce their production costs, seek out developing countries with lax environmental regulations and undertake in those countries productive activities that exacerbate both local and global environmental problems. Fourth, these critics have argued that MNEs, by virtue of investing in low-standard developing countries, are sending a signal to advanced-country governments, unions, and environmental groups that the advanced countries have overly stringent labor and environmental standards and will need to lower those standards if they do not want to see more outflows of investments to the developing countries. Thus, from the viewpoint of these critics, MNEs are a key mechanism by which economic globalization is generating a less just and more dangerous world for millions and millions of people.

Not all observers hold negative views of MNEs, however. For example, although MNEs do pay lower wages to workers in developing-country sites than they pay comparable workers in developed countries, they also pay much higher wages to workers in developing countries than do local firms in the same industry.[23] Furthermore, MNEs are more likely to produce a cleaner rather than a more despoiled natural environment. MNEs, it is suggested, do not have a preference for nations with weak environmental regimes; most MNE investments, in fact, go from one high-standard developed country to another. Moreover, insofar as rich countries prefer environmental protection and foreign investments make recipient countries richer, then foreign investment may be a key motor in developing countries for what is ultimately a stronger national preference for (and capacity to buy) a cleaner environment. In this vein, corporations from rich countries, preferring to have a single set of rules for all competitors, may as a consequence also prefer that developing countries have environmental standards similar to those in the more advanced countries, and may actually press for an enhancement of environmental standards in the developing countries where they operate.[24] Finally, the world's poorest countries may have the worst environmental-protection regimes, but they also receive the lowest levels of foreign direct investment.[25]

On the labor-rights front, labor costs are not that important to the foreign firms that are most active today in developing countries—namely, foreign manufacturing enterprises. To assure that they benefit from highly productive workforces, multinational firms prefer countries where workers have stronger, not weaker, workplace health and safety standards, and better, not worse, social security systems. Furthermore, MNEs prefer to be in countries that are more rather than less respectful of the rights of workers. In other words, MNEs today prefer "Singapore and Costa Rica . . . instead of Bangladesh or Haiti."[26]

In instances when an MNE has exploited its developing-country workforce, the firm has paid a serious price: bad publicity and damage to the firm's goodwill, as unions, human-rights groups, and other concerned nongovernmental organizations (NGOs) have identified the practices of the firm and publicized them around the world. To avoid such costly controversies, many MNEs have negotiated among themselves and with NGOs codes of good conduct for their operations in developing countries and have put into place certification mechanisms to promote compliance with those codes.[27]

Official Finance Flows to Developing Countries

Official capital flows, although generally lower in volume than private flows, still remain important to a large number of the less successful developing nations. Such official flows arise from two basic sources: bilateral and multilateral. In the first case, a single donor provides some form of economic award to the recipient. For example, the United States government provided about $9 billion in direct (bilateral) economic aid during its 2000 fiscal year to developing or other needy countries.[28]

Although there are a number of institutions that are classified as the second type, multilateral sources of financing, such as the Inter-American Development Bank, the Asian Development Bank, and the European Bank for Reconstruction and Development,[29] the two most important sources of multilateral official flows are the World Bank and the IMF. With its headquarters in Washington, D.C., the World Bank has 183 member states and employs 10,000 professional staff members. It supports long-term investment projects, had outstanding loans to approximately 100 countries in 2000, and disbursed approximately $15.3 billion in new loans during its 2000 fiscal year. The bank makes its key decisions on the basis of weighted voting, with the United States, Japan, and the European countries, as the largest contributors to the bank, exercising a clear majority of the total votes.[30]

The IMF is also headquartered in Washington, has 183 member states and 2,700 professional staff members, and makes its decisions on the basis of weighted voting. Its mandate, however, is different from the World Bank's: the IMF provides short-term financing to member countries facing balance-of-payments difficulties. As of early 2001, the IMF had about $65 billion in outstanding credits to 91 member states.

✳ ESSENTIAL ECONOMICS 8.10

Official Financial Flows to Developing Countries, 1970–99

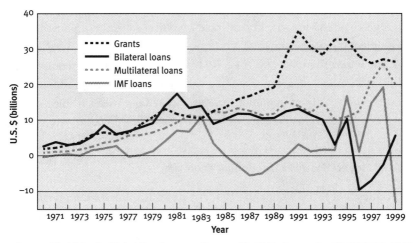

Source: World Bank, *Global Development Finance*, CD-ROM, data series BX.GRT.EXTA.CD.DT (grants), DT.NFL.BLAT.CD (bilateral loans), DT.NFL.MLAT.CD (multilateral loans), and DT.DIS.DIMF.CD and DT.AMT.DIMF.CD (IMF loans, calculated as difference between purchases and repurchases).

Core Principle

Outright grants and multilateral loans comprise the majority of official financial flows to developing nations; bilateral loans and IMF loans are the most volatile types of official flows.

Just as there are two types of sources of official financial flows to developing countries, so too are there two basic categories of official financial flows. ***Official grants*** are financial flows in which a donor provides a certain amount of foreign exchange to a developing country during some period of time, with no expectation of repayment of those resources. ***Official loans***, on the other hand, are financial flows provided to a developing country with the expectation that they will be repaid. These loans may be bilateral in origin (that is, from a developed-country government to a developing-country government) or multilateral (from the World Bank, for example, or another such multilateral institution). Furthermore, loans may be made on ***concessional terms*** (wherein the interest rate is so low and the repayment period is delayed or extended to the degree that at least 25 percent of the loan is effectively a grant), or on ***non-concessional terms*** (wherein the interest rate and repayment schedule more closely match private-market conditions, and there is little or no grant element to the loan).

Essential Economics 8.10 shows the volumes of these four types of official financial flows to developing countries from 1970 to 1999. Two key points emerge from the figure. First, outright grants and multilateral loans (mostly from the World Bank) are the two largest forms of official flows to developing countries. Second, compared to grants and multilateral loans, bilateral loans and especially new IMF credits are highly volatile. Although this may be expected of IMF credits, which are primarily used in response to crises, such volatility is more surprising in the case of bilateral loans and suggests that they, too, have become less a mechanism to promote long-term development and more a tool to respond to immediate crises.

CONTROVERSIES SURROUNDING OFFICIAL FINANCIAL FLOWS

As with private flows, there are several important controversies surrounding the contribution of official flows to the growth prospects of developing countries. It might seem surprising, given the transfer of about $1 trillion of official financing between 1970 and 1999, but the first of these controversies involving official developmental assistance (but not IMF credits, which are discussed later) centers on whether they have actually helped developing countries achieve higher rates of growth. One extended statistical analysis of the transfer by the developed countries of assistance to 96 developing countries has concluded that, although aid might have helped the 14 or so small developing countries for which foreign aid comprised 15 percent or more of gross national product (GNP), for the remaining developing countries "the results imply that most of all aid goes to consumption, . . . increases the size of government, [and] has no significant impact on poverty indicators." Most disturbing, the same study indicates that aid has no greater an impact on developing countries with democratic political systems than it has on developing countries with nondemocratic regimes.[31]

Yet other studies have found that official assistance may promote growth if the developing country is pursuing growth-promoting policies and has representative political institutions. For example, and as we have surmised from the Essential Economics figures presented earlier in this chapter, economists have found that aid by itself does not produce growth. However, they have also found that external aid can promote faster growth in per capita income in a developing country when two other conditions are met: first, the country needs to have government policies aimed at such goals as trade openness, fiscal discipline, and relatively low inflation rates; and second, the country must have high-quality governmental institutions—that is, governments characterized by the strong rule of law and efficient, noncorrupt bureaucracy. Among countries with good policies and institutions (as measured and reported by an NGO, Freedom House), those in the top half in terms of receiving aid as a percentage of GDP enjoyed a growth rate of 3.7 percent in per capita GDP, while those in the bottom half in terms of receiving aid experienced a growth rate of only 2.0 percent in per capita GDP.[32] This finding, relating the efficacy of aid to countries with regimes that are more responsive to the larger public, has been confirmed by supplementary studies by staff at the World Bank and suggests that aid has a positive impact on countries that are democratic, but it has no effect or even a slightly negative effect on countries that are non-democratic.[33]

Perhaps the key conclusion that has emerged in development circles, as the preceding discussion indicates, is that official assistance can foster growth in developing countries only if those countries pursue growth-enabling economic policies and if their governments are reasonably efficient, honest, and responsive to their home publics. This raises the next key question about official assistance: Can it help developing countries acquire governments that are more responsive and more efficient? The record of external donors in promoting policy and institutional reform is mixed; whether such democratic reforms occur in a developing country is more likely to be the result of domestic dynamics that are not readily affected by outsiders. Nevertheless, the World Bank has suggested that external aid can be a "midwife" to internal reform.[34]

Yet some critics suggest that such assistance in fact does *not* promote policy and institutional reform and might even hamper it. According to this line of analysis, external assistance, insofar as it reduces human suffering and improves social conditions in an otherwise corrupt, inefficient, or unrepresentative society, may actually *reduce* pressures for government reform that might otherwise be activated from within the dissatisfied society. Moreover, because most external assistance to developing countries must be channeled through national governmental authorities, corrupt regimes often use their distributive power to enrich and strengthen themselves and to make the availability of aid conditioned on recipients' acceptance of the political status quo. Aid, then, might strengthen rather than weaken the very political forces that are holding back the larger national community from achieving growth and democracy.[35]

Although the criticism reviewed so far has been focused on recipient governments, there are also ample grounds for criticism of the behavior of donor governments. For one thing, as noted above, official assistance flows, especially bilateral ones, exhibit large year-to-year swings. This volatility in aid may translate into higher levels of uncertainty for governments and private firms in developing countries as they consider investment projects, and may lead to a lower level of investment than would be the case were there greater certainty about the availability of external resources. As a result, aid volatility can be detrimental to the growth prospects of recipient developing nations.[36]

Another long-standing problem is that of **tied aid.** As we discussed in Chapter 6, many if not most donor countries use aid to advance their national political, military, and overall economic interests. They may also seek in their assistance policies to promote the commercial interests of firms based in their countries. A donor government can do this by "tying" its aid—that is, by requiring that any aid it gives to a recipient country be used to purchase goods and services from firms in the donor country. As a result, the developing-country government is unable to solicit bids from firms in other countries, thus reducing competition for the contracts and, most likely, raising costs for the developing country. The World Bank has noted that the tying of aid to national producers may reduce the effective value of assistance to recipient countries by as much as 25 percent. During the mid-1980s, perhaps as much as 40 percent of all official assistance from the advanced countries was tied to national producers. Since then, the advanced countries have mutually sought to reduce the tying of aid in their national programs, but, as of the mid-1990s, tied aid still constituted about 20 percent of all bilateral aid.[37]

IMF FINANCIAL SUPPORT OF DEVELOPING COUNTRIES

A country that faces a shortage of foreign currency goes to the IMF to receive short-term loans, which in turn appear as credits in the official settlements account of the country's balance of payments. In order to receive short-terms credits from the IMF, a country must reach an agreement with the fund regarding the terms and timing for repayment and, more important, must agree to a **standby arrangement.** A standby arrangement specifies the actions the country will undertake to ensure that its short-term foreign-exchange shortfall does not become permanent.[38] The IMF (or, more accurately, the major governments who control it) usually requires that a standby arrangement include policy actions that will bring about an improvement in the country's balance of payments. Examples of such policy actions include increasing interest rates, cutting government spending, liberalizing the coun-

PRIMARY DOCUMENT 8.1

Operation of an IMF Standby Arrangement: Turkey, 2001

IMF Home | Search | Site Map | Site Index | Help | What's New

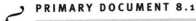
International Monetary Fund

About the IMF | News | Publications | Country Info | IMF Finances | Standards & Codes

News Brief Index for 2001 | 2000 | 1999 | 1998 | 1997 | 1996 | 1995
For more information, see Turkey and the IMF

News Brief No. 01/73
August 3, 2001

International Monetary Fund
700 19th Street, NW
Washington, D.C. 20431 USA

IMF Approves US$1.5 Billion Tranche Under Stand-By Arrangement to Turkey

The Executive Board of the International Monetary Fund (IMF) today completed the ninth review of Turkey's economic program supported by the three-year stand-by arrangement. The Board's decision will enable Turkey to draw SDR 1.2 billion (about US$1.5 billion) immediately from the IMF.

The stand-by arrangement was approved in December 1999 for SDR 2.9 billion (about US$4 billion/see Press release 99/66). In December 2000, SDR 5.8 billion (about US$7 billion) in additional financial resources were made available under the Supplemental Reserve Facility (SRF, see Press Release 00/80). On May 15, 2001, the IMF approved the increase of the stand-by credit by SDR 6.4 billion (about US$8 billion), bringing the total available resources from the IMF to SDR 15 billion (about US$19 billion, see Press Release 01/23). So far, Turkey has drawn a total of SDR 8.1 billion (about US$10 billion) from the IMF.

This Web-based IMF press statement indicates that Turkey had to go to the IMF for financial support on at least three separate occasions between December 1999 and May 2001, in response to which the IMF had provided a line of credit totaling $19 billion. By early August 2001, Turkey had used about $10 billion of that $19 billion. The press statement also makes clear how the IMF exercises discipline over borrowing members. In order to obtain access to $1.5 billion of the $9 billion in credits still available to it (what the IMF terms a "tranche," or slice of the total standby credit line), Turkey had to submit to a review of its economic policies by the IMF Executive Board.

Source: IMF News Brief No. 01/73, August 3, 2001, available at www.imf.org/external/np/sec/nb/2001/NB0173.HTM.

Core Principle

Assistance from the IMF usually comes in stages and is accompanied by a set of economic measures that the recipient country is required to take.

try's economy, and strengthening its regulatory frameworks in finance and other sectors.[39] Primary Document 8.1 shows some details of the operation of a recent IMF stand-by arrangement for Turkey.

This mission of the IMF to support developing countries experiencing short-term balance-of-payments difficulties has produced three main lines of criticism of the fund. The most serious of these criticisms argues that the IMF's lending programs have generally damaged the growth performance and prospects of the countries that have received its support. Some evidence does vindicate the IMF's programs, showing that its standby arrangements do help target countries to ameliorate their balance-of-payments problems, to reduce their inflation rates, and, after a short-term contraction in economic activity, to experience a return to economic growth.[40] Yet certain scholars have found that countries that participated in IMF stabilization programs grew at significantly lower rates than did countries that were in comparably difficult economic circumstances but elected not to pursue IMF support. Moreover, countries that entered into agreements with the IMF do not appear to have grown faster in the years after they completed their stabilization programs than they did before they entered into those agreements, and they do not seem to have attained better growth rates after completing their stabilization programs than the countries that, while comparable in other respects, did not enter into agreements with the IMF.[41]

The second general criticism is related to the first. It holds that the IMF has stunted the growth of many developing countries because it often makes its assistance to them conditioned on their acceptance and implementation of standby arrangements that contain elements that are unnecessary at best and counterproductive at worst. The question of whether the IMF's standby arrangements are appropriate for developing countries became especially acute in the case of the Asian financial crisis of 1997–98. The IMF has reported that it warned Thailand in early 1997 that it was facing a foreign-exchange crisis. Furthermore, when the crisis did strike and spread from July 1997 onward, the IMF points out that it did not seek overly restrictive fiscal and monetary policy responses from the Thai, Korean, or Indonesian authorities in exchange for IMF aid. The IMF has suggested as well that it responded promptly and generously to those countries' requests for help, lending a total of $36 billion to them and "spearheading the mobilization" of an additional $77 billion in support for them from bilateral and other multilateral sources. In addition, the IMF has argued, these countries needed to undertake major reforms of their banking systems because the root cause of the Asian crisis was the fact that the national governments in the region had permitted their banks to borrow too much from abroad and to make extremely imprudent loans to local residents and firms. Finally, the IMF has suggested that although its policy advice to the East Asian countries during the crisis "was not flawless," it adjusted those policies as needed and, for the most part, helped to bring the countries in the region back to financial stability and strong economic growth by the end of 1998.[42]

Yet the IMF's performance during the Asian financial crisis has been strongly criticized from many quarters, as has its performance in managing many other instances in which one or more developing countries experienced foreign-exchange shortfalls and financial panics. Most forceful in criticizing the IMF has been the economist Jeffrey Sachs. He argues that the East Asian countries had basically strong economies at the outset of 1997 (and that even the IMF had said so), that they were not inherently insolvent in mid-1997, and that they were simply facing irrational panics as banks and other short-term investors began to withdraw funds on a massive scale. Furthermore, Sachs has written, the IMF, arriving in Thailand in July "filled with ostentatious declarations that all was wrong and that fundamental and immediate surgery was needed," actually contributed to the crisis in Thailand by issuing "dire public pronouncements" and by demanding solutions so drastic that market participants concluded that "Asia indeed was about to enter a severe contraction." In other words, according to Sachs, "instead of dousing the fire, the IMF in effect screamed 'fire' in the theater." He also has suggested that the IMF repeated this mistake in Indonesia and Korea later in 1997, and that "by then, the panic had spread to virtually all of East Asia."[43] Sachs has claimed that the IMF has made similar mistakes in such countries as Argentina, Bulgaria, and Mexico, and that the IMF insists on severe macroeconomic and institutional responses by a borrowing country, even when what is needed is only short-term liquidity financing, because of the IMF's subservience to the preferences of the United States and other major industrialized countries. Sachs argues that what is needed is for the IMF to be more transparent in its operations and more accountable to external, independent review and criticism.

The third main criticism leveled against the IMF is that it is actually contributing to the likelihood that individual countries and groups of countries might experience a financial panic and possible economic collapse. A commission that was established in 1999 by the U.S. Congress to study the IMF and the World Bank in the wake of the Asian financial crisis issued a highly critical report of the two institutions in March 2000 and suggested that both markedly reduce their operations. The commission's chairperson, the economist Allan Meltzer, in his report to Congress, said specifically that although "the IMF's role as a quasi-lender of last resort is still needed in emergency circumstances," its operations need "fundamental restructuring" because "current practices are rife with moral hazard."

Moral hazard is an example of the law of unintended consequences. Auto insurance companies face this problem acutely: by agreeing to compensate all covered individuals who are in car accidents, they may actually encourage risky driving behavior by those individuals who are prone to taking risks and who know that the company, and not they, will bear the costs of any accidents they may cause. Insurance companies try to manage the problem of moral hazard by being careful about accepting applications for auto insurance, and, most notably, by charging much higher premiums to individuals who have displayed risky driving behavior, as evidenced by their receipt of traffic tickets or being in any sort of accident.

Meltzer has argued that the IMF, by becoming active early in managing financial crises and by imposing costs on the government and public of the borrowing country rather than on either the foreign or the local banks lending to that country, has produced international financial moral hazard. As he suggested in his statement to Congress, "the expectation of future IMF bailouts helps to fuel the volatile short-term capital flows that have played a key role in recent crises."[44] In an earlier article Meltzer and a co-author basically agreed with the IMF that the central cause of the financial crises during the 1990s in such countries as Mexico, Thailand, and Korea had been improvident banking decisions by both local and foreign banks and poor regulation of local banks by national authorities. But the authors went on to explain that, by granting credits to be used by borrowing governments to pay off foreign loans taken on by local banks, "the IMF adds to the problem by fostering the belief that it will bail out the banks, however imprudent or insolvent they may be."[45] The IMF's moral-hazard-producing behavior may be attributable, they suggest, to its subservience to other interests. On the one hand, the United States has pressed the IMF to extend assistance even in circumstances when IMF staff thought such assistance was not warranted. But at the same time, they suggest, IMF staff members may sometimes be reluctant to argue against bad proposals for IMF assistance, because their own career opportunities hinge on their capacity to maintain cordial relations with the governments of the very countries asking for assistance.

The IMF has vigorously disputed the assertion that it has engendered moral hazard in the international banking system. For example, in the framework of a June 2000 review of its performance in the Asian crisis, the IMF sought to demonstrate how its stabilization programs have been hard on borrowing countries (thus creating incentives for them to improve all elements of their political economies, including their banking sectors) and have not saved foreign private investors from losing money (thereby creating incentives for those investors to be more prudent).[46] At the end of 2000, Meltzer and another co-author suggested that the IMF had in fact made some progress in reforming its operations so as to better enable itself to deal with financial crises. However, they argued that the IMF had not yet devised a mechanism whereby foreign private creditors credibly face the prospect of significant losses when they make their loans to developing countries and therefore will be forced to participate in helping that country resolve its financial difficulties.[47]

Conclusion

After reading about the problems that many developing countries have had in achieving economic growth and a decent standard of living for their populations, many of us may tend toward fatalism about the circumstances of those countries and a loss of hope that anything can be done to help those countries and their populations. And yet, it is vital that we who are fortunate enough to live in wealthy countries remain resolute in working with those in poor countries who are motivated to improve their economic conditions.

We should remain resolute in seeking better strategies for development as a practical matter, for although it is unrealistic to believe that inequalities within and between nations can be abolished, persistent poverty and economic turmoil abroad often lead to national and international political instability that even the wealthiest nations cannot fully escape. We should also remain resolute because we know that some countries have escaped poverty even when they seemed to have few resources and were not thought to have a very bright economic future. In 1993, a World Bank analysis of the remarkable economic track record of East Asia usefully acknowledged that the bank itself had not been very effective in picking winners in the region: in particular, a 1957 bank report had been very pessimistic about South Korea's likely growth trajectory.[48] Just as informed observers in the 1950s underestimated what the South Koreans could accomplish by the 1970s and 1980s, so too we today may be underestimating what many developing countries can achieve in the not-too-distant future. The experiences of South Korea, Singapore, and Taiwan for many years, as well as that of China and, to some degree, India and Mexico in more recent times, suggest that the combination of political-economic institutional reform at home and commercial and financial integration abroad can put an otherwise very poor country on a much higher growth trajectory. Thus, as a matter of both prudence and hope, we in the industrialized world should continue to help those in the developing world find their own, more fruitful future in the world economy.

Notes

[1]This review of the evolution of thinking about and policies regarding trade and development relies on Rudiger Dornbusch, "The Case for Trade Liberalization in Developing Countries," *Journal of Economic Perspectives* 6 (Winter 1992), pp. 69–85; Stephan Haggard, *Pathways from the Periphery: The Politics of Growth in the Newly Industrializing Countries* (Ithaca: Cornell University Press, 1990); Anne O. Krueger, *Trade Policies and Developing Nations* (Washington, D.C.: Brookings Institution Press, 1995); Anne O. Krueger, "Trade Policy and Development: How We Learn," *American Economic Review* 87 (March 1997), pp. 1–22; and Barbara Stallings, ed., *Global Change, Regional Response: The New International Context of Development* (Cambridge: Cambridge University Press, 1995).

[2]For the main elements of the Washington consensus and controversies surrounding it at the end of the 1990s, see Moises Naim, "Washington Consensus or Washington Confusion?" *Foreign Policy*, No. 118 (Spring 2000), pp. 87–103.

[3]See, for example, "Globalization and the Opportunities for Developing Countries," in International Monetary Fund (IMF), *World Economic Outlook, May 1997: A Survey by the Staff of the International Monetary Fund* (Washington, D.C.: IMF, 1997), available at www.imf.org/search97cgi/s97is_eng.dll/search97cgi/inetsrcheng.ini?action=FilterSearch&filter=spquery.hts&QueryText=weorepts. For other arguments about the utility of open markets for growth, see IMF, *World Economic Outlook, May 2000* (Washington, D.C.: IMF, 2000), especially Chapters 4 and 5, available at www.imf.org/external/pubs/ft/weo/2000/01/index.htm. In addition, see the various articles at www.wto.org/english/tratop_e/devel_e/devel_e.htm.

[4]Rodrik's key work on this matter is *The New Global Economy and Developing Countries: Making Openness Work* (Washington, D.C.: Overseas Development Council, 1999). In addition, see Rodrik, "The Limits of Trade Policy Reform in Developing Countries," *Journal of Economic Perspectives* 6 (Winter 1992), pp. 87–105; Dani Rodrik, "Trading in Illusions," *Foreign Policy*, No. 123 (March–April 2001), pp. 55–62; and Francisco Rodriguez and Dani Rodrik, "Trade Policy and Economic Growth: A Skeptic's Guide to the Cross-National Evidence," National Bureau of Economic Research (NBER) working paper 7081 (April 1999), available at www.nber.org/papers/w8081.

[5]See Sebastian Edwards, "Openness, Trade Liberalization, and Growth in Developing Countries," *Journal of Economic Literature* 31 (September 1993), pp. 1358–93; Jeffrey A. Frankel and David Romer, "Does Trade Cause Growth?" *American Economic Review* 89 (June 1999), pp. 379–99; and Sebastian Edwards, "Openness, Productivity and Growth: What Do We Really Know?" *Economic Journal* 108 (March 1998), pp. 383–98.

[6]See, for example, Krueger, *Trade Policies and Developing Nations*, pp. 61–66; Krueger, "Trade Policy and Development," p. 1; World Bank, *Entering the 21st Century: World Development Report, 1999–2000* (Washington, D.C.: World Bank, 1999), p. 21; IMF, *World Economic Outlook, May 2000*, especially pp. 114–15 and 123–37; and *Eliminating World Poverty: Making Globalisation Work for the Poor* (London: Her Majesty's Stationery Office, 2000), p. 67, available at www.globalisation.gov.uk.

[7]World Bank, *Global Development Finance*, CD-ROM (Washington, D.C.: World Bank, 2000).

[8]See Uri Dadush, Dipak Dasgupta, and Dilip Ratha, "The Role of Short-Term Debt in Recent Crises," *Finance and Development* 37 (December 2000), available at www.imf.org/external/pubs/ft/fandd/2000/12/dadush.htm.

[9]Such crises, it should be emphasized, are not restricted to emerging-market economies.

[10]For the best single report on the Asian and ancillary crises during this period, see Stephan Haggard, *The Political Economy of the Asian Financial Crisis* (Washington, D.C.: Institute for International Economics, 2000). Also very helpful are IMF, *World Economic Outlook Interim Assessment, December 1997: Crisis in Asia: Regional and Global Implications* (Washington, D.C.: IMF, 1997), available at www.imf.org/external/pubs/ft/weo/weo1297/index.htm; and Council on Economic Advisers, *Economic Report of the President 1999* (Washington, D.C.: U.S. Government Printing Office, 1999), pp. 225–35.

[11]IMF, *World Economic Outlook, October 1999* (Washington, D.C.: IMF, October 1999), pp. 64–67.

[12]Friedman, *The Lexus and the Olive Tree*, pp. 93–119.

[13]See IMF, *World Economic Outlook, October 1999*, p. 52.

[14]Sebastian Edwards, "The Americas: Capital Controls Are Not the Reason for Chile Success," *Wall Street Journal*, April 3, 1998, p. A19.

[15]See Ethan Kaplan and Dani Rodrik, "Did the Malaysian Capital Controls Work?" NBER working paper W8142 (February 2001).

[16]See Barry Eichengreen and Michael Mussa, "Capital Account Liberalization and the IMF," *Finance and Development*, December 1998, available at www.imf.org/external/pubs/ft/fandd/2001/06/index.htm.

[17]For an introduction to the large literature on MNEs and developing countries, see Joseph M. Grieco, "Foreign Direct Investment and Third World Development: Theories and Evidence," in Theodore H. Moran, ed., *Investing in Development: New Roles for Private Investment?* (New Brunswick: Transaction Books, 1986), pp. 35–60.

[18]For a concise statement of his "obsolescing bargain" thesis, see Raymond Vernon, *Sovereignty at Bay: The Multinational Spread of U.S. Enterprises* (New York: Basic Books, 1971), pp. 46–59.

[19]Gary Gereffi, "Global Production Systems and Third World Development," in Stallings, ed., *Global Change, Regional Response*, pp. 100–142.

[20]Peter Evans, "Transnational Corporations and Third World States: From the Old Internationalization to the New," in Richard Kozul-Wright and Robert Rowthorn, eds., *Transnational Corporations and the Global Economy* (New York: St. Martin's, 1998), pp. 195–224.

[21]See Terry Collingsworth, J. William Gould, and Pharis F. Harvey, "Time for a Global New Deal," *Foreign Affairs* 73 (January–February 1994). For a careful analysis of how civil-society groups worked to forestall the negotiation of a multilateral agreement on investment (MAI), see

Edward M. Graham, *Fighting the Wrong Enemy: Antiglobal Activists and Multinational Enterprises* (Washington, D.C.: Institute for International Economics, 2000); and Stephen Kobrin, "The MAI and the Clash of Globalizations," *Foreign Policy*, No. 112 (Fall 1997). For a sympathetic treatment of these groups, see Peter Evans, "Fighting Marginalization with Transnational Networks: Counter-Hegemonic Globalization," *Contemporary Sociology* 29 (January 2000).

[22]Two recent studies suggest that MNE outflows from developed countries to developing countries are positively related to increases in developed-country labor costs. See Jan Hatzius, "Foreign Direct Investment and Factor Demand Elasticities," *European Economic Review* 44 (2000), pp. 117–43; and Magnus Blomstrom, Gunnar Fors, and Robert Lipsey, "Foreign Direct Investment and Employment: Home Country Experience in the United States and Sweden," NBER working paper 6205 (October 1997), available at papers.nber.org/papers/W6205.

[23]See Graham, *Fighting the Wrong Enemy*, 92–95.

[24]See Ronnie Garcia-Johnson, *Exporting Environmentalism: U.S. Multinational Chemical Corporations in Brazil and Mexico* (Cambridge: MIT Press, 2000).

[25]Graham, *Fighting the Wrong Enemy*, pp. 137–44.

[26]Debora Spar, "Foreign Investment and Human Rights," *Challenge*, January–February 1999. See also Debora Spar and David Yoffie, "Multinational Enterprises and the Prospects for Justice," *Journal of International Affairs* 52 (Spring 1999).

[27]Gary Gereffi, Ronnie Garcia-Johnson, and Erika Sasser, "The NGO-Industrial Complex," *Foreign Policy*, July–August 2001, pp. 56–65.

[28]U.S. Office of Management and Budget, *Budget of the United States Government* (Washington, D.C.: U.S. Government Printing Office, 2000), Table 22.2, section 150, available at www.whitehouse.gov/omb/budget/fy2002/bud22_2.html.

[29]For helpful information on the Inter-American Development Bank, see www.iadb.org; for the Asian Development Bank, see www.iadb.org; and for the European Bank for Reconstruction and Development, see www.ebrd.org.

[30]A good overview of the World Bank may be found at www.worldbank.org/html/extdr/about/. For an introduction to the IMF, a good place to start is www.imf.org/external/about.htm.

[31]See Peter Boone, "Politics and the Effectiveness of Foreign Aid," *European Economic Review* 40 (1996), pp. 315, 319.

[32]See World Bank, *Assessing Aid: What Works, What Doesn't, and Why* (Washington, D.C.: World Bank, 1998), esp. pp. 12–14, 36, and Appendix, available at www.worldbank.org/research/aid/. See also Craig Burnside and David Dollar, "Aid, the Incentive Regime, and Poverty Reduction," available at www.worldbank.org/research/bios/burnside.htm; Craig Burnside and David Dollar, "Aid Spurs Growth—In a Sound Policy Environment," *Finance and Development* (December 1997), pp. 4–7; and David Dollar and William Easterly, "The Search for the Key: Aid, Investment and Policies in Africa," *Journal of African Economies* 8 (1999), pp. 546–77.

[33]See Jakob Svensson, "Aid, Growth, and Democracy," *Economics and Politics* 11 (November 1999), pp. 275–97, esp. 285–87.

[34]World Bank, *Assessing Aid*, pp. 17–27, 47–59.

[35]For an overview of this issue, see Arthur A. Goldsmith, "Foreign Aid and Statehood in Africa," *International Organization* 55 (Winter 2001), pp. 123–48.

[36]See Robert Lensink and Oliver Morrissey, "Aid Instability as a Measure of Uncertainty and

the Positive Impact of Aid on Growth," *Journal of Development Studies* 36 (February 2000), pp. 31–49.

[37]World Bank, *Assessing Aid*, p. 6. See also Catrinus J. Jepma, *The Tying of Aid* (Paris: Organization for Economic Cooperation and Development, 1991); and Howard White and Lois Woestman, "The Quality of Aid: Measuring Trends in Donor Performance," *Development and Change* 25 (July 1994), especially pp. 542–44.

[38]On IMF lending procedures, see www.imf.org/external/np/exr/facts/howlend.htm.

[39]IMF lending procedures are described in IMF, "Conditionality in Fund-Supported Programs—Policy Issues," (February 16, 2001), available at www.imf.org/external/np/pdr/cond/2001/eng/policy/021601.pdf; and Michael Musa and Miguel A. Savastano, "The IMF Approach to Economic Stabilization," IMF working paper WP/99/104 (July 1, 1999), available at www.imf.org/external/pubs/cat/longres.cfm?sk&sk=3177.0. For a discussion of IMF conditionality over time, see Harold James, "From Grandmotherliness to Governance: The Evolution of IMF Conditionality," *Finance and Development* 35 (December 1998), available at www.imf.org/external/pubs/ft/fandd/1998/12/james.htm.

[40]See Nadeem Ul-Haque and Mohsin S. Khan, "Do IMF-Supported Programs Work? A Survey of the Cross-Country Empirical Evidence," IMF working paper WP/98/169 (December 1, 1998), available at www.imf.org/external/pubs/cat/longres.cfm?sk&sk=2837.0.

[41]See Adam Przeworski and James Rayment Vreeland, "The Effect of IMF Programs on Economic Growth," *Journal of Development Economics* 62 (2000), pp. 397–403.

[42]See IMF, "Recovery from the Asian Crisis and the Role of the IMF," IMF working paper (June 2000), p. 2, available at www.imf.org/external/np/exr/ib/2000/062300.htm. For additional IMF analyses of its performance in the Asian crisis, see IMF, "The IMF's Response to the Asian Crisis: A Factsheet," (January 19, 1999), available at www.imf.org/external/np/exr/facts/asia.htm; Timothy Lane, Atish Ghosh, Javier Hamann, Steven Phillips, Marianne Schulze-Ghattas, and Tsidi Tsikata, "IMF-Supported Programs in Indonesia, Korea, and Thailand: A Preliminary Assessment," IMF occasional paper 178 (June 30, 1999), available at www.imf.org/external/pubs/cat/longres.cfm?sk&sk=3099.0; Bijan B. Aghevli, "The Asian Crisis: Causes and Remedies," *Finance and Development* 36 (June 1999), available at www.imf.org/external/pubs/ft/fandd/1999/06/aghevli.htm; and Timothy Lane, "The Asian Financial Crisis: What Have We Learned?" *Finance and Development* 36 (June 1999), available at www.imf.org/external/pubs/ft/fandd/1999/09/lane.htm.

[43]Jeffrey Sachs, "The IMF and the Asian Flu," *American Prospect* 37 (March–April 1998), p. 2. See also Steven Radelet and Jeffrey Sachs, "The Onset of the East Asian Financial Crisis" (March 30, 1998), available at www2.cid.harvard.edu/cidpapers/caer/paper27.pdf. For additional commentary on the IMF and the Asian financial crisis of 1997–98, see "The Debate on the Role of the IMF in the Crisis: Did the IMF Plans Worsen the Crisis?" at www.stern.nyu.edu/globalmacro.

[44]"Statement of Allan H. Meltzer on the Report of the International Financial Institution Advisory Commission," Committee on Banking, Housing, and Urban Affairs, U.S. Senate, March 9, 2000, p. 3, available at www.gsia.cmu.edu/afs/andrew/gsia/meltzer/.

[45]Charles W. Calomiris and Allan Meltzer, "Fixing the IMF," *National Interest* (Summer 1999), p. 4.

[46]See Jack Borman et.al., "Managing Financial Crises: The Experience in East Asia," IMF working paper WP/00/107 (June 1, 2000), p. 14, available at www.imf.org/external/pubs/cat/

shortres.cfm?TITLE=managing+financial+crises&auth_ed=&subject=&ser_note=Working+ Paper&datecrit=During&YEAR=Year&Lang_F=All.

[47]See Adam Lerrick and Allan Meltzer, "Slow Progress in Prague: The IMF Is Moving in the Right Direction but the World Bank Is Still in a Muddle," *Financial Times,* October 10, 2000, p. 19.

[48]World Bank, *Sustaining Rapid Development in East Asia and the Pacific* (Washington, D.C.: World Bank, 1993), p. 15.

Chapter 9

Mechanisms for Governance, Reform, and Expansion of the World Political Economy

Introduction

OBJECTIVES

- Determine how states pursue order and reform of world markets.
- Understand the role that institutions play in governing the world political economy.
- Explore the trade-offs that states face as they balance national autonomy with institutional agreements that bind them to the larger world political economy.
- Understand how the mechanisms and politics of global economic governance are changing with the rise of transnational issues and new political actors.

Throughout this book we have traced the ways in which states use world markets as instruments of power and purpose and the ways in which the world economy shapes and constrains the choices of states. In this chapter we will look more closely at the strategies and mechanisms by which states—together or alone—seek to govern the world political economy.

For most of modern history, the world economy—fragmented and weakly integrated—was not governed at all. Beginning in the nineteenth century, the United Kingdom assumed the leading role in promoting trade and open markets and supporting the gold standard, which provided a stable monetary order that allowed capital and trade to flow among the industrialized states of Europe and around the world. But aside from the gold standard and scattered trade agreements, there was little in the way of explicit and agreed-upon institutional mechanisms for the governance of the expanding world economy. The Great Depression of the 1930s, the rising conflict between rival economic blocs, and world war all brought questions of global economic governance to the forefront of relations among the great powers. As World War II came to an end, the United States, the United Kingdom, and the other major powers debated and eventually agreed upon an array of institutions with which to govern the world economy.

As noted in Chapter 5, the United States was the prime mover in the establishment of this post–World War II economic and political order. U.S. power, interests, and ideals were all at work in shaping the rules and institutions that eventually emerged. But the most striking feature of the governing arrangements of the postwar world political economy was the prominence of multilateral institutions—or ***international regimes***—themselves. Never before had states built an international order organized around such a dense and multifaceted array of institutions. Between 1944 and 1951, the United States and the other industrial democratic states spun an elaborate web of institutions through which the world economy would be reopened and managed. The **Bretton Woods agreements**—signed by more than 40 countries in 1944—established the International Monetary Fund (IMF) and the World Bank, which formed the core of this new institutional order. Along with the General Agreement on Tariffs and Trade (GATT), which was agreed to in 1947 at a conference in Havana, Cuba, these were the first permanent international institutions dedicated to the stable functioning of an interdependent world economy.

In the half-century since this postwar turning point, governance mechanisms have become increasingly varied and integral to the functioning of the world economy. Three types of mechanisms are most prominent. First are the formal, multilateral rules, norms, and institutional agreements that prescribe and proscribe specific types of economic policies and relationships for states that are part of the governance arrangement. GATT and its successor, the World Trade Organization (WTO), are the most important institution of this sort. Second are informal, small-group mechanisms, whereby groups of states meet regularly to consult and occasionally coordinate their economic policies. The Group of Seven (G-7), a regular gathering of officials from the world's leading industrialized democracies that was created in the early 1970s, engages in ongoing intergovernmental consultations that allow its member governments to tackle problems of exchange rates, trade imbalances, and monetary and fiscal policy. Third and finally, regional economic governance is pursued through economic integration and the harmonization and liberalization of trade and investment policies between neighboring countries. The European Union is the most prominent and advanced regional grouping today, but many countries around the world—in North America, South America, East Asia, and elsewhere—have formed or are forming a variety of large and small regional cooperative arrangements.

With the rise of newly industrializing countries and with nongovernmental organizations (NGOs) championing labor interests, human rights, and the environment, the governance of the world economy is also expanding beyond the intergovernmental arena. NGOs are seeking to have their voices heard within the established multilateral institutions. These groups, activated in part by the globalization of the world economy, have ignited a lively debate on the reform of global governance.

This chapter untangles the impulses and dilemmas behind state efforts to provide order and governance to the world economy. It explores the varied ways that governance is achieved in the contemporary world economy by focusing on the logic of rule-based economic governance, on the informal coordination provided by the G-7 process, and on regionalism. At the end of the chapter we will look at the challenges to the post–World War II order of multilateral governance.

International Economic Institutions

States face a basic trade-off in their dealings with the world economy. A country that opens itself up to trade and investment with other countries can anticipate economic gains, but it also risks a loss in government policy autonomy and control over its national economy. Openness can also bring political vulnerabilities and insecurities. A similar trade-off exists as states grapple with building institutions for global economic governance. Institutional agreements, by their very nature, restrict the policy choices and autonomy of states that are party to the institutions. Agreeing to operate within a multilateral institution such as the WTO or the IMF requires an acceptance of restraints and obligations on government policy in return for the anticipated cooperation of other states. So government leaders must ask themselves whether the gains of institutional agreement are greater than the costs of lost autonomy.

The Uses of International Institutions

States establish institutions to govern economic relations for a variety of reasons. First, institutional agreements can establish durable trade arrangements that create a steady stream of mutual gains for the states involved. The underlying gains are, of course, economic: as we saw in Chapter 2, trade and investment create efficiency gains in the employment of capital, labor, and resources.[1] The institutional agreement simply turns these specific efficiency gains from individual agreements into an ongoing stream of gains. Under an institutional framework, states do not need to continuously negotiate their economic relationships with other states—and this itself is an efficiency gain.[2]

Second, institutional agreements can facilitate economic exchange by creating mechanisms that allow states to share the gains and costs of openness. As we also saw in Chapter 2, neoclassical trade theory argues that states will gain by reducing barriers to trade regardless of what other countries do. But states are also political actors operating in a competitive international environment, and therefore they care about the relative gains and risks from economic exchange. Thus institutional rules and mechanisms can be useful as cost- and benefit-sharing agreements. A state that is party to an institution knows that other states are bound by the same rules and regulations that govern its own trade and economic policies. It also has greater confidence that it will be treated fairly and not be isolated or discriminated against by others. This is a basic assumption behind the postwar trading rules and norms embodied in GATT and the WTO: all states agree to abide by norms of multilateralism and nondiscrimination as well as to share the gains and burdens of economic expansion and dislocation. In making this mutual commitment, each state reduces its political risks in operating within an open world economy.

Third, institutional agreements can actually create or enhance the capacity of states to manage their own national economies. International institutions can pool resources (such as exchange reserves) and create standby capacities to help national governments in times of economic difficulty. This was the ultimate rationale behind the Bretton Woods institutions. When leaders of the industrialized countries met in Bretton Woods, New Hampshire, in the summer of 1944 to agree on postwar monetary rules, they were not just ceding some state authority to international agencies, thereby reducing their own policy autonomy, they were also creating monetary reserves and other tools that national governments could use to manage exchange-rate crises.[3] The new instruments and capacities that they created could be employed to stabilize their economies and help them weather monetary crises with a minimum of economic dislocation and contraction. Today, the IMF provides capital reserves for developing countries to help stabilize their exchange rates, although its borrowing requirements typically entail elaborate restrictions on the government's macroeconomic and regulatory policies. The IMF provides resources for states to manage an economic crisis, at the expense of the recipient government's policy autonomy.

Fourth, international institutions can play a more general role in binding and constraining states. A powerful state may promote institutional agreements as a way of locking weaker states into a predictable policy orientation well into the future. This was in part what motivated the United States after World War II to help set up the array of multilateral economic institutions. The United States was in an unprecedented position to shape economic relationships after the war. It had an abundance of power resources that it could use to induce other states to participate in a postwar economic order with rules and norms that favored the United States over the long term. Because of its large domestic economy and pre-eminent military standing after the war, the United States had the capacity to extend favorable economic terms to other states and to use its occupation policies in Germany and Japan to open and integrate the industrialized world. The IMF and GATT created institutional rules and mechanisms that shaped and constrained the basic terms by which postwar states could operate within the world economy. In this sense, international institutions are not just instruments that allow states to overcome collective-action problems and achieve joint gains. They are also instruments of political control, mechanisms by which leading states manage the world economic order in ways that accord with their own long-term interests.

But if institutions are mechanisms that can be used to bind and constrain states, these mechanisms can also be used to reduce the arbitrary and indiscriminate actions of leading states. Powerful states may want to lock other states into a predictable and agreeable policy orientation, but weaker states may well want to do the same to strong states. Moreover, strong states may occasionally have an incentive to bind and constrain themselves through institutional agreements, particularly if in doing so they are able to persuade other states to cooperate. The result is a potential bargain: the leading state agrees to operate within an institution that limits its ability to act in arbitrary and exploitative ways and, in return, weaker states agree to participate in the open economic order.[4] Each state—strong and weak—gives up some policy autonomy but in return gets a more predictable and congenial international environment. The United States has made its economic and political preferences more acceptable to weaker states around the world because it has agreed to operate within the rules and norms of multilateral institutions. It has lost some of its discretionary power over economic policy but succeeded in establishing a stable and open economic order willingly accepted by other states.

Types of Institutional Mechanisms

There are a variety of ways in which governments can cooperate to mutually govern the world economy. When states seek ways to govern the world economy they are in effect looking for ways to coordinate their national economic policies. This can be done at the global, multilateral level or in smaller, regional groupings of states. It can be done through formal institutions or by ad hoc agreements between a few states. Each type of mechanism—formal/rule-based, informal/ad hoc, and regional—has its strengths and weaknesses.

In exploring the dilemmas of economic cooperation between states, it is useful to make a basic distinction between two types of policy coordination: rule-based and discretionary coordination. ***Rule-based policy coordination*** is determined by ongoing rules of economic relations. This coordination is autonomic. Governments do not need to make continuous choices about whether to cooperate with another country; the rules ensure that this happens. A fixed exchange-rate regime is a rule-based form of coordination, wherein national macroeconomic policies adjust automatically to the pressures of fixed currency relations. The nineteenth-century gold standard is another good example of this rule-based logic. Each country's national currency was pegged to the price of gold, which itself was fixed in value. Traders could buy and sell currencies and capital could move between national economies at predictable exchange rates. The terms of monetary relations were fixed, and this rule-based system facilitated trade and capital integration around the world. In today's world economy, the WTO, with its judicial-like dispute-resolution mechanisms, is the most ruled-based of the various institutions that govern the world economy.

In contrast, ***discretionary policy coordination*** entails more specific, one-at-a-time agreements. States offer to make policy adjustments or concessions in exchange for policy adjustments or concessions made by other states. This is the type of policy cooperation that is most often exercised at the annual G-7 economic summits, where the leaders of the largest industrialized economies gather to discuss their common economic problems and the wider problems of global economic governance.[5] Sometimes these leaders discuss the establishment of new rules for world markets—the exchange-rate regime, a new trade round, or IMF lending practices. But at other moments they are seeking to settle specific policy disputes and tackle new problems in the management of political-economic relations.

Developing Rule-Based Governance: Bretton Woods Regime

The great postwar multilateral institutions are the most important and far-reaching attempts by states to govern global markets through rule-based institutions. Half a century after their founding, the IMF and the WTO (which replaced GATT in 1995) continue to operate as the core organizing mechanisms of the world economy. These monetary and trade regimes embody the most ambitious efforts by advanced industrialized states to build a formal structure for world economic governance. The agreements produced at Bretton Woods combined a vision of a liberal world economy with a rule whose primary purpose was to constrain national economic policies in cases where otherwise the interaction of different national strategies might cause disaster for the world as a whole (such as in competitive devaluations of national currencies or in the application of protectionism).[6] The postwar agreements reflected a commitment to rule-guided economic openness.

The monetary and trade regimes were both shaped by the United States and its partners as they grappled with the reconstruction of the world economy after World War II. Both regimes were shaped by strong reactions to the failures of earlier eras of the world economy, particularly the tumultuous 1930s. Over the decades, the monetary regime has lost some of its rule-based character, as the Bretton Woods pegged-dollar standard broke down in the early 1970s and evolved into a floating exchange-rate system.[7] The GATT regime, however, has become increasingly rule-based since its transformation into the WTO in the mid-1990s and the development of new, judicially oriented dispute-settlement mechanisms.

Rule-Based Monetary Policy

When the United States, the United Kingdom, and 40 other countries met at Bretton Woods in 1944 to agree to a postwar monetary order, the inadequacies of the nineteenth-century gold standard and the turmoil of the 1930s loomed large. The gold standard did provide for decades of stable exchange rates and facilitated the flow of capital and trade, but it also exacted a heavy toll on the economies of the Western world.[8] Countries that experienced balance-of-payments pressures were forced to raise interest rates to slow their economies in order to bring their accounts back into balance. Unemployment, the inevitable result of increased interest rates, was the mechanism by which countries stabilized the world economy.[9] In the wake of the Great Depression, the leading economies abandoned the gold standard and began a decade of competitive currency devaluations. Governments manipulated their currencies in an attempt to retain trade advantages in a shrinking world market. The convertibility of currencies declined and the world economy fractured into regions.

It was the search for a middle path between these extremes that motivated the famous British economist John Maynard Keynes to work with U.S. officials to devise a new set of rules. The United States was interested primarily in free trade and the convertibility of currencies, and it resisted the most ambitious proposals by Keynes, who wanted to establish an international currency that would allow governments to pursue expansionary fiscal policies and to obligate the United States, as the world's leading capital-account surplus country, to aid capital-account deficit countries. Nonetheless, the Bretton Woods monetary rules did respond to the problems that had wrecked the world economy. The formerly pegged exchange rates became adjustable, subject to agreement between the major economies on the need for realignments. Countries were permitted to institute controls to limit the flows of capital. Most important, however, was a new institution, the IMF, created to monitor national economic policies and provide balance-of-payments financing for countries at risk.[10] The IMF gave governments tools

PRIMARY DOCUMENT 9.1

Purposes and Policies of the International Monetary Fund

The Fund will be guided in all its decisions by the purposes and policies set forth below:

1. To promote international monetary co-operation through a permanent institution which provides the machinery for consultations on international monetary problems.

2. To facilitate the expansion and balanced growth of international trade and to contribute in this way to the maintenance of a high level of employment and real income, which must be a primary objective of economic policy.

3. To give confidence to member countries by making the Fund's resources available to them under adequate safeguards, thus giving members time to correct maladjustments in their balance of payments without resorting to measures destructive of national or international prosperity.

4. To promote exchange stability, to maintain orderly exchange arrangements among member countries, and to avoid competitive exchange depreciation.

5. To assist the establishment of multilateral payments facilities on current transactions among member countries and the elimination of foreign exchange restrictions which hamper the growth of world trade.

6. To shorten the periods and lessen the degree of disequilibrium in the international balance of payments of member countries.

This document which appeared as a White Paper reflected the work of American and British experts and provided the basis for agreements reached at the Bretton Woods conference in July 1944.

Section one of the "Joint Statement by Experts on the Establishment of an International Monetary Fund," 22 April 1944, reprinted in *The Collected Writings of John Maynard Keynes*, Vol. 25 (Cambridge: Cambridge University Press, 1980), Appendix 4, pp. 469–77.

Core Principle

The IMF was initially created to counteract financial crises (such as those that were experienced throughout the 1930s) by offering balance-of-payments financing for at-risk countries. It has grown into a major international lending and financial-consulting institution.

to stabilize their economies and ease their payment flows back into balance without having to resort to deflationary interest-rate policies (see Primary Document 9.1).[11]

As discussed in Chapter 5, the establishment of new monetary rules after World War II was an outgrowth of the Bretton Woods conference of 1944. It was at this meeting that economic specialists from the United States, the United Kingdom, and other major countries met with the assignment to create a stable world economic order that would prevent the return to the economic nationalism and conflict of the 1930s. The Bretton Woods agreements resulted in the establishment of the International Monetary Fund and the International Bank for Reconstruction and Development (now called the World Bank). The IMF was created as a facility that would assist governments in balance-of-payments crisis, and the World Bank was charged with providing loans for long-term economic development. In the decades that followed, regional development banks—such at the Asian Development Bank, the African Development Bank, the Inter-American Development Bank, and the European Bank for Reconstruction and Development—were established to provide loans within specific regions.

The officials who met at Bretton Woods in 1944 envisioned rules for the world economy that would provide governments with a great deal of freedom to pursue national economic objectives, yet with a monetary order that would be based on fixed exchange rates so as to prevent a repeat of the destructive competitive depreciations of the 1930s. The principle of currency convertibility for current-account transactions was also enshrined at Bretton Woods in order to prevent a resurgence of the exclusive economic zones and ruinous regional conflict of the earlier era.

The agreement between British and American monetary planners was particularly important because it helped build a broad coalition in favor of an open and rule-based postwar world economy. Government leaders were given instruments with which they could achieve multiple objectives. Monetary rules provided for economic openness with the commitment to currency convertibility. These rules minimized the ability of states to remain closed within regional economic zones or currency blocs. But the rules also provided governments with access to newly created international financial reserves, which allowed them to manage financial crises and bring their national economies back into equilibrium without triggering recession. It is this innovative "third way" between closure and openness—call it "managed openness"—that allowed states to foster economic growth by expanding trade but also to pursue economic security by building social supports and safety nets.

In the early 1970s, the Bretton Woods exchange-rate rules came under intense pressure. The stability of exchange rates was tied to what emerged as a dollar-gold standard. The breakdown of the system was ultimately due to the expansion of international capital flows. Capital controls, which were left in place with the original Bretton Woods agreements, provided some insulation from balance-of-payments pressures. These capital controls, which made the outflow from and inflow of capital to the economies of the advanced countries, allowed governments to formulate fiscal policy and stimulus programs without having to worry about the pressure such policies would put on interest rates. Thus the controls provided some breathing space for governments to respond to crises and to adjust the pegged exchange-rate system to address the crises. But the gradual decline of controls and the growing mobility of capital doomed the old regime. As one scholar has noted, "in a world of high capital mobility, defending [a pegged exchange rate] required unprecedented levels of foreign-exchange-market intervention and international support."[12] Generating financial support of this magnitude was generally impossible when creditors doubted the ability or the willingness of governments to make the adjustments necessary to eliminate the payments imbalance. With the breakdown of the fixed but adjustable Bretton Woods regime in August 1971, the world's monetary system moved toward floating exchange rates.[13]

The breakdown of hard rules launched monetary officials on a search for ways to maintain stability in a more complex world of fast-moving capital flows and divergent national economic policies. The IMF shifted its duties to include greater focus on surveillance over its members' exchange-rate policies and greater active cooperation to manage shifts in currency rates.[14]

Rule-Based Trade Policy

The other major rule-based international regime established after World War II was the General Agreement on Tariffs and Trade. The multilateral trade rules reflected a single-minded concern by United States and European governments to avoid the protectionism and instability of the 1930s. The errors of that era were not due to flaws in economic theory; economists and many political leaders fully understood the mutual advantages of trade. The errors instead arose from the national rivalries that led to a spiral of protectionism and the inability of governments to agree on procedures and rules of open trade. The high tide of this protectionist scramble was marked by the Smoot-Hawley tariff of 1930, passed by the U.S. Congress and signed into law by President Herbert Hoover over the protests of government and academic economists (a thousand of whom signed a warning letter to the president). Across the industrialized world, governments responded to the U.S. tariff with restrictions of their own, and the world economy lurched toward closure.[15]

The counterattack on protectionism began as early as 1934 with the passage by the U.S. Congress of the Reciprocal Trade Agreements Act (RTAA), which delegated authority to the executive branch to pursue trade negotiations. Five years later the Franklin Roosevelt administration had secured agreement with 20 countries to reduce tariffs on more than half of U.S. trade. The driving force behind the RTAA, Secretary of State Cordell Hull, continued to push for free trade during the wartime discussions of the postwar economic order.[16] As we noted in Chapter 5, the administrations of Franklin Roosevelt and, later, Harry Truman were motivated by the conviction that the war-causing political turmoil of the 1930s was rooted in nationalist and protectionist economic practices. Economic openness was necessary to ensure stable and cooperative postwar political relations. Multilateral rules would be necessary to ensure that competitive national economic policies would not trigger trade wars or spiral downward into protectionism.

The Bretton Woods negotiators called for an International Trade Organization to sit alongside the IMF, the World Bank, and the United Nations as a pillar of postwar order. But their effort failed. The U.S. Congress feared the loss of economic sovereignty and worried that agricultural interests would be hurt under the proposed new multilateral organization.[17] However, a rump organization, GATT, which did not require congressional approval, did survive to operate as a vehicle for multilateral trade reductions. Its mandate was the reduction of tariffs on the trade of manufactured goods. In the decades following the war, a sequence of trade rounds—eight altogether—was pursued, each round expanded on its predecessor to include more countries in the negotiations. The most recent rounds—the Tokyo round, concluded in 1980, and the Uruguay round, concluded in 1994—pushed tariff levels to an all-time low.

The rules that GATT enshrined were aimed at establishing an open trading system that was seen by all as fair and flexible. Toward this end, the GATT regime encompassed a number of norms:

- Nondiscrimination:[18] the best trade arrangement that a country makes with another country should be extended to all other countries participating in the regime; countries should not be singled out for trade discrimination, and tariff levels should be applied equally to all trade partners.
- Liberalization: all participating states should strive toward tariff reductions and economic openness.
- Reciprocity: if one country makes a tariff concession, each state that benefits from it should make a concession of its own; this norm is more political than economic, but is necessary to make the trade rounds work.
- Legitimacy of safeguards: countries that are in serious deficit or faced with severe economic dislocations can be exempt from liberalization agreements this loophole norm gives governments some breathing room to protect their economies under dire circumstances.
- Multilateralism: all countries of the world should be brought into the process, and barriers to trade should be lowered together.
- Major interest: the leading industrialized countries have special obligations to work together and make deals that can be turned into more general agreements.

These norms formed the underpinnings of the rule-based trade regime. They articulate an ideal vision of trade between countries (see Primary Document 9.2). Trade negotiations are to be built on multilateral negotiations rather than bilateral or other partial agreements. Trade is to be conducted by private business actors in a market in which prices are set by a free play of supply and demand. Government intervention is seen as a distortion of the market, aimed at delaying domestic adjustment to international price signals. Governments are expected to set the rules for trade but remain outside the trading arena. Free trade is expected to stimulate the expansion of all economies as long as national economies bear the strains of international growth and adjustment.

The multilateral trade rules enshrined in GATT have been useful in facilitating tariff reductions. Tariff barriers can be measured and monitored and they are relatively easy for governments to reduce. As tariffs have been brought down to very low levels, however, **nontariff barriers** have been used more frequently as obstacles to trade. Nontariff barriers, such as government procurement codes, health standards, subsidies, product regula-

PRIMARY DOCUMENT 9.2

An Ideal Vision of Trade

The trading system should be

- **without discrimination**—a country should not discriminate between its trading partners (they are all, equally, granted "most-favoured-nation" or MFN status); and it should not discriminate between its own and foreign products, services or nationals (they are given "national treatment").
- **freer**—with barriers coming down through negotiation.
- **predictable**—foreign companies, investors and governments should be confident that trade barriers (including tariffs, non-tariff barriers and other measures) should not be raised arbitrarily; more and more tariff rates and market-opening commitment are "bound" in the WTO.
- **more competitive**—by discouraging "unfair" practices such as export subsidies and dumping products at below cost to gain market share.
- **more beneficial for less developed countries**—by giving them more time to adjust, greater flexibility, and special privileges.

Source: www.wto.org/english/thewto_e/whatis_e/ti_efact2_e.htm.

Core Principle

The rules of the WTO revolve around the principles of consistency, fairness, and competition—the iron laws of liberal economics.

tions, and so forth, are more difficult to identity and eliminate. Complex issues of domestic law and legislation are brought into the negotiations, hampering the ability of governments to make commitments to reduce such barriers and actually carry out those commitments. Starting with the Tokyo round in the late 1970s, trade negotiators began seeking ways to deal with these new, thorny problems, and agreements were reached among small groups of countries on reducing specific nontariff barriers in various sectors of their economies.[19] The rules of the GATT regime also tended to be soft. When governments brought charges of trade discrimination or the violation of other trade rules to the Geneva-based GATT, the mechanisms for dispute resolution were never definitive. Governments could ignore or contest the findings of trade-dispute panels. It was difficult to expand the authority of GATT rules beyond tariff barriers to agriculture, services, and other economic sectors, and the mechanisms for enforcing rules and settling disputes were limited.

Confronted with these new challenges to open trade, the United States and its partners agreed to new rules and mechanisms for the management of world trade with the launching of the World Trade Organization. Agreed to as part of the Uruguay round of trade negotiations that culminated in 1993, the WTO formalized and strengthened GATT rule-making and dispute-settlement mechanisms.[20] This new institution marked a major step in establishing a judicial basis for international trade law. A formal organization was established with a legal personality, an independent secretariat, and an expanded institutional framework for international trade cooperation. By creating procedures for the rendering of binding decisions, the WTO constitutes a form of compulsory jurisdiction in international trade law. The WTO was championed by countries seeking to strengthen the legal basis of policy obligations as a way to discipline the resort to unilateral measures, particularly by the United States.

The most far-reaching change introduced by the WTO was the mechanism for the resolution of trade disputes. The GATT dispute-settlement approach operated according to consensus practices that allowed losing parties in trade disputes to block the issuance of reports by investigative panels. Under the WTO framework, however, dispute settlement has been upgraded by providing for cross-retaliation and the automatic adoption of panel reports.[21] The dispute-settlement constraints on national policy autonomy embodied in the WTO are quite specific. States are bound only by settlements that involve disputes over agreements they have already made based on general trade principles. The WTO cannot create obligations that states—or "contracting parties," in the language of the WTO—do not themselves agree to in principle. But member states are obliged to obey rules in practice that they negotiate over in principle. States may also lose some sovereign right to determine the standing of the dispute: they agree that rules will be applied by a legal-technical body that they do not control. As a result, as one analyst concludes, "under the WTO it [is] less easy for the United States and other countries to avoid the implementation of trade rules they agreed to in the past, with some resulting loss of flexibility in national commercial policy-making."[22]

The United States supported the launch of the WTO because it advanced the long-standing U.S. goal of strengthening the dispute-settlement system, which U.S. officials argued would help protect American businesses and reinforce multilateral trade rules.[23] The Europeans saw the WTO dispute-settlement proposal as a way to guard against the unilateral excesses that the United States had practiced in the past. Other, smaller trading countries also supported the WTO because it was seen as a step forward in the development of a rules-based system that would protect them against arbitrary trade discrimination by stronger states.[24] In the end, the world's trading partners made the determination that the gains from the Uruguay round of trade negotiations and the strengthening of the system of trade rules outweighed the restrictions that would be imposed on their policy discretion (see Primary Document 9.3).

Small-Group Governance

Despite the benefits brought by institutions such as the IMF and the WTO, there are limits to the willingness and ability of states to operate within a multilateral rule-based economic order. Often countries choose instead to work within smaller, less-comprehensive groups of states to achieve economic goals. A number of other, smaller institutional mechanisms have therefore evolved to respond to the changes in the world economy and the dilemmas of interdependence.

Institutional mechanisms outside of the Bretton Woods system emerged soon after World War II to help governments reconcile international economic order with the domestic concerns of nation-states. The Organization for European Economic Cooperation was created in 1948 to coordinate the process of European economic reconstruction; it was later turned into the Organization for Economic Cooperation and Development (OECD) to provide technical support and facilitate policy coordination among the world's industrialized countries. The Group of 7 process emerged in the mid-1970s as an annual forum where finance ministers from the advanced industrialized countries would discuss monetary and financial relations among their governments. A group of 10 forum also was formed as a gathering of finance officials who would work outside the IMF to coordinate the supply of financial resources to deal with periodic monetary crises and imbalances, supplementing the work of the Bank for International Settlement, international organization based in Switzerland that promotes cooperation and coordination of the activities of the world's central banks. In 1999, a new grouping—the G-20—was launched by the G-7 countries to encourage international cooperation on financial and economic problems. This group, formed in part

✐ **PRIMARY DOCUMENT 9.3**

Ten Benefits of Rules-Based Trade

In the WTO's view: Ten reasons why we are better off with the multilateral trading system

1. The system helps promote peace.
2. Disputes are handled constructively.
3. Rules make life easier for all.
4. Freer trade cuts the costs of living.
5. Free trade provides more choices of products and qualities.
6. Trade raises incomes.
7. Trade stimulates economic growth.
8. The basic principles embodied in the WTO make life more efficient.
9. Governments are shielded from lobbying.
10. The system encourages good government.

Source: "10 Benefits of the WTO Trading System," www.wto.org.

Core Principle

The World Trade Organization argues that multilateralism—bringing all countries into the global market through lowering tariffs—should became standard economic policy for all nations. In the WTO's view, this prevents the protectionism that catapulted the global economy into depression in the 1930s and facilitated the march to World War II. The WTO's opponents, on the other hand, argue that such unrestricted market forces erode national cultures, widen the gap between rich and poor and between developed and underdeveloped nations, and increase the chances of a global economic crisis.

as a response to the Asian financial crisis of 1997–98, brings together the 7 leading industrialized countries with several large developing countries and representatives from the European Union, the IMF, and the World Bank to discuss the stability and reform of the international financial system.[25]

The developing countries have created their own institutions to deal with economic problems. The United Nations Conference on Trade and Development, along with the UN caucus of developing countries called the G-77, became a vehicle for cooperation within the UN framework, and in the

1990s the G-24 became a forum to coordinate policy with the IMF and the World Bank. The Committee of 20 and later the Interim Committee of the IMF—later renamed the International Monetary and Financial Committee—have operated as a gathering to discuss international economic problems, as well. Around the world at the regional level, a growing variety of associations has been established to facilitate economic cooperation. The result has been a proliferation in recent decades of informal institutions dedicated to discussion and cooperation on facets of the world economy.

The G-7/G-8 Process

The G-7/G-8 summit is the most encompassing and important of these various coordination and consultation institutions. The G-7/G-8 process is a mechanism for the regular discussion of world economic issues and, increasingly, political and security issues, by the leading industrial economic powers. Some see it as a central governance mechanism for the world political economy. One analyst argues that "the G-7 Summit System has become the effective centre of global governance, replacing the order earlier provided by the 1919–1945 [League of Nations and] United Nations and 1947 Atlantic family of institutions, and recurrently creating consensus and inducing compliance among its members and other states and international institutions."[26]

The annual summits of the leading industrialized democracies began in the mid-1970s when the Bretton Woods monetary regime broke down and these countries were pressed to consult more closely on monetary and financial policies.[27] The first meeting was held in Rambouillet, France, in 1975, and was attended by the leaders of France, the United States, the United Kingdom, Germany, Japan, and Italy. The event became an annual gathering the following year when President Gerald Ford called a meeting held in San Juan, Puerto Rico, and invited Canada to join the group. During the 1970s, the focus of the meetings was primarily the management of the international economy: the reform of the monetary order, macroeconomic policy coordination, the liberalization of trade, and the stabilization of oil supplies and prices. During the 1980s, the summit agendas expanded to discuss political and security issues (see Primary Document 9.4), including relations with the Soviet Union. Microeconomic policy and economic restructuring also were added to summit consultations. In the 1990s, the focus shifted again to include new global and transnational issues such as democratization, the envi-

G-7 Statement on Political Issues

Chairman's Statement (Political)

July 10th, 1994

1. This occasion has been given added meaning by the full participation in the political discussions of the President of the Russian Federation. This partnership, which is a reflection of the reforms that have taken place in Russia, reaffirms our wish to tackle together today's problems in a constructive and responsible manner. . . .

2. Following the death of [North Korean leader] Kim Il Sung, we must continue to seek a solution to the problem created by North Korea's decision to withdraw from the IAEA [International Atomic Energy Agency]. We urge [North Korea] to continue to engage [South Korea] and the international community, including a continuation of the talks with the US and going forward with the scheduled summit with [South Korea]. We also urge [North Korea] to provide total transparency in its nuclear program through full and unconditional compliance with its nonproliferation obligations and to remove, once and for all, the suspicions surrounding its nuclear activities. We support the renewed efforts to resolve the North Korean nuclear issue through dialogue and we stress the importance of [North Korea's] ensuring the continuity of IAEA safeguards and maintaining the freeze on its nuclear program, including no reprocessing spent fuel or reloading its nuclear reactors.

3. We have welcomed the Israeli-Palestinian Declaration of Principles and the signing of the Gaza-Jericho agreement as a first step in its implementation. We recognize the need to speed up the delivery of assistance and create the circumstances for a real improvement of living conditions. Progress on the other bilateral tracks and in the multilateral negotiations is now essential in order to achieve a lasting and comprehensive settlement of the Arab-Israeli dispute and a wider process of peace and cooperation in the whole Middle East/Mediterranean region. We call upon the League of Arab States to end their boycott of Israel. We support the efforts of reconstruction of a prosperous and independent Lebanon.

    We reiterate our resolve to enforce full implementation of each and every relevant UN Security Council resolution concerning Iraq and Libya until they are complied with, and recall that such implementation would entail the reassessment of sanctions.

    We call upon the government of Iran to participate constructively in international efforts for peace and stability and to modify its behavior contrary to these objectives, *inter alia* with regard to terrorism.

We support the Algerian government's decision to move forward on economic reforms, which must be pursued with determination, while urging Algerian leaders to continue a political dialogue with all elements of Algerian society rejecting violence and terrorism. We condemn the recent massacre of Italian sailors and other victims, and express our condolences to their families.

We call upon the government of the Republic of Yemen to resolve political differences within the country through dialogue and by peaceful means, and to ensure that the humanitarian situation, particularly in and around Aden, is addressed. International obligations, including sovereignty and territorial integrity, should be respected.

Source: Statement released by the Naples Summit, July 10, 1994, available at www.g7.utoronto.ca/g7/summit/1994naples/chairman.html.

Core Principle

The G-7 and its successor, the G-8, have expanded their role to deal equally with economic and political issues.

ronment, terrorism, and the drug trade.[28] The 2000 summit in Okinawa, Japan, focused on globalization and the digital divide, or the growing economic and technological gap between rich and poor countries.

Interestingly, the G-7/G-8 process exists with very little formal structure. The British government, prior to the hosting of the 1998 G-8 summit in Birmingham, described the annual summit process as "an informal organisation, with no rules or permanent Secretariat staff."[29] But a set of institutional routines and traditions does guide the workings of the summit process and the growing variety of activities that are guided by the G-7/G-8 process. The meetings began as informal discussions by government leaders and their finance ministers. Over the decades they have grown in their preparations and formality. At the 1991 London summit, the British proposed that the summits should have an official chairman, rotating each calendar year, assumed by the government leader of the host country. The background planning and thematic focus of the summits have increased as a result. On occasion, summit leaders have urged the return to the informality of the early summits. At the 1998 summit meeting in the United Kingdom, the summit process officially expanded to include Russia as a full member—turning the G-7 into the G-8—although the original seven countries continue to dominate the ministerial-level process. The G-7/G-8 process has also evolved to include much more than simply the annual meetings of government leaders (see Timeline 9.1). The finance ministers have periodic meetings between summits, often during the annual meetings of the IMF and the World Bank. Central bankers and other international economic officials are often included in these gatherings.[30] Foreign ministers of the G-8 members have also increasingly consulted together in regular meetings. In the eight or nine months leading up to the annual summit, designated representatives (called

> **TIMELINE 9.1**

The Expansion of the G/7-G/8 System

1973	Finance ministers begin irregular meetings
1975	Finance ministers begin to meet annually on summit site
1975	Foreign ministers begin to meet annually on summit site
1975	Sherpa meetings begin to be held 3–4 times per year
1977	International Nuclear Fuel Cycle Evaluation Group begins to meet
1978	Trade ministers quadrilateral meet on summit site
1979	International Energy Technology Group created
1982	Trade ministers quadrilateral convene annual stand-alone summit and also meet on summit site
1984	Foreign ministers begin to conduct an annual stand-alone meeting
1985	Expert Group on Aid to Sub-Saharan Africa is created
1986	Finance ministers begin to meet 3–4 or more times per year
1989	Financial Action Task Force is created
1990	Permanent Working Group on Assistance to Russia is created
1990	Chemical Action Task Force begins to meet
1992	Nuclear Safety Working Group is created
1993	Trade ministers quadrilateral meet on summit site

1993	Finance and foreign ministers meet regarding aid to Russia
1994	Environment Group convenes annual summit
1994	Meeting is held to discuss economic aid to Ukraine
1995	Trade ministers quadrilateral meet on summit site
1995	Counterterrorism Experts' Group begins to meet
1995	Senior Experts' Group on Transnational Organized Crime is created
1996	Employment Group begins to meet annually
1997	Experts' Group on Financial Crime is created
1998	Meeting is held to discuss energy

Source: Adapted from Peter I. Hajnal, *The G7/G8 System: Evolution, Role, and Documentation* (Aldershot: Ashgate, 1999), pp. 36–37.

"sherpas") meet to prepare the agenda and coordinate activities for the formal meeting.

In the 1990s, in perhaps the most important innovation in the G-7/G-8 process, the summit leaders have acted to create an array of task forces and working groups to tackle specific international problems. In the late 1970s, steps in this direction were taken with the establishment of the International Nuclear Fuel Cycle Evaluation Group and the International Energy Technology Group. In 1989, at the Paris summit, the G-7 leaders established the Financial Action Task Force to coordinate government efforts to fight drug-related money-laundering. In 1992 the summit leaders established a Nuclear Safety Working Group, the 1995 Halifax summit created a Senior Experts' Group on Transnational Organized Crime that became known as the Lyon Group, and the 1997 Denver summit created an experts' group on financial crime.[31] A wide range of other groups, some accountable to the G-7/G-8 summit leaders and others created in partnership with other international organizations, provide coordinating groups working on aid to Russia, nuclear proliferation, and international development problems. Increasingly, the summit process is only one small part of a larger network of experts and working groups. The new governance mechanisms that are emerging in the world are doing so in this decentralized and loose organizational fashion.

Policy Coordination among the G-7/G-8

Policy coordination within the G-7/G-8 process has taken a variety of forms. In its weakest version, coordination is really only consultation. States pursue their own policies without formal international coordination, but those policies reflect the results of interactions with other states. During the 1980s, for instance, when the United States was running a huge and growing budget deficit that was putting upward pressure on interest rates around the world and imperiling economic growth in many countries, the leaders of the other industrialized countries pressed their concerns on the administration of President Ronald Reagan. Prime Minister Yasuhiro Nakasone of Japan raised the issue directly with Reagan at the 1987 G-7 summit in Venice, Italy. Such coordination involves no explicit deals or institutional agreements, but does involve an exchange of views that can influence policy and allow mutual adjustment to take place among the major economies.

Another way in which implicit coordination takes place is through the reinforcement of national economic policy directions at international meetings and declarations. When government leaders seek to steer the national economy in ways that meet the approval of foreign governments, the international support for these policies can be used to bolster the prospects of success in domestic politics. British prime minister Margaret Thatcher used statements issued at G-7 summits in the 1980s as a source of support and reinforcement for her domestic privatization and austerity program. Government leaders around the world have made pointed criticisms of U.S. unilateral trade sanctions, such as the Helms-Burton Act that retaliates against foreign firms trading with Cuba. This pressure does not in itself change U.S. policy, but it does raise the stakes and sharpen the choices for the U.S. president. The views of foreign governments are added to the domestic mix of forces that are shaping national economic policy.

Policy coordination can also take place through the growing use of intergovernmental mechanisms. Government bureaucrats in a wide range of departments and ministries conduct routine consultations with their counterparts in other countries. U.S. Justice Department officials, regulatory agencies, environmental officials, and many other government bureaucracies are continuously working on a transgovernmental basis on specific issues.[32] This type of coordination occurs largely out of public view. The intergovernmental process is typically focused on quite specific and technical issues of regulatory law or public policy, particularly as these government officials are involved in the implementation and administration of policy. Policy coordination—just like the devil—is in the details.

Finally, the most full-blown type of policy coordination is what might be called the "package deal," a form of conditional policy cooperation. In such arrangements, national policy is determined as part of a conditional international agreement involving mutual commitments, either within a given policy area, such as trade or energy, or across a swath of policy areas. One government makes a policy change only if it is matched by a policy change by other states. States thereby trade concessions, each getting something in exchange for its own reluctant or difficult shift in policy.

The classic example of this type of coordination unfolded at the Bonn G-7 summit in 1978. In the years between 1976 and 1979, the world was reeling from oil-price shocks and a slowing international economy. "Stagflation" was the word coined to describe the painful combination of rising inflation and slow growth that plagued the industrialized world during these years. The administration of President Jimmy Carter sought a coordinated plan for global "reflation," in which the leading industrialized economies—the United States, Germany, and Japan—would simultaneously stimulate their economies to foster greater growth and trade. It was hoped that this "locomotive" plan would pull the other industrialized countries along and together the world economy would move to a higher and healthier growth path. The weaker countries and many economists, including those at the OECD in Paris, supported this plan. But it was opposed by Japan and Germany, who did not want to jeopardize their own relatively low inflation rates to bail out other governments. The issue of what to do about the deteriorating world economy dominated Western economic diplomacy in the year before the 1978 summit.[33]

At the London summit in the summer of 1977 a vague commitment was made by the G-7 government leaders to pursue higher growth, but the necessary expansionary policies were not carried out. The United States did, however, move to stimulate its domestic economy, and as a result the dollar started to decline in value and inflation started to rise. The United States looked like the only country exercising world economic leadership.

But the other industrial countries had a major complaint about the United States: its huge appetite for oil imports, a demand that put upward pressure on world oil prices. The root cause of the problem was the U.S. government's price controls on domestically produced oil. These price controls, a legacy of the Richard Nixon administration and implemented before the

1973 oil shocks, had perverse effects on world oil markets. The price controls indirectly subsidized U.S. oil consumption because U.S. consumers could buy gas and oil below world price levels. Price controls also dampened domestic oil production because U.S. producers were reluctant to pump oil out of the ground for a price below world levels. Finally, the price controls stimulated U.S. oil imports, to a point where, in 1977, the oil-import bill soared to more than $45 billion. Germany, Japan, and other countries that were heavily dependent on imported oil suffered higher costs than they would have if the United States had not been operating under a price-control regime. Complaints abounded and everyone agreed that the world economy was in trouble.

In the months leading up to the 1978 Bonn summit, political leaders searched for a way forward. British prime minister James Callaghan proposed a bargain: the Germans would agree to specific reflationary measures in return for specific U.S. commitments to eliminate the ceiling on oil prices. At Bonn the deal was elaborated: German chancellor Helmut Schmidt agreed to pursue a fiscal stimulus program and President Carter agreed to let domestic oil prices rise to the world level by 1980. British and French leaders also agreed to make efforts to conclude the Tokyo round of GATT trade negotiations. In the end, all parts of the agreement were implemented. Over the opposition of his domestic advisers and factions in his own political party, Carter used his administrative authority to lift controls on oil prices. Over the opposition of the German Finance Ministry, factions of his political coalition, and the business and banking community, Schmidt stimulated the German economy with public spending. The United States and its G-7 partners found a package of mutual concessions that allowed contentious but constructive steps to be taken to manage a troubled world economy.

Although the agreement between the United States and Germany was announced to the world as a deal involving mutual concessions, in each government there were political factions who actually wanted to pursue these policy changes. The entire group of senior foreign policy and international economic officials in the Carter administration urged that oil prices be decontrolled regardless of what the Germans might offer in return. Controlled oil prices were serving to postpone necessary economic adjustments to changed international conditions and were harming U.S. foreign policy interests. Likewise, leading figures in the Schmidt government, including officials in the Economics Ministry and the Social Democratic Party, were in favor of more stimulative fiscal policies. The agreement in Bonn for these key insiders was not an exercise in

MAP 9.1

Regional Trade Agreements around the World, 2000

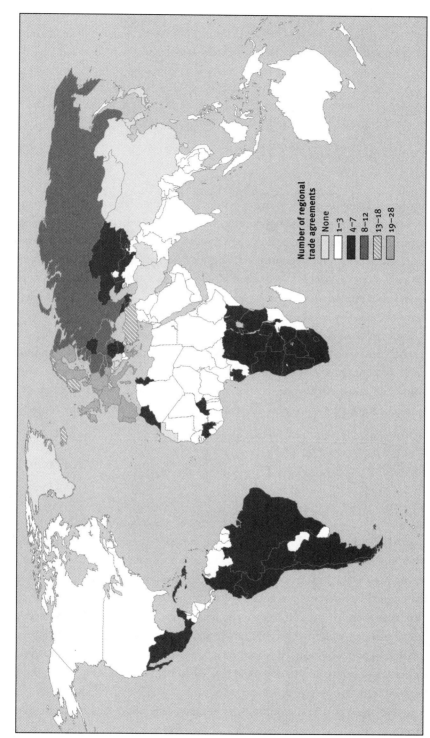

Number of regional
trade agreements

None
1–3
4–7
8–12
13–18
19–28

Source: World Trade Organization, Committee on Regional Trade Agreements, "Mapping of Regional Trade Agreements: Note by the Secretariat," WTO document WT/REG/W/41 (Geneva: WTO, 2000), p. 35, available at www.wto.org/english/tratop_e/region_e/region_e/wtregw41_e.doc.

> *Core Principle*
>
> **S**ome parts of the world have been more active than others in building regional trade arrangements. This map shows the dispersion of regional trade pacts around the world in 2000. It highlights Europe's particularly intense institutionalization of trade relations, as well as the relative absence of such institutionalization in Asia and northern Africa.

concessions, but a way to strengthen their position as they struggled with opponents of these policy changes within their own government. Carter's ability to come home from Bonn and declare that he had received concessions from Germany in return for decontrolling oil prices strengthened his ability to carry the policy out. Likewise, Schmidt was in a stronger domestic position as he moved to stimulate his economy, for he could show the concessions he had received from the United States in return.

Policy coordination, of course, hinges on the ability of government leaders to make policy changes at home. The G-7/G-8 governments are continuously working with one another on a wide range of policy issues. But the ability of large and open democratic countries to implement sweeping economic changes in accord with broad international agreements is more problematic.

Regional Economic Governance

Countries are also seeking to build governance mechanisms within regions (see Map 9.1). Indeed, it could be argued that regional institutions and groupings have been the most creative and noticeable aspect of world economic diplomacy in the last 15 years. There are currently 80 regional deals that provide preferential access to countries within the regional grouping. The most prominent examples are the European Union, the North American Free Trade Agreement (NAFTA), the Association of Southeast Asian Nations (ASEAN), and Mercosur in South America. Many others also exist. Indeed, all but a few of the 142 members of the WTO belong to at least one of these regional trade groupings.

These regional trade groupings have many objectives, but most of them aim to stimulate economic growth through the expansion of trade and in-

✳ **ESSENTIAL ECONOMICS 9.1**

Regional Trade Agreements Notified to GATT and the WTO, 1948–2000

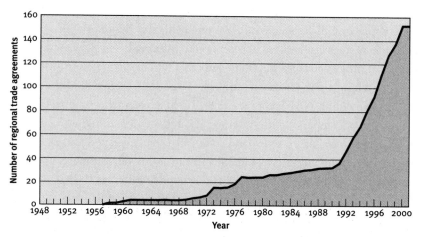

Source: World Trade Organization, "Regionalism: Notified Regional Trade Agreements," available at www.wto.org/english/tratop_e/region_e/regfac_e.htm.

Core Principle

The number of regional trade agreements that have been notified to GATT and, since 1994, the WTO has markedly increased since the end of the Cold War.

---

vestment. For the most part, then, they demonstrate a liberal economic orientation. In contrast to the regional blocs of the 1930s, today's economic regionalism has a more modest political agenda, geared primarily toward the expansion of economic integration within the group by lowering internal barriers rather than raising external barriers. Economic regionalism today is largely a response to three impulses, all largely compatible with global economic openness.

Essential Economics 9.1 shows that the number of regional trade agreements burgeoned starting in the 1980s. This wave of regional agreements emerged as a result of a number of trends, the first of which is the watershed shift that has taken place in the economic development strategies of developing countries around the world. The most remarkable development in the world economic system in the last several decades has been the striking shift in the economic views of emerging countries—in Asia, Latin America, and elsewhere. Chapter 8 highlighted this shift, which is showcased by countries as different as Brazil, Turkey, and Mexico. The result is that developed and developing countries more closely embrace similar views of markets, government policies toward the economy, and the workings of the world economy. New opportunities to cooperate have emerged, and the developed countries have taken steps to "lock in" the economic reforms being pursued in developing countries with regional trade agreements. The invitation for Mexico to join in creating NAFTA can be understood in these terms, and the discussion of expanding NAFTA into a Free Trade Area of the Americas, which would also encompass South America, also reflects this thinking. The opportunities that have arisen to expand trade between developed and developing countries also provide new political incentives for developing countries to consolidate their domestic political and economic reforms.

A second reason for the rise of regional economic agreements is that the liberalization of world trade through global multilateral negotiations has become more problematic. Regional trade deals allow more progress to be made more quickly on trade barriers that are difficult to negotiate within a multilateral setting. As the big, multiyear trade-negotiation rounds have expanded over the decades, they have become more difficult to bring to a successful conclusion. This difficulty arises from the rising number of players involved and from the more complicated nontariff issues that must be confronted. The new trade-liberalization issues are ones that require difficult changes in domestic law. They are more fundamentally political, legal, and regulatory in nature. The Australia–New Zealand free trade agreement, for example, deals with competition policy, which the WTO has not taken up yet. It is more difficult for trade negotiators to make such agreements without close cooperation from the legislative branch. For all these reasons, smaller groupings of states are often seen as a more effective way to make progress. States that are geographically close together typically have more immediate trade-barrier problems at stake and often face similar problems. Progress is more likely and the payoff is more immediate and substantial.

Such regional trade deals can eventually be expanded to more countries. NAFTA is likely to be expanded to include Chile and eventually other countries. There is even discussion of a trade agreement between the EU and NAFTA. There is some evidence that regional trade agreements do discriminate between members and nonmembers. Mercosur's high external tariffs have been shown to cause its members (Argentina, Brazil, Paraguay, and Uruguay) to import from one another even when it would be more efficient to buy goods elsewhere. The EU may have the same effect.[34] But if trade groups can merge and if agreements reached between a few countries can be folded into wider multilateral negotiations, the regional gains can be spread outward and these instances of discrimination can be eliminated.

A third reason for the emergence of so many new regional agreements is related to the ongoing evolution of the world economy. For many industrialized countries, as we saw in Chapter 3, it is increasingly difficult to use traditional macroeconomic tools to manage their economies and stimulate growth. Keynesian policies (deficit spending aimed at stimulating domestic economic growth) have not been possible for many countries in the last decade because so many countries already have huge public debts and budget deficits. Monetary policy has become less effective as countries have developed increasingly internationalized economies and relaxed their capital controls. In this context, regional trade agreements can be attractive: they allow political leaders to get some measure of growth from a government policy. If politicians are motivated chiefly by the search for economic growth—which is, after all, the surest way to be re-elected—then regional trade agreements may provide one vehicle to achieve immediate gains. The big, multilateral trade rounds can take years to negotiate. Regional agreements, on the other hand, can be achieved quickly and their effects can be felt in the short term. They also provide governments with an excuse to tackle microeconomic liberalization problems that, without a trade-negotiation mandate, might be politically unacceptable or impossible.

Together, these three reasons for regional economic agreements suggest a deep compatibility with continued global economic openness. They are part of a wider push to expand and integrate national markets into larger wholes. They are policy tools rather than policy goals. In this view, it is possible to argue that both regional and global economic agendas and institutions are important, and each has its own role to play. Global economic institutions, such as the WTO, are important in enshrining global norms of economic cooperation: reciprocity, most-favored-nation trade status, multilateralism. These global institutions are also important in providing dispute-settlement mechanisms. They cut across regions and help to diminish regional antagonisms. Global institutions also are important in helping to aggregate resources and leadership to deal with global economic crises. The G-7/G-8 process and the large, multilateral organizations are necessary to deal with financial crises that transcend specific regions.

But regional agreements and institutions are also useful. Regional groupings can tackle problems that are unique to a region. This can be seen in the role that the Asia-Pacific Economic Cooperation forum (APEC) is creating for itself within the Asia-Pacific region. APEC provides the only institutional venue in which China, Taiwan, and Hong Kong can sit together around a table as equal participants. Regional organizations can also help integrate rising economic powers and reassure weaker or declining powers that cooperation will prevail. Together, it is important for governments to see regional and global groups and institutions in a larger perspective: they can be used both for conducting business and for managing foreign relations. Each type of group has a role to play. Practical and functional reasons are at work in sorting out which type is most appropriate for which goals, but in the end regional and global economic organizations are part of the same integrated whole.

The Future of Global Economic Governance

In the years since the end of the Cold War, the governance institutions of the world economy have come under more assault than at any time since the early 1970s. The street demonstrations in Seattle during the ministerial meeting of the WTO in late 1999 provided dramatic testimony to the political struggles and intellectual debates that swirl around global multilateral institutions. Part of the criticism is really a reaction to globalization: many protesters worry about the loss of control over their economic future. But the wide variety of controversies and changes that are currently unfolding are changing the ways in which the leading industrialized countries and multilateral institutions are managing world markets.[35]

One of the criticisms of the existing governance institutions is focused on the unfair and unequal operation of world markets and the growing power of multinational enterprises. The rise of global economic integration is creating winners and losers and increasing the inequality between the developed and the developing worlds. Governance institutions such as the IMF and the WTO are the immediate cause of these growing socioeconomic disparities, because they are the tools that spread and enforce liberalization and openness. A recent report by a UN-appointed team of developing-world experts has concluded that the WTO is a "nightmare" for developing countries and argues that the trade organization should be brought under the control of the United Nations. It argues that the WTO's open-trading rules are based "on grossly unfair and even prejudiced" assumptions. It calls for a "radical review of the whole system of trade liberalization" and a search for new ways in

ESSENTIAL ECONOMICS 9.2

Weighted Voting in the IMF

Country	Number of votes	Percentage of total
United States	371,743	17.16
Japan	133,378	6.16
Germany	130,332	6.02
France	107,635	4.97
United Kingdom	107,635	4.97
Saudi Arabia	70,105	3.24
China	63,942	2.95
Russia	50,704	2.76
174 other nations	1,124,192	51.48

Source: www.imf.org/external/np/sec/memdir/eds.htm.

Core Principle

Voting in the IMF is heavily weighted toward the industrialized countries, which received more votes because they provided more initial funding to the IMF. Aside from the 8 countries listed, the remaining 174 nations vote in groups, which are usually also weighted in favor of the industrialized countries within each group. World Bank voting is similarly weighted.

which the benefits of trade can be shared more equally between rich and poor countries.[36]

The problems of economic inequality are difficult to tackle at the global level, if only because the leading industrialized countries resolutely resist radical new mechanisms to transfer wealth between countries. In the mid-1970s, the G-77 group of developing countries proposed ideas for what was called a New International Economic Order (NIEO), an ambitious reworking of the world economy that would obligate the advanced countries to more equally distribute the gains from trade and investment to the developing world. The specific mechanisms for doing so were somewhat ambiguous in the NIEO proposal, but the agenda included the creation of international regimes that would move away from market-based relations to more interventionist rules aimed at regulating and redistributing trade and capital flows.[37] A new array of international regimes would operate to equalize economic gains and provide a more stable world economic setting in which developing countries would operate. The risks inherent in a rapidly evolving world economy would be tamed by wrapping that world economy in a more institutionalized and regulated framework. Today, however, the movement for radical institutional changes is more scattered; the critics of the existing order no longer march under a unified banner.

Another set of proposals suggests strengthening the United Nations and its role in the management of the world economy. The United Nations, with its more equalitarian political orientation, is seen by many developing country as a more attractive venue in which to promote development-friendly international agreements then by IMF and the World Bank, whose weighted voting arrangements favor the United States, Europe, and Japan (see Essential Economics 9.2). Some activists propose that the UN could be strengthened by taxing capital flows or the arms trade and using the resulting revenue to radically upgrade UN rules and institutional authority. The so-called Tobin tax is a proposal, originally advanced by the Nobel Prize–winning economist James Tobin, to tax currency-exchange transactions to dampen the rapidly expanding flows of "hot" capital around the world. The immediate objective of such a tax would be to discourage speculative money flows into and out of weak economies. But even the most modest tax would also generate a huge amount of revenue that could be used for agreed-upon purposes. Proposals along these lines envision genuinely radical change in the world political economy. The ability of a global institution such as the United Nations to actually tax transactions and develop its own economic base would radically loosen the supervisory grip of nation-states over the international political economy. The transfer of aspects of state sovereignty, as such a tax would imply, to a global political body would be much more profound than anything currently existing today, except perhaps for the "sharing" of sovereignty within the Europe Union.

Short of the building of new or newly empowered global institutions to redirect or regulate world markets, other proposals aim at reform of regional or national governance. Malaysia has been one of the most outspoken critics of the IMF/WTO governance order, and its prime minister, Mahathir Mohamed, has proposed the building of an Asian regional bloc—headed by Japan—as a counterweight to the dominance of the United States over global capital markets. Japan has resisted suggestions for an exclusive Asian regional grouping, preferring the more decentralized and inclusive arrangements of APEC. But, as we noted earlier, regionalism can be used both to facilitate and strengthen global economic markets and to block those global forces. In the early 1990s, it appeared that regions might emerge to block and divide the world economy, but by the end of the 1990s this characteristic of regionalism had become less pronounced.

Other responses are occurring at the national level. The liberalization of capital markets that began in the 1970s has been a cutting-edge force in the globalization process, but the capital flows that resulted have also been responsible for the financial crises that have plagued Mexico, Brazil, and East Asia. Some governments, most notably that of Malaysia, have moved to restrict the free movement of capital. Other countries have sought to counter the destabilizing effects of rapid capital flows into and out of their economies by reforming domestic banking and financial institutions. More transparency in financial accounting and greater supervision of banking conduct provide some protection against disruptive surprises in capital flows. In the meantime, the G-7/G-8 countries have worked with the IMF to reform its role in monitoring financial conditions in the developing world and to improve its ability to respond to currency crises.

Finally, reform is also taking place in terms of the participants within governance institutions. This involves changing not the rules of global governance but who precisely gets to make those rules. The G-7/G-8 process has expanded to include Russia, and it is all but inevitable that China will eventually join this group as well. Asia has become a dynamic center of the world economy, but Asian countries are not well represented within the organizations that manage the world economy. The leaderships of the IMF and the World Bank have been dominated by Europeans and Americans, but there will be increasing pressure to expand Asia leadership in these organizations. The Japanese bid to lead the IMF failed in 2000, but Japanese efforts toward that end are likely to continue.

There is also pressure to include more nonstate actors in governance institutions. The rapid growth of NGOs dedicated to the advancement of women's rights, human rights, labor standards, and environmental protection has thrown into question the traditional state-centered character of the multilateral economic institutions. The NGOs are knocking at the door of the WTO, the IMF, and the World Bank, and these institutions have only begun to rethink their processes of participation and decision-making. The new multilateralism that is emerging seeks to accommodate the growth of these NGOs as representatives of what some see as global civil society. One study argues that the world is undergoing a "transformation in the nature of global economic governance"—what the study's authors call "complex multilateralism"—due to the growing activism of transnational social movements.[38]

Absent an abrupt and dramatic crisis in the world economy that reverses the forces of globalization, the search for new governance arrangements will continue to be a struggle among the leading industrialized states, the newly developing countries, and groups and countries that see themselves as disadvantaged by the transformation of the world economy. A historical event equivalent to a new Bretton Woods agreement—one in which the world's government leaders come together to remake the entire structure of governance—is unlikely. Some groups will seek to block further advances in global openness and integration, and others will seek to expand the rules of openness and integration to more fully include social and political norms and values. A political struggle is unfolding today that will surely have an impact on the future character of global economic governance.

Conclusion

Governance of the world economy has taken on a variety of forms. The most ambitious has involved the establishment of formal rules that commit countries to specific economic policies. Since the 1940s, the United States and other countries have made efforts to create a rule-based international economic order in the areas of exchange rates, finance, and trade. The IMF, which was created as part of the Bretton Woods agreements of 1944, was set up to help support stable currency relations by providing financial support for countries in economic trouble. It continues today to provide financial assistance to countries, even though the rules on monetary order have evolved. The WTO is the best example of rule-based economic governance. Members of that trade organization agree to operate within a quasi-legal framework of rules and norms that specify the terms of free and fair trade. A set of dispute-resolution rules gives governments legal mechanisms with which to settle trade conflicts.

Informal, small-group mechanisms have also been established that give governments venues for consultation and cooperation. The G-7 gathering of advanced industrialized countries is the most prominent example of this approach to governance. But today a wide variety of gatherings provides regular meetings for leaders from the developed and the developing world—along with officials from multilateral organizations and central banks—to discuss economic issues. These gatherings do not always produce explicit agreements but they provide opportunities for officials to exchange ideas and information.

Regional cooperation has emerged in the post–Cold War era as an important tool of governance. In Europe, North America, South America, East Asia, and elsewhere, governments have made new commitments to integrate their economies with neighboring countries. Regionalism is driven primarily by desires to reduce trade barriers and stimulate economic growth. The ambitious agenda to integrate Europe has provided a major stimulus for regional ideas and actions by governments around the world. The types of regionalism being pursued today tend to be consistent with global economic openness.

The challenge ahead for economic governance is to find ways to address the growing problems of poverty and economic inequality. The less-developed world tends to be the object of policies made in the developed world, rather than participants in global policy-making. New thinking is needed to devise governance arrangements that are inclusive and that help realize global economic goals.

Notes

[1]On the benefits of open markets, see Organization for Economic Cooperation and Development (OECD), *Open Markets Matter: The Benefits of Trade and Investment Liberalisation* (Paris: OECD, 1998).

[2]This is one rationale for international regimes: they simplify the process of international negotiations. See the classic statement of this view in Robert Keohane, *After Hegemony* (Princeton: Princeton University Press, 1984).

[3]G. John Ikenberry, "Creating Yesterday's New World Order: Keynesian 'New Thinking' and the Anglo-American Postwar Settlement," in Judith Goldstein and Robert Keohane, eds., *Ideas and Foreign Policy: Beliefs, Institutions, and Political Change* (Ithaca: Cornell University Press, 1993), pp. 57–86; and Ethan B. Kapstein, *Governing the Global Economy: International Finance and the State* (Cambridge: Harvard University Press, 1994).

[4]This institutional bargain is discussed in G. John Ikenberry, *After Victory: Institutions, Strategic Restraint, and the Rebuilding of Order after Major War* (Princeton: Princeton University Press, 2001).

[5]The G-7, formed in 1975, comprises Canada, France, Germany, Italy, Japan, the United Kingdom, and the United States. At the end of the 1990s the group began inviting Russia to participate in its meetings, thereby forming what is now referred to as the G-8. The G-7/G-8 grouping will be discussed at length later in this chapter.

[6]Harold James, *International Monetary Cooperation since Bretton Woods* (New York: Oxford, 1995), pp. 587–88.

[7]Under the pegged-dollar standard, major world currencies were tied at a fixed rate of exchange to the dollar, which in turn was fixed to the price of gold.

[8]The gold standard was a fixed exchange-rate regime. Countries set the value of their currencies in terms of a specific, fixed quantity of gold, and promised to exchange gold for currency

at that official rate. As a result, each currency had a fixed rate of exchange against all other currencies in terms of gold. Adjustments in national balances of payments would be carried out in principle by movements of gold and associated changes in national money stocks, prices, and economic activity. If a country were running a balance-of-payments deficit with a trading partner, for example, residents in the partner could present unwanted currency to the country's central bank in exchange for gold; as the country's money supply (founded on its holdings of gold) declined, economic activity would contract, domestic prices would decline, and therefore exports would increase and imports decrease. At the same time, the partner's gold stocks and therefore its stock of money would expand, economic activity would increase, as would domestic prices, and therefore exports would decrease while imports would increase. As a result, the country's external payments position with respect to the partner would return to balance.

The Bretton Woods system acted as a gold-dollar system: the United States fixed the value of its currency in terms of gold, and other countries fixed their currencies in terms of the dollar. This system depended on the capacity of the United States to exchange dollars for gold, which it ceased to be able to do in 1971. For a full treatment of the operation of these two systems, see Beth V. Yarbrough and Robert M. Yarbrough, *The World Economy: Trade and Finance*, 3d ed. (Ft. Worth: Dryden, 1994), pp. 715–22.

[9]The most famous critique of the tyranny of market forces that were unleashed by the gold standard is Karl Polanyi, *The Great Transformation* (New York: Rinehart, 1944).

[10]The IMF itself has many rules unrelated to exchange rates, including liquidity requirements for members and myriad borrowing requirements.

[11]See Barry Eichengreen, *Globalizing Capital: A History of the International Monetary System* (Princeton: Princeton University Press, 1996).

[12]Eichengreen, *Globalizing Capital*, p. 137.

[13]See James, *International Monetary Cooperation*.

[14]For an overview of issues, see John Williamson and C. Randall Henning, "Managing the Monetary System," in Peter B. Kenen, ed., *Managing the World Economy: Fifty Years after Bretton Woods* (Washington, D.C.: Institute for International Economics, 1994).

[15]The classic study of the Smoot-Hawley tariff is E. E. Schattschneider, *Politics, Pressures and the Tariff* (New York: Prentice-Hall, 1935). See also Barry Eichengreen, "The Political Economy of the Smoot-Hawley Tariff," *Research in Economic History* 12 (1989), pp. 1–43; and John Conybeare, "Trade Wars: A Comparative Study of Anglo-Hanse, Franco-Italian and Hawley-Smoot Conflicts," *World Politics* 38, No. 1 (October 1985), pp. 147–72.

[16]See Stephan Haggard, "The Institutional Foundations of Hegemony: Explaining the Reciprocal Trade Agreements Act of 1934," *International Organization* 42, No. 1 (Winter 1988), pp. 91–119; and Michael Lusztig, *Risking Free Trade: The Politics of Trade in Britain, Canada, Mexico, and the United States* (Pittsburgh: University of Pittsburgh Press, 1996), Chapter 3.

[17]See Douglas Irwin, *Against the Tide: An Intellectual History of Free Trade* (Princeton: Princeton University Press, 1996).

[18]For an overview of GATT norms and rules, see Jock A. Finlayson and Mark W. Zacker, "The GATT and the Regulation of Trade Barriers: Regime Dynamics and Functions," in Stephen D. Krasner, ed., *International Regimes* (Ithaca: Cornell University Press, 1983), pp. 273–314. Also see Bernard Hoekman and Michael Kostecki, *The Political Economy of the World Trading System: From GATT to WTO* (Oxford: Oxford University Press, 1995).

[19]See Gilbert Winham, *The Evolution of International Trade Agreements* (Toronto: University of Toronto Press, 1992).

[20]For descriptions of the WTO agreement, see Raymond Vernon, "The World Trade Organization: A New Stage in International Trade and Development," *Harvard International Law Journal* 36 (1995), pp. 329–40; Ernest H. Preeg, *Traders in a Brave New World: The Uruguay Round and the Future of the International Trading System* (Chicago: University of Chicago Press, 1995); John H. Jackson, "Managing the Trading System: The World Trade Organization and the Post-Uruguay Round GATT Agenda," in Peter B. Kenen, ed., *Managing the World Economy* (Washington, D.C.: Institute for International Economics, 1994), pp. 131–51; John H. Jackson, "The World Trade Organization, Dispute Settlement, and Codes of Conduct," in Susan M. Collins and Barry P. Bosworth, eds., *The New GATT: Implications for the United States* (Washington, D.C.: Brookings Institution Press, 1994), pp. 63–75; and Gilbert R. Winham, "The World Trade Organization: Institution-Building in the Multilateral Trade System," *The World Economy* 21, No. 3 (May 1998), pp. 349–68.

[21]See Preeg, *Traders in a Brave New World*, pp. 207–10.

[22]Winham, "The World Trade Organization," p. 363.

[23]"Testimony of U.S. Trade Representative Michael Kantor," Committee on Commerce, Science, and Transportation; U.S. Senate, June 16, 1994, pp. 9–19.

[24]Winham, "The World Trade Organization," pp. 352–53.

[25]Alan Beattie, "New Forum to Supplement G7 Work," *Financial Times*, August 27, 1999.

[26]John J. Kirton, "The Diplomacy of Concert: Canada, the G-7 and the Halifax Summit," *Canadian Foreign Policy* 3, No. 1 (Spring 1995), p. 65.

[27]See Robert D. Putnam and Nicholas Bayne, *Hanging Together: Cooperation and Conflict in the Seven-Power Summits*, rev. ed. (Cambridge: Harvard University Press, 1987), p. 25.

[28]See Peter I. Hajnal, *The G7/G8 System: Evolution, Role and Documentation* (Brookfield, VT: Ashgate, 1999), pp. 19–21.

[29]U.K. Foreign and Commonwealth Office, "G-8 Structure: An Informal Club," available at birmingham.g8summit.gov.uk/brief0398/what.is.g8.shtml.

[30]See C. Fred Bergsten and C. Randall Henning, *Global Economic Leadership and the Group of Seven* (Washington, D.C.: Institute for International Economics, 1996).

[31]Hajnal, *The G7/G8 System*, pp. 42–43.

[32]Some scholars argue that this is the most important way in which the growing political interdependence between the industrialized democracies is being manifested. See Anne Marie Slaughter, "The Real New World Order," *Foreign Affairs* 76, No. 5 (September–October 1997).

[33]See Robert D. Putnam and C. Randall Henning, "The Bonn Summit of 1978: A Case Study in Coordination," in Richard Cooper, Barry Eichengreen, Gerald Holtham, Robert Putnam, and C. Randall Henning, eds. *Can Nations Agree? Issues in International Economic Cooperation* (Washington, D.C.: Brookings Institution Press, 1989).

[34]See "A Question of Preference," *Economist*, August 22, 1998, p. 62.

[35]For a good overview of the growing political struggles over trade, see Susan Ariel Aaronson, *Taking Trade to the Streets: The Lost History of the Public Efforts to Shape Globalization* (Ann Arbor: University of Michigan Press, 2001).

[36]"WTO is 'Nightmare' for Developing Nations," *Financial Times*, August 15, 2000.

[37]Stephen Krasner, *Structural Conflict: The Third World against Global Liberalism* (Berkeley: University of California Press, 1985).

[38]See Robert O'Brien, Anne Marie Goetz, Jan Aart Scholte, and Marc Williams, *Contesting Global Governance: Multilateral Economic Institutions and Global Social Movements* (Cambridge: Cambridge University Press, 2000). See also Steve Charnovitz, "Participation of Nongovernmental Organizations in the World Trade Organization," *University of Pennsylvania Journal of International Economic Law* 17 (Spring 1996), pp. 331–57; Christophe Bellman and Richard Gerster, "Accountability in the World Trade Organization," *Journal of World Trade* 30, No. 6 (December 1996), pp. 31–74; and Gabrielle Marceau and Peter N. Pedersen, "Is the WTO Open and Transparent? A Discussion of the Relationship of the WTO with Non-governmental Organizations and Civil Society for More Transparency and Public Participation," *Journal of World Trade* 33, No. 1 (1999), pp. 5–49.

Chapter 10

Conclusion

The international political economy is a work in progress. States and markets are constantly changing, and the economic fortunes of states continually rise and decline. Ideologies and models of political economy—social democratic, laissez-faire, or statist—come into and out of fashion. The issues that command the attention of world leaders, such as energy shortages, trade conflicts, financial crises, monetary instabilities, and geopolitical struggles, also change over time. The logics of comparative advantage, economic exchange, supply and demand, state power, and political conflict and cooperation play out in new places and situations. As the twenty-first century unfolds, the existing organization of the world political economy will be challenged and perhaps transformed.

It is useful to end this inquiry into states and markets by looking to the future. What are the great issues of international political economy that confront the world community in the years ahead? The following are some of the most important developments to watch. Each is a sort of real-world "experiment" in political economy; the way each of these experiments is resolved will tell us a great deal about the changing character of the world political economy.

The Economic Engagement of China

In the twenty-first century, China's world position is likely to change more rapidly and radically than that of any other country. But where precisely is China headed? What sort of country will it be in the decades ahead? Will it gradually integrate into and cooperate with the existing, Western-oriented international political economy, or will it emerge as a powerful revisionist state bent on challenging and overturning the existing order? The answers to these questions are unknown today, but regardless of the way in which China develops, the implications of its transformation are profound.

The United States and the other major industrial countries have recently been trying to engage China and draw it into the existing world order by expanding its commercial ties and institutional affiliations. Western governments hope that expanded trade and investment linkages with other countries will encourage China's leaders to pursue economic and political reform within their country and thereby bolster their incentives to be a cooperative partner in world politics.[1] Expanded trade and investment will strengthen the position of China's private sector and civil society, it is believed, thereby providing a greater counterweight to the Communist Party–controlled state. As a middle class emerges within China, engagement proponents also anticipate that this segment of society will tender demands for expanded political rights and freedoms. The result may not be a Western-style democracy, but the hope is that it will be a more open and pluralistic political system.

Engagement also involves seeking China's integration into the world's multilateral economic institutions, particularly the World Trade Organization (WTO), to which China has recently been admitted. Participation in these multilateral institutions, it is hoped, will socialize Chinese elites into the norms and practices of the world economy and provide venues through which disputes can be settled. As a member of the WTO, China will also be subject to its rules and norms, and this provides a mechanism by which the outside world can pressure China to adopt international standards of state-market relations.

The expectations of engagement proponents, however, may be wrong. Economic engagement with China could simply provide opportunities for China to become a bigger and stronger global superpower capable of challenging the vital interests of the other major countries. It is also not clear whether Chinese membership in the WTO will change China or the WTO.

China's $475 billion in annual trade indicates that it is already emerging as a global trading power. Will the Chinese government adapt to existing universal standards, or will it use its market power to push for different rules and norms of trade? The expansion of market society within China also is not necessarily destined to foster political liberalization and democracy; it could just as easily generate domestic conflict and disarray. "Rather than the unstoppable juggernaut often perceived in the West, in many respects China is a fragile reed," wrote one China specialist. "Its partly transformed society is burdened by its socialist legacy and caught between the demands of globalization and the needs of 1.3 billion people."[2] Growing regional economic inequality between the wealthy coastal provinces and the poorer inner provinces could provide a line along which China's political system could fragment. The ruling Communist Party has all but abandoned the Leninist-Maoist ideology that provided its legitimacy. In its attempt to hold onto power, the government could turn to stoking the flames of nationalism and militarism, triggering heightened conflict with the outside world. The movement toward democracy is never smooth and often is accompanied by more, rather than less, belligerence in foreign policy.[3]

The impact of a rising China on the international political economy depends ultimately on whether China is undergoing a single or a double transformation: is it simply becoming a more powerful state with its existing political interests and ambitions intact, or is the political character of the country also transforming? Proponents of engagement hope for a double transformation, but skeptics remain.

The Uniting of Europe

Will Europe succeed in its ambitious plans for further integration, and what does this mean for the United States? The 15 countries and 376 million people that make up the European Union (EU) are embarked on a bold experiment in building a union of states. The most recent efforts began in 1985 with the launching of the "single market" initiative and took a decisive step forward with the signing of the Maastricht Treaty in 1991, which laid the groundwork for monetary and political integration. Most of the members of the EU have adopted a single currency, the euro, which fully replaced the national currencies in January 2002. Yet it is still unclear what sort of entity Europe is in fact becoming. European leaders themselves do not embrace a singular vision: some seek to build a federal state not unlike the United States, whereas others envisage a more mixed order in which national governments would retain important sovereign and legal powers. Europeans also disagree on whether the EU should emphasize a deepening of the union (that is, expanding it beyond the economic realm) or a widening to include more members at the current level of integration.

One implication of the rise of a united Europe is in the realm of political imagination. Europe was the birthplace of the nation-state: it was in Europe that Westphalian sovereignty and the modern bureaucratic state were invented. Now Europe is the location for a new experiment in shared sovereignty and post-nation-state political engineering. As such it provides a great deal of inspiration and guidance for new forms of interstate cooperation. The most advanced areas of political integration in Europe are in the area of law. The European Court of Justice and the European Court for Human Rights, for example, have rendered verdicts in recent years that have obliged member countries to reconsider or revise their own national laws and policies in the areas of the environment, trade, human rights, and worker conditions.[4] This evolving European legal order is making Europe the political epicenter for the wider, global movement toward greater legal and rule-based cooperation in areas of the environment and human rights. Europe is pioneering a more complex political order and providing the world with new ideas and models.

Another uncertainty about a unified Europe is how this emerging political entity will interact with the United States. For the last 50 years, the United States has dealt with Europe in an alliance partnership characterized by enormous disparities of power. The United States dominated Europe both in military and in economic terms. Europe's relative weakness was further exacerbated by its political fragmentation. Indeed, a Europe of separate nation-states sometimes frustrated U.S. policy-makers. In the 1970s, Secretary of State Henry Kissinger complained that "Europe" had no telephone number. But the fragmentation of Europe also meant that American leadership could not easily be challenged. Europe was not in a position to stand up to the United States. Will the more powerful and united Europe that is emerging today provide a better partner for the United States or will it create a powerful adversary that generates new transatlantic tensions? The answer depends on both Europe and the United States. If European unity—and political identity—is built in part on opposition to the United States, greater conflict can be expected. Likewise, if the United States is unwilling to adjust to a more equal partnership, political and economic conflict also is likely to rise.

Managing International Financial Contagion

What can be done to reduce the risks of international financial contagion? Since the end of the Cold War, the world economy has been hit by periodic financial crises, most notably the Mexican peso crisis of 1995 and the East Asian crisis in 1997–98, which spread to Latin America and threatened American financial institutions, as well. The causes of these crises are multi-faceted and widely debated, but in each case currency instability in one country or a small group of countries has threatened to destabilize the world financial system. "Trouble in one emerging economy can serve as a 'wake-up call' to investors to look more discriminatingly at others with similar problems."[5] The Asian crisis, as we saw in Chapter 8, began with the collapse of the Thai baht in the summer of 1997 but soon spread to the Philippines, Indonesia, South Korea, and other countries around the world. Sharply rising interest rates and the drying up of credit pushed these countries into a cycle of recession and soaring unemployment.[6] Twenty-five years ago, such fluctuations in the Thai baht or Korean won would have been little noticed, but today, because of the increased globalization of trade and finance, such events trigger alarm bells in capitals around the world.

In the years since the Asian crisis, political leaders and experts have debated how to strengthen the stability of the world's financial system. The underlying factor, of course, is the growing magnitude of international flows of capital. Private capital flows into the emerging-market countries increased in the ten years before the Asian crisis from $25 billion to $304 billion. The deregulation of capital markets has brought both great economic gains and significant economic risks. Global capital markets have enormous capabilities to finance investment and growth in the developing countries, but they are also fickle and will punish countries that are deemed to be pursuing unsound policies. In the wake of the 1997–98 crisis, the leaders of the advanced economies have urged a variety of reforms, emphasizing the importance of reform of domestic financial institutions. One goal is greater transparency, so that investors have better information on which to base their decisions. Western investments in the emerging markets of Southeast Asia, for example, were often made with remarkably little knowledge of the nature of the investment or the local situation. Another goal is to promote the adoption of sound financial-sector policies and new global standards and the establishment of more capable institutions of supervision and surveillance within domestic financial systems. Finally, the International Monetary Fund

(IMF) and other international financial institutions must become better equipped to identify and respond quickly to financial crises.

The question remains, however, whether the world community can develop an international financial architecture that is adequate to the challenge of rapidly expanding flows of trade, capital, and information. Deep differences of opinion remain across the developed and developing world about where the burden lies for management and crisis-prevention. Debates continue about the proper role of the IMF and the conditions under which it should lend to member states. How intrusive should international financial managers be in mandating domestic financial reforms and the conduct of national macroeconomic policy? Should there be global standards of reform or should the conditions imposed by the IMF be more regionally and locally contingent? What should be the role of regional monetary facilities? Ultimately, the proper balance between market openness and regulation in ensuring optimal levels of stable economic growth is still undetermined.

The "Seattle Syndrome" and the World Trading System

Will the street demonstrations that have erupted at international economic summits of the WTO, the IMF, and other trade groups usher in an era of growing political opposition to globalization, or will they lead to a new world consensus on the rules and management of economic openness? One of the most dramatic symbols of the controversy over globalization are the crowds of demonstrators that have become loud and uninvited guests at global economic meetings. Talks between trade or finance ministers today have become venues for protests by a confusing array of activist groups denouncing free trade and the WTO as threats to labor, the environment, and national sovereignty. These protests have clearly captured the international headlines. What is less clear is the exact character of the political movements that lie behind the activism. How deep does the dissatisfaction with an open world economy run? Aside from disrupting international summits, how are these activist groups affecting the politics and policies of national governments?

It is increasingly clear that most of these groups are not simply old-style advocates of protectionism. Within the advanced industrialized countries, the origins of the new antiglobalization politics can be traced back to the 1970s and the Tokyo round of trade negotiations, at which liberalization ef-

forts moved away from tariff reductions (which had been reduced over
the previous decades to historically low levels) and toward the lowering of
nontariff barriers such as health and safety regulations. The new trade-
promotion agenda is aimed at reducing nontariff barriers whose source is not
explicit protectionism but simply a country's social and economic regulatory
structure. Free-traders see these regulations as barriers to trade, while others—including the protesters in the streets—see them as part of a healthy
and secure society. Accordingly, most of today's anti-WTO demonstrators are
not traditional trade protectionists but activists who see such current trade
agreements as threats to domestic social and environmental quality.[7] Their
agenda is not to roll back globalization but to better manage it.

The battle lines are not always clear. Some of the demonstrators are in
fact angry at the ceding of national sovereignty to multinational enterprises
and international bankers. They sense that their ability to control their own
destiny and protect their national culture and values is threatened by the im-
personal global forces of capitalism. The banner of national sovereignty is
often hoisted to reflect this sentiment. But ironically, to protect national sovereignty the practical political course of action is to push for more interna-
tionally-accepted rules to manage trade and capital flows. The battle
between free-traders who embrace deregulated markets and the trade-
agreement critics is over the type and amount of supranational governance
that is needed to manage globalization.[8] The challenge for both the government leaders inside summit conference halls and the demonstrators on the
street outside is to find a way to make trade liberalization consistent with social and environmental protection. The proponents of new forms of supranational regulation may look like the enemies of free trade, but this is a
political misunderstanding. If support for an open world economy is to remain strong, both groups must be brought together into a wider political
coalition in favor of an open, but managed, trading system.

Global Economic Inequality and Political Instability

Will growing economic inequality create new and dangerous conflicts between rich and poor countries? The grand liberal vision of globalization is
that greater world economic integration brings with it increased prosperity
and cooperation to all corners of the world. But globalization does not produce only winners. It also creates losers, and there is evidence of growing

economic inequality within and between many countries today. The twenty-first century promises to bring even greater extremes of wealth and poverty. What will be the implications of growing inequality for the stability of the existing international order? Can globalization be made to benefit those who are today hurt or left behind in its wake? What can the international community—the advanced states, nongovernmental organizations, and global international institutions—do to address the problem of rising economic inequality?

The 1990s created more wealth on a global scale than any other decade in world history, but they also saw an expanded gap between the rich and the poor. The rise of the so-called new economy and the advent of the information-technology and knowledge economy is only making the gap wider, not only in terms of economic disparities—the material standard of living and life changes—but also in terms of disparities in power and freedom and the ability of people to control their destiny and improve their circumstances.

The evidence of growing inequality and disparities in living standards is quite dramatic. It is true that overall during the last half-century the average human being's lot has improved. Life expectancy rose from 46.4 years in 1950–55 to 64.4 in 1990–95, and the absolute number of people who were chronically undernourished fell from 941 million in 1970 to 786 million in 1990. This improvement was realized despite a rising global population. But the rich have benefited disproportionately during this period. The ratio of per capita income between the top fifth and the bottom fifth of the world's population was 30 to 1 in 1960, 45 to 1 in 1980, and 60 to 1 by the 1990s.[9] The United Nations reports similar evidence of rising gross inequality: some 358 global billionaires have wealth equal to the combined incomes of the world's 2.3 billion poor people—nearly half of the global population. Likewise, 80 percent of the world's people live in Third World countries, but they have just 22 percent of the world's wealth. In a sign of growing inequality, the UN reports that the lowest one-fifth of nations held 2.3 percent of the world's wealth 30 years ago; now they possess exactly 1.4 percent. Of some 4.4 billion people in the Third World, three-fifths lack access to safe sewers, two-thirds lack toilets, one-third have no access to clean water, and one-fifth lack any kind of modern health care. About one-quarter of Third World peoples are illiterate, and of these, two-thirds are women.[10] Overall, the number of people around the world who are living on less than one dollar a day has risen from 1.2 billion in 1987 to around 1.5 billion today.[11]

There is reason to think that the transformation of world capitalism is it-self making inequality more profound. Those who argue that we are moving into a "new economy" seem to be making the claim that capitalism is moving from an economy based on the production of physical goods to an economy based on the production and application of knowledge. This transition may be happening gradually, but there is clear evidence that the role of "knowledge goods" is increasing relative to that of traditional industrial goods. If this is true, the gap between rich and poor will continue to grow.

It is not yet clear how these massive disparities in life opportunities will manifest themselves in world politics. In the advanced societies this grim picture of poverty and underdevelopment is not visible. Their inequality is distributed in a way that does not immediately lend itself to great global struggles between the haves and the have nots. But the very process of glob-alization is making it easier for dissatisfactions to be communicated around the world. How the advanced countries respond to the plight of the poor will help shape the character of the international political economy in the decades ahead. A growing divide between a few rich societies and a vast ex-panse of poor and uneducated peoples will not serve anyone's interests.

Unipolarity and Global Leadership

Will the United States continue to identify its own national interest with the stability and openness of the world political economy or will it, because of its hegemony or a coming decline in its position, turn inward and unilateral? American power today is unprecedented. The United States began the 1990s as the world's only superpower and ended the decade in an even more powerful position. "The United States of America today predominates on the economic level, the monetary level, on the technological level, and the cul-tural area in the broadest sense of the word," French foreign minister Hubert Vedrine observed in a 1999 speech. "It is not comparable in terms of power and influence, to anything known in modern history."[12] After World War II, the United States enjoyed a similar position of global dominance and used its power and influence to construct institutions and partnerships that served to open and stabilize the world economy. It saw its own economic interests advanced over the long term by creating rules and institutions that integrated the advanced industrialized societies and established mechanisms to manage conflict and crisis. Many people around the world today worry that the United States is not quite as motivated to provide enlightened global leadership as it was 50 years ago.

The rise of American unipolar power has altered the terms of cooperation. The common external threat of the Cold War facilitated cooperation among the allies and gave the United States strategic incentives to open itself up to consultation and mutual adjustment to the ideas and interests of its partners. Containment and alliance solidarity disciplined the United States and created incentives for it to raise its sights above domestic politics and listen to its partners. The creation of multilateral economic rules and institutions facilitated trade liberalization and openness and infused the postwar economy with a sense of fairness. The United States never acted completely selflessly during the Cold War, but all the advanced industrialized societies were committed to maintaining a stable and cooperative noncommunist order and they readily reminded each other of their common interests and shared "free world" identity. U.S. power was tamed and made acceptable because U.S. officials agreed to operate within an agreed-upon postwar political and economic framework.

Can the United States and its European and Asian partners find ways to recreate this cooperation and joint decision-making, even while the new realities of international power challenge joint governance? This question is particularly pressing today, when issues such as global warming, management of financial crisis, and trade in genetically modified foods have exposed even among advanced industrialized countries deep differences in ideas and interests that must be overcome. It is easier today for the United States to act unilaterally or to define its interests in more narrowly national terms. And European and Asian countries also have fewer reasons to defer to the United States and the goal of alliance solidarity.

The intensification of U.S. predominance in the 1990s exacerbates this problem. It is possible that European and Asian governments will slowly come to view American unipolar power as a dangerous reality that must be countered. Europe and East Asia may increasingly seek protection against the vagaries of an unpredictable and unilateral United States by moving toward more regionally centered governance. Europe and Japan could begin to conceive of their own security relations in regional terms rather than as part of the extended American security order. The construction of an open world economy after World War II was facilitated by the far-flung alliance system that the United States and its allies constructed. Strategic partnership reinforced trade and economic partnerships. If U.S. hegemony today is unsatisfactory to America's partners, the movement toward regional orders and fragmented security relationships will undercut the open world economy. There are opportunities in the U.S. "unipolar moment" to reinforce the rules and institutions that provide the supports for the world political economy, but there are also risks and dangers in an international system where one state predominates. How the United States and its partners deal with unipolarity will help shape the landscape of international political economy in the decades ahead.

The more diffuse challenge for U.S. leadership is to respond to the hatred and terrorist violence that emerges from parts of the world that are geographically distant from but increasingly capable of inflicting damage on the Western way of life. The terrorist bombing of the World Trade Center in New York City and the Pentagon in Washington, D.C., are the most dramatic and dangerous instances of this new reality. U.S. power—manifest in economic, political, cultural, and military realms—is itself a target of this dark violence. How the United States and its partners respond to these terrorist dangers will help determine the health and stability of the global political economy in the twenty-first century.

Notes

[1] There is some evidence that the importance that China attaches to trade and investment ties to the United States is already serving to temper Chinese foreign policy. See Erik Eckholm, "China Grins and Bears It," *New York Times*, July 30, 2001, p. A1.

[2] Robert A. Manning, "Beijing Rules, but It's Got a Host of Problems," *Washington Post*, July 15, 2001, p. B1.

[3] See Jack Synder, *From Voting to Violence: Democratization and Nationalist Conflict* (New York: W. W. Norton & Co., 2000).

[4] Roger Cohen, "A European Identity: Nation-State Losing Ground," *New York Times*, January 14, 2000, p. A3.

[5] "How the Bug Can Spread," *The Economist*, July 21, 2001, p. 21.

[6] For a discussion of the origins and responses to the crisis, see Stephan Haggard, *The Political Economy of the Asian Financial Crisis* (Washington, D.C.: Institute for International Economics, 2000).

[7] See Susan Ariel Aaronson, *Taking Trade to the Streets: The Lost History of Public Efforts to Shape Globalization* (Ann Arbor: University of Michigan Press, 2001).

[8] See Robert Wright, "Continental Drift," *New Republic*, January 17, 2000.

[9] Joel E. Cohen, "How Many People Can the Earth Support?" *New York Review of Books*, October 8, 1998.

[10]UN, *Human Development Report, 1998,* as cited in "News of the Week in Review," *New York Times,* September 27, 1998.

[11]Martin Dickson, "The Gap between the Rich and the Poor Is Increasing," *Financial Times,* September 22, 2000, p. xxiv.

[12]Quoted in Craig R. Whitney, "NATO at 50: With Nations at Odds, Is It a Misalliance?" *New York Times,* February 15, 1999, p. A7.

Appendix: **Studying International Political Economy through the Internet**

The Internet is revolutionizing the way in which we study international political economy. The following are some of the key Web sites relating to international political-economic matters.

Current News and Analysis

The *Financial Times* (www.ft.com) may be the best daily source of information on international economic and political developments, and the *Economist* (www.economist.com) provides superb in-depth weekly reporting, analysis, and educational supplements on international economic-policy matters. The *International Herald Tribune* (www.iht.com/frontpage.html), co-published by the *New York Times* (www.nytimes.com) and the *Washington Post* (www.washingtonpost.com), is an excellent daily source of world news, as are the *Times* and the *Post* themselves. Also informative is Bloomberg.com (www.bloomberg.com).

International Institutions

All of the major international economic institutions provide useful and important materials on world economic matters. For example, the International Monetary Fund (www.imf.org) provides free access to a broad range of materials, including its biannual *World Economic Outlook,* which contains very good quantitative materials on world economic and monetary developments as well as interesting and useful analyses of those developments. In addition, the IMF and the World Bank co-publish a very helpful monthly, *Finance and Development,* which can be accessed on the Web at no charge at www.imf. org/external/pubs/ft/fandd/2001/06/. The World Bank also publishes other materials relating to developing countries and their international economic linkages; the entry point is www.worldbank.org. The World Trade Organization (www.wto.org) publishes important documents on international trade negotiations and on dispute-settlement activities taking place under its auspices, and it provides a critical annual report on international trade at www.wto.org/english/res_e/statis_e/statis_e.htm. In addition, the WTO Web site has a very useful section relating to developing countries, including an "Interactive Electronic Guide to WTO and Developing Countries." The United Nations Conference on Trade and Development (www.unctad.org) provides partial access to the statistical information it collects and the analytical studies it completes; particularly important are its annual reports on international investment and development and trade and development, found at www.unctad.org/en/pub/pubframe.htm. The Organization for Economic Cooperation and Development (www.oecd.org), the European Union (europa.eu.int), and the Bank for International Settlements (www.bis.org) also provide useful materials for students of international political economy.

U.S. Government Agencies

The U.S. government publishes a vast amount of Web-based materials relating to the international economy. A key U.S. government repository of statistical materials relating to U.S. trade and investment abroad is maintained by the Office and Trade and Economic Analysis, which is a part of the Department of Commerce; the entry point for these materials is www.ita. doc.gov/td/industry/otea/. Web portals that may be used to locate materials published by Congress and by the executive branch are maintained by the National Institute of Standards and Technology at nii.nist.gov/ ext_links/gov/govt.html and by Louisiana State University at www.lib.lsu. edu/gov/exec.html. Particularly helpful materials, including the annual *Economic Report of the President,* are provided online by the president's Council of Economic Advisers; see www.whitehouse.gov/cea/index.html. Researchers interested in the official positions of the U.S. government on international economic matters can find speeches and other useful materials at the Web sites maintained by the Office of the U.S. Trade Representative at www.ustr.gov, the U.S. Department of State at www.state.gov, and the U.S. Department of the Treasury at www.ustreas.gov.

Research-Oriented Policy Institutes and Academic Sources

New York University business school professor Rouriel Roubini maintains a remarkable Web site on international financial and macroeconomic policy matters (www.stern.nyu.edu/globalmacro). A prominent policy research institute in Washington D.C., the Institute of International Economics, provides a great deal of useful, interesting, and accessible analyses of international economic policy issues (including those with a focus on U.S. foreign economic policy) at no charge through its website, www.iie.com. Three other Washington, D.C., organizations provide important works on international economic matters: the Brookings Institution (www.brookings.org), the Cato Institute (www.freetrade.org on trade matters, and www.cato.org/research/mon-st.html on money and banking issues), and the Heritage Foundation (www.heritage.org). The quarterly journal *Foreign Policy* maintains a superb Web site at www.foreignpolicy.com, including a top-quality set of links to other useful Web sites in the fields of international relations in general and international political economy in particular (www.foreignpolicy.com/resources/worldwide_links.html). The University of Michigan library maintains a superb inventory of Web-based statistical data sets on international economic matters at www.lib.umich.edu/libhome/Documents.center/stecfor.html.

Business Associations, Labor Organizations, and Nongovernmental Organizations (NGOs)

The key U.S. business association, the U.S. Chamber of Commerce, provides commentary on its Web site (www.uschamber.com) that is usually supportive of international economic integration; in contrast, the major U.S. labor organization, the AFL-CIO, maintains a Web site (www.aflcio.org)

that provides a more critical perspective on such integration. Among the many important NGOs and their Web sites to consult, we would suggest the Sierra Club (www.sierraclub.com); Friends of the Earth (www.foe.org), particularly its section on international issues (www.foe.org/international); Oxfam (www.oxfam.org.uk); and Greenpeace (www.greenpeace.org).

GLOSSARY

Accommodative monetary policy   Policy whereby a government, usually working through its central bank, seeks to bolster aggregate demand by increasing the supply of money in the economy (and thus reducing interest rates), thereby facilitating expenditures by consumers and business, and as a result increasing national income to a level that more closely matches the country's productive capacity.

Anarchy   Characteristic of the international system emphasized by realist theories, referring to the absence of a centralized government or authority.

Appreciation   A market-induced increase in the value of a currency in a flexible exchange-rate regime.

Atlantic Charter   Joint statement of war aims prepared by British prime minister Winston Churchill and U.S. president Franklin Roosevelt in 1941 that emphasized the goal of creating a stable and open world economy and peaceful political order after the war.

Autarky   Economic condition in which a country does not engage in international trade and instead remains self-sufficient.

Autonomous transactions   Transactions recorded in a country's current and capital accounts that are undertaken without regard for their impact on the balance of payments.

Balance of payments   Summary of the economic transactions of a country's residents with residents of countries in the rest of the world during a fixed period of time, such as a quarter or a year; consists of the current account and the capital account.

Balance-of-payments deficit Situation in which total autonomous credits in the current and capital accounts are less than total autonomous debits.

Balance-of-payments surplus Situation in which total autonomous credits in the current and capital accounts exceed total autonomous debits.

Blockade Economic sanction wherein the initiator state seeks to stop all commerce between the target state and the outside world and is willing to use force to enforce the target state's economic isolation.

Boycott Economic sanction wherein the initiator state prohibits some or all imports from the target state.

Bretton Woods agreements Historical agreements reached between the United States, the United Kingdom, and several dozen other countries in 1944 that established the International Bank for Reconstruction and Development (the World Bank) and the International Monetary Fund as core institutional mechanisms to assist economic reconstruction and management of the international monetary and financial system after the war; created the first permanent institutions to facilitate economic openness and stability.

Capital account Portion of a country's balance of payments summarizing autonomous transactions involving financial instruments, that is, financial transactions undertaken for purposes other than bringing the country's payments position into balance.

Coercion Efforts to take or threats to take military or economic measures to force a target state to stop or reverse and action that it has already taken.

Comparative advantage Situation in which a country faces opportunity costs in the production of a given good that are less than the opportunity costs faced by another country in the production of the same good.

Concessional terms Loan terms wherein the interest rate of the loan is so low and the repayment period so delayed or lengthened that at least 25 percent of the loan amount is effectively a grant.

Consumption indifference curve Graphical representation of market baskets representing different combinations of two goods that provide an individual with a constant level of satisfaction; often called a "consumer indifference curve" or an "indifference curve."

Currency attack Economic sanction wherein the initiator state undertakes operations in the foreign-exchange market designed to undermine the value of the currency of the target state.

Current account Portion of a country's balance of payments summarizing transactions involving trade in goods and services, income receipts, and unilateral transfers.

Declining marginal utility from consumption   Assumption in economic theory that, as an individual consumes more and more of one good, he or she derives less and less satisfaction from consumption of the next fixed increment of that good.

Depreciation   A market-induced decrease in the value of a currency in a flexible exchange-rate regime.

Deterrence   Efforts to take or threats to take military or economic measures (such as sanctions) to prevent a target state from taking a particular action or actions.

Devaluation   A decrease in the value of a currency in a fixed exchange-rate regime.

Discretionary coordination   Form of governance in the international system whereby governments cooperate in coordinating their policies in an informal and ad hoc manner.

Economic globalization   Growing integration since World War II of the national economies of most of the advanced industrialized countries of the world and of an increasing number of developing nations, to the degree that there may be emerging a single worldwide economy.

Economic incentive   Policy instrument wherein the initiator state promises or actually extends an economic benefit to a target state in exchange for compliance by the target state with a political demand of the initiator.

Economic sanction   Policy instrument wherein the initiator state threatens or actually interrupts economic relationships with a target state in order to force the target state to meet a specific political demand of the initiator.

Embargo   Economic sanction wherein the initiator state seeks to prohibit some or all of its own exports to and imports from the target state, but does not interfere with financial contacts between its residents and those of the target and does not interfere with economic ties between the target and third countries.

Exchange rate   The price that a resident of one country must pay in terms of a particular currency (usually that of the resident's country) to purchase one unit of a foreign country's currency.

Export-led growth (ELG)   Strategy for economic development wherein a government relaxes import restrictions and other biases in favor of production solely for the local market and encourages growth through exports by providing preferential access for exporters to credit and foreign exchange.

Financial-crisis contagion   Cross-national transmission of a financial crisis wherein, as one country goes into a crisis due to a sudden reversal of liquid capital flows, other countries also experience rapid outflows of such foreign capital.

Fiscal policy   Policy that involves government spending and taxes.

Fixed exchange-rate regime   Policy whereby a government specifies the exchange rate at which its currency will trade against a key currency or group of currencies and undertakes financial interventions in the foreign-exchange market to keep those rates in place; also termed a "pegged exchange-rate regime."

Flexible exchange-rate regime   Policy whereby a government allows market forces to determine the exchange rate for its currency; also termed a "floating exchange-rate regime."

Foreign direct investment   Investment made by an investor residing in one country to acquire a 10 percent or greater management interest in an enterprise operating in another country.

Freeze on financial assets   Economic sanction wherein the initiator state denies residents of the target state access to financial assets they hold within the initiating country.

Gross domestic product (GDP)   Money value of the final goods and services produced in a country during some period of time by residents working within that country; equal to GNP less the value of goods and services produced by a country's residents working abroad.

Gross national product (GNP)   Money value of the final goods and services produced by residents of a country during some period of time, regardless of whether those residents are working at home or abroad.

Heckscher-Ohlin theorem   Proposition suggesting that a country will have a comparative advantage in, and thus will tend to export, those goods whose production requires the intensive use of the factor of production that that country has in relative abundance.

Hegemonic stability theory   Explanation for the openness and stability of the international economy emphasizing the critical role of a hegemonic state and its exercise of power in organizing the rules and regimes of the system; when the hegemonic state declines, the rules and regimes are expected to weaken.

Hegemonic state   Overwhelmingly powerful state that organizes and controls the wider international system.

Import-substituting industrialization (ISI)   Strategy for economic development in which a government temporarily restricts imports of manufactured goods, subsidizes local private and state-owned firms that were or could become local producers of such goods, and, by so compelling a substitution of local for foreign products, promotes the rapid industrialization and long-term growth of the country.

Infant-industry argument   Argument holding that, if an industry that might be opened to trade, or that is already under pressure by imports, is given temporary protection, it will become (or gain become) as competitive as foreign suppliers.

Inter-industry trade   Exchange between countries of goods in different industries.

International regime   Set of principles, rules, norms, and decision-making procedures around which actors' expectations converge; often used interchangeably with international rules, agreements, and institutions.

Intra-industry trade   Exchange between countries of goods in the same industry.

Long-term financial flows   Capital flows that are intended to be available to residents and entities in the recipient countries for a period of one year or more.

Macroeconomic stabilization policy   Government actions aimed at affecting the level of aggregate demand in the economy and thus the generation of national income within its borders; may consist of fiscal policy or monetary policy.

Marginal rate of product transformation   Amount of one good whose production must be forgone in order to produce one additional unit of another good; measured as the absolute value of the slope of the production possibility frontier at any given point.

Marginal rate of substitution   Amount of one good a consumer is willing to forgo in order to consume one additional unit of another good; measured as the absolute value of the slope of the consumption indifference curve at any given point.

Monetary policy   Policy that involves changes in the money supply, and therefore in interest rates.

Moral hazard   The risk that economic aid, rather than stimulating reform on the part of the recipient, will instead encourage the perpetuation of the unsound behavior that created the need for aid in the first place.

Most-favored-nation status (MFN)   Stipulation wherein each of two or more countries agrees to extend to the other country or countries the best possible treatment with regard to imports that it is offering its other trade partners; WTO members automatically extend MFN to one another.

Multilateral sanctions   Economic sanctions imposed by a group of states against a target state

Multinational enterprise (MNE)   Firm that has significant operations not just in the country in which it is headquartered, but also in other countries, and that pursues global strategies as a result of which it views the world as a single, integrated market.

National income (Y)   Total income earned during some period by the owners of a country's different factors of production (most importantly, labor, capital, and land) as they produced the country's GNP.

Neoliberal institutionalism   Perspective on the role of institutions in the international system that emphasizes their usefulness to states in reducing obstacles to cooperation, such as uncertainty and transaction costs.

Nonconcessional terms   Loan terms wherein the interest rate and repayment schedule closely match private-market conditions, and there is little grant element to the loan.

Nontariff barrier   Policy instrument other than a tariff that has the effect of increasing the cost and hence the economic attractiveness of importing goods into a country; can include environmental and health standards, procurement codes, and a host of other government laws and regulations.

Official grants   Financial flows in which a donor state or organization provides a certain amount of foreign exchange to a country during some period of time, with no expectation of repayment of those resources.

Official loans   Financial flows in which a donor state or organization provides foreign exchange to a country with the expectation that the amounts provided will be repaid; may be made on concessional terms or nonconcessional terms (the interest rate and repayment schedule more closely matches private-market conditions, and there is little or no grant element to the loan).

Official settlements account   Portion of the balance of payments of a government with a fixed exchange-rate regime wherein transactions are recorded to compensate for imbalances in autonomous transactions summarized in the current or capital accounts.

Official transactions   International financial transactions undertaken by a government with a fixed exchange-rate regime to offset its current-account or capital-account imbalances (that is, surpluses or deficits); also called *compensatory transactions*.

Opportunity cost   Amount of a good whose production or consumption is forgone in order that another good may be produced or consumed.

Portfolio bond investment   Capital flow wherein an investor from one country purchases a bond that is issued by an entity in another country.

Portfolio equity investment   Capital flow wherein an investor acquires an ownership interest in a foreign firm, usually by buying common stock shares issued by the firm or traded in a local stock market, but does not acquire a stake sufficiently large to exercise control over the firm's operations.

Primary sanction   Type of economic sanction wherein the initiator state seeks directly to interrupt bilateral economic ties between itself and the target state and thereby to impose costs directly on the target.

Production possibilities frontier   Graphical representation of the different combinations of goods that a country may produce during some period of time, given the full exploitation of the productive resources available in the country during that period of time.

Quota   Quantitative limit imposed by government on the amount of a good or service that may be imported during a period of time.

Real income   Income adjusted for inflation—that is, income measured by what it can actually buy, rather than by the amount of money involved.

Realism   Multifaceted perspective on foreign policy and international relations emphasizing the anarchic nature of the international system and the power-oriented goals of states.

Restrictive monetary policy   Policy whereby a government, usually working through its central bank, seeks to reduce aggregate demand by decreasing the supply of money in the economy (and thus increasing interest rates), thereby discouraging consumption and investment and as a result bringing national income down to a level that more closely matches the country's productive capacity.

Returns to scale   Change in the average cost of production relative to the change in the scale of production; may be constant, increasing, or decreasing.

Revaluation   An increase in the value of a currency in a fixed exchange-rate regime.

Rule-based coordination   Form of governance in the international system whereby governments agree to formal rules and norms of cooperation that bind them to specific policy commitments and constraints.

Sanctions fatigue   Belief by citizens and policy-makers of the initiator state that sanctions their country has imposed ought to be abandoned because they are failing to change the target state's behavior and are hurting only innocent civilians in the target country.

Secondary sanction   Type of economic sanction wherein connection the initiator state seeks to impose economic penalties against third countries as a way of forcing them to curtail their economic transactions with, and thus indirectly to hurt, the target state.

Short-term financial flows   Capital flows intended to be available to residents and entities in recipient countries for a period of less than one year.

Social clause   Element of a trade agreement wherein signatories to the agreement can withdraw trade concessions or impose trade sanctions against other signatories found not to be faithfully implementing certain labor and other social standards.

Sovereignty   A country's ability to exercise ultimate political authority.

Standby agreement   Agreement reached between the IMF and a borrowing country that specifies the program of actions the country will pursue, in return for receiving IMF financial support, to ensure that its short-term foreign-exchange shortfall does not become permanent.

Stolper-Samuelson theorem   Argument suggesting that, in a country that is specializing in production of a given good as a result of trade liberalization, the owners of the relatively abundant factor of production in that country will experience a gain in their returns and real incomes, and the owners of the relatively scarce factor of production will sustain a drop in their returns and real incomes; implies that the first group will favor trade liberalization and the second will oppose it.

Tariff   Tax that is imposed by a government on imported goods or services.

Tied aid   Aid given by a donor who requires that the aid be used to purchase goods and services provided by firms from the donor country.

Unilateral sanctions   Economic sanctions imposed by only one state against a target state.

Washington consensus   View that, to achieve sustainable growth, countries should pursue macroeconomic stability, rely on private enterprise rather than state-owned firms, and reduce barriers to trade and investment to allow international market forces to direct the country to the most efficient employment of its human and natural resources.

BIBLIOGRAPHY

Aaronson, Susan Ariel. *Taking Trade to the Streets: The Lost History of the Public Efforts to Shape Globalization.* Ann Arbor: University of Michigan Press, 2001.

Alesina, Alberto, and David Dollar. "Who Gives Foreign Aid to Whom and Why?" *Journal of Economic Growth* 5 (March 2000): 33–63.

Baldwin, David. *Economic Statecraft.* Princeton: Princeton University Press, 1985.

———, ed. *Neorealism and Neoliberalism: The Contemporary Debate.* New York: Columbia University Press, 1993.

Baldwin, Richard E., and Philippe Martin. "Two Waves of Globalization: Superficial Similarities, Fundamental Differences." NBER Working Paper 6904, January 1999, available at www.nber.org/papers/w6904.

Barbieri, Katherine. "Economic Interdependence: A Path to Peace or a Source of Interstate Conflict?" *Journal of Peace Research* 33 (February 1996): 29–50.

Baumol, William J., and Alan S. Blinder. *Macroeconomics: Principles and Policy,* 7th ed. Ft. Worth: Dryden Press, 1997.

Bellman, Christophe, and Richard Gerster. "Accountability in the World Trade Organization." *Journal of World Trade* 30 (December 1996): 31–74.

Bergsten, C. Fred, and C. Randall Henning. *Global Economic Leadership and the Group of Seven.* Washington, D.C.: Institute for International Economics, 1996.

Bernauer, Thomas, and Dieter Ruloff, eds. *The Politics of Positive Incentives and Arms Control.* Columbia: University of South Carolina Press, 1999.

Blanchard, Jean-Marc F., Edward D. Mansfield, and Norrin Ripsman, eds. *Power and the Purse: Economic Statecraft, Interdependence, and National Security.* London: Frank Cass, 2000.

Block, Fred. *The Origins of International Economic Disorder.* Berkeley: University of California Press, 1977.

Boone, Peter. "Politics and the Effectiveness of Foreign Aid." *European Economic Review* 40 (February 1996): 289–329.

Bordo, Michael D., Barry Eichengreen, and Douglas A. Irwin. "Is Globalization Today Really Different Than Globalization a Hundred Years Ago?" NBER Working Paper 7195, June 1999, available at www.nber.org/papers/w7195.

Braudel, Fernand. *Civilization and Capitalism: 15th–18th Century*, Vol. II: *The Wheels of Commerce*. New York: Harper and Row, 1982.

Brewer, John. *The Sinews of Power: War, Money and the English State, 1688–1783*. New York: Knopf, 1989.

Buchanan, James M. *The Limits of Liberty*. Chicago: University of Chicago Press, 1975.

Calvo, Guillermo A., and Enrique G. Mendoza. "Mexico's Balance-of-Payments Crisis: A Chronicle of a Death Foretold." *Journal of International Economics* 41 (December 1996): 235–64.

Cameron, David R. "The 1992 Initiative: Causes and Consequences," pp. 23–74 in Alberta Sbragia, ed., *Euro-Politics*. Washington, D.C.: Brookings Institution Press, 1992.

Charnovitz, Steve. "Participation of Nongovernmental Organizations in the World Trade Organization." *University of Pennsylvania Journal of International Economic Law* 17 (Spring 1996): 331–57.

Chipman, John S. "International Trade," pp. 922–55 in *The New Palgrave: A Dictionary of Economics*, Vol. 2, ed. John Eatwell, Murray Milgate, and Peter Newman. London: Macmillan, 1991.

Conybeare, John. "Trade Wars: A Comparative Study of Anglo-Hanse, Franco-Italian and Hawley-Smoot Conflicts." *World Politics* 38 (October 1985): 147–72.

Cortright, David, ed. *The Price of Peace: Incentives and International Conflict Prevention*. Lanham: Rowman & Littlefield, 1997.

Crowley, James. *Japan's Quest for Autonomy: National Security and Foreign Policy, 1930–1939*. Princeton: Princeton University Press, 1966.

Cumings, Bruce. "Trilateralism and the New World Order." *World Policy Journal* 8 (Spring 1991): 195–222.

——. "Japan's Position in the World System," pp. 34–63 in *Postwar Japan as History*, ed. Andrew Gordon. Berkeley: University of California Press, 1993.

Dollar, David, and William Easterly. "The Search for the Key: Aid, Investment and Policies in Africa." *Journal of African Economies* 8 (December 1999): 546–77.

Doremus, Paul, William Keller, Louis Pauly, and Simon Reich. *The Myth of the Global Corporation*. Princeton: Princeton University Press, 1998.

Dornbusch, Rudiger. "The Case for Trade Liberalization in Developing Countries." *Journal of Economic Perspectives* 6 (Winter 1992): 69–85.

Dower, John. *Embracing Defeat: Japan in the Wake of World War II*. New York: W. W. Norton & Co., 1999.

Drezner, Daniel W. "Conflict Expectations and the Paradox of Economic Coercion." *International Studies Quarterly* 42 (December 1998): 709–31.

———. *The Sanctions Paradox: Economic Statecraft and International Relations.* Cambridge: Cambridge University Press, 1999.

Dunn, Robert M., Jr., and James C. Ingram. *International Economics,* 4th ed. New York: John Wiley, 1996.

Eckes, Alfred E., Jr. *Search for Solvency: Bretton Woods and the International Monetary System, 1944–71.* Austin: University of Texas Press, 1975.

Edwards, Sebastian. "Openness, Trade Liberalization, and Growth in Developing Countries." *Journal of Economic Literature* 31 (September 1993): 1358–93.

———. "Openness, Productivity and Growth: What Do We Really Know?" *Economic Journal* 108 (March 1998): 383–98.

Eichengreen, Barry. "The Political Economy of the Smoot-Hawley Tariff." *Research in Economic History* 12 (1989): 1–43.

———. *Globalizing Capital: A History of the International Monetary System.* Princeton: Princeton University Press, 1996.

Elliott, Kimberly Ann. "The Sanctions Glass: Half Full or Completely Empty." *International Security* 23 (Summer 1998): 50–65.

Elliott, Kimberly Ann, and Gary Clyde Hufbauer. "Ineffectiveness of Economic Sanctions: Same Song, Same Refrain? Economic Sanctions in the 1990's." *American Economic Review* 89 (May 1999): 403–8.

Evans, Peter. "Fighting Marginalization with Transnational Networks: Counter-Hegemonic Globalization." *Contemporary Sociology* 29 (January 2000): 230–41.

Feenstra, Robert C. "Integration of Trade and Disintegration of Production in the Global Economy." *Journal of Economic Perspectives* 12 (Fall 1998): 31–50.

Finlayson, Jock A., and Mark W. Zacker. "The GATT and the Regulation of Trade Barriers: Regime Dynamics and Functions," pp. 273–314 in *International Regimes,* ed. Stephen D. Krasner. Ithaca: Cornell University Press, 1983.

Finnemore, Martha. *National Interests in International Society.* Ithaca: Cornell University Press, 1996.

Frankel, Jeffrey A., and David Romer. "Does Trade Cause Growth?" *American Economic Review* 89 (June 1999): 379–99.

Friedman, Thomas L. *The Lexus and the Olive Tree.* New York: Farrar, Straus and Giroux, 1999.

Garcia-Johnson, Ronnie. *Exporting Environmentalism: U.S. Multinational Chemical Corporations in Brazil and Mexico.* Cambridge: MIT Press, 2000.

Gardner, Lloyd C. *Economic Aspects of New Deal Diplomacy.* Madison: University of Wisconsin Press, 1964.

———. "The Atlantic Charter: Idea and Reality, 1942–1945," pp. 45–81 in *The Atlantic Charter,* ed. Douglas Brinkley and David R. Facey-Crowther. London: Macmillan, 1994.

Gardner, Richard. *Sterling-Dollar Diplomacy: The Origins and the Prospects of Our International Economic Order.* New York: McGraw-Hill, 1969.

Gillingham, John. *Coal, Steel, and the Rebirth of Europe, 1945–1955: The Germans and French from the Ruhr Conflict to Economic Community.* Cambridge: Cambridge University Press, 1991.

Gilpin, Robert. *U.S. Power and the Multinational Corporation: The Political Economy of Foreign Direct Investment.* New York: Basic Books, 1975.

————. "Economic Interdependence and National Security in Historical Perspective," pp. 19–66 in *Economic Issues and National Security,* ed. Klaus Knorr and Frank N. Trager. Lawrence: Regents Press of Kansas, 1977.

————. *The Political Economy of International Relations.* Princeton: Princeton University Press, 1987.

Goldsmith, Arthur A. "Foreign Aid and Statehood in Africa." *International Organization* 55 (Winter 2001): 123–48.

Gould, David M., and Roy J. Ruffin. "What Determines Economic Growth?" (Federal Reserve Bank of Dallas *Economic and Financial Review* Second quarter 1993): 25–40.

Gowa, Joanne. *Allies, Adversaries, and International Trade.* Princeton: Princeton University Press, 1994.

Graham, Edward M. *Fighting the Wrong Enemy: Antiglobal Activists and Multinational Enterprises.* Washington, D.C.: Institute for International Economics, 2000.

Grieco, Joseph M. "Anarchy and the Limits of Cooperation." *International Organization* 42 (Summer 1988): 485–507.

————. "The Maastricht Treaty: Economic and Monetary Union and the Neo-Realist Research Programme." *Review of International Studies* 21 (January 1995): 21–40.

————. "State Interests and Institutional Rule Trajectories: A Neorealist Interpretation of the Maastricht Treaty and European Economic and Monetary Union." *Security Studies* 5 (Spring 1996): 261–306.

Griffith, Robert. "Forging America's Postwar Order: Domestic Politics and Political Economy in the Age of Truman," pp. 57–88 in *The Truman Presidency,* ed. Michael J. Lacey. Washington, D.C.: Woodrow Wilson Center Press, 1989.

Grossman, Gene M., and Elhanan Helpman. "Endogenous Innovation in the Theory of Growth." *Journal of Economic Perspectives* 8 (Winter 1994): 23–44.

Grubel, H. G., and P. L. Lloyd. *Intra-industry Trade: The Theory and Measurement of International Trade in Differentiated Products.* New York: Wiley, 1975.

Haass, Richard N., ed. *Economic Sanctions and American Diplomacy.* New York: Council on Foreign Relations Press, 1998.

Haass, Richard N., and Meghan L. O'Sullivan, eds. *Honey and Vinegar: Incentives,*

Sanctions, and Foreign Policy. Washington, D.C.: Brookings Institution Press, 2000.

Haggard, Stephan. "The Institutional Foundations of Hegemony: Explaining the Reciprocal Trade Agreements Act of 1934." *International Organization* 42 (1988): 91–119.

——. *Pathways from the Periphery: The Politics of Growth in the Newly Industrializing Countries.* Ithaca: Cornell University Press, 1990.

——. *The Political Economy of the Asian Financial Crisis.* Washington, D.C.: Institute for International Economics, 2000.

Haggard, Stephan, and Beth Simmons. "Theories of International Regimes." *International Organization* 41 (Summer 1988): 491–517.

Hajnal, Peter I. *The G7/G8 System: Evolution, Role and Documentation.* Brookfield: Ashgate, 1999.

Harrod, R. F. *The Life of John Maynard Keynes.* London: Macmillan, 1951.

Hart, Jeff. *Rival Capitalism: International Competitiveness in the United States, Japan, and Western Europe.* Ithaca: Cornell University Press, 1992.

Hirschman, Albert. *National Power and the Structure of Foreign Trade.* Berkeley: University of California Press, 1980 [1945].

Hoekman, Bernard, and Michael Kostecki. *The Political Economy of the World Trading System: From GATT to WTO.* Oxford: Oxford University Press, 1995.

Hogan, Michael. "European Integration and the Marshall Plan," in *The Marshall Plan: A Retrospective,* ed. Stanley Hoffman and Charles Maier. Boulder: Westview, 1984.

——. *The Marshall Plan: America, Britain, and the Reconstruction of Western Europe, 1947–1952.* Cambridge: Cambridge University Press, 1987.

Hufbauer, Gary Clyde, Jeffrey Schott, and Kimberly Ann Elliot. *Economic Sanctions Reconsidered: History and Current Policy,* Vol 2, 2d ed. Washington, D.C.: Institute for International Economics, 1990.

Huntington, Samuel P. "Trade, Technology, and Leverage: Economic Diplomacy." *Foreign Policy* 32 (Fall 1978): 63–80.

Ikenberry, G. John. "A World Economy Restored: Expert Consensus and the Anglo-American Postwar Settlement." *International Organization* 46 (Winter 1991–92): 289–321.

——. "Creating Yesterday's New World Order: Keynesian 'New Thinking' and the Anglo-American Postwar Settlement," pp. 57–86 in *Ideas and Foreign Policy: Beliefs, Institutions, and Political Change,* ed. Judith Goldstein and Robert O. Keohane. Ithaca: Cornell University Press, 1993.

——. *After Victory: Institutions, Strategic Restraint, and the Rebuilding of Order after Major War.* Princeton: Princeton University Press, 2001.

Ikenberry, G. John, and Charles Kupchan. "Socialization and Hegemonic Power." *International Organization* 44 (Summer 1990): 283–315.

Irwin, Douglas A. *Against the Tide: An Intellectual History of Free Trade*. Princeton: Princeton University Press, 1996.

————. "The United States in a New Global Economy? A Century's Perspective." *American Economic Review* 86 (May 1996): 41–46.

Jackson, John H. "Managing the Trading System: The World Trade Organization and the Post-Uruguay Round GATT Agenda," pp. 131–51 in *Managing the World Economy*, ed. Peter B. Kenen. Washington, D.C.: Institute for International Economics, 1994.

————. "The World Trade Organization, Dispute Settlement, and Codes of Conduct," pp. 63–75 in *The New GATT: Implications for the United States*, ed. Susan M. Collins and Barry P. Bosworth. Washington, D.C.: Brookings Institution Press, 1994.

James, Harold. *International Monetary Cooperation since Bretton Woods*. Oxford: Oxford University Press, 1995.

Jentleson, Bruce W. *Pipeline Politics: The Complex Political Economy of East-West Energy Trade*. Ithaca: Cornell University Press, 1986.

Kaplan, Ethan, and Dani Rodrik. "Did the Malaysian Capital Controls Work?" NBER Working Paper W8142, February 2001, available at papers.nber.org/papers/W8142.

Katzenstein, Peter J. *Small States in the World Economy*. Ithaca: Cornell University Press, 1989.

————, ed. *Between Power and Plenty*. Madison: University of Wisconsin Press, 1978.

Kegley, Charles W., Jr., and Steven W. Hook. "U.S. Foreign Aid and U.N. Voting: Did Reagan's Linkage Strategy Buy Deference or Defiance?" *International Studies Quarterly* 35 (September 1991): 295–312.

Keohane, Robert. "The Theory of Hegemonic Stability and Changes in International Economic Regimes, 1967–1977," pp. 131–62 in *Change in the International System*, ed. Ole Holsti, Randolph M. Siverson, and Alexander L. George. Boulder: Westview, 1980.

————. *After Hegemony: Cooperation and Discord in the World Political Economy*. Princeton: Princeton University Press, 1984.

Keohane, Robert, and Joseph Nye. *Power and Interdependence*. Boston: Little, Brown, 1977.

Kildegaard, Arne. "Foreign Finance and the Collapse of the Mexican Peso." *Journal of Economic Issues* 31 (December 1997): 951–67.

Kindleberger, Charles P. *The World in Depression, 1929–1939*. Berkeley: University of California Press, 1973.

Kirshner, Jonathan. *Currency and Coercion: The Political Economy of International Monetary Power*. Ithaca: Cornell University Press, 1995.

————. "The Political Economy of Realism," pp. 69–102 in *Unipolar Politics: Realism and State Strategies after the Cold War*, ed. Ethan Kapstein and Michael Mastanduno. New York: Columbia University Press, 1998.

Krasner, Stephen D. "State Power and the Structure of International Trade." *World Politics* 28 (April 1976): 317–47.

———. *Defending the National Interest: Raw Materials Investments and U.S. Foreign Policy.* Princeton: Princeton University Press, 1978.

———. *Structural Conflict: The Third World against Global Liberalism.* Berkeley: University of California Press, 1985.

———. *Sovereignty: Organized Hypocrisy.* Princeton: Princeton University Press, 1999.

———, ed. *International Regimes.* Ithaca: Cornell University Press, 1981.

Krueger, Anne O. *Trade Policies and Developing Nations.* Washington, D.C.: Brookings Institution Press, 1995.

———. "Trade Policy and Development: How We Learn." *American Economic Review* 87 (March 1997): 1–22.

Krugman, Paul R. "Intraindustry Specialization and the Gains from Trade." *Journal of Political Economy* 89 (October 1981): 959–73.

———. "Growing World Trade: Causes and Consequences." *Brookings Papers on Economic Activity* 1 (1995): 327–77.

Krugman, Paul R., and Maurice Obstfeld. *International Economics: Theory and Policy.* New York: HarperCollins, 1991.

Lake, David. "British and American Hegemony Compared: Lessons for the Current Era of Decline," pp. 106–22 in *History, the White House, and the Kremlin: Statesmen as Historians,* ed. Michael Fry. New York: Columbia University Press, 1991.

Leffler, Melvyn P. "The American Conception of National Security and the Beginning of the Cold War, 1945–48." *American Historical Review* 48 (1984): 349–56.

Lipson, Charles. "The Transformation of Trade: The Sources and Effects of Regime Change," pp. 258–62 in *International Regimes,* ed. Stephen D. Krasner. Ithaca: Cornell University Press, 1983.

Long, William J. *Economic Incentives and Bilateral Cooperation.* Ann Arbor: University of Michigan Press, 1986.

———. "Nonproliferation as a Goal of Japanese Foreign Assistance." *Asian Survey* 39 (March–April 1999): 328–47.

Lundestad, Geir. *"Empire" by Integration: The United States and European Integration, 1945–1997.* Oxford: Oxford University Press, 1998.

Lusztig, Michael. *Risking Free Trade: The Politics of Trade in Britain, Canada, Mexico, and the United States.* Pittsburgh: University of Pittsburgh Press, 1996.

Maddison, Angus. "The Nature and Functioning of European Capitalism: A Historical and Comparative Perspective." *BNL Quarterly Review* 203 (December 1997): 431–79.

———. *The World Economy: A Millennial Perspective.* Paris: Organization for Economic Cooperation and Development, 2001.

Maier, Charles S. "The Politics of Productivity: Foundations of American International Economic Policy after World War II," pp. 23–49 in *Between Power and*

Plenty: The Foreign Economic Policies of Advanced Industrial States, ed. Peter J. Katzenstein. Madison: University of Wisconsin Press, 1978.

———. "The Two Postwar Eras and the Conditions for Stability in Twentieth-Century Western Europe," pp. 153–84 in *In Search of Stability: Explorations in Historical Political Economy.* Cambridge: Cambridge University Press, 1987.

Marceau, Gabrielle, and Peter N. Pedersen. "Is the WTO Open and Transparent? A Discussion of the Relationship of the WTO with Non-governmental Organizations and Civil Society for More Transparency and Public Participation." *Journal of World Trade* 33 (February 1999): 5–49.

Martin, Lisa L. *Coercive Cooperation: Explaining Multilateral Economic Sanctions.* Princeton: Princeton University Press, 1992.

———. "An Institutionalist View: International Institutions and State Strategies," pp. 78–98 in *International Order and the Future of World Politics,* ed. T. V. Paul and John A. Hall. New York: Cambridge University Press, 1999.

Mastanduno, Michael. "Do Relative Gains Matter? America's Response to Japanese Industrial Policy." *International Security* 16 (Summer 1991): 73–113.

———. *Economic Containment: COCOM and the Politics of East-West Trade.* Ithaca: Cornell University Press, 1992.

Mastanduno, Michael, David Lake, and G. John Ikenberry. "Toward a Realist Theory of State Action." *International Studies Quarterly* 33 (December 1989): 457–74.

Milward, Alan S. *The Reconstruction of Western Europe, 1945–1951.* Berkeley: University of California Press, 1984.

———. *The European Rescue of the Nation-State.* London: Routledge, 1993.

Murphy, Craig. *International Organization and Industrial Change.* Oxford: Oxford University Press, 1994.

Moravcsik, Andrew. "Negotiating the Single European Act: National Interests and Conventional Statecraft in the European Community." *International Organization* 45 (Winter 1991): 19–56.

———. *The Choice for Europe: Social Purpose and State Power from Messina to Maastricht.* Ithaca: Cornell University Press, 1998.

Morgan, T. Clifton, and Valerie Schwebach. "Fools Suffer Gladly: The Use of Economic Sanctions in International Crises." *International Studies Quarterly* 41 (1997): 27–50.

Naim, Moises. "Washington Consensus or Washington Confusion?" *Foreign Policy* 118 (Spring 2000): 87–103.

Newnham, Randall. "The Price of German Unity: The Role of Economic Aid in the German-Soviet Negotiations." *German Studies Review* 22 (October 1999): 421–46.

———. "More Flies with Honey: Positive Economic Linkage in German *Ostpolitik* from Bismarck to Kohl." *International Studies Quarterly* 44 (March 2000): 73–96.

North, Douglass C. *Structure and Change in Economic History.* New York: W. W. Norton & Co., 1981.

North, Douglass C., and Robert Paul Thomas. *The Rise of the Western World: A New Economic History.* Cambridge: Cambridge University Press, 1973.

O'Brien, Robert, Anne Marie Goetz, Jan Aart Scholte, and Marc Williams. *Contesting Global Governance: Multilateral Economic Institutions and Global Social Movements.* Cambridge: Cambridge University Press, 2000.

Obstfeld, Maurice. "The Global Capital Market: Benefactor or Menace?" *Journal of Economic Perspectives* 12 (Fall 1998): 9–30.

Obstfeld, Maurice, and Alan M. Taylor. "The Great Depression as a Watershed: International Capital Mobility over the Long Run," pp. 353–402 in *The Defining Moment: The Great Depression and the American Economy in the Twentieth Century,* ed. Michael D. Bordo, Claudia Goldin, and Eugene N. White. Chicago: University of Chicago Press, 1998.

Oneal, John, and Bruce Russett. "The Classical Liberals Were Right: Democracy, Interdependence, and Conflict, 1950–1985." *International Studies Quarterly* 41 (June 1997): 267–94.

———. "Assessing the Liberal Peace with Alternative Specifications: Trade Still Reduces Conflict." *Journal of Peace Research* 36 (July 1999): 423–42.

Papayoanou, Paul A. "Interdependence, Institutions, and the Balance of Power." *International Security* 20 (Spring 1996): 42–76.

Pape, Robert. "Why Economic Sanctions Do Not Work." *International Security* 22 (Fall 1997): 90–136.

Parlberg, Robert L. *Food Trade and Foreign Policy: India, the Soviet Union, and the United States.* Ithaca: Cornell University Press, 1985.

Preeg, Ernest H. *Traders in a Brave New World: The Uruguay Round and the Future of the International Trading System.* Chicago: University of Chicago Press, 1995.

Polanyi, Karl. *The Great Transformation.* New York: Rinehart, 1944.

Pollard, Robert A. *Economic Security and the Origins of the Cold War, 1945–1950.* New York: Columbia University Press, 1985.

Porter, Michael E. *The Competitive Advantage of Nations.* New York: Free Press, 1998.

Przeworski, Adam, and James Rayment Vreeland. "The Effect of IMF Programs on Economic Growth." *Journal of Development Economics* 62 (2000): 397–403.

Putnam, Robert D., and C. Randall Henning. "The Bonn Summit of 1978: A Case Study in Coordination," pp. 12–140 in *Can Nations Agree? Issues in International Economic Cooperation,* ed. Richard Cooper, Barry Eichengreen, Gerald Holtham, Robert Putnam, and C. Randall Henning. Washington, D.C.: Brookings Institution Press, 1989.

Reinicke, Wolfgang H. *Global Public Policy: Governing without Government?* Washington, D.C.: Brookings Institution Press, 1998.

Rittberger, Volker, ed. *Regime Theory and International Relations*. Oxford: Oxford University Press, 1995.

Rivera-Batiz, Luis A., and Paul M. Romer. "Economic Integration and Endogenous Growth." *Quarterly Journal of Economics* 106 (May 1991): 531–55.

Rodman, Kenneth R. "Sanctions at Bay? Hegemonic Decline, Multinational Corporations and U.S. Economic Sanctions Since the Pipeline Case." *International Organization* 49 (Winter 1995): 105–37.

Rodrik, Dani. "The Limits of Trade Policy Reform in Developing Countries." *Journal of Economic Perspectives* 6 (Winter 1992): 87–105.

———. *Has Globalization Gone Too Far?* Washington, D.C.: Institute for International Economics, 1997.

———. *The New Global Economy and Developing Countries: Making Openness Work*. Washington, D.C.: Overseas Development Council, 1999.

———. "Trading in Illusions." *Foreign Policy* 123 (March–April 2001): 55–62.

Romer, Paul M. "Increasing Returns and Long-Run Growth." *Journal of Political Economy* 94 (October 1986): 1002–37.

———. "The Origins of Endogenous Growth." *Journal of Economic Perspectives* 8 (Winter 1994): 3–22.

Ruffin, Roy J. "The Nature and Significance of Intra-industry Trade." *Federal Reserve Bank of Dallas Economic and Financial Review* (Fourth quarter 1999): 2–8.

Ruggie, John G. "International Regimes, Transactions, and Change: Embedded Liberalism in the Postwar Economic Order," pp. 195–231 in *International Regimes*, ed. Stephen D. Krasner. Ithaca: Cornell University Press, 1983.

———. "Embedded Liberalism Revisited: Institutions and Progress in International Economic Relations," pp. 201-34 in *Progress in Postwar International Relations*, ed. Emanuel Adler and Beverly Crawford. New York: Columbia University Press, 1991.

———. "Multilateralism: The Anatomy of an Institution," pp. 8–14 in *Multilateralism Matters*, ed. John G. Ruggie. New York: Columbia University Press, 1994.

———. *Winning the Peace: America and World Order in the New Era*. New York: Columbia University Press, 1996.

Sachs, Jeffrey, Aaron Tornell, and Andres Velasco. "The Mexican Peso Crisis: Sudden Death or Death Foretold?" *Journal of International Economics* 41 (December 1996): 265–83.

Sagan, Scott D. "From Deterrence to Coercion to War: The Road to Pearl Harbor," pp. 57–90 in *The Limits of Coercive Diplomacy*, 2d ed., ed. Alexander L. George and William E. Simons. Boulder: Westview, 1994.

Sandholtz, Wayne, and John Zysman. "1992: Recasting the European Bargain." *World Politics* (October 1989): 95–128.

Schaller, Michael. "Securing the Great Crescent: Occupied Japan and the Origins of Containment in Southeast Asia." *Journal of American History* 69 (September 1982): 392–414.

Schattschneider, E. E. *Politics, Pressures and the Tariff*. New York: Prentice-Hall, 1935.

Schraeder, Peter J., Steven W. Hook, and Bruce Taylor. "Clarifying the Foreign Aid Puzzle: A Comparison of American, Japanese, French, and Swedish Aid Flows." *World Politics* 50 (January 1998): 294–323.

Schwabe, Klaus. "The United States and European Integration: 1947–1957," in *Western Europe and Germany, 1945–1960*, ed. Clemens Wurm. Oxford: Oxford University Press, 1995.

Schwartz, Thomas A. *America's Germany: John J. McCloy and the Federal Republic of Germany*. Cambridge: Harvard University Press, 1991.

Skalnes, Lars S. "Grand Strategy and Foreign Economic Policy: British Grand Strategy in the 1930s." *World Politics* 50 (July 1998): 582–616.

Skocpol, Theda. "Bringing the State Back In: Strategies of Analysis in Current Research," pp. 3–37 in *Bringing the State Back In*, ed. Peter Evans, Dietrich Rueschemeyer, and Theda Skocpol. Cambridge: Cambridge University Press, 1985.

Smith, Wayne S. "Our Dysfunctional Cuban Embargo." *Orbis* 42 (Fall 1998): 533–45.

Spar, Debora. "Foreign Investment and Human Rights." *Challenge* 42 (January–February 1999): 55–80.

Spar, Debora, and David Yoffie. "Multinational Enterprises and the Prospects for Justice." *Journal of International Affairs* 52 (Spring 1999): 557–81.

Spykman, Nicholas. *America's Strategy in the World: The United States and the Balance of Power*. New York: Harcourt, Brace, 1942.

Stallings, Barbara, ed. *Global Change, Regional Response: The New International Context of Development*. Cambridge: Cambridge University Press, 1995.

Stone, Peter H. "K Street Musters for the Middle Kingdom." *National Journal* 32 (March 25, 2000): 944–45.

Svensson, Jakob. "Aid, Growth, and Democracy." *Economics and Politics* 11 (November 1999): 275–97.

Tilly, Charles. "War Making and State Making as Organized Crime," pp. 169–91 *Bringing the State Back In*, ed. Peter B. Evans, Dietrich Rueschemeyer, and Theda Skocpol. Cambridge: Cambridge University Press, 1985.

———. *Coercion, Capital, and European States: AD 990–1990*. Cambridge: Blackwell, 1990.

Van Der Beugel, Ernst H. *From Marshall Plan to Atlantic Partnership*. Amsterdam: Elsevier, 1966.

Vernon, Raymond. "The World Trade Organization: A New Stage in International Trade and Development." *Harvard International Law Journal* 36 (Spring 1995): pp. 329–40.

Viner, Jacob. "International Finance and Balance of Power Diplomacy, 1880–1914." *Southwestern Political and Social Science Quarterly* 9 (June 1928): 407–51.

Waltz, Kenneth N. "The Myth of National Interdependence," pp. 205–23 in *The International Corporation: A Symposium,* ed. Charles P. Kindleberger. Cambridge: MIT Press 1970.

———. *Theory of International Politics.* Reading: Addison-Wesley, 1979.

Williamson, John, and C. Randall Henning. "Managing the Monetary System," pp. 83–111 in *Managing the World Economy: Fifty Years after Bretton Woods,* ed. Peter B. Kenen. Washington, D.C.: Institute for International Economics, 1994.

Wang, T. Y. "U.S. Foreign Aid and UN Voting: An Analysis of Important Issues." *International Studies Quarterly* 43 (March 1999): 199–210.

Winham, Gilbert R. *The Evolution of International Trade Agreements.* Toronto: University of Toronto Press, 1992.

———. "The World Trade Organization: Institution-Building in the Multilateral Trade System." *The World Economy* 21 (May 1998): pp. 349–68.

Woods, Randall Bennett. *A Changing of the Guard: Anglo-American Relations, 1941–1946.* Chapel Hill: University of North Carolina Press, 1990.

World Bank. *Assessing Aid: What Works, What Doesn't, and Why.* Washington, D.C.: World Bank, 1998.

Yarbrough, Beth V., and Robert M. Yarbrough. *The World Economy: Trade and Finance.* Fort Worth: Dryden Press, 1994.

Young, Oran. *International Cooperation: Building Regimes for Natural Resources and the Environment.* Ithaca: Cornell University Press, 1989.

———. "Political Leadership and Regime Formation: On the Development of Institutions in International Society." *International Organization* 45 (Summer 1991): 281–307.

Zelikow, Philip, and Condoleezza Rice. *Germany Unified and Europe Transformed: A Study in Statecraft.* Cambridge: Harvard University Press, 1995.

Zysman, John. *Governments, Markets, and Growth: Financial Systems and the Politics of Industrial Change.* Ithaca: Cornell University Press, 1983.

INDEX

Note: Page numbers in italics refer to graphs, charts, and other illustrative materials.

Samuelson, Paul, 47
    Stolper-Samuelson theorem, 47–49,
        53, 227
sanctions, economic, see economic sanc-
    tions
sanctions fatigue, 349
Sandanistas, 165–66
Saudi Arabia, 178
Schmidt, Helmut, 312
Schuman, Robert, 151
Schuman Plan, 144, 151
secondary sanctions, 170, 350
Second World, 244, 245
services, growth in trade of, 210
short-term financial flows to developing
    countries, private, 264–66, 265,
    266–70, 350
signaling of intention, economic sanc-
    tions used for, 171
Singapore, 211, 212
    economic growth in, 245, 282–83
    international trade and, 252, 255–56
Skocpol, Theda, 95
Smith, Adam, 30
Smoot-Hawley tariff, 111, 299
social clause, 350
social security, welfare programs and,
    139–40, 141, 222
societies and states, relationship be-
    tween, 95–97
software companies, transnational na-
    ture of, 15
South African apartheid policy, eco-
    nomic sanctions and incentives
    and to influence, 168, 178
South Asia:
    economic growth in, 246, 247
    financial flows to, 262–64, 263, 264,
        270
South Korea, 157, 189, 211, 212
    economic growth in, 245, 282–83
    financial crisis in, 13, 268–69, 279,
        280, 281, 331
    international trade and, 252, 255,
        256, 257

invasion by North Korea, 151
sovereignty, 350
Soviet Union:
    Cold War and, see Cold War
    collapse of, 245, 251
    containment policy, 144
    economic decline of, 251
    gas-pipeline project, Reagan adminis-
        tration economic sanctions and,
        176, 181
    grain sales to, 189, 190, 191
        embargo on, 165, 168, 170, 174,
            180, 181
    invasion of Afghanistan, 165, 180,
        189
    sales of military goods and technology
        to, 179
    technology transfers to, 189, 192
    testing of atomic weapons, 151
    West German food sales to, 182, 190
    withdrawal of troops from eastern
        Germany, 182–83, 191
    see also Russia
Spain, fiscal policy of, 86–87
specialization:
    neoclassical model of international
        trade, 37–40
    partial, 39, 40
    Ricardian (classical) model of interna-
        tional trade and, 29–36
Spykman, Nicholas, 130
stagflation, 310
standby agreement, 350
states, see nation-states
statistical discrepancy, 75
"sterilization" operations, 79
Stimson, Henry, 131
Stolper, Wolfgang, 47
Stolper-Samuelson theorem, 47–49, 53,
    227, 350
strategic interdependence, 126–27
sub-Saharan Africa:
    economic deterioration in, 245
    financial flows to, 262–64, 263, 264
    international trade and, 252